Men, Women, and History

Men, Women, and History

A Biographical Reader in Western Civilization Since the Sixteenth Century

Roland N. Stromberg
University of Wisconsin—Milwaukee

Prentice Hall, Englewood Cliffs, New Jersey 07632

Library of Congress Cataloging-in-Publication Data

Stromberg, Roland N.
    Men, women, and history : a biographical reader in Western
  civilization since the sixteenth century / Roland N. Stromberg
      p. cm.
    Includes bibliographical references (p.) and index.
    ISBN 0-13-146671-2
    1. Civilization, Western—History. 2. Biography—17th century.
  3. Biography—18th century. 4. Biography—19th century.
  5. Biography—20th century. I. Title.
  CB245.S84 1995
  920'.009182'1—dc20
  [B]   94-15410
                                       CIP

Editorial/production supervision and interior design: Shelly Kupperman
Acquisition editor: Steve Dalphin
Buyer: Nick Sklitsis
Editorial assistant: Tamara Mann
Cover designer: Ray Lundgren

© 1995 by Prentice-Hall, Inc.
A Simon & Schuster Company
Englewood Cliffs, New Jersey 07632

Printed in the United States of America
10 9 8 7 6 5 4 3 2 1

ISBN   0-13-146671-2

Prentice-Hall International (UK) Limited, *London*
Prentice-Hall of Australia Pty. Limited, *Sydney*
Prentice-Hall Canada Inc., *Toronto*
Prentice-Hall Hispanoamericana, S.A., *Mexico*
Prentice-Hall of India Private Limited, *New Delhi*
Prentice-Hall of Japan, Inc., *Tokyo*
Simon & Schuster Asia Pte. Ltd., *Singapore*
Editora Prentice-Hall do Brasil, Ltda., *Rio de Janeiro*

Contents

Preface

I owe the inception of this book to discussions with my colleague, Professor Glen Jeansonne of the University of Wisconsin-Milwaukee, and subsequently with Steve Dalphin, the history editor at Prentice Hall. The goal of enlivening and humanizing the way of presenting that familiar, essential, but sometimes debatable and always difficult course, the History of Western Civilization, as well as of United States history, has led some to think of a biographical approach.

Such a method should enable us to make history vivid and interesting. Biographies are seldom boring. The concrete details of real human experiences cannot fail to enlist our interest, more so than statistics or generalities. There is surely no need to justify this strategy of studying history through selection of key individuals, for it has been used from Plutarch's "Lives" in ancient times down to Emerson's "Representative Men," and beyond. One has of course the difficult task of choosing who is "representative," a question I address in the Introduction.

It should be added that this text is intended as a supplement to a general survey textbook for the Western Civilization or Modern History course, not a substitute. Though for many readers this book can stand by itself, it tends to assume that they have gotten basic historical directions from a central text; it aspires only to clothe that skeleton with some real flesh and blood.

Did not the master of World History himself, Karl Marx, once say that "the microscopic world" was more interesting than the "macroscopic?"[1]

To Steve Dalphin I also owe the process of having the manuscript read critically by qualified reviewers, themselves involved with Western Civilization: Donald McKale, Clemson University; Ronald Coons, University of Connecticut; and Rita Victoria Gomez, Anne Arundel Community College. These readers made many helpful suggestions, in small things and in large, and even when I failed to follow their excellent advice (again, who could agree on the choice of subjects?) they helped me clarify my thinking. Of course, any surviving errors are my fault alone.

I have written a number of books in European history, chiefly intellectual history, and once taught Western Civilization as well as European Intellectual History and Twentieth Century Europe. I hope that this long experience has helped me to make this one a success. Students must judge.

Roland N. Stromberg

---

[1]David McLellan, *Karl Marx: His Life and Thought* (Harper and Row: New York, 1973), p. 449.

Men, Women, and History

Introduction

If as Thomas Carlyle claimed "History is the essence of innumerable biographies," it must be an elusive thing, for each one of these millions of lives is unique, we cannot possibly tell them all, and if we could they would add up simply to an enormous unstructured mass. From this swarm of lives can we extract a common denominator that is the "essence" of history? We could doubtless identify certain activities that virtually all people have in common. They are born, work, eat, breed, sicken, and die; they live in societies together and often these societies fight each other. What they have in common are only those bald quantitative features that social historians have recently bored us with as they supply statistics on average length of life, age of marriage, number of children, etc. This kind of history is stripped of all excitement, action, drama—even of significance.

It is more plausible to think that we can choose lives that are representative of humanity at any particular place or moment. By telling particular lives we can bring out the dreams, actions, and ideas most typical and in some sense most important for the whole of a society. They would show the crowning achievements, or the crucial defects, of an age, identify the biggest changes, the issues and ideas that most shaped the human condition.

Some have questioned whether private lives really matter in the great human achievements. The irrelevance of the life to the work is a strong theme in recent interpretation. Thus Carl Dahlhaus, writing about Ludwig van Beethoven, declares that the subject who speaks through the great composer's

1

music is not the same as Beethoven the man. Who Beethoven's friends were, and what he thought about Napoleon, are as irrelevant to his music as when he was born and how he died. The music is autonomous. Beethoven inherited a musical structure from his predecessors and added formal elements to it; this is all we should attend to.

In our group, at least of Shakespeare, of Newton, of Curie and Kafka, one might say, as Herman Broch once said of himself and Robert Musil, "that neither of them had a real biography; they merely lived and wrote and that was all." What counted was their achievements, which had little to do with the events of their private lives. It may be interesting to learn that Marie Curie had an affair with a married man, and that her son-in-law became a Communist; but obviously we would never have remembered her for these things, and they hardly bear on her genius as a chemist.

In the name of humanity we must surely reject such a bloodless kind of history. We are interested in people for their own sake, or we are not historians; indeed, one is tempted to say, we are not human beings. And assuredly, private and public lives do intertwine and sometimes coincide in fascinating ways. Many histories leave the impression that political decisions are always taken for reasons of state or at the least because of a general, rational purpose, like economic self-interest or power. But did Napoleon invade Russia because Tsar Alexander I refused to let the Corsican upstart marry the tsar's sister? Did Alexander write the Holy Alliance treaty because he had fallen in love with a mystical lady? Did Rousseau revolutionize the consciousness of Europe because he pined for the lost happiness of his early childhood? Did Mazzini sublimate his libidinous impulses into love for the Motherland? Did Hitler hate the Jews because he blamed a Jewish doctor for his mother's death? These are among innumerable questions that touch on the relationship between public and private lives, between "history" in the old-fashioned sense and psychology. We should keep them in mind in this book.

To select a cast of characters to represent the enormous terrain of Western history over the last four centuries is an impossible task. Every historian would choose a different cast, in part or even in whole. This may not matter, if we can justify those chosen on grounds of typicality and human interest. Of course, all of these men and women must be important and imposing figures; though the "Diary of a Nobody" once achieved literary success, people wholly obscure can hardly qualify for a book such as this one, aimed at presenting to students the essentials of their civilized tradition. Perhaps I should have included one Nobody, but I didn't.

At the same time, we do not need to read about just the supermen (or women). Sometimes a secondary figure can tell us more about an age or an issue. And it is important to present a broad spectrum of types—not just political and military leaders but also scientists, poets, engineers, inventors, businessmen, workers and, ideally, all the main areas of human achievement. If our group falls short of this goal, that is because of limitations of space. No history can reveal—it can at best suggest—the inexhaustible richness of human experience. My goal was to select people who were outstanding, representative, and interesting in their private lives; to get a variety of types, sexes, nationalities; and to show some connection between the private and public dimensions.

My own professional bias in favor of intellectual history doubtless shows through, as critics kind enough to read the manuscript have not failed to point out. But there is a strong case for the purveyors of words and ideas having exerted a stronger effect on humanity than any others. I asked myself who had influenced more people both great and small, literary and nonliterary, than anyone else, and I came up with Shakespeare. (The Bible is excluded because of the time period.) I wondered what intellectual discovery had changed the world more than any other, and came up not unreasonably with Newton's physical laws and scientific methods. I thought about social and political change, and found Jean-Jacques Rousseau. All of these, along with Karl Marx, are surely justifiable, even inevitable choices, not because they were writers but because they so obviously "made history." As for Max Weber, he is not only the greatest of sociologists but also a commentator on the modern age without peer.

For strategic reasons, we need a balance of nationalities and of sexes as well as occupations and professions, and time periods. Gender is a difficult point—for who can deny either that female achievements have unjustly suffered in most past histories, or that in fact males have heretofore dominated the public side of Western societies, which is the main subject of historical works? Among the fourteen people featured in this book, spread over the centuries from about 1600 to near the present, there are only three women, but another, Queen Elizabeth, shares the stage with Shakespeare, and women appear prominently in most other chapters. (Two of these women, in addition to Queen Elizabeth, were political leaders, rather challenging the notion that this region belongs exclusively to males.)

As for overall balance: Two of the fourteen were pure creative writers, each one with qualities that typify an age. Two great scientists make their appearance, three if we count the social science of Max Weber. There are a pair of activist philosophers, or thinkers who impacted strongly on the history of their times. In terms of national distribution, we have five British, three Germans, two Russians, two French (if we count the Polish-born Curie), one Italian, one from Central Europe. Clearly an English-language bias appears, but this is inevitable.

The evil side is represented by Adolf Hitler; the misguided by Anthony Blunt. The choice of Blunt may be considered idiosyncratic; but an author is surely entitled to one, and what deviant is more alluring than the spy? Blunt additionally typifies a highly important ideological debate of the twentieth century. Left-wing ideologists may cavil at Mrs. Thatcher, but her chapter features a general discussion of the present clash of economic ideas and political values.

Issues and causes represented include nationalism, socialism, capitalism, fascism, communism, feminism, science both physical and social, and the alienated artist. Among our types there are highly liberated women and "gay" men. As a matter of balance, we have included not just the victories but the defeats, not just the splendid achievements but also the failures, not only heroes but villains. These, surely, ought to get some recognition, unless we are to leave a false impression about the human past, which Voltaire thought a record of "crimes, follies, and misfortunes."

It is more than that; it is also a story of achievement and progress. But sometimes the achievement is misguided, and progress turns sour. Bertrand Russell once wrote, and published, a history of the world that ran (in toto) as follows: "Since Adam and Eve ate the apple, man has never refrained from any folly of which he was capable." That "the wings of time are black and white" (Emerson) is a truism that comes closer to the truth than either the pure black or the pure white.

Some of our heroes (or villains) arouse interest because they attempted that most difficult of goals, namely the integration of thought and action. Mazzini and Marx were both ideologues and activists, or tried to be. Hitler was a person who seized hold of an idea and tried to carry it out. Rousseau, by nature a solitary writer, managed to make himself by proxy a vital part of the actions of his day and after—his ideas proved far more than empty dreams. Ideas were important to the Russian rulers, Catherine and Alexander, who attempted with varying degrees of success to apply them to public questions. This theme is a prominent one in human history. Are Augustine's two Cities, of God and Man, the ideal and the practical, destined to be separated in this world, and should they be, or is Marx's praxis, the notion of creatively integrating theory and action, a possibility? If so, how can it be achieved? The theme appears in all our specimens, as it must perhaps in every human life.

We can only hope that the fourteen lives presented in this book are interesting as well as instructive, providing us with key issues in the history of our civilization along with enough human interest to make these issues living realities. If no fourteen people can speak for all human history, they can at least bring to life a significant number of its foremost themes.

The shades of all our protagonists live on in the contemporary world. Karl Marx may seem to have been vanquished, and Newton superseded; but in a deeper sense the issues they raised and the methods they pursued remain as our inheritance. Rousseau's self-conscious individualism is as pervasive as is Weber's analysis of the modes of political action. Franz Kafka's uncanny stories have become a part of the human consciousness. The ghost of Hitler continues to haunt us. The oldest and greatest of them, Shakespeare, seems never to fade. The present poet laureate of England has just written a complicated book about him.

1

Shakespeare and Elizabethan England

SHAKESPEARE'S MISSING LIFE

William Shakespeare was born in 1564, probably on April 23 (it is typical that we do not know the precise date), the same day on which he died fifty-two years later. He entered the world in the sixth year of the long reign of Queen Elizabeth I, a political and economic achievement of the first magnitude in both English and world history. What connection Elizabeth and the Elizabethan Age had with the literary art of its leading ornament, one of the all-time great figures of world literature, is problematic. Legend—one of the many that surround Shakespeare, few of them, alas, verifiable—had it that the queen herself often came to sit behind the scenes or even appear on the stage of the Globe Theater at performances of Shakespeare's plays, in which he himself acted. This is extremely improbable, but Shakespeare's plays were evidently performed before Elizabeth, who may even have commissioned *Merry Wives of Windsor* after having been so delighted by Sir John Falstaff, the comic knight in *Henry IV*, that she wanted a sequel.

We know much about the life of Queen Elizabeth, and of many of her famous courtiers and servants such as Francis Bacon, Walter Ralegh, the seadogs Drake and Hawkins, her advisors Walsingham and the Cecils. We know little about Shakespeare's life, which is so little documented that some have doubted that he even existed; perhaps Francis Bacon wrote his plays. A whole school dedicated to this view arose in the nineteenth century; later, there were advocates of the Earl of Oxford, Derby, Queen Elizabeth herself, or a committee! The believers in someone other than William Shakespeare of Stratford writing almost all the plays attributed to him (there are a few cases of collaboration) have, however, been overwhelmingly an amateur fringe group; it is hard to find a qualified scholar who accepts the case for any of the proffered substitutes.

If William Shakespeare did exist and did write plays—as few informed people doubt—he was remarkably obscure for so great a genius; this is one of the world's great mysteries. In the eighteenth century, George Steevens declared: "All that is known with any degree of certainty concerning Shakespeare" could be told in a few words.

> He was born at Stratford upon Avon, married and had children there, went to London, where he commenced actor, and wrote poems and plays,—returned to Stratford, made his will, died, and was buried.

Two centuries of almost frantic efforts to increase this knowledge have not turned up a whole lot more. This has not prevented a host of Shakespeare biographies, often massive ones, a total that swells annually. The entire remarkable story tells us as much about us, and about the alleged science of history, as it does about Shakespeare.

In the sixteenth century few records were kept of most commoners' lives beyond the bare facts of birth, marriage, death, perhaps property transactions and law cases. If records existed, they were scattered and inaccessible to scholars. Serious biographies of anyone other than important men of state such as kings or high nobles or bishops just were not written; it was a time when books were rare and most people illiterate, as Shakespeare's father apparently was. Shakespeare's friend and fellow playwright Ben Jonson was more famous at the time than he, but we know as little about Jonson's life as about Shakespeare's.

No one even attempted what could be called a biography of Shakespeare for almost a century after his death, even though his fame had spread. By the time his earliest biographer appeared, people whose memories of Shakespeare might have supplied evidence were dead; only hand-me-down tales remained. Any existing family documents had long since been lost or destroyed. (Shakespeare's direct line died out by 1670, with the second generation of his descendants.) Even his will—an extensive and carefully drawn document—was not recovered until 1747. In the absence of any real information, a rich store of legends about Shakespeare had emerged. No doubt some kernels of truth had been greatly embellished and distorted as a good story was passed on from person to person; but how to know what truth there was in this mass of folklore and literary invention would baffle the critical scholar. The same tendency for legends to mount up about a great man may be seen in other cases, of course—cf. Abraham Lincoln. But today we have ways of checking them, in part at least, because of the abundance of records.

Whether to accept, reject, or partly discount "traditionary" evidence drawn from undocumented folk memory is a question of considerable importance to anyone aspiring to be a historian. In some African countries today it is almost the only kind of evidence that exists for earlier periods. All the stories about Jesus recorded in the New Testament rest on oral traditions written down several decades after Jesus' death; thus, Western civilization's greatest writer is in the same boat with the founder of its chief religion. Hence, should such evidence be credited, on the grounds that persistent tales in oral tradition usually reflect some real happening, or be rejected on the grounds that such tales are as unreliable as most gossip and rumor? Scholars are not of one mind about this.

The first serious investigators of Shakespeare's life went to Stratford toward the end of the seventeenth century, three-quarters of a century after his death, and found some people alive who remembered someone who had known Will or his children. Or who said they did, perhaps to please the visitor. Pub gossip of this sort provided many of the stories still presented in Shakespeare biographies, the leading example being the deer-poaching story, about how young Will was arrested and had to flee Stratford because he defied the law against killing game on the lord's preserve. Visitors to Stratford later were shown the very barn where Shakespeare was detained after being apprehended! None of these stories stand up very well to critical examination. Research finally disclosed that Sir Thomas Lucey did not even have a reserve for deer at that time! The deer-poaching story may reflect an urge to glamorize Shakespeare as a lively youngster, or a rebel.

To find out something about the man, Shakespeare, became one of the greatest of scholarly inquiries. Scholars still occasionally discover some minutiae as they ransack obscure records. Some of them spent their entire careers laboriously pawing through archives searching for some clue, and occasionally finding one. Through this process of gradual accretion far more has been learned than once could have been hoped for. Still, the greatest of writers remains a mystery, "out-topping knowledge," as Matthew Arnold wrote: "We ask and ask—Thou smilest and art still."

Shakespeare was one of eight children, it was finally decided; his father's occupation was that of glover. (Confusion with another Shakespeare, a butcher, once gave rise to fanciful portraits of young William killing calves.) John Shakespeare dabbled in wool trading, the largest business in Elizabethan England, and got in trouble with the law over this—usury and speculation still being suspect; he held village offices; evidently he fell upon lean times in his later years.

That young William at the age of eighteen rather hastily married a woman eight years his senior from a neighboring village is perhaps the most interesting fact about him we know for sure. But whether after this apparent shotgun wedding his thirty-four years of married life with Anne Hathaway were blissfully happy or bitterly unhappy is still subject to complete disagreement. You may find both opinions in recent Shakespeare scholarship. Obviously both are just guessing. Bits and pieces of evidence are themselves mystifying.[1] It may be theorized that Shakespeare fled to London from domestic unhappiness, or that he returned happily to his nest after making his fortune. Under what circumstances he joined a London acting company is totally unclear, despite manifold theories. So are estimates of his qualities as an actor.

The decade or so following his marriage, roughly his twenties, are Shakespeare's "lost" years, about which virtually nothing is known for certain. In 1588 he joined his father and mother in a lawsuit. The first clear reference to him as a London playwright was in 1592. One thin thread of evidence points to his teaching school and joining a company of private players for a great Catholic family at a country house in distant Lancashire. It is an interesting example of how any shred of possible fact about Shakespeare can become the basis of elaborate speculation. A will drawn by or for one Alexander Hoghton of Lea, Lancashire, turned up in 1860, dated August 1581, when Will was seventeen, a year before his marriage (which would of course have to put him back in Stratford at that time); the will included a request that the heirs treat well a William Shakeshafte, "now dwelling with me." In those days of wild orthographic disorder (Shakespeare's name was spelled eighty-three different ways, someone has counted), *shaft* for *spear* is by no means impossible as a variant. Lancashire is a good ways from Shakespeare's native Warwickshire, but his schoolmaster, John Cottom, was a native of that county, and a "John Cotham" is also mentioned in the will. An early mention of Shakespeare, by the seventeenth-century antiquary John Aubrey, on the basis of what evidence we do not know, says that Shakespeare "had in his early years been a schoolmaster in the country." The first acting company of which Shakespeare is known to have been a member, the Lord Chamberlain's Men, evolved from a group of actors known as Lord Strange's Men. *Strange* was of the Stanley family, of Lancashire.

There is a persistent tradition, backed by a little circumstantial evidence, that Shakespeare's family was Roman Catholic. In the 1580s such an allegiance implied danger. The great Protestant Reformation, begun by Martin Luther in Germany in the 1520s, cast its shadow over the entire century and beyond; it forced people to choose between two basic branches of the ancestral faith, and often to decide between loyalty to their ruler and to their conscience or custom. It did not then seem possible that a person could separate

---

[1]Thus the notable question of how to interpret a clause in Shakespeare's will leaving his "second-best bed" to Anne. This has been construed as a gesture of scorn, yet evidence from other wills suggests it may have been a token of affection. The curious student will find a whole shelf-ful of furious debate on this point alone.

his or her religion from one's political loyalty. Henry VIII, and even more pronouncedly his daughter Elizabeth, had chosen the Protestant side for England. As Shakespeare came of age, war between Protestant England and Catholic Spain was approaching. In 1587 Queen Elizabeth had her cousin Mary, Queen of Scots, put to death for involvement in conspiracies against the throne related to the international power struggle between the Catholic and Protestant causes.

Religion and politics were so closely tied together then as to be inseparable. The trouble with being a papist from Elizabeth's point of view was that an Englishman who gave his primary loyalty to the Roman Church was a potential traitor. The "bloody question" put to English Catholics was where their loyalty would lie in a war with Spain. This resembled the situation of Communists devoted to the Soviet Union in the twentieth century (see Chapter 12). It might have been prudent for a young English Catholic to seek sanctuary with a powerful Catholic family of the north. Such a theory runs counter to Shakespeare's fervent loyalty to Elizabeth as revealed in the plays, but they were written after the glorious victory over Spain in 1588 and the subsequent surge of patriotic joy.

The entire story rests on flimsy evidence, as is clear, and if true it still does not tell us a whole lot about Shakespeare. Other Shakespearians have been so impressed by the knowledge of various subjects revealed in the plays that they suppose their author must have once worked in a law office, as a sailor, a soldier, a schoolteacher; or that he lived in Italy. One might as well, citing *The Merchant of Venice*, assume that young Will was a businessman or banker. It seems much more likely that he pulled all this exact information, with which the plays are filled, from books and conversation. Still, we do not know.

Those who questioned whether Shakespeare wrote any of the works attributed to him argued that it was unlikely that a barely educated provincial could write the most profound and exquisite lines in all literature, as well as exhibit so much knowledge of the world. They generally assumed that he had had little or no education; but William received a decent grammar-school education—which might have taught him as much as some colleges do today. Modern scholars have exhaustively examined this traditional humanistic curriculum. Shakespeare may have taught in such a school. He did not, in any case, need to know much Latin or Greek to absorb a great deal of literature handed down from the ancients, for, as modern research has established, English translations were available.

Some of the surviving evidence about Shakespeare, a matter of property deeds and other legal records, exhibits him as a man much concerned with improving his social status. In 1597, not too many years after he went to London as a member of a company of actors (this may have been as early as 1587), he bought one of the grandest houses in his native Stratford; five years later he added a substantial area of farmland nearby. He acquired other properties, and by 1613 was able to retire to Stratford as a gentleman of considerable estate. In London he had become part owner of the Globe and Blackfriars theaters, where his plays were mostly performed, and he bought other property as well. His income was evidently substantial by the standards of his day; it came less from any royalties on his writing than from sharing in the proceeds of the theater performances; perhaps also from wealthy patrons.

This prudence as a man of business mixes oddly with the image of the divine master of the imagination. Here was no modern "accursed poet" fleeing the busy haunts of men, a dropout or dreamer withdrawn from society, but a very practical citizen. Shakespeare was capable of suing to recover a rather petty sum of money from a friend. This Shakespeare trait may seem to support the opinion that he could not have written such sublime plays; someone else must have. But our surprise at a poet and playwright being something other than an eccentric outcast is anachronistic, reflecting a social context that scarcely existed in Shakespeare's time. The great divorce between popular and elite culture, or lowbrow and highbrow culture, had not yet happened in 1600; in some ways it did not occur until the late nineteenth century. Shakespeare's theater was an integral part of everyday Elizabethan life, not an arty defiance of it—that is part of the secret of Shakespeare's immortality.

Given the scarcity of data about Shakespeare's life, people have looked at the writings for possible clues to the history of the man who wrote them. This is especially true of the sonnets, which appear to be autobiographical. But are they? These stunning poems might well be complete fictions; people in Shakespeare's own time seem to have thought of them as literary exercises. Not until the Romantic era did it occur to anyone that the sonnets were autobiographical. Even if we decide that these poignantly personal statements must have had something to do with their author's own experiences, no one has ever been able to identify for certain the people to whom they were addressed, or about whom they speak. They express adulatory love, jealousy, separation, cautious reunion, and falling in love with a woman whose sexual attractiveness is mingled with features that inspire the poet's exasperation and even disgust: "The expense of spirit in a waste of shame." The most famous and radiant of the sonnets evidently speak of homosexual love: They are addressed to a beautiful youth, perhaps the author's patron as well as friend, whose identity remains uncertain, although generations of scholarship narrowed the search down to a probable two—only to see the rival advocates of the Earl of Pembroke and the Earl of Southampton hopelessly at odds.[2] The Southampton-Pembroke controversy has proved so puzzling that one might suspect Shakespeare of creating a composite portrait, the better to

---

[2]In *The Portrait of Mr. W.H.* (1889), Oscar Wilde took up the candidacy of a boy actor named Will Hughes; the book shocked the Victorians with its frank presentation of Shakespeare as a Platonic homoerotic.

mystify posterity. One reason for the lack of information about him is that he seems to have been, by nature, secretive and self-effacing.

Are we to believe, to adopt the vulgar language of our times, that Shakespeare was "gay"? What then of his enduring marriage, his three children, his years as a respectable squire? Rather, was he not writing in a tradition of spiritual love that went back to Plato and had been revived in the Italian Renaissance, from which the sonnet form came?

Search for the identity of the "Dark Lady of the sonnets" has fared no better, indeed worse; there have been countless nominations but no election or even narrowing of the field. Each decade sees a new candidate brought forward, only to be rejected. Did Shakespeare have an affair with the mistress of an inn at Oxford where he frequently stayed en route between London and Stratford, and who bore him a son? Was she in fact the sultry brunette of the sonnets? Or was this a black prostitute of Clerkenwell? Such questions have been raised, but their answers can only be guessed at.

Shakespeare retired to his native Stratford in 1613 and died there three years later at what today we would regard as the almost youthful age of fifty-two, although at that time it was greater than the average life expectancy. It is typical of our maddening lack of knowledge about him that we do not know the cause of his death, although we do know that his son-in-law practiced medicine in Stratford. There is a conjecture, based on two allusions in the sonnets, that Shakespeare was lame. Perhaps like Byron he had a club foot. We simply do not know.

Does it matter? Modern critics are apt to dismiss the biography as irrelevant and say that this man was immersed in a sea of language. His writings are part of the history of discourse, or of consciousness. The real question is why did someone (or perhaps more than one), whatever we call him, at this particular time, create such a world of words?

SHAKESPEARE'S WRITING

Almost half of the forty or so plays, written between 1591 and 1613, were not published until after Shakespeare's death, in the First Folio of 1623. It took generations of relentless scholarship to settle the authorship of some of the plays, and to decide on the order of their composition and performance—indeed, some of these points are still in dispute. Establishing accurate texts for many of the plays was and remains a vexed question. To the heroic toil of two of Shakespeare's fellow actors we owe the crucial 1623 collection, which may have saved the plays, or many of them, from disappearing entirely or from being utterly unreconstructible. But one cannot be sure that these texts are just as Shakespeare wrote them; indeed, it is highly improbable that they are.

Some of the published plays were evidently derived solely from the recollections of actors—these were the "bad quartos," perhaps pirated editions.

Others came to the printer from copies of theatrical prompting books, or from copies of the author's often disorderly original. Maybe there was more than one original. Shakespeare is now thought to have written two different versions of *King Lear*. Reading difficult handwriting while tired or in a hurry, the compositor might make mistakes; or, fresh and frisky, he might decide to become an editor, offering improvments to Shakespeare. So might the proofreader. The number of possible intermediaries between Shakespeare's original manuscript (itself with words scratched out, scribbled in, written in the margin) would include one or more copyists plus compositor and proofreader. "When we get a chain of transmission like this, the end result is still recognizably Shakespeare," writes the textual scholar Fredson Bowers, "but we can be positive it is not exact Shakespeare in every detail." To this muddle later were added the forgeries of those who could not refrain from finding the right text even if they had to invent it—a story itself of much interest. All this makes the editing of Shakespeare a task compared to which nuclear physics sometimes looks like child's play.

We will never have the exactly correct Shakespeare text; too many uncertainties cannot possibly be settled for sure. We may not even accept some clearly established corrections. If the Bard wrote "a rose by any other word" rather than "a rose by any other name," the true text is not likely to replace the corrupt one. "O that this too too solid flesh would melt," we are told, should be *sullied* flesh, but likely never will be in our minds. These textual niceties concern the professors more than the public.

The plays are remarkable in many ways. They cover the entire range of human affairs, run the gamut of human emotions, in a way that makes them a kind of encyclopedia of the human heart, and they are quite timeless. Macbeth, the ambitious nobleman egged on by his wife to commit murder in order to become king, could just as well be a present-day corporate pirate clawing his way to the top. *Hamlet*, staged in modern dress, fits a New York mansion as well as it does a Danish castle. Jealousy, envy, revenge, greed, and ingratitude are the elemental emotions displayed for all times by the Othellos, Iagos, Hamlets, Shylocks, and Lears of Shakespearian tragedy; as for tragic love, we have the ill-starred passion of Romeo and Juliet, and Antony and Cleopatra.

The keen perceptiveness with which such characters are delineated puts modern psychology to shame. Sigmund Freud named Shakespeare as the first and foremost of the poets from whom he said he derived psychoanalysis.[3] The Stratford Bard's words set their seal on the English language for all time, so that we still use Shakespeare's phrases, probably without realizing it; they have become the clichés of popular speech. A list of such phrases could go on

---

[3]Though it must be admitted that Freud, succumbing to that last infirmity of noble minds, came to believe that someone else had written the Bard's plays. He had been fascinated by Shakespeare since childhood.

for many pages. A mere sampling: *green-eyed monster; midsummer madness; brave new world; the lie direct; a lean and hungry look; suffer a sea-change; shuffle off this mortal coil; once more into the breach; what's past is prologue; out, out brief candle; full of sound and fury; the slings and arrows of outrageous fortune; age cannot wither nor custom stale; all the world's a stage; we are such stuff as dreams are made on; let slip the dogs of war. . . .*

Shakespeare also provided us comedy, and here too the themes are eternal and archetypal. For example, the Keystone Kops of early movie renown, who gave way to Peter Sellers's Inspector Clouseau, have their origin in Shakespeare's comic policemen like Dogberry the constable, who advises his men to show their virtue by having nothing to do with criminals (*Much Ado about Nothing*). Dogberry, who speaks of "comprehending all vagrom men," is also a predecessor of Mrs. Malaprop and all the other manglers of the English language. *A Comedy of Errors* is pure Marx Brothers farce. *Taming of the Shrew* transmuted into a successful Broadway musical comedy. The delightful fantasy-romances, *As You Like It, Twelfth Night, Midsummer Night's Dream,* are sex comedies quite outdoing the usual Hollywood variety. The latter, like *The Tempest,* also takes us into a strange realm inhabited by fairies and monsters, akin to subsequent science fiction, today's "creatures from outer space."

Then there are the history plays, featuring seven of England's kings beginning with the target of Magna Carta, King John, and ending with Elizabeth's father, Henry VIII. They are remarkable evocations of historical action, with much psychological insight—e.g., Cardinal Wolsey's great "Farewell, a long farewell to all my greatness" on his career and fall. Shakespeare is passionately pro-Tudor. Exuberant patriotism born of a successful war defending the nation's independence against a more powerful foe is evident in many of Shakespeare's lines, and at the end of the last history play, *Henry VIII*, the birth of Elizabeth brings a prophecy that this royal infant promises

Upon this land a thousand thousand blessings.

This play was written well after Elizabeth's death, so no suspicion of currying favor with the monarch can exist. Shakespeare was an adolescent in 1588, the year of the miraculous defeat of the Spanish Armada, which the king of Spain had sent to punish the English for aiding the Protestant cause and pillaging Spanish treasure ships in the New World. It was then that Elizabeth emerged fully as heroine of her people, courageously leading England's fight for freedom. Just then arriving in London, the young Shakespeare must have been deeply stirred. He catered to public taste in telling the story of the "scepter'd isle's" rise from the depths to the heights under a popular line of rulers. In so doing, he produced some of his most memorable lines and stirring stories. At one time the Shakespeare cycle came close to being the authoritative textbook of English history; the Duke of Marlborough said Shakespeare was the only history he ever read.

The most dramatically successful of the history plays are *Henry V* and *Richard III*, dealing, respectively, with the Tudor founding father and with the defeat of the House of York in 1485 that ended the civil war, the "War of the Roses," and began the succession of Tudor kings. Shakespeare's bias against the Yorkist claimant, who lost to the future Henry VII on the field of Bosworth, has been criticized.[4] Richard III is one of Shakespeare's classic studies in villainy, fit to set alongside Iago and Lear's daughters. As for Henry V, no one questioned his courage when just after World War II the great actor Laurence Olivier brought him inspiringly to the screen to cheer for Britain's "happy few" of those years. The history plays also contained Shakespeare's greatest comic creation, the uproarious Sir John Falstaff, who was Henry V's father's early playmate.

From Shakespeare we as students of history can learn chiefly that some things have no history, in the sense that they do not essentially change. These are most of the matters of everyday private life: love, courtship, marriage, career goals, success, growing old. The seven stages of a man's life, as memorably recited in Jaques's "All the world's a stage" speech in *As You Like It*, do not seem much out of date. The eternal verities of human nature and the human condition are present here: ambition, lust for power, envy, greed, ingratitude, but also the pricks of conscience, courage, loyalty, self-sacrifice. Fully aware of villainy—none can equal Iago or Regan for pure unmitigated evil—and of the fickleness of fortune, Shakespeare's predominant mood is seldom bitter or misanthropic, as one might allege of other Elizabethan writers. A joyous spirit keeps breaking through. "I had rather have a fool to make me merry than experience to make me sad," Rosalind rebukes the melancholy Jaques, and we feel that this marvelous woman speaks for Shakespeare here. In one of the Bard's greatest plays, *Measure for Measure*, a spirit of charity forgives almost all human sins and takes away their sting.

Modern critics have argued that Shakespeare touched deep chords that echo in all people's subconscious minds. Why, asks the writer in Iris Murdoch's *The Black Prince*, is *Hamlet* "the best known work of literature in the world"? "Indian peasants, Australian lumberjacks, Argentine ranchers, Norwegian sailors, members of the Red Army, Americans, all the most remote and brutish specimens of mankind have heard of *Hamlet*," he avers. We could add that almost all the people in our book, discussed in the chapters that follow, were influenced by Shakespeare; most of them idolized him. This includes Catherine the Great, the empress of Russia; the German socialist revolutionary Karl Marx; the Italian nationalist hero Giuseppe Mazzini; and the Prague Jewish modernist writer Franz Kafka. Shakespeare was as well known in Germany, Russia, Poland, and Italy as in England. He truly belongs to the

[4]The pro-Richard cause, appealing to the naturally nonconformist, became virtually a cult; its zealots included such unlikely historians as Josephine Tey, Helen Hayes, and Tallulah Bankhead. The experts are divided; not surpisingly, there is simply not enough evidence to be sure about Richard's complicity in the murder of the little princes and other villainies.

world. Some of the leading interpreters of Shakespeare were non-English, such as the German philosopher Schlegel and the Danish critic Brandes. The great Japanese film director Akira Kurosawa's most celebrated movies were adaptations of Shakespeare ("Ran," 1985, is based on *King Lear*, "Throne of Blood," 1957, on *Macbeth*). There is a book titled *Shakespeare in India*, edited by S. Nagarajan and S. Viswanathan (1987). And so on.

Iris Murdoch's character answers his own question by saying: "Because Shakespeare by the sheer intensity of his meditation on the problem of his identity has produced a new language, a special rhetoric of consciousness . . . a meditation upon the bottomless trickery of consciousness and the redemptive role of words in the lives of those without identity, that is human beings." So Shakespeare becomes a psychoanalyst and an existentialist. But perhaps this is just another example of every age casting Shakespeare in its own image.

Perhaps this is the place to say that bardolatry finally produced the inevitable reaction, and we have individuals from Frank Harris to Anthony Burgess who, with the license to invent one's own Shakespeare that everyone seems to have felt, imagined a sexually promiscuous and drink-sodden wretch. Some Victorians thought Shakespeare shockingly obscene. The range of possible Shakespeares is almost infinite.

Shakespeare's women, many of whom like Rosalind are strong, vibrant creatures, remind us of his defects by standards of modern liberalism. Antifeminism has been detected in *Taming of the Shrew*, anti-Semitism in *Merchant of Venice*. (Though Shylock has occasionally been presented sympathetically, this was surely not Shakespeare's intent.) These were popular prejudices and Shakespeare holds his mirror up to them. Both of these plays are comedies, in which a happy ending throws a mood of reconciliation over everything; but the rebellious female in *Taming of the Shrew* is taught her place as servant of her lord and master, to the annoyance of today's feminists.

In Shakespeare's world this was no sin. Everything in the universe "observes degree, priority, and place," as Ulysses explains in *Troilus and Cressida*. This hierarchy is found in the planets and mirrored in human affairs; "the primogenitive and due of birth,/Prerogative of age, crowns, sceptres, laurels" are part of the natural order of things. The traditional society was a hierarchy in which individuals were unequal because each had his or her functional role to play on the human team. Women and men, as well as subjects and rulers, peasants and lords, young and old, had separate spheres. "Such duty as the subject owes the prince, Even such a woman oweth to her husband." To complain that this is inequality and therefore wrong would have puzzled Shakespeare along with the vast majority of his contemporaries; like the feet, the arms, and the brain in a human organism, or like the instruments in an orchestra, categories of people simply serve different functions. Release them from this rule all to go their own way—the violins, for example, trying to play the brass part—"and, hark, what discord follows!" All would be in chaos, mere force would rule, endless injustice would be done.

In this sense Shakespeare was a conservative. The Jack Cade rebels as he depicts them in *Henry VI, Part II*, are a rascally set ("The first thing we do, let's kill all the lawyers"). Nothing human is absent from Shakespeare's plays, and one can find noble examples of resistance to tyrants, indictments of bad rulers, as for example in *Measure for Measure*. The wisest people in Shakespeare's plays are the fools. But the most dominant political theme is a celebration of English resistance to foreign attacks:

> This England never did, nor never shall
> Lie at the proud foot of a conqueror.

THE ROOTS OF SHAKESPEARE'S GENIUS

Shakespeare borrowed his plots freely from earlier playwrights, reaching back to the Romans and Greeks. What sets his plays apart is the verbal witchery. Here Shakespeare cannot be seen as a lone peak of inexplicable genius towering above everything else. The Elizabethan and Jacobean stage witnessed a creative renaissance in which others participated. Marlowe, Jonson, Webster, Chapman, Daniel, and Middleton were among his contemporaries or predecessors, all of them—while not Shakespeare's equal—showing remarkable command of language and metaphor, along with striking characterizations. There is a magical richness of imagery here that suggests a unique moment in the history of language and sensibility, and/or of society and human relations.

A number of theories have been advanced to explain this unique Elizabethan quality. For one thing, the English language itself had evolved as an amalgamation of Anglo-Saxon, French (the tongue of the rulers after the 1066 Norman Conquest), and Latin. The combination produced a versatile and flexible instrument of communication. Something similar was happening in France, as Rabelais and Montaigne molded the French tongue into its modern shape out of a wilderness of medieval dialects. Latin was still used, well into the seventeenth century, for learned treatises and serious philosophical exercises—indeed, for a variety of other purposes; but the vernacular languages, the national tongues we have today, were beginning to take over "literature," whether poetry or drama or popular histories.

The peculiar quality of Shakespeare's plays had something to do with the contrast between spoken and written language. This may be viewed as a split between emotion and intellect; or between society and the individual. The bards of primitive society who declaimed from memory the epics of the tribe did so to a congregation of the people. The theater, of course, had deep roots in communal experience; its ultimate source was the tribal religious ceremony, perhaps some shamanistic ritual. The Middle Ages had produced religious drama of the sort still preserved in the celebrated Passion Play performed at Oberammergau in Bavaria, and quite familiar in England. Such pageants were traditional and anonymous; they truly belonged to the entire community.

Writing is alienating as well as more rational, permitting difficult analysis to be carried out in the privacy of the scholar's study, as he or she sits down to reason and to comb notes. Modern literature, whether poetry or prose, has typically been written in private by an individual author, printed in a book, then read in isolation by readers. This may have begun with the medieval sonnet, much developed in the Italian Renaissance of the fifteenth century.

Shakespeare's plays fall in between these two extremes of the communal and the individual. His lines, of course, were spoken to a live audience. He wrote them down, it seems, sometimes just minutes before the performance. It was rather like an improvised jazz music session. The actor helped shape the play. It is surely significant that Shakespeare began as an actor and often appeared in his own plays, not however usually taking the leading parts. The plays are filled with the idioms of popular speech. That is chiefly why they are sometimes difficult for modern ears. Shakespeare's own voice, as in the sonnets, in diction and syntax is very similar to the language of our own time. It is when he is mimicking the speech of plain people, with often uproarious and bawdy humor, that the text becomes archaic; nothing dates so quickly as yesterday's slang.

But if this oral, spontaneous element existed, Elizabethan plays *were* written; they bear the marks of literary care and craftsmanship. Shakespeare's sonnets alone testify to a preoccupation with technical esthetic mastery that derived from the mighty impact of the Italian Renaissance. At this moment in time a combination seemed possible that got the best of both worlds: the spontaneity of the oral performance with the refinement of writing. Friedrich Nietzsche was later to argue that great art must combine primitive, "Dionysian" energy with formal, rational structure in just the right proportions. The ancient Greeks of the sixth and fifth centuries B.C. had it; now again in the Renaissance did a magical artistic moment occur.

The above idea appears in a long debate among Shakespearian critics about whether he was simply a child of nature, "warbling his native woodnotes wild," as Milton put it, or a finished artist. In fact, miraculously, he was both. In one other sense Shakespeare seems to stand halfway between the old and the new cultures. The Elizabethan stage owes much to the medieval "morality" plays in which virtues and vices were personified. Shakespeare retained this concern for elemental human moral qualities, but he provided them with vivid individuality; not disembodied abstractions, allegories, and stereotyped figures, but real human beings were presented. In his own phrase, he gave to the eternal verities "a local habitation and a name." The Italian Renaissance had assisted this evolution toward a greater naturalism and realism in the arts. The modern novel, we might argue, has gone too far toward the specific and the individual, losing track of the general. Shakespeare once again stood in-between and gained the best of both worlds.

Theories such as the above have been offered to account for Shakespeare's achievement. Another one points out that extreme specialization had not yet prevented a complete integration of knowledge. Walter Ralegh once remarked that he bought every book that was published! It was still possible to do that in the late sixteenth century. A writer could take all knowledge as his playground. Shakespeare takes the entire universe for his subject. He is not afraid to face the largest issues. William Butler Yeats drew the contrast between then and now in an epigram:

> Shakespearian fish swam the sea, far away from land;
> Romantic fish swam in nets coming to the hand;
> What are all those fish that lie gasping on the strand?

And he could do so without losing touch with the average person. In Shakespeare's day high and low culture had not yet separated as they soon would. The new urban intellectual elite divorced itself from the masses during the seventeenth century. Educated individuals would begin to ridicule the old village culture of unlettered people, with that culture's magic potions and witches and folk medicine. These ancient folkways would seem ignorant and superstitious to the new scientist, as well as to the devout Christian. Shakespeare himself accepted popular notions of natural science. Adversity, he tells us, "like the toad, ugly and venomous, wears yet a precious jewel in his head." In point of fact, toads are neither poisonous nor bejeweled, as popular lore held.

At the end of the sixteenth century, high and low cultures were about to part company but they had not done so yet. There was nothing "highbrow" about Shakespeare; still sharing a common culture, rich and poor alike understood and enjoyed him. It has been questioned whether the people who flocked to the Globe or Blackfriars to see and hear a play, in the peculiar intimacy of those theaters, really included many of the London poor. Perhaps not; but the fact remains that no gulf existed between the general public consciousness and that of a literary elite—at any rate nothing like the distance that later became typical.

THE SOCIAL AND POLITICAL CLIMATE

England entered a golden age during the reign of Queen Elizabeth, 1558–1603, marked by the creation of great wealth, substantial internal peace, victory in war over the powerful kingdom of Spain, and above all a cultural renaissance of which the writings of William Shakespeare were not the only expression. Elizabeth's father, the much-married Henry VIII, had begun this era of success; or perhaps it was his father, the first Tudor monarch, Henry VII. Prior to 1485 there had been an era of civil strife, culminating in a struggle for the throne between rival claimants during the so-called War of the Roses (1455–1485). The victory of Henry Tudor over the white rose of York at the battle of Bosworth Field, of which Shakespeare himself was to give the most stirring account (if not necessarily the most accurate) in his *Richard III*, was a decisive moment in English history. It is perhaps the best place to date the beginning of the modern era and the end of the "Middle Ages." For under able monarchs a centralized state began to replace that diffusion of authority among great nobles, typical of medieval feudalism, which the War of the Roses exemplified. A strong monarchy was the bridge from feudalism to the nation-state, assuredly a hallmark of modern times. If "the modern world as we know it is a seventeenth-century creation," as noted historians have held, that is because it brought to birth not only modern science but modern politics.

The Elizabethan Age was a time of great accumulation of wealth in England. Evidences of this are to be seen in the fabulous country houses of nobles and some gentry, which are among the finest examples of private architecture the world has ever seen. The "gentry," a class that now emerged as dominant, consisted of commercial gentlemen farmers or "squires" who sold their crops on the market and might invest their profits in a variety of other enterprises. There were divisions within the gentry between lesser and greater; all gentry were socially beneath the titled aristocracy, now quite a small if eminent company. They stood a step above the yeomen farmers, although these might be quite well off.

Such investors were the source of the capital that created the great overseas joint-stock trading companies, the Levant, Muscovy, and East India companies. "Never in the annals of the modern world," famed economist John Maynard Keynes declared, "has there existed so prolonged and rich an opportunity for the businessman, the speculator, and the profiteer" as during the sixteenth century. The roots of modern capitalism lie mainly in this era. Booty from the Spanish Main, seized from Spanish treasure ships by English vessels during the conflict with Spain, enriched the land that was becoming the dominant naval power of the world and the foremost trader. The people of England began to take the lead in planting overseas colonies as well as trading abroad. English merchants appeared in Moscow about the same time that Walter Ralegh attempted to plant a colony on Roanoke Island, Virginia, a predecessor to the permanent settlement at Jamestown, founded soon after Queen Elizabeth's death in 1603. While the daring English seadogs pirated Spanish treasure from the New World, Ralegh and Humphrey Gilbert persuaded the queen to look to North America, initially for naval bases on the Spaniard's flank. England had cut her political ties to the European continent, put her resources into her navy, and looked overseas for her commercial opportunities—a famous recipe for economic success that led to Britain pioneering the Industrial Revolution. The late sixteenth century witnessed a burst of mechanical inventions, "projects" in the language of the day, that foreshadowed the more famous ones of the eighteenth century. One of Queen Elizabeth's counsellors wrote the most famous of all anticipations of the scientific age. This was Francis Bacon; he was by no means the only Elizabethan with scientific interests. In 1600 Elizabeth's court physician, William Gilbert, contributed a noteworthy treatise on magnets.

Profound social changes were underway in Shakespeare's England. London, to which about 1590 the Bard repaired from the provincial town of his origin, was already a great city—the largest in northern Europe save for Paris, which it would soon surpass. In 1600 it had a population of about 200,000, and this would double by 1650. No other city in the British Isles came close to it, and it held more than 10 percent of the nation's population by 1700. An urban historian estimates that by the latter date one Englishman in six had lived in London at some time. It was already a huge market stimulating changes in the agricultural economy that supplied it. Growing in "a most straggling and confused manner" (Daniel Defoe), London was filled with criminals, prostitutes, vagabonds, starving urchins, drunkards, miserable housing, and wretched sanitation—already much as Dickens so memorably painted it two centuries later, and rather like many Third World cities of recent decades, growing much too fast for the infrastructure. Plays were given in daylight hours because streets were unsafe after dark. Yet London was charged with excitement, energy, vitality. People went there despite all its horrors, much as they go to big cities today. Some historians think the horrors have been exaggerated; the city was not wholly a wild chaos; it was in part at least a new kind of order, with much more opportunity for advancement than in the countryside.

Writers frequently contrasted the sophisticated Londoner with the simple-minded country folk. In the first decade of the seventeenth century Thomas Middleton's "city plays" portrayed the breakdown of traditional values amid the rise of a new materialism, where wealth commanded all, corruption reigned, and rising tradesmen bought out the old aristocracy: "A mad world, my masters." A good deal of cynicism and pessimism was in evidence: Ben Jonson's Volpone, a greedy and cynical creature, provides a fair example. In this respect Shakespeare was gentler than some other dramatists, including his rival Chapman, and may have been more accurate; for already the alienated writer-intellectual was exaggerating the defects of his society.

The main source of wealth in Tudor times was wool. Though there were some large-scale English clothiers, most of the wool was exported to the weavers of the Low Countries, to be made into clothing and rugs. The lord chancellor of the English Parliament sat on a woolsack as a reminder to all of where the economic heart of England lay. Shakespeare's father did some trading in wool, as many Englishmen of his day did. Sheep have become more important than men, Thomas More had already complained in Henry VIII's time. The process of evicting peasants from their humble niche in the communal village agriculture system in order to enclose the land for raising sheep was held responsible for an increasing number of vagabonds. The Elizabethan state attempted rather feebly to deal with this distressing problem. One cause of the interest in colonizing abroad was a desire to export "the fry of the wandering beggars of England" to North America.

Shakespeare lived a dozen years into the reign of Elizabeth's successor, James I, the first of the ill-starred Stuart kings whose reigns stretching down to 1688 saw two revolutions and a civil war, which forever changed the essentials of English government. A bit of uncertainty about the new monarch may perhaps be glimpsed in *Measure for Measure*, written in the first year of James I's rule, with its plot centering on a good duke who goes on leave putting his country in charge of an unworthy lieutenant. *King Lear* and *Macbeth* also belong to Shakespeare's later years—featuring wicked successors or aspirants to the throne, in the latter case a Scotsman, as was James Stuart, son of the martyred Mary. (Chapman and Jonson were imprisoned briefly for anti-Scottish sentiments in their 1605 *Eastward Hoe*.) But Shakespeare seemingly had good relations with King James, who granted his acting company an important patent. James I's troubles with Parliament began in earnest just after Shakespeare's death in 1616. The next quarter of a century featured constant conflict between a more confident Parliament and the first two Stuart kings, James I and Charles I, ending in regicide and civil war. What a subject that would have made for the Bard!

We do not read much about the House of Commons or the Common Law in Shakespeare's court-centered history. What we read about Puritans tends to be contemptuous (cf. Malvolio in *Twelfth Night*). And although no one yet thought Parliament the sovereign body, ever since the late thirteenth century its lower house had established its claim to be consulted by the sovereign on matters of importance touching the entire realm. The Tudor kings had allowed it this function, even though they were able to dominate it. In Commons sat the proud gentry of England, the knights and squires who themselves were petty sovereigns in local affairs; they were not easily bullied. They resisted new taxes partly because they had gone in debt building those gorgeous mansions, which were a mark of status in this architecture-intoxicated age. The great architect Inigo Jones may have been a friend of Shakespeare's.

James I's quarrels with Parliament foreshadowed the great civil war and revolution his son was to face in the two decades after 1625. These were chiefly over taxation, mixed with concerns about control of foreign policy and about the Church. Underlying these issues, it seemed that a new era required more clarity in defining and locating the sovereign power of the state. "They say miracles are past; and we have our philosophical persons, to make modern and familiar, things supernatural and causeless," Shakespeare has Lafeu remark in *All's Well That Ends Well*. It had long been assumed that king and Parliament somehow shared power. But if two men ride a horse, as political theorist Thomas Hobbes put it, one must ride in front. Resting on a sense of shared community in the political family, the old order had found it possible to avoid this issue. Now it had to be resolved.

THE RISE OF MODERN SCIENCE

Thomas Hardy said that the poet should express the emotions of all ages and the thought of his own. This was very much the case with Shakespeare. In the crucial area of physics and astronomy, a great revolution had just begun. The genius of Galileo and his successors was transforming the very face of nature even as Shakespeare lived. But little of this startling novelty penetrated Shakespeare's mind, or at least his works, most of which had been written before the new cosmos was fully unveiled. The startling message from Italy that alerted Europe to the collapse of the old order of nature came in 1610, when Galileo observed through his telescope phenomena such as the moons of Jupiter and the phases of Venus wholly incompatible with the Ptolemaic model of astronomy. He was to show, additionally, that a sun-centered system, using the elliptical orbits of the planets that Johannes Kepler had discovered, accounted for the observed movements of the planets better than the old earth-centered one. Earth had been displaced from its proud spot as center of the universe. Were there perhaps other worlds, other planetary systems? Giordano Bruno was burnt at the stake for suggesting such a heresy. Some years later (1633), Galileo himself was briefly imprisoned and required to recant his theory. Born in the same year as Shakespeare, the Italian genius lived a quarter of a century longer. In the year he died, Isaac Newton was born.

Shakespeare's picture of the cosmos derived from the ancient Greeks, especially the astronomer Ptolemy of the Hellenistic era. The earth stood solidly at the center of the universe, while around it in circular spheres revolved the planets, including the sun, which were made of a different, weightless substance and carried on crystalline spheres, rather like balloons on strings. The last outlying circle of heavenly bodies carried the fixed stars. When Nicholas Copernicus suggested in 1543 that the sun rather than the earth might be at the center of the planetary system, few took his hypothesis seriously, since he offered no explanation of the dynamics of such a system. It defied common sense to suppose that the earth, a heavy body, could be in motion without any evident mover. True, there were serious problems with the Ptolemaic model as more and more observations forced awkward modifications in it to account for the movement of the planets.

This old Ptolemaic astronomy was tied to an Aristotelian philosophy that blended with medieval Christianity. As the earth was a unique physical body forming the center of the cosmos, so man as lord of the earth was a unique being. Everything in the universe was made for him. Today, as we contemplate a universe consisting of billions upon billions of stars like our own solar system, which is situated somewhere on the edge of one of ten billion or so galaxies, we may well smile at the earth-centered and human-centered outlook of our ancestors of only a few hundred years ago. But the laughter is a little hollow. The universe was then a friendlier place. To the ancients anything that happened in the physical universe was connected with human affairs. Correspondences between the macrocosm and the microcosm, between heavens and humans, were seen everywhere. As the plotters prepare Caesar's assassination, in Shakespeare's *Julius Caesar*, strange portents abound; lightning flashes and wonders are seen. "The heavens themselves blaze forth the death of princes." To Shakespeare's audience this was no mere metaphor but literal reality; nature and humanity were so closely tied together that anything that happened in one arena could not fail to affect the other.

We may well agree with those who have thought that the old worldview suited art and literature better than the new. Modern science disconnected the natural order from the human, depriving the former of life to make its hard, cold matter subject to mathematically stated laws; with Descartes it might put soul and body in separate compartments. In T.S. Eliot's phrase it dissociated the writer's sensibility.

In England during Shakespeare's time, possibly his most illustrious contemporary, Francis Bacon (1561–1626), expressed a new intellectual outlook. Bacon was almost as amazing an intellectual prodigy as Shakespeare. A good deal more prominent, he wrote a half dozen books that helped change the mind of the Western world, in the intervals of a busy life as statesman, lawyer, judge. His essays on a variety of subjects are full of pungent epigrams, like his "apothegms": "Hope is a good breakfast, but a bad supper"; "Money is like muck, not good except it be spread"; "The remedy is worse than the disease." "Be so true to thyself as thou be not false to others" reminds us so much of Polonius's remark in Shakespeare's *Hamlet*, "To thine own self be true, and it must follow . . . thou canst not then be false to any man," that the Baconian authorship of Shakspeare's plays may seem plausible.

But Bacon's most serious project was nothing less than a total intellectual revolution, a "Great Instauration" or completely fresh start toward creating an effective body of scientific knowledge. "Knowledge is power," he knew. From the writings of his later years (1620–1626) emerges a picture of the modern scientist, untrammeled by past authority, conducting experimental research in coordination with many others, and from this basis in factual data framing hypotheses that will guide further research. "Keep the eye fixed steadily upon the facts of nature," he wrote. Bacon served to inspire a wave of seventeenth-century interest in experimentation, culminating in a new kind of plain and clear style and in the Royal Society, an institution for the advancement of learning, something that Bacon had imagined would bring together the work and findings of many researchers. With the slightly later French genius René Descartes, Bacon shared the role of prophet of modern scientific methods, "secretary of nature."

In Shakespeare's next-to-last play, *The Tempest* (1611), Prospero the magician, whom some have thought Shakespeare intended to represent himself, says at the end

> Now my charms are all o'erthrown,
> And what strength I have's mine own. . . .

Perhaps in this passage Shakespeare meant to acknowledge the Galilean revolution, bringing an end to magic and enthroning a rational scientific outlook. The age of the artist was ending. The world was losing its poetry.

Why did Shakespeare leave the following famous lines to be placed on his tomb?[5]

> Good friend for Jesus' sake forbear
> To dig the dust enclosèd here!
> Blessed be the man that spares these stones
> And cursed be he that moves these bones.

Was it because he wanted to stand as a symbol of stability? What he would have made of the momentous changes in society, intellectual thought, and politics that were underway just at the time of his death we cannot know.

Shakespeare's fame began to spread only after publication of the First Folio in 1623, followed by the Second in 1632. That no one bothered to undertake his biography until the end of the century—chief reason for the failure to save evidence about his life—may perhaps be blamed on England's absorption in the political struggles of the seventeenth century. The Puritans banned theatrical productions as immoral during their reign in the 1650s. Another reason was the turn toward science and reason, which made Shakespeare's style seem antique to some. During the Restoration, after 1660, it was thought necessary to rewrite Shakespeare, removing the impurities—a neoclassical arrogance so astonishing that it contributed to the subsequent decline of that esthetic outlook. Though interest in "the national poet" grew during the years after England's Glorious Revolution of 1688, and Dr. Johnson's edition of Shakespeare's works, so long labored over, was a landmark of the late eighteenth century, it was not until the Romantic period of the early nineteenth century that bardolatry came into its own. And indeed the whole Romantic movement in literature, so vital a part of modern consciousness, drew heavily on Shakespeare for its inspiration. For the realm of Shakespeare's mastery was the human heart. It is ironic that we know so little about his own.

---

[5]If in fact he did. Like almost everything else about the Bard, this lacks confirmation. The first recorded observation of the epitaph was seventy-five years after the burial..

2

Newton and the Enlightenment

ENGLAND'S GLORIOUS REVOLUTION AND ITS CONSEQUENCES

England had its great national revolutions in the seventeenth century. The first of these came in the 1640s and 1650s, and led through civil war to the execution of King Charles I following the defeat of his royalists at the hands of the Puritan New Model Army of fighting saints. Conflict between Parliament and monarch, common law and royal courts, Puritan and Anglican had erupted under James I and gained momentum in the reign of Charles I in the 1630s. For English monarchs a critical problem was the deeply planted belief that Parliament must approve any new tax. It would take much space to explain why Parliament, and especially the lower of its two houses—the House of Commons—had come to play a special role in English politics. No one had ever thought it the sovereign body; but since the late thirteenth century Parliament had established its claim to be consulted by the sovereign on matters of importance touching the whole realm.

As previously noted, the House of Commons was the domain of knights and squires, men of substance, who were accustomed to governing their own localities and not easily intimidated. Under the Tudor kings, Parliament, though occasionally restive, did not rebel against these strong and prestigious monarchs. It proved much harder for the less popular and less skillful Stuarts to manage this troublesome body, even more so as they urgently needed to have Parliament provide them with more revenue.

The cause of Parliament tended to run in the same harness as the religious beliefs of Puritanism, for the latter provided a basis for resistance to royal power. Puritans thought Church leaders should be chosen by the congregations, not appointed by the king as head of state. Puritans were not all of exactly the same mind; they ranged from relatively conservative ones to a radical fringe who echoed the outburst of sects in the German world that the Reformation had unleashed. Some of these proclaimed the coming millennium bringing a new, egalitarian social order, when all woes would vanish and people would live together in harmony and peace.

In 1641 a long and dramatic struggle culminated in war between the two standards, the king's and Parliament's. With the victory of the latter side, and the execution of King Charles I, England became a Commonwealth, of which the leading Puritan army general, Oliver Cromwell, was named Lord Protector. Cromwell proceeded to purge and then dismiss Parliament, in whose name his side had come to power. Thus do revolutions "devour their own children," defeating the very purposes for which they were fought.

After the death of brave Oliver in 1658 the Puritan elite negotiated a restoration of the monarchy. Puritanism had worn out its welcome in England. The grim seriousness of the Puritan ethic had waged war on a "merry England" of popular amusements and festivals, including the theater, which was closed down altogether in the 1650s. No more Shakespeare! The character qualities that Puritanism fostered nourished a sturdy middle class of hard workers and savers who brought modern economic society to England and Scotland earlier than anywhere else. But a strong swing in the opposite direction marked Restoration England after 1660. Charles II, son of the Puritans' victim, returned from exile in France to rule for the next twenty-five years. With him returned the Church of England, though not the royal law courts that had battled against the common law judges, and not, on the whole, the Crown's ascendancy over Parliament.

Charles was no Puritan; the merry monarch of many mistresses and a naughty court was not a tyrant either. Parliament retained a number of its rights, and Charles did not attempt to rule without it. It was agreed that the House of Commons must approve taxes, probably the major issue in the long dispute between king and Parliament. Still, the crucial question of which was sovereign had not yet been clearly answered; Charles II was simply too cautious or weak to push the issue. The Restoration era was filled with plots and counterplots, from both sides—extreme royalists and unrepentant commonwealthmen. With good reason people suspected that Charles had converted to Roman Catholicism and that he took subsidies from the powerful king of France. But Charles never attempted to force his secret faith or his royal prerogative on the country. He did once dissolve a Parliament to forestall an attempt to pass a law excluding a Roman Catholic from the throne. Under the names of Whig and Tory the old Parliament-royalist division was continued; not by armed violence in the main, yet not with full acceptance of the rules of democratic politics either.

All eyes were on the next in line for the throne, Charles's brother James, who was an avowed Roman Catholic. Charles had not succeeded in begetting a legitimate son, though he had several illegitimate ones, one of whom, the Duke of Monmouth, tried to seize the Crown when Charles died in 1685. James crushed the Monmouth Rebellion with severity, and proceeded to try to force a French-style royal absolutism on England, along with—so it appeared—the Roman Catholic religion. Within three years he was gone. Perhaps his chief sin was attempting to keep a standing army to enforce his decrees. He also tried to control the universities. Virtually all England, Whigs and Tories alike, joined in opposing him. For, in religious terms, James II represented as much of a threat to the Church of England as to the Puritans, who were represented by several nonconformist sects including Presbyterians and Independents.

The two parties joined in approaching the constitutional king of the Netherlands, William of Orange, who was married to one of James's daughters. She had been raised a Protestant. This Dutchman was the outstanding champion in Europe of Protestant resistance to the great power of France, which threatened to impose its dominance on all of Europe. The relative power of the strong centralized French state had swelled with the ruin of Germany in the Thirty Years' War, along with Spain's dramatic decline. A war pitting France against a Grand Alliance was about to erupt. With a brief interruption from 1698 to 1701 it went on until 1714. The fate of Europe hung in the balance, and this factor strongly influenced British conceptions of politics.

The letter of invitation to William and Mary to come and serve as England's sovereigns mentioned grievous offenses on the part of James II's government against the people's "religion, liberties, and property," and declared that nineteen of every twenty English subjects would welcome James's overthow. When, borne by a Protestant wind, William sailed across the North Sea to England late in 1688 he found this to be true. Abandoned by almost everyone, James fled, hurling the Great Seal into the Thames as he left. For this as well as his illegal acts of government he was held to have sacrificed the throne. But he had an infant son (though some refused to believe this) who by the principle of hereditary succession was the rightful king. Parliament, however, bestowed the crown on William and Mary jointly, exacting from them the pledges contained in the famous Bill of Rights of 1689. It was an apparent example of a contract between people and rulers, based on certain inviolable "natural rights," and containing an implicit right of revolution should the government violate these rights. It would be a model for subsequent declarations of rights in America and France. A century later the American Bill of Rights repeated those of 1689 often in virtually the same language. Planted during the Stuart era, the American colonies grew up in the shadow of the Glorious Revolution and absorbed their political philosophy from John Locke's famous arguments for the social contract.

More concretely, Parliament had established its supremacy over the Crown, ending the long stalemate between the two forces. There would be a monarch, but he or she was bound by law to respect the limitations on royal power solemnized in the Bill of Rights. Never again would a monarch attempt to rule without Parliament or in defiance of it. Parliament proceeded to stipulate that the throne would pass to the nearest Protestant line, ruling out Roman Catholics, and in 1714 after Mary's sister Anne ruled from 1702 to 1714, and like her sister died childless, Parliamentary leaders settled on George of Hanover, husband of a granddaughter of James I. The house has been there ever since. Without departing altogether from hereditary principles, Parliament had set the rules for the royal succession. The German George I's disinterest in English affairs facilitated Parliament's victory. By strict hereditary principles James II's son should have been king, but there were not many of his supporters in England (more in Scotland); in 1715 a Jacobite uprising failed badly.

The Common Law had triumphed along with Parliament. So had the ban on a standing army. The social order had scarcely been touched; the squires remained locally dominant; indeed, their position was strengthened in some ways, for Property was chief of the guaranteed rights. The House of Commons was far from a democratic body; no more than one in ten Englishmen was entitled to vote, and they generally chose the local grandee on whom their welfare depended. But the principle of popular sovereignty might be used later to extend the popular basis of government. The Bill of Rights included a right to bear arms, to have a trial by jury, to be free from taxation without consent. England after the Glorious Revolution enjoyed substantial freedom of the press and religious toleration, although in principle these were not yet complete. The Licensing Act requiring publications to be approved in advance ended in 1695. The 1689 Act of Toleration, while granting non-Anglican Protestants (Unitarians excepted) a right to their religion, left the established Church of England in a privileged position; political rights depended on belonging to it. But nonconformists had little difficulty evading the ban by practicing "occasional conformity," that is, showing up at the Church of England once a year for a few minutes. The mainline nonconformists were free to practice their religion. The coming age would be a "latitudinarian" one, reacting against the inflamed theological passions of the century just about to end.

The British were inordinately proud of their liberty in the eighteenth century. "A land, perhaps the only land in the universe," wrote jurist William Blackstone in 1758, "in which political and civil liberty is the very end and scope of the constitution." The young French writer who called himself Voltaire, visiting England in the 1720s, was deeply impressed with this English liberty, comparing his own country unfavorably to it. Continental great states, from Bourbon France to Peter the Great's Russia, were based on absolute monarchy; nothing like the English Parliament existed on the Continent except in one or two tiny German states. The French *parlements* were courts of law, registering the royal edicts, not representative lawmaking bodies. England stood alone as a major power boasting constitutional liberty and parliamentary ascendancy. Her religious toleration, while not complete, surpassed other countries with the exception of the Netherlands. Louis XIV had rescinded the old edict of toleration of Protestants in France and tried to force religious uniformity on his country.

Under constitutional government and religious liberty England (becoming Great Britain in 1707 through union with Scotland) prospered mightily in the eighteenth century. Most of the years from 1688 to 1714 found England engaged in war at the head of an alliance against Louis XIV's France, whose awesome military power had threatened to upset the European balance of power. In what may be regarded as the first "world war" of modern times, the Grand Alliance checked France, forcing her to yield much of her territorial gains. After 1714 she subsided as a threat to rule the Continent. Though an important state still—indeed, the most important one culturally and intellectually—France for the next seventy-five years was not strong enough to dominate Europe. Some have argued that France was so fatally weakened by the protracted wars of Louis XIV, ending in defeat, that her path led down to the revolution of 1789. Certainly the two Louises that followed the Sun King, as Louis XIV was styled, marked a sad decline.

ISAAC NEWTON

England's example of a successful though bloodless and moderate revolution, leading to ordered liberty under the law, was a powerful source of that cultural and intellectual climate of opinion known as the Enlightenment. As it happened, the Glorious Revolution coincided with another English contribution, by the great mathematician and scientist Isaac Newton, whose epochal work on the laws of physical motion, *Philosophiae Naturalis Principia Mathematica* —to give its full title—*Mathematical Principles of Natural Philosophy*—appeared in 1687. Few books have had so mighty an influence. It signaled the beginning of a new worldview.

Newton was a child of the seventeenth-century passion for a new kind of science. Science offered itself to the seventeenth century as an alternative to religion as well as the older sort of philosophy—a new attitude, a new mode of discourse—at a time when the passions of theology threatened to destroy society. In England, the Royal Society quite consciously presented an approach to knowledge that was calmer, less impassioned, and less dogmatic. The new scientists did not so much reject religion as bypass it. Let us turn away from vain disputations, they argued, and seek plain, useful truths by experimentation. If God exists, this will be manifested in His works. The style of this new breed of inquirer mirrored their mood; they cultivated a plain, clear, unvarnished prose that eschewed the traditional devices of rhetoric, avoiding "enthusiasm" and too much imagination. "Who can behold without indignation how many mists and uncertainties these specious Tropes and Figures have brought on our knowledge?" asked Thomas Sprat, the historian of the Royal Society.

Ever since Galileo overthrew the ancient model of the heavens at the beginning of the seventeenth century, doubt had reigned about the structure of the cosmos; people like John Donne might feel "all coherence gone." Much exciting scientific work had failed to cohere in a new synthesis. If the heavy earth was in motion through space without an evident mover, how it managed to do this was explained only by Descartes's dubious system of whirlpools. There were various models of planetary motion to choose from; the great Danish observer Tycho Brahe suggested, for example, that the planets might be in motion about the sun but the whole of this system around the earth. The Church of Rome tolerated the Galilean system only if it were viewed as an unproven hypothesis. Now a Lincolnshire farm boy was to show how the heliocentric universe worked.

Newton brushed up against the Glorious Revolution when, as the author of a book just about to be published, which every scientist in Europe was scurrying to lay hands on, he found himself involved in the crisis precipitated in 1687 by James II's attempt to pack the colleges of both Cambridge and Oxford universities with Catholics. Though Newton was normally aloof from university affairs, the forty-five-year-old professor of mathematics and fellow of Trinity College at Cambridge lent his pen to the cause of fending off the royal demands. "A mixture of Papist and Protestants in the same University can neither subsist happily nor long together," Newton wrote. Today it would surprise us to be told this; but in 1687 the fact of James Stuart's religion was closely bound up with his dependence on France and his evident desire to install a French-style absolute monarchy.

Newton stuck his neck so far out that he might well have suffered severe penalties had King James II triumphed over the revolutionary forces. As it was, the great scientist became a member of the Convention Parliament that offered the Crown to William and Mary. Although he played no very prominent role in this historic action, Newton was indelibly associated with the great political revolution of 1688/89.

Published in 1687 and eagerly discussed in the ensuing years, Newton's magisterial work, the *Principia Mathematica* as it was familiarly known, emerged from the brain of a stunning mathematical genius. It demonstrated the exact law of universal gravitation and showed that this law applies to all bodies alike: The same force that draws a falling body to earth keeps the moon in its orbit. As early as 1666, when he was twenty-four, Newton had become convinced of the validity of his inverse square law, that every particle attracts every other with a force obtained by multiplying the masses together and dividing by the square of the distance between them—the law of universal gravitation. But he could not prove it at that time, so he shelved the idea.

In every great scientific discovery the suspicion of it seems to precede its proof by some distance. Darwin's evolution by natural selection provides another famous example; this later Cambridge scientist had his theory long before his proof, and for that reason held up publication of *The Origin of Species* for many years, publishing in 1858 only when it seemed another scientist was about to do so. In both cases the interval between the flash of intuition and publication of the fully fleshed out theory was about twenty years. Darwin's *Wunderjähre*, corresponding to Newton's 1665/66, were 1837/1839. One might compare Marx's 1843/44 period leading on to *Das Kapital* in 1867.

Many people, indeed, had hold of the general idea of evolution in the first half of the nineteenth century. Similarly, individuals other than Newton entertained the conception of a law of physical attraction. To prove it was quite another thing. Needed were new mathematical tools. And so Newton worked on differential and integral calculus, the mathematics of moving bodies and changing quantities. But the study of optics, to which he made brilliant contributions, distracted him for a time; so did some largely fruitless researches into alchemy (premodern chemistry). He published his theory of gravitation only when urged to do so by Edmund Halley of the Royal Society (founded in 1662, early in the reign of Charles II, who notably encouraged science). Newton's fault had been that of many a young genius, going off in too many directions; as his biographer Richard Westfall says, he had left a litter of unfinished treatises. Now, in his forties, Newton put it all together. For one priceless moment he managed to focus all his energies and abilities on one great problem and see it through to a conclusion.

Halley, visiting Newton in August 1684, heard him say that he had already proved that the elliptical course of the planets, which the great scientist Johannes Kepler had discovered by laborious means, followed from the inverse-square law of force, and had the proof somewhere in his papers, which he could not find! The discussion seems to have impressed Newton for the first time with the importance of his own discovery and the need for its full development. He worked intensively on the *Principia* from 1684 to 1686, so totally absorbed that he scarcely found time for eating.

The *Principia* gave exact formulation to the laws of motion, demolished Descartes's popular theory of the motion of heavenly bodies, calculated the masses of the sun and planets, and lucidly explained such heretofore mysterious phenomena as the orbits of comets, the precession of the equinoxes, the cause of ocean tides. Suddenly, it seemed, all mysteries had vanished; "God said, Let Newton be, and all was light."

For the first time in Western history the authority of the ancient Greeks had been shown to be wrong, and replaced by better knowledge. People were encouraged to think that this new scientific method might correct all manner of old errors, putting mankind on the road to infinite progress for the first time in history. Only a few cavilled at Newton's failure to offer a mechanical explanation of "attraction at a distance,"[1] or at his assumption of an absolute space and time.[2] Enough to know the exact formula by which physical nature worked. Newton's notes on methods stressed the need to avoid unnecessary hypotheses. The principle of economy ("Occam's Razor," the medieval philosophers had called it after one of their number) dictated that one should not use more of an explanation than is necessary to account for a phenomenon. In Newton's words, "We are to admit no more causes of natural things than are both true and sufficient to explain their appearance."

What kind of man was this creator of the greatest of revolutions? Though there are many mysteries, we know a great deal more about Newton's life than we do about Shakespeare's—a measure of the advances in preserving knowledge in the intervening century. Yet there are some parallels in the lives of the two great English geniuses. One was the rural obscurity of their origins. Newton's father, like Shakespeare's, could not write his name, and when Isaac came to study at Cambridge in 1661 at the age of eighteen he had never before ventured out of his Lincolnshire hamlet. Nor had any of his sheepherding ancestors ever gone to a university. Like Shakespeare he was a natural genius. Not, to be sure, of the same sort! Newton had absolutely no feeling for the arts. The man who described statues as "stone dolls" was reported to have called poetry "ingenious nonsense" and is known to have walked out of the only opera he ever attended. His library contained no Shakespeare or any other classic of literature. Like many another intellectual he was humorless, tactless, wholly absorbed in thought.[3]

Not that Newton's mind dwelt only among abstractions. The secret of his awesome genius lay in the combination of superlative mathematical ability with practical engineering skills. As a child he built all kinds of machines. As an adult he not only designed but built a reflecting telescope (1672), making the tools needed for the job! Unlike many highly theoretical physicists, he had a strong aptitude for visual-spatial relations, along with a hands-on laboratory skill, to go with his mathematical ability.

Newton's disinterest in the humanities did not extend to religion. Biblical studies, at least, were a lifelong obsession. They were indeed a matter of

[1]The Cartesian tradition died hard on the Continent. Christian Huygens, the great Dutch scientist of this era, though he did not doubt the validity of the inverse-square law, thought that Newton had not really explained what gravity is—true in a sense—and in 1690 offered a revised version of Descartes's vortex theory, which attempted to explain the physical process by which gravity takes place.

[2]Einstein's criticism of Newton's law of gravity, two hundred years later, was partly anticipated by some at the time, e.g., Bishop George Berkeley. But little attention was paid to it then.

[3]According to a famous story about Newton the only time he was known to laugh was when someone asked him what use there was in studying mathematics (Euclid)—whereupon he was "very merry."

consuming fascination to Newton's generation. If "the Bible alone is the religion of Protestants," as one English cleric remarked, it was vital to know what it said; but critical scholarship as developed during the Renaissance discovered serious problems in establishing an accurate text of the Judaic and Christian Scriptures. That huge body of writing had been subjected to defective copying and translation for nearly two millennia. As a textual problem, Shakespeare's plays pale into triviality compared to the Bible. Produced in Shakespeare's time by a committee of scholars, the authorized King James Version of the Bible was a marvel of literature and even, for its time, of scholarship, but it was far from impeccable. Textual disputes involved important theological issues. Such issues were raised when, in retreat from Reformation passions, people approved a more rational approach to Christianity.

A few "deists" claimed that all the necessary truths of religion and morality could be found in natural reason alone, without need for the Bible or the organized churches. There was no need for the "revelation" allegedly contained in Holy Scripture; nature was enough of a revelation. Such a credo was much too bold for Georgian England. If one stuck to the Bible, there was enough room for controversy. Newton became deeply interested in the trinitarian controversy, involving the relationship of God the Father and Christ, His sometime human son. The issue was not just a metaphysical one; since ancient times it had been realized that making Christ human and not (altogether) divine meant humanizing and moralizing the Christian religion.

Newton became convinced, probably with some justification, that New Testament texts had been tampered with in order to support the orthodox position on the Holy Trinity. In brief, he was a Unitarian, a mildly heretical position at this time. But Newton kept his doubts pretty much to himself. Of his belief in God there can be no doubt. He strongly disliked Descartes because the Frenchman's view of the cosmos left no place for divine intervention; the universe was a perfect machine that, once created and started, ran by itself thereafter. Newton's refusal to speculate about the nature of the mysterious attraction between bodies, which annoyed the Cartesians, tied in with his firm belief in a divine providence. "Such a wonderful uniformity in the planetary system must be allowed the effect of choice," Newton declared, thus lending his support to the argument from design. So marvelous a system must have had an all-wise Creator. "This most beautiful system of the sun, planets, and comets, could only proceed from the counsel and dominion of an intelligent and powerful Being." It also required the continuing presence of a divine agent to sustain it. Detractors of Newton's system sneered that he made God into a defective manufacturer, who had to stay around to keep making the necessary repairs to His creation.

Eighteenth-century "deism" undoubtedly derived in good part from Newton's success in plumbing the secrets of nature, but Christians fitted Newtonianism easily into their creed. Those who held that human reason alone could provide all that was needed in the way of religious and moral beliefs obviously subverted Christianity, which claimed that God's revelation in Scripture formed the essential foundations of religion. Ridiculing the Bible and assailing the clergy, the deists were shockingly radical and for a time in the 1690s were subjected to censorship in England. Yet a fine line separated orthodox and unorthodox "natural theology." Most good Christians in the eighteenth century held their religion to be rational in the sense that, once revealed, this religion was consistent with reason, though reason alone could never have found it out.

Newton himself subscribed to a rational Christianity that should be distinguished from non-Christian Deism. A popular series of English lectures invoking Newton's name dwelt on the affinities between science and religion; except among a handful of the bolder rationalists, there was no such conflict between science and religion as emerged in the Darwinian nineteenth century. Certainly not in England; after mid-century, it is true, some of the bolder French "philosophers" strayed closer to atheism and materialism. Newtonianism, with a slight shift in emphasis, might serve as the basis of either rational Christianity or anti-Christian deism. If in using Newton as a basis for the latter, Voltaire and the French deists misused the great scientists's authority, it was an easy mistake to make.

NEWTON AND ALCHEMY

Probably the oddest feature, to us, of Newton's formidable intellectual activity was his long pursuit of what today is usually regarded as the pseudoscience of alchemy. This was premodern chemistry, so different from the modern science bearing that name that it had to be completely jettisoned before the latter could come to birth in the late eighteenth century. A revolutionary in his physics, Newton seemed like a reactionary in his chemistry. In formulating his laws of motion and gravity he purged from physical "matter" all the vitalistic qualities that the older philosophy had attributed to it; but in his chemical experiments he accepted such qualities. For alchemists saw metals and rocks as living things, whose changes were related to spiritual qualities—a kind of mysticism of the laboratory. Esoteric alchemists thought that the procedures for steadily purifying metals—to end, they hoped, in creating the elixir or philosopher's stone—should be accompanied by stages of spiritual progress toward perfect knowledge and purity. Stoic and Neoplatonic philosophy, which saw all elements of the universe interconnected, and alleged the similar nature of all being, everything containing both physical and spiritual aspects, had influenced alchemy. In brief, minerals had souls as much as did animals and men. The trick was to tune in on their corresponding spiritual wavelengths, as it were.

Alchemy was an ancient and somewhat arcane study that over the centuries had produced an oddly imposing literature. Newton read all of it, and he conducted many experiments of his own. He accumulated a huge body of papers on alchemy—much more than on all other subjects combined. Most of this obscure mass of Newtoniana was not even read until recent times, and is still far from being understood. Though Newton was a friend of Robert Boyle, the pioneer student of gases (also a kind of universal genius who wrote on religious and philosophical as well as scientific questions), Newton's chemical researches did not bear on the chemical revolution later to be achieved by others. They apparently stand as the aberration of a strange and powerful mind, just as alchemy itself is an odd cul de sac in the history of thought.[4] Newton's commitment to alchemy does testify to his deeply spiritual conception of nature, as well as his compulsion to link all of nature together in a single harmonious totality. This side of Newton stands in strange contrast to the fault that some romantics later accused him of: the conversion of nature into a machine. When Samuel Coleridge asserted that "Newton was a mere materialist," he was quite mistaken.

Much alchemical lore is more relevant to mental than physical science. The great twentieth-century psychoanalyst Carl Jung pointed out alchemy's relevance to depth psychology. This is interesting, because Newton's personality was in fact a neurotic one, the result perhaps of an abnormal infancy, somewhat resembling Bertrand Russell's (see Chapter 13). His father died before Newton's birth, and his mother remarried when the boy was three, leaving him to be brought up by a grandmother. Modern psychological theory might find here a cause of what was evidently a homosexual personality; Newton never married. This may well have been, of course, because of his incessant compulsion to thought; a philosopher cannot give hostages to fortune in the form of wife and children; he is always enchained to his creative life. But in 1693 Newton experienced a nervous collapse related in part, it appears, to his separation from a male friend. He recovered but was never very creative after that, though he tinkered with the projects that were the fruits of his youthful genius. It has been suggested that Newton's late mental problems stemmed from mercury poisoning emanating from his chemical experiments, but the evidence for this is not very convincing.

He pulled together his brilliant earlier work on light and colors for publication (*Opticks*). Newton had conducted experiments with prisms at the same time that he conceived the theory of gravitation, in 1665/66, the wonder years of his youth. Descartes, Boyle, and Hooke had all offered theories of colors, brought into notice especially with the invention of the telescope. Finding himself a prism at a local fair, Newton caused it to diffuse white light into the colors of the spectrum, and he offered a totally new theory to account for this phenomenon, one that broke sharply with the older tradition just as did his laws of gravity and motion (but not his chemistry), and which form

---

[4]Some scholars recently have given Newton's alchemy more sympathy than it formerly received. See the bibliographical notes for this chapter.

the basis of modern theories of light. Newton was as modern as Einstein in holding to a particle or "corpuscle" theory of light—the nineteenth century would revise him here in favor of waves, but the twentieth century came back to him. With the same secretiveness or fearfulness that led him to delay publication of the inverse-square law for twenty years, Newton withheld his *Opticks* until 1704, and then published it only in a Latin edition. But this was justified inasmuch as there was much controversy in this area, and Newton's unorthodox view of light had been anything but universally accepted.

NEWTON'S LATER YEARS

Although not creative in his later years, Newton lived to the ripe age of eighty-five, held in awe and much honored. Stories about his incredible mathematical ability—solving with ease puzzles that had baffled others for centuries—made him a living legend. The last thirty years of his life he spent at the Royal Mint, first as Warden and then as Master, a highly remunerative position. Newton seems to have shared one trait at least with Shakespeare—a keen sense of his own material interests. He died a wealthy man.

His main blemish was "that last infirmity of noble minds," as his older contemporary John Milton called it: jealousy about his entitlement to credit for important discoveries. This led him into some venomous quarrels with other scientists. He spent an inordinate amount of time in self-justification. Then as now the scientific community was filled with oversize egos avid for fame and wildly jealous of competitors. Newton's ego was certainly not the least of these.

Chief though by no means the only one of Newton's rivals was the German genius G.W. Leibniz, who fiercely disputed with him the claim to priority in the invention of the calculus. Neither of these scientific superstars showed much magnanimity in the dispute, which would seem to have been a case of independent discovery rather than of one plagiarizing the other as each charged. The public controversy between "two of the greatest philosophers and mathematicians of Europe," one dismayed scientist wrote in 1714, was a scandal that might prove "fatal to learning." This did not prevent the dispute from going on with increasing fury. Newton wrote biased accounts that he had published in several languages. Various would-be peacemakers met the usual fate of their kind, earning the hostility of both sides. The argument, indeed, still endures; it is hard to say that it has ever quite been settled. It is the classic example of a controversy involving claims to priority in scientific discovery. Similar disputes would surround other famous scientific or technological innovations, including those of Darwin and even Einstein. In most cases the discovery of a great scientific fact or principle is a complex process to which many minds contribute, and which more than one may bring to fruition at about the same time. Sometimes the discoverers express the law in differing symbols or language, giving rise to almost irreconcilable disputes about priority.[5]

Newtonianism did not triumph without a struggle over the strongly entrenched Continental schools, especially Cartesianism, but with the aid of Voltaire and others it gradually did. The eighteenth century worked out more fully the implications of Newtonian mechanics and astronomy. The general Newtonian philosophy left a deep mark, in part because it was more compatible with religious conservatism than Descartes. In the end, and to a considerable degree in his own lifetime (some innovative scientists are not so fortunate), Newton's triumph was conceded. The myth of Newton grew; in 1837 the authoritative Victorian historian of science William Whewell spoke for virtually everyone in declaring that Newton was "altogether without a rival or neighbour," his work on universal gravitation "indisputably and incomparably the greatest scientific study ever made." Today, even after Einstein's theories have modified Newtonianism in some respects, this judgment is seldom questioned.

JOHN LOCKE AND THE EIGHTEENTH-CENTURY ENLIGHTENMENT

The spirit of the Enlightenment drew heavily on the new scientific philosophy; Voltaire wrote a popularization of Newton, and the leading publication of the French *philosophes* was a multivolume Encyclopedia designed to replace all previous repositories of knowledge by drawing on recent technical and scientific advances. But the writers who with Voltaire formed the *philosophe* movement were at pains to distinguish themselves from all previous philosophers; they were not fruitless "metaphysicians." Not usually practicing scientists, they were literary propagandists for a scientific order of things. The new philosophy was in effect the scientific method. The basis of this assumption was in fact a far from indisputable assertion, that reality is phsyical matter and its qualities may be discovered; but this implicit metaphysics was mainly concealed.

Equally as great an influence as Newton on these propagandists of the Enlightenment was his friend John Locke, with whom Newton was often paired. A versatile intellectual with a famous library and a sometime practitioner of medicine, Locke was interested in science though not a mathematician. His own epochal publication, which acknowledged the influence of Newton, was the 1690 *Essay Concerning Human Understanding*. Before that he had been identified with the liberal cause in the events leading up to the Glorious Revolution—indeed, he found it prudent to leave England for a time

[5]In the 1980s French and American teams of medical researchers found the virus that causes the disease AIDS at about the same time, giving rise to a heated argument about priority in which charges of plagiarism were made.

just before 1688. His widely read tracts on politics made a case for the basis of government in a social contract between rulers and citizens; though he was not directly involved in the events of 1688, Locke's *Treatises on Government*, along with his *Letter on Toleration*, seemed to many to sum up the Glorious Revolution's meaning, and in the eighteenth century these were treated as almost the sacred oracles in political theory. The deep impact of Locke on the Americans who made the 1776 Revolution against British rule has always been conceded, the only controversy being about whether Locke stood alone or at the head of a group in the estimation of Thomas Jefferson's generation.

In criticizing the old patriarchal justifications for monarchy (the king as father of his people) Locke offered a view of society as made up of equal individuals establishing political society in a deliberate rational act, choosing to endow government with certain powers in order to serve their own higher self-interest, but reserving other rights that government could not legally infringe. In such an idea one might see an analogy with Newton's separate particles obeying a general rational law.

Extending this idea to the sphere of economics was to be a great eighteenth-century project; some of Locke's writings pioneer this enterprise of political economy. It remained for two Scottish disciples, David Hume and especially Adam Smith, to show that the action of individual human agents, based on self-interest, add up to a social order governed by general laws. Growing up in the shadow of Newton, the Scotsman Adam Smith as a student in the 1740s was keenly interested in physical science, and once embarked upon a history of astronomy. But his more mature work, that for which he became almost as famous as Newton, was *The Wealth of Nations*. Here we meet a conception of society as a collection of individuals whose rational pursuit of their own material interests leads to a society in which wealth is maximized. The writer Bernard Mandeville had already presented in less rigorous form this thesis that "Private vices equal public benefits."

The Newtonian analogy was ever-present in the eighteenth-century mind. Thus, one of the intellectual leaders of the French Revolution of 1789, the Abbe Sieyes, saw the legislative process as one in which "all particular interests must be allowed to jostle and collide with one another," after which "they finally come together and fuse into a single opinion, just as in the physical universe a single and more powerful force can be seen to result from a mass of opposed ones."

Locke largely shared Sir Isaac's views on religion. They were both Unitarians, and they both believed in a religion of nature, which strayed close to the boundaries of deism. One of Locke's disciples became the leading deist of his day, but Locke himself never went that far.

Locke's *Essay Concerning Human Understanding* supplied the Enlightenment with a key philosophical manifesto. Armed with the dual honors of being the philosopher of the Glorious Revolution and the friend of Newton, Locke in this essay undertook to explain the foundation and methods of the new scientific philosophy. The vain visions and gropings of the past must give way to an precise, careful analysis of exactly how the mind works and what it is we are fitted to know. Locke treats the mind as though it were a box containing Newtonian particles, in the form of "ideas," which are related according to certain laws of association. From experience come simple ideas or sense impressions that combine in the mind to form more complex ideas.

It is difficult to know whether Locke was an empiricist, rooting knowledge in experience, or a rationalist, locating it in the reasoning structures printed in our minds. He sometimes spoke of the mind as a "blank tablet," void of "innate ideas" such as his rival Descartes had argued for. But he assumed there is a power in the mind able to associate and compare the sense data it receives from outside. There are inconsistencies in Locke, who was far from a profound thinker. Promising to establish clear and certain foundations of knowledge, he stumbled into skepticism; evidently we do not know the external world directly, but through our senses. These may deceive us, and in any case sense impressions are not the same thing as the "real" objects outside our perceptions. David Hume would soon draw attention in a most disconcerting way to this feature of the Lockean "way of ideas."

Again, many of Locke's Enlightenment followers took him to mean that human nature is infinitely malleable and so may be reshaped via education, but he did not consistently hold this either. It was chiefly the French *philosophes* who drew this conclusion. It was an almost intoxicatingly radical idea; human nature may be redeemed from its natural depravity through proper education and other benign social influences.

If Locke himself did not go this far, nevertheless his persuasive rhetoric radiated confidence in a method of thought freed from the errors of the past and leading on to more perfect knowledge. Practicality, rootedness in solid facts, clarity in identifying what the human mind is suited for and what it should abjure as fruitless—these were the features of Locke's "common sense" philosophy that appealed to the eighteenth-century *philosophes*. Voltaire will make wicked fun of all the old philosophies, lost in a fog of unanswerable questions and useless metaphysics. "The proper study of mankind is man," the poet Alexander Pope wrote. The first rule of knowledge is to find out what the human mind is equipped to learn, and forget about the rest. The Encyclopedists will focus their new collection of knowledge on the practical arts. French materialists like Diderot and La Mettrie derived from Locke as they construed him. If Newton was their idol, Locke was their bible.

THE PHILOSOPHES

The intellectual fire started in England in the amazing 1680s, with the Glorious Revolution, Newtonian science, and Lockean philosophy spread to cause more of a blaze across the English Channel a generation or two later. The *philosophe* movement in France flowered in the 1740s and 1750s as a thing of such brilliance that few alert minds were untouched by it. This was the time of Denis Diderot and the *Encylopédie*, of Rousseau's emergence, Voltaire's zenith, Montesquieu's immensely influential writings. In the wake of these big vessels a host of lesser craft produced a literary culture heretofore unequaled in Europe. It was nourished in Paris in aristocratic salons where literary and scientific people of all sorts met to exchange ideas, but also in the bookstalls of Port-Royal where ambitious scribblers on the make competed for the rewards of a new literary marketplace.

The emergence of the *philosophe* "movement"—it was scarcely a "party," though some of its enemies called it a "church"—dates from the 1740s. The initial impact of Voltaire and Montesquieu goes back to 1734. An influential essay by the ex-Oratorian priest Dumarsais in 1743 hailed "The New Freedom of Thought." There were other popularizers, such as the impecunious Provençard noble Argens, who doubled as a pornographer. The year 1745 brought the Breton physician La Mettrie's provocative *Natural History of the Soul*; he would later speak of man as a machine. Montesquieu's 1748 *Spirit of the Laws* soon became an enduring classic of social and political thought. Diderot's first writings followed, so antireligious that an alarmed orthodoxy demanded a crackdown. It was on his way to visit Diderot in prison in 1749 that Jean-Jacques Rousseau conceived the essay that won a prize and launched his literary career. It was an unexpected answer to a question about the value to civilization of the arts and sciences.

From then on despite rather half-hearted censorship efforts—which in any case could be circumvented by slipping across the border to Holland— the tide of bold, often irreverent publications became a flood. Paris was the center. A much more cosmopolitan place than insular London, its cultural influence extended all over Europe. To it came German barons and Russian princes, Italian musicians and Swiss scholars, even some from the Orient or the New World. The attraction of the "city of lights" was partly its beauty and architectural splendor, but mainly a quality of civilization. All of France's intellectual energies were focused there, as was hardly the case with London for the British Isles; and France was then a more populous and wealthier land than any other in Europe. The French language established itself as the modern *lingua franca* of civilized discourse; French styles in art and architecture dominated the Continent all the way to Catherine the Great's Russia, whose ruler was the friend and admirer of Diderot and Voltaire. Was not Reason the same for all people everywhere, caring nothing for its place of origin? That is why Catherine of Russia could patronize Scottish architects and French writers without resenting their being non-Russians. She herself was a German by birth, brought to Russia via marriage to the prince she later replaced on the throne after his murder. The royalty and nobility of Europe, intermarrying across national lines, provided a solid basis for the Old Regime's internationalism.

The eighteenth-century style was international, its ideas cosmopolitan. Neoclassicism reigned in the arts, teaching that reason determines the standards of beauty that are the same for all times and places. If the Enlightenment found its leading voices in Paris, they were not French nationalists but "citizens of the world." The *illuminés* were in fact an international crowd, counting among their most illustrious members the American Benjamin Franklin, the Italian Beccaria, and the German monarch Frederick the Great. Rousseau himself was a Swiss by birth. The Enlightenment caught fire in Edinburgh and St. Petersburg, in Switzerland and northern Italy, even in Spain and the Hapsburg domains.

The *philosophes* were numerous, and, as one of their number once remarked, it is impossible "to find in them a philosophy common to all." He (André Morellet) mentioned Fontenelle, Vauvenargues, Montesquieu, Voltaire, Rousseau, Buffon, Condillac, Mably, d'Alembert, Turgot, Saint-Lambert. . . . No two had exactly the same opinions, but, he added, they did have in common some general qualities. These might be summed up as a faith in reason, a confidence in the scientific method, a belief that there are natural explanations for all phenomena. Chains of cause and effect can be traced; the proper methods of reasoning can correct errors and reach the truth. Much of this general spirit of the Enlightenment can be traced back to Newton.

The Enlightenment ideologues sought to convert the monarchs to principles of government that were universally valid: orderly, equal, and just laws; religious toleration; government support for projects useful for human happiness. It is sometimes said that the French Revolution came about because eighteenth-century intellectuals had undermined so many pillars of ancient authority. They ridiculed the clergy, in the name of a kind of rational Christianity that needed no miracles and was accessible to natural reason; though they did not often assail the monarchy they wanted the ruler to be a prince of reason, dedicated to maximizing the happiness of his people. They were hardly democrats, for they wanted policy decided not by the irrational populace but by the enlightened few, not by numbers but by Reason. Yet they disapproved of an idle aristocracy. They preached all manner of reforms to make government more efficient and people more productive.

Yet the Enlightenment leaders of thought never contemplated violent revolution and were both astonished and dismayed when it came. Voltaire, Rousseau, Diderot, Montesquieu were all dead by 1789; their many disciples included quite a few who were to be involved in the tumultuous events of 1789–1794. But in general they had expected gradual, orderly change as principles of reason made their slow but inevitable progress. Newton's universe was one governed by natural law. The model that the Scientific Revolution supplied for the social and political order was one of harmony and order, not turmoil and upheaval.

NEWTONIAN SCIENCE
AND THE INDUSTRIAL REVOLUTION

It would be wrong to suppose that the important technological innovations of the eighteenth century derived simply and entirely from theoretical break-throughs in science. Historians of the so-called Industrial Revolution find it extremely difficult "to trace the course of any significant theoretical concept from abstract formulation to actual use in industrial operations" (Charles Gillispie). Thus, when James Watt added a condenser to the Newcomen steam engine, possibly the one most crucial step in the growth of power over nature in the eighteenth century, he was acting less as the applier of scientific principles of heat than as a practical engineer tinkering with a piece of machinery. Still, he did consult with his friend, the chemist Joseph Black, about heat. Science and technology did interact. But they did not run together in perfect harness; a great amount of science had no immediate bearing on anything practical and most of the mechanical "inventions" came from people who were not scientists. The history of technical knowledge is a separate one; it involves the accumulation of practical skills among artisans and craftsmen whose names for the most part were left unrecorded, because they lived and worked among people who were not literate. If a Newton of the carpenters or the metal workers existed we do not know his (or her) name.

But it is important to note that a new kind of scientific outlook became popular in the eighteenth century. Not only were books written popularizing science—the poet and dramatist Oliver Goldsmith produced one—but societies sprang up that brought together amateur scientists from many walks of life. Benjamin Franklin's Philosophical Society in Philadelphia supplies one example; the Lunar Society of Birmingham, England, was a notable British case. Lecturers enthralled large audiences with scientific demonstrations. Making static electricity became a popular parlor game, while the brothers Montgolfier amazed Frenchmen by floating around in their hot-air balloon in 1783. It is no accident that the highly important Enlightenment social institution the Freemasons, whose clubs, perhaps originating in Scotland, spread from one end of Europe to the other in the eighteenth century, derived from an old guild of architects and builders, a repository of consummate technical skill.

Toward the end of the century, chemistry, in which Newton had dabbled so fruitlessly, began to come into its own and was a source of knowledge with practical applications: witness the bleaches and dyes that found a place in the important cotton textile industry, the first industry to develop the "factory" system of production; and chemistry's uses in purifying iron ore to make a harder metal.

It remains to be explained why Great Britain (Scotland prominently included) pioneered in the Industrial Revolution, engendering the first great cotton textile mills and iron-smelting blast furnaces. There is no reason to suppose British artisans were any more skillful than their Continental counterparts. Medieval building arts had seemed to flourish most in France, clockmaking in Germany. In earlier times the English had sent their wool over for the Flemish weavers to work into cloth. In some ways England was less advanced in popular scientific education than was France. Searching for reasons why the Midlands of England led the way toward a new kind of industrial environment, and why Great Britain preceded other countries in taking off into sustained economic growth, economic historians invoke all kinds of possible influences, from climate to religion. But the most obvious ones are related to the political and social stability of post-1688 England.

Not only technical development but also capital accumulation require a long period of time in which people can be reasonably sure that no disruption will deprive them of their property, guaranteed by secure laws. Britain was to base its economic order on private enterprise. During the eighteenth and nineteenth century many a company grew from the back room of some individual artisan to a great industrial corporation, gradually accumulating skills, customers, and capital. The incentive to persist in working and investing rested on the assurance that the business would be handed down intact to the next generation; no greedy and arbitrary government would seize it, no invading armies or revolutionary mobs would destroy it. English Common Law gave property unusual protection, while the Royal Navy and the English Channel protected England from war.

If this favorable environment for the entrepreneur was one basic cause of British economic success, another was the strong interest in science and technology. This was the heritage of Newton, just as the first was a bequest of the seventeenth-century political revolution. A remarkable circle of engineers, scientists, and businessmen appeared in England in the late eighteenth century; among their number along with James Watt were the famous potter Josiah Wedgwood; the chemists Joseph Priestley and Humphrey Davy; and Charles Darwin's father. Their number would later include the pioneer of electrical energy, the self-taught Faraday. This circle also to some extent took in the poets Wordsworth and Coleridge, and the great essayist and historian Thomas Carlyle. Erasmus Darwin, who was a physician, attended the English king. Against a background of the country-home sociability of England's landed gentry, this Wedgwood Circle, linked closely to the Lunar Society, was almost an extended family (Charles Darwin was to marry one of his Wedgwood cousins). It reflected the interests of England's intellectual elite as the eighteenth century led into the nineteenth. Newton and Locke were its spiritual ancestors. They would have been very much at home in it.

3

Jean-Jacques Rousseau: The Self and Society

ROUSSEAU'S EARLY LIFE

Our third case provides an exception to the rule we thus far appear to have encountered, namely that great geniuses whether scientific or literary had a tendency to grow wealthy. Jean-Jacques Rousseau was probably poorer at the end of his life (largely by choice) than at the beginning. His father was an artisan, with a rather elegant house that came from his wife's family; lack of success in his trade led the elder Rousseau, however, into serious financial difficulties early in Jean-Jacques's life. Jean-Jacques, as all Europe was to call him, became identified with simple living in rural solitude, close to nature; in fact, born in the city of Geneva, of an old French Huguenot family, he lived his last years in a tiny apartment in Paris. Once he was nearly run down by a carriage in the narrow streets of that city—vehicle accidents existed long before the automobile—and no one recognized the most influential writer in Europe.

Paradoxically, he was also in some ways the best-known person in Europe. That is because in writing his *Confessions* he virtually invented the psychological autobiography. Of this book he said, "I was determined to make it a work unique of its kind, by an unexampled veracity, which, for once at least, would enable the outside world to behold a man as he really was in his inmost self." He just about did so. A recent scholar remarks that while Rousseau did not invent the genre of autobiography, "in a single stroke he realized almost all its possibilities." The word autobiography itself does not appear until after his time. It has been said that "no one before Rousseau had concentrated on the formation of personality in such an intense way." Even the wider claim that Rousseau "invented the self" is defensible. "The self was invented shortly after the middle of the eighteenth century," John O. Lyons has argued. That is to say, for the first time people became self-conscious, in the literal meaning of that term; aware of a "me," different from others, unique, and worth recording just for that reason. De Tocqueville, the great nineteenth-century French analyst of society, said that "individualism" was a concept unknown before the French Revolution.

A good many of the revelations about the intimate self, startling for their time, contained in Rousseau's *Confessions*, probably happened to everyone, but they were too embarrassed to reveal them. The eager response of his innumerable readers was a chapter in the history of growing individualism. Rousseau had already become an interesting person to countless people before he wrote his *Confessions*—that is why they wanted to read it. He had become perhaps the best-known writer in Europe, equaled only by his rival, often enemy, Voltaire. Both of them were arch-examples of the way literature could be an avenue to fame under new conditions of book publication. Rousseau's success was part of a "reading revolution" that occurred in the middle to late eighteenth century. Books were not new, of course, but they had changed into something like a mass media, no longer just rare objects treasured by a small elite. Though nothing like the present in absolute numbers—Rousseau's editions were numbered in the thousands rather than the millions—books became available to a far wider audience through cheaper production and extensive distribution. Rousseau's novel was rented out by the hour as well as purchased by readers.

There is evidence that literacy increased considerably in Western Europe in the eighteenth century. For example, in 1790, 80 percent of the men and 64 percent of the women in one French village apparently could read and write. This silent revolution was preparing the way for the great political uprisings and the growth of a national consciousness.

Unhappy with his apprenticeship, Rousseau left his native city of Geneva, Switzerland, at the age of sixteen to wander about for some years. One of the striking things about him, certainly a key to his unique success as an autobiographer, was a combination of introversion and extroversion. Shy, awkward, a loner in many ways, Jean-Jacques was also adventurous and had the ability to get involved in unusual incidents. Introverts understand themselves but often have little external life to write about; extroverts have adventures but cannot write about them insightfully. Somehow Jean-Jacques could do both.

His rather picaresque existence led him to encounter the person who did most to shape him, an amiable woman named Mme. de Warens, who initiated him into sex when he was twenty-one and she thirty-three. Having first met her in Annecy, over the French border not far from Geneva, Jean-Jacques stayed with the lady he called "Maman" in her home in Chambéry, just down the road from Annecy, and at a nearby farm, for several years on and off, until at length that relationship tired. Jean-Jacques's discovery of a woman who was for him both a substitute mother—he had lost his real one in infancy—and also a mistress piques our curiosity; after Freud, we must wonder whether in mysterious ways this did not unlock streams of creativity in Rousseau. Certainly this idyllic life in the beautiful countryside near the Alps gave him that vision of an Edenic existence that always haunted his imagination.

But Rousseau's relationship with Mme. de Warens was tinged with ambivalence; in his *Confessions* he says that he always felt guilty in their sexual relations, and to his annoyance she finally eased him out in favor of another partner. After he left her, Rousseau continued to correspond with "Maman" and, fifteen years later, he saw her during a return visit to the Geneva area. She was then facing bankruptcy and poverty, and, as Rousseau bitterly regrets in his *Confessions*, he was not able—or willing?—to give her much help. She is the tragic and unsung heroine of the Rousseau saga.

Mme. de Warens found him a post as tutor in a wealthy and refined Lyon family, but as a teacher Jean-Jacques was something less than a success; nevertheless, he used the opportunity to make notes about the educational process that he later would exploit in literature. During these years both in Chambéry and Lyon, Rousseau conducted a most successful self-education project, gorging himself on the intellectual and literary feast that the new book trade was bringing to the public. He bought and devoured books of every sort, from mathematics to poetry. Both *Maman* and the Mablys of Lyon indulged his appetite; they must have sensed something remarkable in this young man. In Lyon he met members of the intelligentsia in that cultivated city on the Rhone, the second city of France after Paris.

He was employed for a time in Venice as secretary to the French ambassador to Italy, with whom, predictably, he soon quarreled, before making his way to Paris, where he failed in his attempt to establish a new system of musical notation. He had already written an abortive opera or two, and thought music was to be his career. This only partly worked out. But, meeting Diderot and others of the Paris intelligentsia at the very moment when the *philosophe* movement was being born, Rousseau won an important literary prize in 1749 that launched him on a spectacular career as writer. His wonder years were 1761/62, when, at the age of fifty, he published three books that were to change the world.

In Paris in the 1750s the always paradoxical Jean-Jacques managed to be both very famous and very poor, very popular and very unpopular. Parisian hostesses on the lookout for interesting additions to their *salons* lionized him, but he was more like a bear—rough-hewn, ungracious, ill-dressed, suspicious of all this wealth and ostentation. This very roughness made him all the more attractive; he was an anomaly, a curiosity, almost another "noble savage" like those American Indians and South Sea natives who visited the drawing rooms. His creed of rustic simplicity became a fashion. Yet for Rousseau this was no pose, and eventually he had to break with a world in which he did not belong except as some kind of freak. Making a virtue of necessity perhaps, he declared his contempt for wealth and resolved on honest poverty. He really meant this.

An outsider to the brittle world of Parisian sophistication, Rousseau condemned its decadent immorality. His 1749 Dijon prize essay, which vaulted the obscure Swiss wanderer to Parisian fame, took the surprising line that the arts and sciences had done more harm than good, because they corrupted natural human society. Rousseau came to think this early essay jejune, but its assumption of a "golden age" in the precivilized past, when people lived unspoiled in a Garden of Eden, never strayed far from the center of his thought. It echoed one of humanity's most basic myths or archetypes.

In opting for rural simplicity against urban sophistication Rousseau chose feeling over intellect, religion over reason, and community over individualism; in all these ways he affronted the reigning doctrines of Voltaire, Diderot, and the other main Enlightenment "philosophers." Soon he quarreled with them.

The essay with which Rousseau followed up his initial success may have been equally brilliant, but it was less enthusiastically received. Jean-Jacques asked: "What had corrupted the simple, natural society to bring it to its present sad state?" His version of original sin, which disrupted primitive happiness and innocence, was private property. Someone fenced in a plot and declared he owned it. Selfishness had reared its ugly head; its offspring was inequality. The human family had fallen apart early, it seemed. Rousseau's *Discourse on the Origins of Inequality*, which did *not* win a prize, was an important anticipation of socialism; Friedrich Engels once said it contained all of Karl Marx in embryo. Civil society ever since the initial act of transgression has been illegitimate; the problem is to reestablish it on a valid basis. And so Rousseau was led to write his famous *Social Contract*, a work that went far to justify Lord Acton's remark that its author was "the most powerful political writer that ever lived."

THE INVENTOR OF SENSIBILITY

The book that made Rousseau most famous was a "novel," though the distinction between fact and fiction, the real and the invented, was not so clear in the eighteenth century as it later became. Indeed, the "novel" as it arose in the eighteenth century was distinguished from the medieval romance largely by its greater realism, its tendency to observe and carefully describe actual human beings rather than abstract and generalized types. Few readers of *Julie, ou la Nouvelle Héloise*—whose title recalled the familiar medieval story of

Abelard and Héloise, a true tale—doubted that the characters in *Héloise* were
real people.

Said to have been the biggest best-seller of the century, *La Nouvelle
Héloise* went through seventy editions in the four decades after its publication
in 1761 and was translated into every European language. A Russian translation appeared in 1769, after an imitation in 1766, the first of many. Rousseau's tale reduced all Europe to tears. Its readers suffered with the characters as the story unfolded in serial form; people were rendered ill or nearly
mad. "Julie dying was no longer an unknown person," a French marquise
wrote. "I believed I was her sister." Children were named Juliette, later Emile
after another Rousseau creation. People wrote to Jean-Jacques from all over
Europe, sometimes bringing him their real-life problems; he was the first Dear
Abby. "You know the human heart too well not to understand all the emotions that can agitate it," one unhappy woman wrote to Rousseau. People assumed he would understand their problems. Certainly they took his characters to be real.[1]

That words on paper can become more real than flesh-and-blood persons was a discovery not so surprising as it may seem. There is a sense in
which we can know the characters in a book better than living people. The
latter's interior thoughts are concealed from others, but in a novel, provided
one accepts the author's omniscience—as readers were prone to do—one can
know them fully, inside as well as out. One could have the illusion of knowing not only what Julie said and did but what she thought and felt. She was
only the first of a parade of literary figures so vividly realized that they assumed the status of historic personalities: Wilhelm Meister, David Copper-
field, Emma Bovary, Anna Karenina, and many others. (Perhaps Cervantes's
Don Quixote, who himself could not distinguish things in books from real life,
was the first.) These characters moved into their readers' lives and deeply influenced them. Today this function is more likely to be filled by motion picture or television characters.

Reading a book, especially one that introduces characters and tells a
story, is a private, intimate experience in which the reader's imagination encounters the printed page. The "novel" as it developed in the eighteenth century escaped from the strict rules of composition and classification of genres
decreed by Classicism; in doing so it reflected the new social and political
equality. Rousseau's work was not the first sensation in this exciting new literary field. In England seemingly the entire nation eagerly followed Samuel

[1]Robert Darnton, "Readers Respond to Rousseau" (in *The Great Cat Massacre*), gives
many examples including a woman who wrote: "People who have read your book . . . assert that
it is only a clever fabrication on your part. I can't believe that. . . . I implore you, Monsieur, tell
me: did Julie really live? Is Saint-Preux still alive? What country on this earth does he inhabit?
Claire, sweet Claire, did she follow her dear friend to the grave? M. de Wolmar, milord Edouard,
all those people, are they only imaginary as some want me to believe? If that is the case, what
kind of a world do we inhabit, in which virtue is but an idea?"

Richardson's *Pamela* as it was serialized. This epistolary novel by an English book publisher resembled Rousseau's success in detailing the afflictions of a lovely and virtuous woman. An "age of sensibility" seems to have arrived in the 1760s. In England this decade produced Laurence Sterne's *Tristram Shandy*, Horace Walpole's *Castle of Otranto*, and Oliver Goldsmith's *Vicar of Wakefield*.

Rousseau's Julie carried a bit more of a social message. Though once succumbing to temptation, this beautiful and sensitive heroine in the end is virtuous, dismissing her lover to submit to familial and filial duty. Julie conquers her own passionate indiscipline to accept social order at the price of marriage to a man she does not really love—a rather unromantic message in the work that supposedly started Romanticism. In this work Rousseau rejected the claims of the emancipated individual ego, while sharply raising the question of its conflict with society. This exciting ambivalence was the key to much of Rousseau's strange power, whether as social theorist or novelist. The community at Clarens in which Julie and her family lived in *La Nouvelle Héloïse* was a model of this idyllic human society—a community marked by "harmonious order in which each person has his place" (Hugh M. Davidson), "an organic society held together by fairness and responsibility" (Warren Roberts). Having lost his mother in infancy, Rousseau constructed from his imagination a happy family for the human race.

Natural purity redeemed from urban decadence; the heart speaking again directly and simply rather than with the tongues of alienated abstraction: Europe was ready for this message after too much "civilization." Even the French queen, Marie-Antoinette, pretended to be a dairymaid and nursed her own children. Rousseau's conversion of the Old Regime aristocracy to radical simplicity, at least as a kind of parlor game, may remind us of Karl Marx's appeal to the capitalists he condemned.

"Strip off the artificial habits of civilized man, his superfluous wants, his false prejudices . . . return to your own heart, listen to its intimate sentiments . . . and you will rediscover that primitive Adam, long buried under a crust of mold and slime, but which rescued from its enclosing filth can again be placed on its pedestal in all the perfection of its form. . . ." Thus did the French critic Hippolyte Taine summarize Rousseau. It was a shocking message to those long accustomed to believe that human nature is naturally corrupt until civilized, and redeemed by religion from Original Sin.

Rousseau, whose first trade was copying music, also wrote some music. His chief contributions to the famous *Encyclopédie* edited by his sometime friends Diderot and d'Alembert were articles on music. Rousseau had a fine voice, played several instruments, and wrote a good deal about music. His operatic works fitted his general theme in exalting rustic simplicity. Rousseau's composition was amateurish, as he knew, yet melodious, a kind of beginning of the "popular song" so significant in modern mass culture. "Any music that does not sing is boring," Jean-Jacques declared, rejecting the contrapuntal harmonies of the older composers. In a long and acrimonious argument with Rameau, the celebrated classicist composer, Rousseau argued for the supremacy of content over form, melody over harmony. Music must "speak to the heart" of the individual listener. His opera "The Village Soothsayer," presented at court, was a great success; the king, who found himself humming Rousseau's tunes, wanted to give the author a pension, which Rousseau refused!

In this opera, a courtier tries to corrupt an innocent village girl. Rousseau began a trend that persisted in many a subsequent operetta or ballet—for example, the popular ballet *Giselle*. (The most famous of the Russian Heloises was "Poor Liza," by the historian N. Karamzin, in which a peasant girl is seduced and betrayed by an aristocratic lover.) It is emblematic of Rousseauism. Its message was democratic in implying that "plain people also have feelings," and aristocrats are arrogant. In celebrating the simple virtues of village life, Rousseau's opera began the Romantic quest for folk themes in art.

In an essay on the origins of language, Rousseau, with the fascination that attaches to all his writings, argued that music actually preceded language; it is the voice of the emotions, and these emotions—love, joy, anger, fear, etc.—were present among human beings before logic and reason. People sang or chanted before they spoke; speech, and writing even more so, is the medium of a corrupt civilization. Nevertheless, Jean-Jacques made much more of an impact with his writing than with his music.

THE SOCIAL CONTRACT *AND* ÉMILE

Appearing in 1762, just a year after Julie's sensational debut and about the same time as his almost equally popular tale *Émile, Du Contrat Social* demonstrated the Genevan's versatility; it was not a romance but a closely reasoned exercise in politcal theory. "Man is born free, but is everywhere in chains"— the famous beginning was not a rhetorical invitation to revolt but a statement of the problem. How can the unjust and illicit political order be reshaped to make it just and proper?

Rousseau was aware of earlier versions of the "social contract" in which government or organized society originated, or was presumed in some sense to have originated. The greatest of these came from the suspicious brain of Thomas Hobbes, writing in the era of the English civil war and concerned to make the point that, without a strong central authority, people are wolves to each other. In the original or hypothetical "state of nature" there was perpetual warfare between individuals, who lived an existence that was "nasty, solitary, brutish, and short." Sheer self-interest drove them to agree to set up a government and give it complete power to end this intolerable anarchy. People have no ultimate rights against the state, as long as the state governs effectively. Hobbes's Leviathan state is a mortal god, before whom human beings bow down as the price of civil peace.

Rousseau like Hobbes began with individual humans in a "state of nature," prior to government and, apparently, before organized society. But he sees a happier situation than Hobbes's bitter war of all against all. Rousseau's primitives were solitary and brutish perhaps, but rather tranquil. His view owed something to Montesquieu, the celebrated author of *The Spirit of the Laws*. But Montesquieu had agreed with John Locke in seeing the passage to civil society as natural, humans being by nature social animals. To Rousseau, civilization, at least, was not natural to humans! Human nature flourishes better in peaceful solitude. Rousseau himself seems to have been one of those rare individuals who can do without human society. He was happy in solitary walks and nature projects, as well as in thinking and writing by himself—a natural introvert.

But (he theorized) growing population and material needs forced social organization, at the cost of inequality and injustice. The enemy was scarcity. Jean-Jacques disagreed with Hobbes in refusing to regard civil society as a blessing, because he, unlike the author of *Leviathan*, thought that human beings are naturally peace-loving and unaggressive. They are, in their present form, confused and insecure beings because they have been corrupted by society. But it might be possible to end this unnatural condition by devising a better form of the social contract—indeed, the first true contract, because no legitimate one has ever existed, only a series of frauds and usurpations. Such a contract would not be between subjects and rulers, but among all the people.

Locke's social contract visualized people granting less than total power to society and government, witholding certain "inalienable rights" and liberties as they set up a government for limited purposes. Rousseau's social contract is less liberal. A right cannot exist outside of society, he agreed with Hobbes. His social contract set up a government whose laws, being based on the general will, are absolutely binding on all who enter into the contract. A just social order, Rousseau implied, can be resisted only by the unjust. In this many subsequent critics found the roots of a totalitarian society, suppressing individual dissent in the name of democracy. There is considerable irony in Rousseau the prophet of individualism being also the prophet of socialism and of fascism—engendering, as it were, the entire modern political spectrum.

Whatever logical traps he may have sprung on himself in attempting to reason out the bases of government, Rousseau remained consistently faithful to his vision of civilization as corrupting the lost innocence of social childhood. If *Émile* is, as it has been called, the "basic treatise of modern education," this is because Rousseau clearly recognized the need to treat the child as a developing mind and personality, not as a small adult, a view he attributed to Locke.[2] Educational content and methods must be attuned to stages of growth; there is a logic of emotional development that must be followed in determining what subjects the child is ready for.

In general, Rousseau's "natural education" assumed the innocent virtue of children.[3] What turns this into evil is a false education. "All is well when it leaves the hands of the Creator; all degenerates in the hands of men." Rousseau's enemies, including the leading *philosophes* Voltaire and Diderot, accused him of wishing to return men to savagery. A close examination of Voltaire reveals that the great satirist was not altogether free from traces of Rousseauism; he occasionally condemned luxurious living and deplored the decline of the honest yeoman, in the spirit of Oliver Goldsmith's "Deserted Village":

> Ill fares the land, to hastening ills a prey,
> Where wealth accumulates and men decay.

Perhaps it was envy of Rousseau's success, as well as his difficult temperament, that turned most of the intellectuals against him. His enemies joined forces to get Rousseau expelled from France.

It was as much *Émile* as the *Social Contract* or the *Discourse on the Origins of Inequality* that got him into trouble. *Émile* shocked the clergy as well as the educational establishment, for in it Rousseau inserted, as the creed of a Savoyard vicar, an eloquent statement of deism or natural religion: All the faiths, which are essential to social life, Confucius, Brahma, Muhammad, Jesus, even the religion of American "savages," are at bottom the same. Take away the obfuscation of priests and you have the simplest of creeds: to believe in the existence of a Master Designer, to love's one's fellow men (all are equal), to do one's duty. The creed is written in the human heart, and only the artificial veneer of civilization obscures it.

Here Rousseau affronted orthodox Christians; but in suggesting a need for religion and stressing its rootedness in human emotional life he also annoyed the orthodox *philosophes*. They, the intellectual leaders of the rationalist Enlightenment, were either atheists (though "not in front of the servants") or believers in a rational "religion of nature" that was based on scientific truth. To deplore religious "enthusiasm" was as close to the heart of the Enlightenment as was criticism of priestly "superstition."

Jean-Jacques was forced to flee from France in 1762, not to return to Paris until 1770. He was subject to attack also in his native Switzerland. In 1762 the

---

[2]Nevertheless, Locke had written: "Each man's mind has some peculiarity, as well as his face, that distinguishes him from all others; and there are possibly scarce two children, who can be conducted by exactly the same method."

[3]Rousseau brought up no children of his own; in the most controversial if not shocking feature of his life, he sent his children to an orphanage.

elders of his own city of Geneva publicly burned *Émile* and *The Social Contract!* It is hardly surprising that one who at best was never a perfectly balanced personality began to have paranoid suspicions. "His life was one long war with self-sought foes," Byron wrote. Rousseau indeed managed to affront all the powers that be, including most of his fellow "philosophers," shocked at his apparent attack on their idols of reason, science, and civilization. Rousseau's seeming advocacy of village ignorance went against every instinct of the Age of Reason.

ROUSSEAU AND THE FRENCH REVOLUTION

So peasants and common folk found in Jean-Jacques a spokesman against aristocracy and court life. But of course he was no peasant; he was of fairly humble birth but so were Voltaire, Diderot, d'Alembert (a foundling), and other *philosophes* who generally found Rousseau's anti-intellectualism repellent. And some highly aristocratic personages, like the French queen, became converts to the cult of natural simplicity. Moreover, Rousseau's simplicity was a somewhat phony pastoralism; born in Geneva, he lived most of his adult life by preference in Paris. His pastoralism does not altogether match his equally strong stress on subjectivity, for most peasants are not lonely dreamers given to solitary meditation (see Rousseau's charming *Reveries of a Solitary Walker,* his final book). One has to wonder if Rousseau could ever have understood or been understood by a real peasant. The kind of sensibility that Rousseau displayed in his literary style was the product of an advanced civilization, the sort that in theory he condemned. If he became a noble savage it was only pretending—the attempt of a jaded adult to recapture his childhood innocence, impossible of course except as a fantasy. One might add that the immortal Julie in *Nouvelle Héloïse* was probably based on an aristocratic lady, the charming Sophie d'Houdetot. She was no rough-skinned peasant woman! (There have been other nominees; Rousseau's dream lady is almost as controversial as Shakespeare's dark one.)

Rousseau's appeal according to some was to the middle class or bourgeoisie, but this deduction of Marxian theory bears little relation to reality. Many aristocrats succumbed to his charm; in any case the distinction between a bourgeois and an aristocrat was very fuzzy in eighteenth-century France. The bourgeoisie according to Marxism represented the forward thrust of industrialism and private enterprise, but Rousseau presented an ideology of agrarian communalism and did not believe in progress; he thought that all civilization had been a regress. Likewise, his sentimental subjectivity had very little in common with the individualism of the merchant or the capitalist. Large portions of Rousseau's message transcended class or status. The queen of France and the empress of Russia were among his disciples; if the king of Prussia detested him it was because Friedrich II was a Voltairean, upholding clarity and reason against Rousseau's cult of feeling and his attack on advanced culture. Rousseau's own temperament approved what he saw as the old, traditional nobility (it scarcely existed in a France where most of the nobles were *parvenus*) and rejected the vulgar upstarts who paraded their wealth.

In those cantos from "Childe Harold's Pilgrimage," which contain Byron's tribute to Rousseau, the English Romantic poet declared that

> . . . from him came
> As from the Pythian's mystic cave of yore,
> Those oracles which set the world in flame.

It has long been a hallowed view that between them, Voltaire and Rousseau, especially Rousseau, created or made possible the French Revolution. By 1789 both of the French Enlightenment's intellectual leaders had been dead for a decade, but their words had deeply moved the generation that grew up in the 1760s and 1770s; these were the people who played major roles in the stirring events of 1789–1794. Everywhere during the French Revolution there appeared disciples or admirers of the great eighteenth-century writers, whose phrases were constantly quoted, and who were enshrined in the Pantheon of revolutionary heroes. Voltaire and Rousseau's disagreements showed up to a considerable degree in the revolutionary factions. The politicians and demagogues who came to the top at one time or another during the French Revolution's turbulent years seldom appreciated all the nuances of Enlightenment thought; their specialty was not philosophical analysis but action. It was enough for them to know the larger ideas and some ringing phrases. Still, the vast influence cannot be denied.

But in fact the great majority of the *philosophes* had neither expected nor wanted sudden and violent revolution. "Hardly a survivor among the *philosophes* gave the Revolution his support," a recent scholarly study finds. They thought in terms of a peaceful enlightenment that would operate gradually over a period of time, an intellectual or moral revolution. Violence was on the whole, though not entirely, foreign to their thought. A prominent and relatively radical *philosophe*, Baron d'Holbach, whose famous salon Rousseau once frequented, wrote in his influential *La politique naturelle* (1773) that "In revolutions, men, guided by fury, never consult reason." The riots, lynchings, and use of the guillotine that marked the frenzied course of the Revolution belonged to another sphere of reality than the ideas of the *philosophes*, many of whom themselves fell victim to the Reign of Terror that climaxed the events of 1789 to 1794. Those events had begun sedately enough with the summoning of a great national assembly to deal with a problem many another government has confronted, a huge national debt and budget deficit. But matters quickly got out of hand with violence in the streets of Paris among the *sans culottes*.

Feeding the conflagration were both a mass of penniless wretches who had flooded into Paris in a season of poor harvests, and a crowd of ambitious literary adventurers who conducted attacks on the established order. The latter made a living by popularizing the great *philosophes*, and by producing *libelles*, the scandal sheets of the day, which retailed gossip not about movie and TV stars as today, but about the nobles, the queen, the court favorites. They dealt in book smuggling. Pornography was not excluded. Among these "poor devils" leading a precarious existence in the literary underworld of Paris were some dissident priests who harbored a special grudge against the higher-ups in the First Estate. As Robert Darnton, their leading recent historian, says, most of these scribblers and purveyors of subversive literature were "natural enemies of the state" who "welcomed the revolutionary crisis of 1789 as a gift from Providence." From their ranks came journalists and street orators who were to supply the Revolution with its inflammatory rhetoric; but also some of the more responsible future politicians, like Brissot. Among those who rose to the top—only to fall before long—were people strongly influenced by Voltaire, Rousseau, or others of the Enlightenment heroes of thought.

Standing out among these was Maximilien Robespierre, who as the dominant member of the Committee of Public Safety ruled France and sent thousands to the guillotine in 1793/94. "Divine man, you taught me to know myself," Robespierre said of Rousseau. (He probably was most influenced by the *Confessions*.) An orphan like Rousseau, this provincial lawyer tried to model himself on Jean-Jacques. Whether the Jacobin leader did not seriously misconstrue his idol in using him to sanction revolutionary terror has long been a strenuously debated question. In any case the left-wing of the Jacobins did not supply all the admirers of Jean-Jacques. Manon Phlipon, daughter of a Paris engraver, had read Plutarch before she was ten, Fénelon at fifteen, Voltaire's *Candide* at sixteen—before Rousseau seduced her intellectually. The man she married was a factory inspector, but "definitely a *philosophe*." At their first meeting they argued about Rousseau, Voltaire, and Raynal. "Once I get involved in intellectual matters, in science and study, goodbye love!" the attractive Manon declared. M. and Mme. Roland (as Manon Phlipon later became) went on to become leaders of the Girondist faction that eventually fell victim to the internal battles of the revolutionaries and either went to the guillotine or committed suicide in prison, along with the French royal family and thousands of others. The Rolands' Rousseau was certainly not that of their executioners, Robespierre and Saint-Just.

In general, early in the French Revolution everyone loved Jean-Jacques, who was virtually canonized; a popular play in 1790 reverently portrayed his last moments. Monarchists and republicans alike invoked his name, also a few socialists; so did advocates both of direct democracy and of constitutional restraints on the popular will. The defender of Louis XVI at the king's trial quoted Rousseau on his side, as did those who voted for the death penalty.

But those who worshipped him as a god and used him as a weapon the most often, as the Revolution wore on, were the left-wing Jacobins, or *montagnards*, the latter name being taken from their position in the legislature or Convention, where they sat on the slopes. Their debts to Rousseau included not only deism, expressed in the attempt to establish a Cult of the Supreme Being, and a suspicion of the rich and powerful, but, especially, the notion of the General Will as the basis of popular sovereignty.

The Jacobins mistrusted representative government as a form of democracy because it divides up the community into selfish particular interests. What is needed, they thought, is the will of the whole people, something that transcends the sum of individual wills. This will can be found in the basic moral feelings of the community. Rousseau thought that only a small, tightly integrated society could be democratic; to him it was something like a New England town meeting or the Spartan camp, an assembly that everyone attended and that then found the general spirit of the entire body. "The magnanimous devotion which merges all private interests in the general interest" Robespierre named "virtue." Democracy did not signify the compromises reached in the trade-offs of a mixed group of factions, but rather "the one pure will of a truly virtuous people."

The fatal problem of the French Revolution was how one determined this General Will; who spoke for "the people"? The idea of a nebulous General Will above and superior to the actual majority was a dangerous invitation to autocracy or minority rule. Robespierre convinced himself that *Je suis peuple moi-même*, "I myself am the People, through me the General Will is made manifest." A sinister strain of thought leads from Rousseau through many ultranationalist and *völkisch* thinkers down to Adolf Hitler's National Socialists.

Needless to say it is doubtful if Rousseau would have approved of this. Nevertheless, in their deadly quarrel with the Girondists the Robespierrean *montagnards* relied heavily on their interpretation of Rousseau. They used Rousseau as a weapon against the other intellectuals, most of whom were identified with the Gironde faction. Their interpretation was not entirely fanciful. A recent careful study of Rousseau's thought (by Carol Blum) concludes that Robespierre's reading of Rousseau was "narrow, rigid, unnuanced . . . but nonetheless authentically faithful to a central core of the master's teachings." Rousseau's ideal political community as depicted in *The Social Contract* tolerates no dissent from the tribal creed; it is not democratic in a way most people today would recognize. It is not pluralistic democracy but, as it has been termed, "totalitarian democracy." It is a town meeting of like-minded and equal citizens. Fully sharing a basic set of customs and values, participants reach agreement by consensus. In transforming this process to the level of the nation, Robespierre did violence to its essential localism. Neither Rousseau nor Voltaire nor Montesquieu ever dreamed that democracy was possible except in small and closely knit communities.

But nationalism, a thrust toward making a single people out of the fragments of feudal France that made up the Old Regime, was perhaps the most powerful force present in the French Revolution. All the revolutionary groups shared a yearning for total unity. The historian Michelet wrote that Danton's great dream was "a vast table in which all of France, reconciled, would be seated to break the bread of fraternity, without distinction of class or parties." This was in fact everyone's dream. The Girondist vocabulary featured words like "unity," "universality," "harmony." "religion and the laws . . . , institutions, rituals, customs, letters, arts, manners, and morality" should all be part of a single culture. The Revolution attempted to standardize and nationalize the French language, wiping out the local dialects. The new community was to be the nation, not the village.

Like Jean-Jacques himself, the deputies who supported the Mountain tended to be provincials, from the peripheral regions, suspicious of Parisian sophistication; they were less urban and less educated as compared to the Girondists. But we feel that Mme. Roland's lover, Buzot, was right when from his death cell he wrote that if the *philosophes*, including Rousseau, had been alive, "they would have experienced the same fate. Like us, if they had not emigrated . . . Montesquieu, Rousseau, Mably would have been condemned to death; they would all have perished on the scaffold."

At least one of Rousseau's disciples, the Comte d'Antraigues, turned rather far to the right. It is not difficult to extract from Rousseau something like Edmund Burke's famous and influential indictment of the French Revolution, proclaimed in 1790 by the British orator-essayist in his *Reflections on the Revolution in France*. Political institutions must be rooted deeply in the culture of the community; they cannot be manufactured to order by literary ideologists. Uprooting them violently leads to anarchy followed by dictatorship. Abstract reason is not easily applied to politics. "Abbé Sieyes has whole nests of pigeon-holes full of constitutions ready made," Burke wrote scornfully, "ticketed, sorted, and numbered"; but constitutions are not to be selected from the wares of political theorists. They have to grow like a great tree from the soil of a country over many centuries.

We cannot know, of course, what Rousseau would have thought of the Revolution. Some blamed its bloody excesses on the anticlerical ideas of both Voltaire and Rousseau, who had undermined traditional religious values. Rousseau, of course, felt religion to be a necessity, but preferred a "religion of nature" to Christianity. His disciple Robespierre in 1793 paraded a goddess of reason (a rather scantily clad lady) through the streets of Paris in honor of a Cult of the Supreme Being that was supposed to replace the old faith. It was a bizarre failure. Earlier, in 1791 the revolutionary legislature had enacted a Civil Constitution of the Clergy, which required priests to serve as employees of the state. One can see in this the shadow of Jean-Jacques's "civil religion," which as sketched in *The Social Contract* was supposed to bind together the political community. The Civil Constitution proved to be a great failure;

rebellions against it broke out in regions of France as religious people reacted with outrage at this assault on the Church. This quarrel was one of the first and greatest of those that led the happy revolutionaries of 1789 into bitter animosities against each other. Thus, the Revolution devoured its own children and caused it to collapse into the arms of a military dictatorship by the end of the decade of revolution.

ROUSSEAU'S INFLUENCE

Whatever we may think of Rousseau's political ideas—and they were much more subtle, as is always the case with an important thinker, than the travesties of them held by enthusiastic disciples—he left a very great influence in other areas. Rousseau's style had opened up horizons that were to excite the artists and writers of Europe. He is generally conceded to be the chief if not the only founder of that great movement in literature and the arts known as Romanticism. To Byron "the self-torturing sophist, wild Rousseau" was one

> who threw
> Enchantment over Passion, and from Woe
> Wrung overwhelming eloquence . . . ; yet he knew
> How to make Madness beautiful, and cast
> O'er erring deeds and thought, a heavenly hue
> Of words. . . .

Rousseau's critics down into the twentieth century have tended to echo the rationalist viewpoint of Voltaire, as they accuse Jean-Jacques of fomenting intellectual disorder. They are the Classicists, as opposed to the Romantics—a persistent dichotomy in human nature; the left side of the brain against the right side, we might say. They accused Rousseau of teaching that human nature is altogether good; but Rousseau actually was decidedly ambivalent on this point. He drew a rather precarious distinction between selfishness, which is bad, and self-interest, which is good.

Disparagers of Jean-Jacques's cult of subjective feeling accused Rousseau of subverting clarity and order. "I consider Hugo and Michelet to have been two perverters of men's minds," wrote the French reactionary Leon Daudet, naming two of the leading French Romantics; "almost as pernicious as Rousseau." The whole "stupid nineteenth century" with its vulgarity, democracy, socialism, and moral decay had stemmed from the poison secreted by the Genevan. But this rather gloomy neoclassicism labored in vain against the great tide of individualism that spread through the modern world.

Those who thought with some justification that Rousseau believed human nature wholly benevolent until corrupted by society sometimes became philosophical anarchists, like his English disciple William Godwin: Remove the incubus of government from humanity and it will revert to its initial and natural virtue. "Government, like dress, is the badge of lost innocence," said Tom Paine. But Rousseau had wanted a new social contract, not none at all. Educators down to Montessori or A.S. Neill in recent times have followed *Émile* in seeking to free the child from too much structuring and to allow for individual differences.

And so, like all great thinkers, Rousseau's influence stretched in many directions. Romanticism, socialism, liberal individualism, anarchism, nationalism, fascism—all have looked to one facet or another of his writings. Fledgling political scientists still read *The Social Contract* among the handful of acknowledged classics. Environmentalist "greens" of recent vintage should find Rousseau congenial, except that he would probably deplore the destruction of a natural environment more for social than biological reasons—more because a harmonious human society is lost than because plant and animal species are destroyed. He was, however, a delighted lover of nature.

His most widely known book in his time, *Nouvelle Héloise*, is no longer much read except by specialists. "One can only feel sorry for the modern reader who is totally insensible to the spell of Jean-Jacques," a recent student of Rousseau commented. Julie was a heroine for her age, destined to fade with the years like many another beautiful woman. To Byron she was still the quintessence of love, "wild and sweet"; to later generations she seemed rather insipid.

Feminists have problems with Rousseau, who thought that females were "made for man's delight" and existed chiefly to help males be creative. Julie is the prototype of the noble, self-sacrificing woman who tends to set feminist teeth on edge; she reappeared in the works of Dickens and other nineteenth-century novelists. Rousseau himself preferred, as his consort, "a simple and uneducated girl to a woman with intellectual and literary pretensions," and he followed this precept in his long relationship with Thérèse Levasseur (they never formally married). He would probably have agreed with a later French writer, Octave Mirbeau, who wrote that "Woman is not a brain. She is sexuality, which is far more beautiful. She has only one role, to make love and to perpetuate the species." Rousseau might have also agreed with Sigmund Freud that women "have come into the world for something better than to become wise." Feminists may find it annoying that the apparently sexist Rousseau was enormously appealing to women, many of whom offered him their all, while the "emancipated" Condorcet found his views far from popular with the other sex.

Rousseau's Jacobin followers at the peak of the Reign of Terror banned women from politics (they could come to meetings if they sat quietly and knitted) and sent Olympe Gouges as well as Manon (Phlipon) Roland to the scaffold. It was their foes among the Girondists, such as Condorcet and the Rolands, who proclaimed the equality of men and women. Rousseau's equality did not extend that far; his was the equality of patriarchal families. Clarens, the ideal community where Julie lived, is quite patriarchal.

But this was hardly what people then learned from Rousseau. In a very popular novel written in the next generation by a Rousseauist, Bernardin de Saint-Pierre's *Paul et Virginie*, two women, both victims of society, one an aristocrat and one a commoner, go off to Mauritius to bear their children and raise them together in natural virtue. In France, they believe, civilization is hopelessly corrupt; money has replaced virtue. This attempted return to a simpler social world—flight from Europe to some imagined purer, uncorrupted, unpolluted society—has been a persistent motif for the last two centuries. A century after Rousseau, Paul Gauguin tried to find it in Tahiti, and Robert Louis Stevenson sought it in Samoa. The quest still goes on, as unspoiled primitives become ever scarcer. Claude Lévi-Strauss thought he found the last of these unspoiled primitives in Amazonian Brazil in the 1930s. In the 1960s unbelievably naive "flower children" formed California communes or roamed the roads of India looking for some escape from urban industrial civilization, even as they drove their parents' automobile or took the TV along to Eden.

A Rousseauist analysis can be found in Prince Mikhail Shcherbatov's *Corruption of Morals in Russia* (c. 1786–1789). Peter the Great's violent break with the Russian past uprooted ignorance, superstition, and coarseness, but at the cost of simplicity, loyalty, faith, implicit religious belief. The result would be decay of morality and hence of the state, Shcherbatov feared. Monarchy and aristocracy and people are no longer bound together in trust but alienated from each other. The prince adopted Rousseau's ideas because they seemed to correspond to the situation in Russia. The conflict between advanced civilization, based on science and reason, and the deepest ties of human community has been a poignant one for modern humanity. Rousseau touched its very center.

Two of Rousseau's French disciples who managed to survive the Revolution (it was not easy) can be cited as examples of the antirationalist impulse. Sylvain Maréchal led the de-Christianizing campaign during the Reign of Terror, and in 1796 he joined the Conspiracy of the Equals, a fruitless insurrection that has frequently been seen as the beginning of modern socialism. Its leader, "Gracchus" Babeuf, wanted to divide up wealth equally. Maréchal came to believe that a new revolutionary religion must replace Christianity. The cold rationalism of the Enlightenment is not enough; people need religion, and one must invent one suitable for an age of civil equality. It must have its rituals, its symbols, its holy days. Maréchal, "the man without God," wrote lyrics for some patriotic hymns. Nationalism did indeed subsequently create holidays, "anthems," symbols like Marianne or John Bull or Uncle Sam, which became enormously popular and functioned as a sort of quasi-religion. Nationalism in fact became the great nineteenth-century faith; some of this is related to Rousseau's vision of a republic of equal citizens bound together by a common "civil religion."

Claude Saint-Martin, "the unknown philosopher," became the leader after 1794 of a mystical cult that combined Freemasonry with Christianity.

During the eighteenth century the Masons, spreading from Scotland, had multiplied all over Europe with their "lodges" closely related to the Enlightenment. Liberal people joined the Freemasons to express their acceptance of *philosophe* thought, deism, civil equality; many attributed the Revolution itself to Masonic influence. The Masons split into many branches, some of them attracted to occultism. Saint-Martin was a prominent example of the kind of mystical religious teaching that swept through Europe in the aftermath of the French Revolution, sometimes announcing the end of the world, the Second Coming of Christ, the Apocalypse. Saint-Martin, who saw Rousseau as a messenger sent from heaven, fully developed the side of the Geneva sage that had appalled the Enlightenment rationalists: Instinct and intuition, the imagination, may be used to discern truths that escape the analyzing scientific intellect. There is a realm of deeper truth that opens itself to the spontaneous feelings of uncorrupted souls. A new religion, transcending Christianity, should result from the exploration of subjective consciousness.

If numerous far-out prophets drew on Jean-Jacques, so did perhaps the greatest of all pure thinkers, a German just a dozen years younger than Rousseau. This was Immanuel Kant, author of works in the late eighteenth century that ushered in the modern age of philosophy. The chief problem Kant set out to resolve stemmed from David Hume's critical reading of John Locke's empiricism, which cast doubt on the possibility of certain knowledge. But in far-off Königsberg, Kant felt the impact of Rousseau. The only time he missed his famous morning walk, by which the locals could set their watches, was to read the last episode of *Nouvelle Héloise*! He was deeply moved by Rousseau at about the same time as he was shaken by David Hume; the two roused him from his "dogmatic slumbers" to undertake his memorable Critical Philosophy. The Rousseau influence appeared in Kant as a limitation on scientific reason, which in its own domain of the phenomenal (that which is experienced by the senses) can attain exact knowledge. But that is not the only domain; the noumenon also exists, a realm of essences and purposes, of God himself, which is not precise but can be approached through ways of knowledge different from the scientific. The aesthetic life as well as the moral is autonomous, standing apart from the counting and analyzing methods of science. God's existence can never be proven, and to seek logical proofs of it in the manner of the Scholastics and Newtonians is a categorical error. But in moral experience we can discern strong hints of it.

One can view Kant as rescuing some of the Enlightenment from the skepticism of Hume and the sentimentalism of Rousseau[4]; but one can equally well see him as surrendering the citadels of Pure Reason in which he had been reared, to admit the poet and the seer into the sacred temple of truth.

---

[4]Kant, as Karl Jaspers writes, "held that Rousseau was wrong in demanding a return to nature," though right in pointing out the conflict between nature and civilization. "It is only through this conflict that man can develop all his powers and faculties and progress toward rational freedom."

Science is all very well within its limits, but there are "more things in heaven and earth than are dreamed of in its philosophy." The philosophy of the Romantic movement stemmed from Kant as developed by his immediate successors in German philosophy—Fichte and Schelling. They taught that the ultimate reality in the world is a single spiritual substance, of which material objects are only the outward shell. Our minds are a part of this world soul and can attain knowledge of the spiritual essences—values, freedom, God—when we use our higher reason or Imagination. Coleridge transferred this heady philosophy to the English Romantic poets. Coleridge, Blake, Wordsworth, and Shelley believed that the poetic imagination penetrates into deeper truths than does the scientist's.

So the great Romantic movement owed much to Kant, even if he himself was not wholly a romanticist. And the Romantic aspects of Kant's thought clearly came to him chiefly from Rousseau. In the last decade or two of the eighteenth century the younger generation began to weary of the dry rationalism of Voltaire's age. Goethe described how he and his friends found it simply boring. The future master of German literature wrote his early *Sorrows of Werther* as an exercise in sentimentality that rivaled Rousseau's Julie in reducing all Europe to tears. A few years later, between 1801 and 1805, René Chateaubriand emerged as Rousseau's major successor in France, with his romantic novels set in the forests of the New World, and his deeply religious spirit. The Romantic generation was underway; Rousseau was its acknowledged source.

Romantics like Chateaubriand were enemies of the French Revolution. It is odd that Rousseau should have been the chief inspiration both of the Revolution and of those who rejected it. But, as we have seen, he had this power to be all things to all people. Nietzsche spoke of the "Janus face" that the greatest thinkers present. Virginia Woolf, reading Coleridge, remarked on ideas that "explode" and give rise to all sorts of others. Rousseau was such a player with ideas, one of the most influential in a lineage that stretches in the West from Jesus and Plato down through Machiavelli and Luther and so, after Voltaire and Rousseau, to Marx, Nietzsche, and Freud. They emit sparks and cause explosions. People read different meanings into them, but the electrifying effect is always there. Probably the most electrifying of all was the penniless wandering artisan from near Lake Geneva, who came bearing the message of a return to simplicity, poverty, and love, for which he was persecuted. His career bears a strange resemblance to that of Christ.

4

Catherine the Great and Imperial Russia

In the early eighteenth century Tsar Peter the Great labored with gargantuan energy, often with incredible cruelty, to drag sluggish Mother Russia into the mainstream of European development. He built—or compelled tens of thousands of conscripted laborers to build—a stunning new capital, literally out of a swamp on the shores of the Baltic. He sought to bring in Europe's more advanced technology along with, some stubborn reactionaries held, the Continent's corruptions and decadence. Peter's thirty-five-year reign made Russia into a major power and something like an organized state—at the cost, some held, of her freedom. It was an old story, and it is still going on at the end of the twentieth century.

Russia first emerged distinctly out of the mists of the East, as part of a European complex of power, at the beginning of the eighteenth century during the Northern War for control of the Baltic Sea. Peter visited Europe in 1697 and 1698 to learn chiefly about its military and naval technology. Improving both his army and navy, in 1709 he defeated the then formidable Swedes in the struggle for the Baltic.

The vast and diverse land of Russia had once been dominated by Asiatic Mongols; nomadic tribes still inhabited large parts of it. Russia's main principle of unity since medieval times rested in the concept of Moscow as the Third Rome, heir via the Orthodox Church to the ancient keys of the Christian kingdom. The second Rome, Constantinople, fell to the infidel Turks in 1453. Since 1589 the Russian Orthodox Church had been centered at Moscow, heading the largest number of Eastern Christians. But Peter the Great was strikingly secular in his goals; he reduced the Church as well as the nobility to dependence on the state. The absence of a Roman tradition of law and of independent noble houses strengthened the Russian Crown.

With superhuman energy and absolute ruthlessness Peter followed the example of Western European monarchies in building a strong centralized state around the autocratic emperor. In fact, as tsar (caesar) he was both caesar and pope, far more despotic than anything Latinized Europe ever dreamed of. The "absolute monarchy" that arose in France in the seventeenth century was by comparison extremely limited in its powers. Only total and unrestrained power could cope with the immense problems of this huge, sprawling, and backward region known as Russia.

The chief problem of any autocracy is the succession: how to replace a strong, able ruler with another one. This problem had plagued Russia before. The first Grand Duke of Moscow to assume the title of tsar, Ivan the Terrible, was an able if tyrannical contemporary of Queen Elizabeth; but debilitating struggles for the throne followed his death in 1584, including a period in the early seventeenth century poignantly characterized in Russian history as a Time of Troubles. Peter's death in 1725 opened another era of political instability, lasting for thirty-seven years. He had murdered his son Alexis for allegedly conspiring against him. A half dozen incompetents spent brief periods on the throne, installed usually by the palace guards who then speedily terminated their miserable reigns. The scenario was reminiscent of later imperial Rome when the Pretorian guards made and unmade emperors. Little respect was paid to the principle of hereditary descent; Peter himself had decided that each tsar should choose his successor.

Peter the Great's daughter Elizabeth became empress in 1741, installed by the bayonets of the guards, and she soon summoned to Russia from Germany her nephew Peter, son of her sister, Anne, the Duchess of Holstein. This Peter impressed everyone as feeble of intellect, narrow-minded, and childish. He was an obsessive admirer of all things Prussian, especially Frederick the Great's military organization and practices. This obsessiveness was to be repeated in Peter's presumed son by Catherine the Great, Tsar Paul. The half-witted, capricious Peter was established at the court as Grand Duke and heir apparent or, in the Russian term, *tsarevich*.

In 1744 Elizabeth brought him a fourteen-year-old bride from Germany, Princess Sophia of Anhalt-Zerbst, daughter of one of the field marshals of Frederick the Great. The clever and adaptable German girl started to learn the Russian language, which she soon mastered. One day she would tartly inform Frederick that it was a far richer tongue than either German or French. She studied the Russian religion too; renouncing her native Lutheranism, she entered the Orthodox Church receiving the name of Catherine, the name of Peter the Great's second wife. Actually, her beliefs were more nearly those of the Enlightenment deists, but she was quite willing to go along with local customs for political reasons. Given the title of Grand Duchess after her marriage to Peter, she quickly realized that her husband was an immature nonentity who took no interest in her whatsoever. He played with toy soldiers on their honeymoon.

In compensation, Catherine curled up in bed with the books of Voltaire, Diderot, Montesquieu, Bayle, Mme. de Sévigné, and other exciting French writers, with their sparkling style and their fund of new ideas among which the notion of "enlightened despotism" was prominent. This German girl with a French education had, as she recorded in her memoirs, a burning ambition to become "an autocratic empress of all the Russians." A budding beauty, she began to cultivate the people who could help her achieve this ambition, chiefly the officers of the two key guard regiments. In 1754 Catherine gave birth to a son, Paul, whom Peter recognized as his own but whose father was probably an officer named Saltykov, the first of Catherine's many lovers.

Upon succeeding Elizabeth in 1762, as Tsar Peter III, Catherine's husband proceeded to reveal his incompetence. He ended Russia's hitherto successful participation in the Seven Years' War, as the enemy of Prussia. During this war, which Russia had conducted since 1756 at the side of the French and Austrians, Russian troops had captured most of East Prussia and even Berlin itself. When Peter came to the throne, Frederick was at the end of his resources; but the new tsar ordered the Russian commanders in Germany to abandon their conquests and switch sides! The Russian troops evacuated all their territorial conquests. With momentous consequences for future world history, Frederick's Prussia was miraculously saved from total defeat. Otherwise it would assuredly have vanished from the picture and some other scenario would have been enacted in the muddled realm of Central European politics.

In his obsessive adulation of Frederick, Peter III went so far as to kneel publicly before the bust of the Prussian ruler, crown it with a wreath, and kiss it. At the same time Peter surrounded himself with Germans from his native Holstein, ordered the Orthodox priests to dress like Lutheran pastors, and talked loudly during religious ceremonies at the court. He once stuck out his tongue at the bishop officiating at a High Mass! No wonder that many influential Russians thought him a disaster as ruler. His scintillating wife, from whom he was now totally estranged, was an obvious choice to supplant him. The younger officers of the guards, with Catherine's approval, formed a conspiracy to seize power. In June 1762, when Peter's secret agents arrested one of the conspirators, bringing the danger that torture might compel him to reveal the names of other plotters, the conspirators hastened to put their plans into effect. Supported by his two brothers and other conspirators, the empress's reigning lover Gregory Orlov brought two guard regiments and other units to St. Petersburg. At the head of some 14,000 troops Catherine marched to the capital dressed in the green and red uniform of the Semenovsky regiment. Speaking from the scaffolding of the still unfinished Winter Palace, Catherine with her eight-year-old son Paul at her side addressed the troops in Russian, urging them to defend her against her cruel and insane husband: "I am a poor woman. . . . My husband, a foreigner who didn't even bother to learn our language, has not only dishonored our sacred national banners, but vilified our holy Orthodox religion, and now he wants to murder me. . . . Together with my little son I throw myself under your protection. Help me and my son!"

At the same time Catherine's agents distributed a printed manifesto that proclaimed the dethronement of the incompetent and treacherous Peter III and Catherine's accession to the throne, "by the grace of God and the choice of the Russian people." She claimed to stand for the defense of Orthodoxy, the honor of Russian arms and for the land's public security, menaced by the flood of often contradictory decrees that had flowed from her husband's suburban palace of Oranienbaum. Cheering soldiers, under orders from their officers, surrounded her, while officers, priests, and nobles approached to swear allegiance to the new empress. Meanwhile, the indolent and confused Peter waited passively at Oranienbaum; he was soon arrested without much resistance by some of Catherine's supporters. Ordered to abdicate, he made a humiliating submission asking only to retain his fiddle, his black servant, his dog, and his favorite mistress. His surrender did not save him; the Orlov brothers murdered him. The world was told that Peter had died of colic.

The heir-apparent to the throne vacated by Peter's death was the eight-year-old Grand Duke Paul, whom Peter had officially acknowledged as his son. But Catherine took advantage of the legal ambiguity about the succession to proclaim herself Empress, with the approval of almost everyone of importance at the court. She immediately took charge of affairs of state with remarkable energy and ability. She considered herself an expert in the art of statecraft. She was as resourceful, Machiavellian, often unprincipled (but seldom cruel) as she was highly intelligent and literate. She would write plays and even histories as well as state documents. She presided over a glittering court. She was a tireless worker, a brilliant diplomat, a skillful administrator. Her passion for men and ideas never slackened, to say the least. She earned the title of Catherine the Great and became a legend for all times. Two hundred years later, people were still talking about her, rewriting her biography, even making films about her.

The stream of lovers continued. Gregory Orlov, the handsome artillery captain who had helped her to the throne, gave way to the eccentric Potëmkin, who received envoys in bed clad only in a robe, and wandered the palace in his dressing gown or a cloak with a pink bandana around his head. Did he secretly marry the empress? She always seemed to defer to him as to a husband. "A crooked, squinting, huge, swarthy, sweaty, filthy giant," Tolstoy later described him; his honesty was questionable, but he was a man of great energy and knowledge. While always treating Potëmkin with special regard, Catherine eventually moved from him as lover to a succession of younger men. When she was past sixty she had a lover in his early twenties.

Historians have alleged that during the thirty-four years of her rule she had some forty bed companions. But this is probably an exaggeration. Only twelve major lovers can be documented, and these tended to be serial, not overlapping: Catherine was passionately devoted and usually faithful to her companion of the moment. Gossip characteristically inflated her sexual appetites, the legends about which became a kind of masculine mythology.

Catherine presided over a resplendent court. She was always preceded and followed by an immense retinue of courtiers. Her bodyguards, composed of tall, handsome young men, wore sumptious attire. At official functions all the men were adorned as richly or even more so than the women.

But Catherine was much more than a gilded butterfly. A child of her times intellectually, she was correspondent and friend of the great French *philosophes*, one of whom, Denis Diderot, chief editor of the great French *Enyclopédie*, visited her at St. Petersburg. Catherine brought a new kind of intellectual and cultural life to Russia, at least to the St. Petersburg part of it. She encouraged music as well as literature; she subsidized the translation of foreign books, but also scholarly works to clarify the much mixed-up Russian language and thus lay the foundations of a Russian literary culture. She was a promoter and pioneer in the field of education, including women's education, founding the first institution of secondary education for girls of noble families. Private theaters presented popular comedies and musicals at court, some with Russian folk themes, and Catherine herself wrote plays of this sort, as well as historical dramas "in imitation of Shakespeare," one of her favorites. She also composed a number of comic operas using Russian folk material, which she helped collect and preserve. Here she was the disciple of Rousseau, whom she also cited in planning the education of her royal grandsons.

The Russian court resounded with brilliant talk, with songs and plays and operas. The exciting fruits of that breathtaking intellectual renaissance known as the Enlightenment flowed into Russia, even though Catherine was at times inclined to blow the whistle on ideas that were too dangerous for Russia: Voltairean attacks on the Church, or Rousseau's creation of a cult of subjective sentiment and the common man. In 1781, advised by her friends among the European intelligentsia, Catherine would select as tutor for her son Paul's children a young Swiss disciple of Voltaire and Rousseau and Montesquieu.

Catherine's choice of a religious instructor for her grandsons was a quite unconventional Orthodox priest, Father A.A. Samborsky, who had married an Englishwoman, taken a liking to the Anglican ritual, and shaved his beard. Catherine even allowed him to wear secular garb. The Orthodox hierarchy suspected the purity of his faith, and some bishops refused to conduct services with him, considering him a libertine and a heretic. The court chaplain was in fact more interested in economics than religion, and he pioneered in bringing to Russia some understanding of the new science that the French Physiocrats and the Scotsman Adam Smith were creating. His house was the meeting place for all those interested in English ideas, and for all visitors from the British Isles. Their presence in Russia was of considerable significance both culturally and economically.

CATHERINE'S RUSSIA

Catherine's taste in the arts and architecture ran to the French neoclassical, as befitted her Enlightenment outlook. The French architect Vallin de la Mothe designed many of the buildings in St. Petersburg and at Tsarskoe Selo, a complex of residences and parks a few miles outside the capital that served as the Russian court's summer residence. There were also British influences. A Scot, Charles Cameron, added Palladian decor to pure classicism. (Followers of the sixteenth-century Italian architect called Palladio included Shakespeare's contemporary and possibly friend, Inigo Jones, but this elegant classical style came into its own as a model for English country homes in the eighteenth century.) Catherine liked "Capability" Brown's landscaping ideas, another favorite of eighteenth-century neoclassical taste; Brown's gardens summoned up visions of Roman imperial dignity. Her preference for neoclassicism in architecture could be seen in the Hermitage Theater, built for her by the north Italian Quarenghi; also in the English Palace at Peterhof. The influence of British eighteenth-century taste could be seen also in the leading literary satirist of Catherine's era, Nicolas Novikov, who modeled his style on that of the celebrated English weekly *The Spectator*. But by the end of the century, Russia was producing its own architects. Bazhenov designed the Tsaritsyn Palace in 1784/85.

It would be hard to overrate Catherine's contributions to high Russian culture. But some Russians always resented the foreignness of St. Petersburg, that artificial city built by Peter the Great to give backward Russia a "window on Europe" and force her to adopt Western ways. Catherine disliked Moscow, the old capital, and deplored the "superstition" of old Russia: "Never had a people before its eyes more objects of fanaticism" (churches, icons, relics, etc.). Russia, looking abroad to the West for all that was cultured and progressive, suffered from an identity crisis, or a split personality. "We have become citizens of the world, and so we have in some ways ceased being citizens of Russia," thoughtful Russians lamented.

The spirit of the age was changing in the later years of Catherine's reign. The taste of the Enlightenment admired reason, clarity, order. This Classical canon with its dislike of anything base and popular was at high tide in the

1750s; after that it gradually receded. In the later years of the eighteenth century a new passion, something eventually to be labeled Romanticism, began to seep in. The Russian court was torn apart by this. For it involved the very identity of Russia, what it meant to be a person living under the Tsarina, to be talking and writing, or perhaps painting, designing buildings, in St. Petersburg. The capital city itself became controversial. Some muttered that it was a great blunder, even a crime, for Peter to have built this unnatural city, and at a frightful cost. Its impressive, monumental neoclassical architecture was cold and alien. Moscow is the real heart of Russia, they said. In St. Petersburg people spoke French or German rather than Russian. The implication was that Russia was miserable and savage, and must be made over in the image of foreigners.

Answers ran along this line: "True, we should not blindly imitate the French or English. But what are we to do? Not a single truly Russian novel exists—one in which Russian manners, customs, features are realistically depicted. How can we have a cultured society without the great French, English, German writers to read? To return to Moscow is to revert to a miserable savagery. We have got to keep in touch with the thought of the West." In this debate Rousseau's glorification of popular culture and the countryside, Romanticism's delight in folklore and folk identity, reenforced, against the Westernizers, those who were soon to be called Slavophiles.

Catherine herself, child of the Enlightenment as she had been, became deeply interested in Russian folk culture. In 1784 her close friend, Princess Dashkova, to entertain an English visitor, gave a village feast on her estate that included features of both Marie Antoinette pastoral idylls and Russian comic opera. Peasants dressed in holiday costumes danced on the green; Russian food was served. Catherine kept *gusly* (dulcimer) players at her court. Her court conductor Kozlovski collected songs from marketplaces and taverns. Numerous Russian songbooks were published. Catherine liked I. Bogdanovich's play *The Slavs* (1781) in which Alexander the Great declares that he prefers the superior qualities of the Slavs, these noble barbarians, to the depraved Athenians.

Reflected in the battle of the capitals, Russia's uncertain identity appeared above all in language. Princess Dashkova said, "We were instructed in four different languages, and spoke French fluently." But she and her aristocratic friends knew Russian only badly. Some Russians complained: "They never read the old Slavonic Russian books but only French comedies, novels." False to Russia's deepest spirit, this desertion of cultural roots seemed to some people as corrupting. But what *was* the Russian language? The old Slavonic was a "high" language that now seemed pompous and archaic, much as Latin might have seemed to a Frenchman. Low Russian, the speech of the people, was too crude and lacked a written canon. In the eighteenth century, writers and scholars labored with the Empress's aid to create an acceptable middle

Russian. There were no rules, grammars, dictionaries. Founded in 1783 on the model of the French Academy, the Russian Academy produced the first Russian dictionary between 1789 and 1794.

The linguistic division reflected the social gap in Russia between upper class and low, between nobility and peasant-serfs. A small group of powerful noblemen, families like the Golitsyns, the Shuvalovs, the Yusupovs, owned thousands of "souls" and lived in luxury, occupying most of the lucrative positions of state as well. The gap between the bonded peasant grinding out his or her life in the fields, and the Europeanized nobles isolated in their manors or in the palaces of St. Petersburg or Moscow, was practically unbridgeable. Subsequently, this sorry alienation preyed on the consciences of some guilt-stricken aristocrats, who became the most unlikely but dedicated of revolutionaries.

It is true that, as in the American Old South, a lesser slaveholding gentry was much less opulent. In 1772, roughly 32 percent of the landholders owned fewer than ten serfs each, while only 25 percent owned more than twenty serfs. For most landowners life was a struggle for survival. State service in the armed forces or government administration offered the only way of bettering their lot.

Catherine has been criticized for doing nothing to mitigate the evils of serfdom. Prince Dmitri Alexandrovich Golitsyn produced a plan to permit peasant ownership of land; but the Empress, by no means uninterested in reforms and improvements, was doubtful that the nobles could be persuaded to give up their human assets, and she was in no position to compel them to do so. In practice, as in most feudal societies, the theoretically all-powerful monarch was heavily dependent on her nobles and landlords. The latter in the vast majority strongly opposed any liberation of the serfs, whom they believed to be happier in subjection than they could possibly be in freedom. The great majority of the landlords, like the slaveowners of the Old South in the United States, regarded the serfs as happy and well off. Catherine herself thought that "under a good master, the Russian peasant was as well off as any in the world." Under Rousseau's influence a good many Russian plays and operas, one by Catherine the Great herself, depicted the peasant as filled with simple bucolic joy and virtue; such idealization was soon countered by a celebrated picture presented in 1790 by Alexander Radishchev, first of the "repentant nobles," a picture of misery and savage mistreatment —for which the author of *Journey from St. Petersburg to Moscow* got himself banished to Siberia.

In Catherine's era the Ukrainian free settlers and warriors (Cossacks) were turned into serfs attached to the soil. Local folksongs and ballads reviled Catherine as the wicked woman who crushed the Cossacks and fastened the Ukrainian peasant to the soil: "Katerina, devil's mother, what have you done? To the wide steppes and the happy land you have brought ruin and serfdom." Some scholars have disputed the view that Catherine's policy of extending serfdom (in order to assure food production) was the cause of the series of savage peasant uprisings that marked her reign; but the uprisings happened. A colorful, charismatic Don Cossack, Yemelian Pugachev, led the largest and most famous of these, one that caught the imagination later of the great Russian writer Pushkin. Proclaiming himself to be Peter III, miraculously saved from the hands of Catherine's henchmen, Pugachev raised the standard of rebellion first in 1773 in the Urals, from which the revolt spread over a vast area of southern and central Russia. It was one of the greatest rebellions of all time. Pugachev's followers succeeded in capturing Kazan, Penza, Soratov, and many other cities, until he was betrayed by rivals, captured, and taken to Moscow to be tortured and executed in 1775. Massive and barbarous reprisals ensued, as serfdom in all its severity was reimposed. Catherine exhorted the squires to "Treat your serfs at least as well as you treat your cattle." She herself followed the practice of bestowing thousands of "souls" as gifts on nobles who performed meritorious state service, or on some current favorite.

Her critics alleged an inadequacy also in Catherine's halting attempts to introduce other basic political and social reforms to backward Russia: a constitution, a just and humane code of laws. In 1766 she called together a commission of elected representatives of all social classes, except the serfs, and all national groups, except the nomads; the commission was to prepare the foundations of a new legal code. The Empress herself prepared the guidelines for this body, using European Enlightenment sources including Montesquieu's *Spirit of the Laws.* "For two years I read and wrote," Catherine declared. "I consulted no one, but was guided by my head and heart." Yet, as Catherine became aware, such abstract principles of reason did not match the realities of Russia. "You write only on paper," she told Diderot. "I have to write on the skins of real men." Though some delegates frankly exposed the evils of corrupt and inefficient administration, the commission achieved few practical reforms.

Despite Catherine's evident, and hardly surprising, failure to remove all evils, the best historians of Catherine's reign give it high marks. "Intelligent, educated, charming, and ruthless," one of them remarks, "she is one of the greatest figures in European history, and the obsession with her nocturnal activities which has filled one biography after another is the most telling commentary on our ignorance of Russian domestic history." The sex bias implicit in this tendency to disparage Catherine because of her active sexual life becomes evident when we reflect that similar habits in a long list of male leaders, from Caesar to Kennedy, have not prevented recognition of their political abilities.

CATHERINE THE MOTHER

Catherine's treatment of her son, Paul, hardly showed her at her most magnanimous. To be sure, Paul seemed destined to be unloved; an ugly and awkward child, he grew into a short, fat adult with an unappealing face. He disliked his mother as much as she appeared to dislike him, and he was an obvious target for disaffected members of the nobility to use as a weapon against Catherine. Relations between mother and son grew extremely tense, despite mutual attempts to preserve outward appearances. In 1773, when he was nineteen, she did attempt to tutor him in the art of statecraft, on which Catherine considered herself an expert. She supervised the search for an appropriate wife for him, sought among German princesses. Paul's first marriage, to a Hessian princess, ended in tragedy and scandal when the young Grand Duchess died in childbirth, evidently, as it subsequently appeared, pregnant by a man not her husband. (The Russian court was an extremely dangerous place for attractive women. Catherine would later remark, about protecting the virtue of grandson Alexander's betrothed, that "These guard officers are ravening wolves, savage tigers, capable of all sorts of devilish tricks to seduce an innocent thing like Louise, as long as her position at the court is not well defined. Even I would be helpless to prevent it.")

Paul then found a happier marriage to a charming Württemberg princess, who soon bore him two sons, the older of whom was born December 12 (old style date), 1777, and christened Alexander in honor of Alexander Nevsky, the Muscovite national hero who had defeated the Swedes and the Teutonic Knights in the twelfth century. Alexander, a handsome blonde, blue-eyed infant, immediately captured his imperial grandmother's affection. Born two years later, the second son, named Constantine, was less attractive than Alexander; chubby, red-haired, with a Mongoloid face and a ridiculously small nose, he more resembled his ugly father. Yet Catherine paid considerable attention also to this lively child, destined in his life to be a counterfoil to his famous older brother.

The Empress wanted to supervise Alexander's education—one of the many areas in which Catherine considered herself an expert. Thus, she sent the boys' parents—Grand Ducal couple—on a tour of Europe in 1781 and in their absence transferred the boys to the Winter Palace and then to Tsarskoe Selo. They were to be educated for the future under the watchful eye of their grandmother and the tutors she chose for them. Alexander was to be prepared for the throne of Russia. Constantine one day, perhaps, would live up to his name by ruling from Constantinople over a reestablished Byzantine Empire, wrested from the Turks. Catherine ordered that the parents were to see their sons only with her permission, which often would not be granted for months. The boys' parents protested in vain. When the Grand Duchess wept and insisted on recovering her own children, Catherine stamped her royal foot and cried, "The children belong not to you but to Russia. It is my duty to raise them as they should be raised to fulfill their sublime destinies." When Maria Fyodorovna gave birth subsequently to other children—she had four daughters—Catherine told her, "Now you have four children to assuage your grief. Isn't that enough for you? The boys are state property."

Increasingly estranged from his mother, Paul fell under the influence of the Panin brothers, which strengthened his Prussian, militaristic ideas. Nikita and Peter Panin argued that Russia should ally with Prussia, not Austria, a policy contrary to Catherine's. The reign of Catherine and Potëmkin, they told Paul, was corrupt and immoral as well as despotic. "I wouldn't mind throwing her into the Neva [River] with a stone around her neck!" Paul was heard to mutter regarding his mother, now widely regarded as the first royal personage in Europe, especially after the death of Frederick the Great in 1786.

After 1783, in the last decade of the great Empress's life, Paul more and more isolated himself and his family at Gatchina, given to him by Catherine after the death of Gregory Orlov in 1783, a place some forty kilometers from St. Petersburg. There, she thought, Paul would be less dangerous, as well as less uncomfortably present to her sight. He lived there in a world of military play-acting. Paul hired architects, engineers, ballistic experts, and others to fortify the residence and build enormous barracks, where he trained his own little army, a force of five small battalions (some 2,400 men) known as His Imperial Highness's Battalions. He dressed them in Prussian uniforms and drilled them daily—to exhaustion—as his private army, separate from the rest of the Imperial forces. He governed the village of Gatchina as his own tiny kingdom, while he nursed his bitter hatred of his mother, her court, her urbane, intellectual ways, all she stood for. Prussianism stood in his mind for opposition to Catherine's Enlightenment ideas about religion, morals, behavior (even though Frederick the Great of Prussia, his idol, himself was very much influenced by Voltaire and the French Enlightenment). Many thought Paul now insane. "A maniac whose sound qualities are only brief interruptions of his delirium," a Russian general described him.

With their parents out of the way, Catherine proceeded to pay passionate attention to the education of her two grandsons, even designing their toys and writing stories for them. She adored Alexander, calling him pet names, and watched over his every move. This suffocating attention proved counterproductive: Alexander's adolescent rebellion was directed against his surrogate parent, the fussy old lady whom he came to view with aversion.

POLITICS AND IMPERIAL EXPANSION

Under the Empress Catherine the Russian Empire expanded enormously. During the seventy years after the death of Peter the Great, who had dreamed more of Asia than of Turkey or Poland, it increased its population from 18 million to 30 million, mostly as a result of Catherine's conquests. Such indeed was the Russian habit; from the original nucleus of Moscow it had long been a natural, a "manifest destiny," as with the Americans, to fill the vast, almost empty spaces stretching out in all directions. But Catherine's was a golden age of imperial expansion. The weakness of her neighbors aided her plans. The keys were a weak Polish state and a declining Ottoman (Turkish) Empire.

The Polish problem stemmed from a troublesomely democratic kingship. "Good God," Frederick the Great of Prussia grumbled in 1764, "We have to make a king of Poland." It was the signal for international intrigue, and even war. Catherine tried to get her lover, Stanislas Poniatowski, elected to the Polish throne; a Polish revolt aided by the French spread to bring in the Turks also, but the Russians defeated them soundly and took not only the Romanian provinces but part of the Crimea from the slipping Ottomans (1769/70). The road to Constantinople seemed to lead through Poland! The battle of Chesme in the Aegean Sea became as famous in Petersburg as Lepanto had been and Trafalgar would be, among the great naval victories of world history. A *Te Deum* was sung to it; Alexei Orlov added "Chesmensky" to his name, and the halfway house, resembling a medieval fortress, that Catherine built midway between St. Petersburg and Tsarskoe Selo was named Chesme Palace. This victory, which destroyed a Turkish fleet, took place in 1770.

Thinking to forestall other troubles, Frederick then proposed to Catherine and to Maria Theresa of Austria the famous, or infamous, partition of Poland, and the first of three banquets at which these three monarchies made a meal of the hapless Poles occurred in 1772. The two strong German states had arisen in the seventeenth century out of the ruins of a Germany ravaged by the Thirty Years' War and plagued by the absence of any strong central authority among a wilderness of *Kleinstaaten*—small states—more than a hundred of which in varying sizes cluttered the anachronistic Holy Roman Empire. The new state of Prussia rose rapidly in the rather bleak environment of northern Germany, brilliantly led by a sequence of four outstanding Hohenzollern rulers. Its original nucleus was the duchy of Brandenburg, an electoral province within the Holy Roman Empire.

Joining the anti-French coalition that checked Louis XIV, the electorate of Brandenburg was rewarded in the Treaty of Utrecht of 1713 by being elevated to a kingdom and renamed Prussia. Frederick the Great's father, the grim Calvinist Frederick William I, watched jealously over the celebrated Prussian army, which in his son's time became the most effective fighting force in Europe. Frederick the Great (Frederick II) was a musician and intellectual who did battle in his youth with his narrow-minded father—one of the all-time leaders, surely, in this perennially popular category of combat—but later settled down to become a great soldier and an "enlightened despot." The growth of military force in this age of expanding state power may be gauged by the Prussian "progress" in this line: from 6,000 in 1660 the standing army grew to 39,000 in 1713, the year of the Utrecht treaty, and to 83,000 by 1740, when Frederick assumed the throne. By the time he departed the army had reached 200,000, and its quality was regarded as foremost in Europe. Napoleon's crushing of it twenty years later was one of history's greatest surprises.

By the time the rest of Poland was swallowed up, in the second and third partitions of 1793 to 1795, both Frederick and Maria Theresa had passed from the scene, and Catherine gained for Russia the lion's share of the once large Polish kingdom: Courland, Lithuania, Volynia, Podolia, Belorussia. This cynical greed shocked much of Europe; Edmund Burke took it as a sign that chivalry was dead. But sharing the Polish spoils cemented an alliance among the three accomplices—who were to combat France during the wars of the French Revolution, form the nucleus of the Holy Alliance after 1815, and stay together until near the end of the nineteenth century—when their breakup exposed Russia to tragedy.

A century later, the rivalry of Russia and Austria-Hungary over the spoils of the Ottoman Empire led to the disastrous Great War of 1914–1918 (World War I). But under Catherine and Joseph II of Austria, son and successor of Maria Theresa and also a notable Enlightened despot, the two eastern powers cooperated. Catherine had a genius for foreign policy. In diplomacy she combined keen intelligence, and an almost ruthless realism characteristic of the age, with the compelling charm of her personality. It must be admitted that she thought little of the peasant soldiers who died in battle or from disease—the plague was a constant worry of Catherine's—in behalf of her vision of a greater Russia.

From the wars with Turkey, Russia gained a firm hold on the northern shores of the Black Sea. Catherine looked forward to further conquests. She thought her second grandson, the roly-poly Constantine, was destined one day to sit on the Byzantine throne of the Paleologues, after wresting from the Turks the city which bore Constantine's name. In 1774 the Turks were forced to recognize a Russian right to act as protector of the Christian Orthodox peoples who lived under their rule, in Greece, Romania, and the Balkans: This was a magnificent excuse for intervention any time Russia felt like it.

Catherine kept up pressure on the Turks; Austro-Russian schemes to dismember the Ottoman Empire filled the 1780s, checked somewhat by an anxious England joined by Prussia and Sweden. The Austrian alliance led to an almost bloodless conquest of Crimea in 1783/84, with Potëmkin managing the operation. Three years later, Russia was again victorious in a war with the Ottomans, who had found an ally in the king of Sweden.

The key rivalry between Russia and Britain centered on the Straits connecting the Black Sea to the Mediterranean—and eventually all the other oceans. The rivalry was to have a long history. Brittania the ruler of the waves had bases all over the Mediterranean, which she regarded as essential to her trade and security.

CATHERINE'S LAST YEARS

The French Revolution drove Catherine considerably away from such liberal views as she had once entertained. It ended forever her flirtation with the Western intellectuals. The bust of Voltaire moved from her study to the cellar. When the French ambassador took his leave in the fall of 1789, Catherine remarked that he would do better to remain in Russia and not expose himself "to the tempests." "Your penchant for the new philosophy and for liberty will probably lead you to support the popular cause. I shall be sorry. I shall remain an aristocrat. That is my *metier*," she told him proudly. Initially not without sympathy for the constitutional cause in the first, milder phase of the French Revolution, Catherine watched with increasing horror the events of the next several years in France—the riots and massacres climaxed by the execution of the king and queen; the beheading of Marie Antoinette moved her more than that of Marie's husband, Louis XVI. By 1793, it seemed to Catherine that the French people had become infected with a madness for which the *philosophes* and *illuminati* were responsible.

She broke off relations with France and decreed six weeks of court mourning after the regicide early in 1793. To Melchior von Grimm, her old *philosophe* friend who had fled from France early in the Revolution, Catherine wrote early in 1794: "You were right to not wish to be included among the *illuminés* and *philosophes*, since experience proves that all this leads to destruction." She supported Grimm after the revolutionary government confiscated his wealth in France. She closed the Masonic lodges in Russia in 1794, and forced French people living in Russia on pain of expulsion to take an oath of allegiance to the Russian state. A tight censorship now forbade the publication of books "likely to corrupt morals" or indeed dealing with the French Revolution at all, and it became illegal for Russian subjects to import French books, newspapers, even French wines and perfumes. The most famous victim of the censorship was Alexander Radishchev, exiled to Siberia for venturing to criticize serfdom in his now classic 1790 work, *Journey from St. Petersburg to Moscow*.

Yet though she wished them well Catherine did not join the monarchs of Austria and Prussia in making war on the revolutionary French regime. She was far too interested in Poland and Turkey for that. While this western war was going on the wily Empress would seize more of Poland and try also to terrorize the Ottomans.

Meanwhile the Empress continued her domestic tyrannies. She selected Alexander's wife, a Baden princess, still almost a child when she married Alexander in 1793 to the accompaniment of enormous pageantry in St. Petersburg. Alexander was only a year older than his bride. Their sexual union was evidently a disaster because of their mutual shyness and inexperience.

Catherine's schemes to bypass her son Paul and make her grandson Alexander the next Russian ruler had not been completed when she died. Alexander himself was an obstacle; he disliked his grandmother and had drifted back somewhat into his father's entourage. He shrank from politics and talked privately of his desire to renounce his claim to the throne and live a quiet life in some rural retreat (Rousseau-like). He was nineteen in 1796, a rather bookish and naive youngster, though with something of a passion for military dress and parades, which gave him a chance to display his good looks. Catherine had tried to get F.-C. Laharpe to influence Alexander toward her wishes for the succession, but the Swiss tutor would not do so; he thought this one reason why his thirteen-year-old job was terminated in 1794. (Another reason, surely, was the French Revolution; Laharpe was a staunch republican.) When Catherine died she had a letter of abdication on her desk for Paul to sign but he had not done so and surely would not have.

In her mid-sixties Catherine had grown old and stout, and she had lost her figure if not her sexuality. The death of Potëmkin in 1791 stunned her; he was the man on whom she had long most depended. On November 5, 1796, soon after rising and drinking five cups of coffee, she suffered a stroke and died the following day without regaining consciousness. The major figures of government and court, including Alexander, quickly did their obeisances to Paul, who was anxious to rule. He yearned to undo all his hated mother's policies!

It was a crucial moment for Europe. In 1796 Napoleon Bonaparte's Italian campaign announced the arrival of a new force that would transform Europe out of all recognition in the next dozen years. The age of Catherine ended just as that of Napoleon began. In that next memorable epoch, Catherine's grandson Alexander was destined to play a notable part.

PAUL'S DEBACLE

All too predictably, Paul's brief reign was a disaster. A letter from Alexander to his old tutor Laharpe, now back in Switzerland, reported the tsar losing his grip in 1798, unable to govern coherently. "An order given today will be revoked in a month. . . . The interest of the State counts for nothing. Absolute despotism leads to absolute disorder. . . . In brief, my poor father is in an indescribable state." Paul's foreign politics, at least, had failed. He had the misfortune to be up against a formidable adversary.

Paul hated the French Revolution as much as his mother, a rare case of agreement. And he became furious with Napoleon when the latter turned his attention to the Mediterranean and Egypt. Declaring himself protector of Malta and of Naples, Paul sent the Russian Black Sea fleet through the Bosporus into the Mediterranean, offering to support the Turks in rescuing Egypt from Napoleon. Paul liked the Turks because his mother had waged unremitting war on them. Allying with Austria, and encouraged by British Admiral Nelson, who had cut off Napoleon in Egypt, Russia prepared for war against France. Russian troops entered Italy and southern Germany.

But the French under Massena defeated the Russians in Switzerland. Paul blamed the Austrians for this debacle at Zurich in which Generals Suvorov and Korsakov lost 50,000 of 80,000 men. At the same time an Anglo-

Page

Russian landing in Holland also failed. Returned from Egypt, Bonaparte punched the Austrians out of the war at Marengo and Hohelinden in 1800. These defeats brought to an ignominious end, for the anti-French side, the second war of the coalition. As Napoleon took over the reigns of France, initially as First Consul, later as Emperor, he would pursue in earnest, armed with even greater strength, his crusade to export the French Revolution throughout Europe. In 1801 the Peace of Amiens brought what both sides knew would be only a truce.

Abruptly, Paul deserted the coalition to make friends with Napoleon, and he placed an embargo on British goods in line with Napoleonic desires. Anger at the Austrians and disillusionment with the English had pushed the unstable emperor toward a complete reversal of his previous policies. Paul rationalized his abrupt change to the French side by deciding that Napoleon "is no longer the head of the French Revolution; he is its vanquisher!" Abandoning the French royalist emigrés, Paul spent the last days of his brief and inglorious reign on a grandiose plan to oust the British from India by an overland invasion from Orenburg to the Khyber Pass.

Was Paul so insane in this policy, or was his madness a myth of his enemies, led by the English, who used it as a pretext to get rid of him? In thinking that Napoleon had ceased to be a revolutionary, Paul found many to agree with him. Paul's assassination corresponded with a British naval attack on St. Petersburg, a commercial blockade, a near panic about the Franco-Russian offensive aimed at India, Egypt, and the Straits. The news of Paul's death staggered Napoleon, who always blamed it on the "dirty English." There were indeed hints of British money behind the conspiracy to kill Paul. The British had financed much of the Russian war effort and were appalled at the tsar's desertion of the cause. But the master mind of the coup, Count Peter van der Pahlen, headed a group that evidently believed sincerely in constitutional reforms to limit the tsar's autocratic powers.

Paul was murdered in his bedroom on the night of March 11–12, 1801. Alexander thought that he could replace his father without killing him; he consented to the coup but not the murder, which took place anyway. It seems clear that nearly everyone had given up on Paul, who had alienated one supporter after another. The morose and paranoid tsar had destroyed the gaiety and brilliance of Catherine's court, replacing it with a joyless militarism. People said that the survival of Russia depended on finding a more popular and competent "little father" for the Russian people and state.

Such happenings, after all, were not new in Russia. Its political system seemed to be despotism tempered by assassination. Catherine's husband and son were both victims of this system. Now her grandson, whom she had yearned to see on the throne, would have his chance.

5

Alexander I of Russia and the Napoleonic Wars

THE APPRENTICESHIP OF A TSAR

A link to Rousseau in the life of Tsar Alexander I was Alexander's Swiss tutor F.-C. Laharpe (originally La Harpe, an aristocratic form he dropped under the influence of the French Revolution). Born near Rousseau's Geneva and educated there, as a law student the young Laharpe fell under the influence of *philosophe* ideas; he was particularly attracted to the simpler, more natural kind of education made famous in Rousseau's *Émile*. He entered politics as a champion of social equality against the patrician outlook dominant in Swiss cities. Laharpe became a Freemason, a significant expression of antiaristocratic sentiment in that era. Catherine, the Empress of Russia, learned of Laharpe through Baron Grimm, the German friend of Voltaire and Diderot, and, as we will recall, engaged him to teach her grandsons.

Caught to some extent between the feuding family factions, Laharpe managed to stay on good terms with almost everyone; certainly he was very close to his pupil Alexander. After Laharpe returned to his native Switzerland in 1794, he kept up a correspondence for a long time with the future tsar, who sought his advice and confided in him. Tsar Alexander I became estranged from Laharpe only in the last years of his life and reign. Alexander, who was a conscientious student, learned from his teacher Enlightenment ideas of rational government, constitutionalism, and humanitarianism, concepts hardly at home in a Russia governed by an autocrat and filled with serfdom.

In the beginning of his incredible life the child Alexander's scene was a family psychodrama such as not even Freud could have imagined: a neurotic if not psychotic father, an adoring and beautiful mother, but, always near, a prying and potent grandmother. And it was between Catherine and her son— Alexander's father, Paul—that a deep animosity existed. Catherine saw her heir in this handsome boy and at length virtually kidnapped him while his parents withdrew to another residence. The influence of all this on Alexander's personality would provide a psychoanalyst with abundant material for a Freudian analysis.

An ambivalence in Alexander's attitude toward his imperial destiny was evident from the start. Throughout his life he periodically expressed a desire to renounce public affairs and retreat to private quietude. Many times in his youth he said the throne was "not my vocation. If I could honorably change my condition, I would do so willingly." In a letter of 1797 to Laharpe, Alexander speculated that if he did become tsar, after having given Russia "a free constitution" he would "withdraw into some corner," and live happily, watching the happiness of his country. "I am sick and tired," he would tell his friend Adam Czartoryski, "of the artificiality and hypocrisy of the Court. Wouldn't it be lovely to retire, for instance, to an old castle on the Rhine, reading interesting books and cultivating an orchard or a vineyard?" Even after he had become ruler, led his country through the greatest war yet in history, and emerged as Europe's foremost political personality, Alexander reverted to fantasies of retirement. For example, in 1819 he wrote his sister-in-law: "I have decided to lay down my duties and retire from the world. Europe has more need of young sovereigns. . . . I believe it is my duty to withdraw." He also told Prince William of Prussia four years later that he would abdicate at age fifty. In 1825 he informed the Prince of Orange that he would abdicate and live a simple life. It was Alexander's lifetime vision, formed no doubt when he listened in his childhood to Laharpe speaking of Rousseau and Switzerland, and encouraged by the gulf between his ideals and Russian realities, as well as by his highly ambivalent feelings about his parents and grandparent. But in fact he never carried out this retirement plan—unless we accept the story that he faked his death and reappeared as a Siberian holy man. Of this more later.

Laharpe infused Alexander with a republican idealism of sorts. "An enlightened prince," Laharpe insisted, "should be a benevolent father to his subjects, the first servant of his country, and not their oppressor. . . . Ideally there should be no princes. Each country, under the rule of just and impartial laws, should elect its most worthy citizens to fill the offices of government." Russia was not ready for such an ideal state, but an enlightened tsar would help Russia prepare for it.

Leo Tolstoy, the famed Russian novelist of a later generation, in his notes toward a biography of Alexander that he never completed, wrote of the tsar's ambivalence; from the start he "wanted sincerely to be good and moral, but also wanted to reign at all costs." This dualism of power and virtue the great writer saw as characteristically human, at bottom a struggle between St. Augustine's two Cities, of God and Man, always in contradiction on earth. It is clear that Alexander in some ways was far from well suited to political life; he was much more comfortable with ideas than with people, with abstract and bookish things than with human realities. Yet he enjoyed the admiration of the multitudes. He liked dressing up for military parades and ceremonies. He showed, to use a more recent psychological term, a tendency toward narcissism. He was self-centered, people noticed, and a bit stubborn. Narcissists can be charming, as Alexander undeniably was. They are sociable, desperately needing the approval of other people, even as they are manipulative of others, valuing only their own basically insecure egos. Seemingly pliant, they have a core of determined ego protection that makes them in the end quite stubbornly their own person. They can sublimate their egoism and become good world-savers. The description fits Alexander. His strange childhood, including separation from his mother, easily accounts for his psychological aberrations.

Laharpe said of Alexander that "His physical beauty is on a par with his moral beauty." Everyone said the same of the handsome, polite, well-spoken lad, who at the age of four spoke French and English fluently, as well as some German. Like most people at the Russian court, Alexander knew French, English, and German better than Russian, which was not yet a suitable language of civilized discourse. In addition to languages, including Latin and Greek as well as French, German, and English, and history, Alexander learned mathematics, drawing, fencing, music; also scientific subjects, very agreeable to Laharpe as a man of the Enlightenment. Tutoring took place largely in the pleasant surroundings of Tsarskoe Selo, where the various imperial residences stood amid massive greenery, in a large, scenic, English-type park, adorned in typical eighteenth-century manner with a vast artifical lake and studded with picturesque pseudo-ruins of ancient temples, along with ornamental "medieval" bridges and replicas of a mosque and a Chinese village. Members of the high nobility and officers of the imperial household occupied the villas that surrounded the park. The community had its own high school or *lycée* for children of the elite families. All this formed a special world of its own dominated by the imperial palace. Hardly a place to meet the Russian "people."

Twelve years old when the French Revolution began, Alexander followed the unfolding of that great revolutionary drama with keen interest and some initial sympathy, encouraged by Laharpe. But the execution of the French royal couple and the Reign of Terror sobered his enthusiasm. He regarded the execution of Louis XVI as a warning to monarchs to change their ways; it was another encouragement to carry out his own plans to resign the throne and settle down to cultivate his garden as a private individual.

We have mentioned previously the unsatisfactory state, sexually at least, of Alexander's marriage at a tender age to an even younger girl he barely knew, who was selected by his grandmother, Catherine the Great, for reasons of state. Such marriages, according to the code of the Old Regime aristocracy, were not expected to be romantic successes; their rationale was wholly political. Between Alexander and the future Empress Elizabeth there evolved an understanding based on friendship and an agreement to find sexual fulfillment with others. Alexander's real sexual initiation seems to have come via his regimental comrades in the company of women of easy virtue. Throughout his life he was to evince a considerable appetite for lovely ladies. His grandmother, Catherine, would have been proud of him. The most enduring of these affairs was with the Countess Maria Naryshkin, who bore him three children; the Count was one of those tolerant eighteenth-century aristocratic husbands who never dreamed his wife would be faithful—he wasn't— and who was more than pleased that she found such a distinguished lover.

Meanwhile, Alexander had enough to do watching the unraveling of his father's brief and ill-starred reign, and wondering what his role was to be. After the coup d'etat of March 1801, which we recounted in the previous chapter, some thought the new tsar a prisoner of those who had organized the assassination of his father. But it was not long before Alexander asserted his authority. The handsome tsar was undeniably popular. And the country was urgently in need of strong leadership to deal not only with domestic reform but with the volatile international situation.

Alexander through much of his reign affirmed his commitment to constitutional government while, in reality, never doing anything about it—for which he had some good excuses. A leading scholar (Allen McConnell) notes a "conflict between [the] liberal idea of representative government and the paternalistic way of introducing and controlling it." The new tsar began his reign with a series of salutes to individual freedom and constitutional government. He freed Alexander Radishchev together with some 700 others imprisoned or exiled for political reasons, and even appointed the liberal his grandmother had banished to head a commission to codify the laws—something Catherine had once tried to do herself. Alexander also abolished restrictions on free movement in and out of Russia, and he ended prohibitions on foreign books.

If none of his reforms proved durable, so that by 1820 observers found him an autocrat walled off from the people, governing by ukases, a plausible excuse might be found in the international storms that were brewing just as his reign began. Napoleon Bonaparte was on the prowl. "The fermentation of spirits is universal over all the Continent," Alexander noted as he postponed plans for constitutional reform so as to deal first with foreign affairs.

ALEXANDER AND NAPOLEON

There was only a short interlude of peace after the 1801 Treaty of Amiens. The struggle for the world and the minds of men was sharpening. Italy, Switzerland, the Low Countries all lay under the control of Napoleon. Napoleon became First Consul for life; then Emperor! Alexander responded: "The veil is lifted. Napoleon has revealed himself as one of the most accomplished tyrants that history has produced." In England, Prime Minister William Pitt aroused the spirit of his countrymen to defy the French. He refused to evacuate Malta as Napoleon thought Britain had promised to do.

Napoleon Bonaparte seemed destined to be Alexander's rival on the stage of world history. Just eight years older than the tsar, he became the supreme ruler of a great nation at the same time as Alexander, but arrived there by a very different route. Napoleon was born to no higher status than the lesser Corsican gentry; the Russian equivalent might have been a Cossack outlaw. Napoleon's fabulous luck started when the Italian-speaking island of Corsica became a part of France just before his birth. Then as a young military officer he was flung into the turmoils of the French Revolution. Dissolving the old noble-officered army and creating a new revolutionary one meant unprecedented opportunities for advancement, and the little Corsican found himself a general well before he was thirty years old!

Getting involved in the French Revolution's factional struggles was the chief danger, and Bonaparte came close to being condemned as a follower of Robespierre at the time of the latter's fall in 1794. But another stroke of good fortune put the young captain in Paris to quell a Royalist uprising in 1795. Here was a man of impeccable revolutionary credentials who nevertheless stood for law and order. Here also was an artillery commander who understood the recent improvements in gunnery, which actually had taken place in the last years of the Old Regime.

Napoleon obtained the command of the Army of Italy in 1796 at a time when the tide of battle was beginning to turn in France's favor in the war that had broken out in 1792 and was to rage with few interruptions for the next twenty-three years. Though he took advantage of favorable political and military developments, Napoleon's military genius was never in doubt. His greatest good fortune was that he sprang to the fore at a moment when, as he put it, "France needs a master." Trying to live without a monarch since the regicide of 1793, revolutionary France struggled through several unsatisfactory regimes of turbulent legislatures, a Reign of Terror, and a kind of Board of Directors (the Directory), until almost every one agreed that France did indeed need an enlightened dictator, a new king but one made by the Revolution and pledged to carry out its social program.

After sensational successes in Italy in 1796/97, during which Napoleon defeated the Austrians and forced them to yield northern Italy to France, the popular commander's expedition to Egypt turned out badly, when England's Admiral Nelson destroyed the French Mediterranean fleet, leaving Bonaparte and his army stranded. But this untoward adventure did not prevent Napoleon from making his way back to France in time to take part in the coup of November 9–10, 1799 (the eighteenth and nineteenth Brumaire of the year VIII of the revolutionary calendar), which overturned the unpopular Directory. For a time as First Consul he nominally shared power with two others, but by 1802 he had become unquestioned master of France. He would soon be the master of most of Europe. Perhaps he was a tyrant—a valiant band of Frenchmen of high ideals thought so—but the French people voted for him overwhelmingly in a plebescite that confirmed his powers. Here was a democratic despot, a tsar of the Revolution, as such wielding immense and unprecedented power.

Alexander delivered a lecture to Napoleon on political manners on the occasion of the murder of the Duc d'Enghien, an event that produced shock waves in European aristocratic circles. Kidnapped from the chateau d'Ettenheim near the French border, the French *emigré* leader was taken to Vincennes where he was judged, convicted, and shot the same night. It is offensive to maintain relations with a government that does such things, the tsar declared. The Russian ambasssador at Paris was recalled. In his irritated reply, Napoleon mentioned the way Alexander came to his throne!

Alexander had become a good friend of the young Prussian king Frederick William III, whose wife, Louise, thought the Russian tsar sublime. They met at Memel in June 1802. Alexander now saw friendship with Prussia as the foundation of European reconstruction. He regretted that the rather passive Prussian king did not fight in 1803 when Napoleon, as the war was renewed, occupied Hanover and blockaded the Elbe and Weser rivers. Alexander was all for Prussia fighting Napoleon, but this was easy for him to say. He visited Berlin to stiffen the Prussian spirit, and he signed a Russian-Prussian treaty of alliance on November 3, 1805. The new allies made sweeping demands for Napoleon to liberate Naples, the Low Countries, the German states, and Switzerland. (Back in Switzerland Laharpe, pro-Revolution and initially hopeful about Napoleon, had now become convinced that the latter was a tyrant who had betrayed the Revolution.)

But the euphoria of the Allies was quite unrealistic. Napoleon proceeded to smash the Austrians at the great battle of Ulm in southern Germany. He preferred for the moment to avoid battle with Russia, but he found that Alexander was still hostile; Napoleon fumed that "the fool speaks to me as if I were one of his boyars." At the memorable battle of Austerlitz the French forces annihilated Alexander's army, which lost 45,000 of 70,000 men. Alexander called it "the hardest day of my life." Some claimed that General Kutuzov lost Austerlitz on purpose, not having wanted the battle. Alexander was actually on the battlefield, his first real military experience. Napoleon spoke patronizingly but not disdainfully of Alexander's youth and inexperience and the bad influences around him. Napoleon wanted a meeting but Alexander returned in shame to St. Petersburg.

Napoleon then drove a hard bargain with Prussia, which retreated to its former neutrality. William Pitt died, gloomily saying it was time to roll up the map of Europe. It was the nadir of the Coalition, Napoleon's zenith. He went on to provoke war with Prussia, launch a surprise attack, and smash the proud Prussian army at Jena in 1806, a scar that remained on the German psyche for decades. Queen Louise barely escaped capture by Napoleon, who wanted to seize her. "Of my great and valiant army only shattered fragments remain," Frederick wrote sadly to Alexander. "The French are entering Berlin. If the conditions of the victor are too harsh, I count on your aid." Alexander replied that he would come through. It is darkest before the dawn, he chirped; perhaps things will turn out—a Pollyannyish streak in Alexander, perhaps, but he did not crack. And the Russians soon won a victory, attacking the French army in its winter quarters at Eylau and inflicting heavy losses.

Bonaparte moderated his tone toward Prussia, expressing a desire for peace. His line with Prussia and Russia was to blame the war on the greedy British. Alexander met the Prussian ruler again at Memel, where Queen Louise found him as charming as ever, and he signed another treaty of alliance with her husband. But again another defeat lay ahead, at Friedland. The Russians now (June 1807) retired behind the River Niemen, leaving Prussia to her fate.

Before Friedland, the tsar's brother, Constantine, spoke for a group of army officers in asking Alexander to negotiate with Napoleon. They did not share his romantic illusions; they thought the French too strong. Alexander's friend, Adam Czartoryski, the Polish prince, also disapproved of the Prussian alliance, for pro-Polish reasons. So did the queen-mother. No good ever came of the attachment to Berlin, the old Catherinists believed. After Friedland this tide of opposition was too strong for the tsar to resist, and he agreed to discuss terms with the upstart French emperor, who was engaged in completely restructuring a Europe that largely lay at his feet, a triumph marred only by the British fleet's smashing victory over the French at Trafalgar near the Strait of Gibraltar.

On June 25, 1807, a memorable meeting took place between Tsar Alexander I and Napoleon on a military craft in the middle of the Niemen River near Tilsit, which was to be the boundary between their two spheres. Bonaparte in the green uniform of the infantry guard, wearing the Legion of Honor cross, galloped up between rows of soldiers; the elegant and handsome Alexander joined him from the right bank, and the two heroes conferred for two hours. The unstable Frederick William also arrived, at Alexander's insistence, but promptly quarreled with Napoleon. The beautiful Prussian empress flirted with Napoleon too.

Napoleon said only the tsar's intervention saved Prussia, otherwise he would have given the Prussian crown to his own brother Jerome; Napoleon was engaged in distributing lands of the new Europe to various of his relatives. As it was, Prussia was reduced to a third of its former size. Some Germans blamed Alexander for surrendering too easily; blessed are the peacemakers. Attached to Saxony, a Napoleonic satellite, was a Duchy of Warsaw, reawakening Polish desires for independence.

Alexander and Napoleon impressed each other. Bonaparte tempted the tsar to take Constantinople, also to wrest Finland from Sweden. Napoleon believed that at Tilsit he had made himself the master of the Continent. But the shrewd Prince Metternich, then the Austrian ambassador at Paris, observed that "If Napoleon thinks that after Tilsit he is master of Europe, he deludes himself. . . . In partitioning Prussia Napoleon has suppressed a potent *glacis protecteur*," that is, a buffer between his Europe and Alexander's Russia.

England reacted by blockading Copenhagen and sinking the Danish fleet. Alexander, following Napoleon's lead, declared war on Sweden and annexed Finland. He also declared war on England! He seemed to be recapitulating the about-face of his unfortunate father. But soon the insatiable French conqueror was cheating on the Tilsit agreement terms, and reaching in the sensitive direction of Turkey. For Napoleon, too, coveted Constantinople; to him it was the center of world power and of the ancient Roman Empire he hoped to reestablish. "Only then would he be *the* Emperor, and not simply *an* emperor" (essentially self-proclaimed), as the historian Edouard Driault remarked.

When the two leaders met again at Erfurt in 1808 there was less cordiality. Bonaparte had shown his contempt for royalty by deposing the Spanish monarch, as well as by abolishing the Holy Roman Empire. Nevertheless, Alexander remained aloof from the Fifth Coalition, which British initiative managed to put together in 1809, only to see Napoleon smash this one up too. In that year Napoleon, soon to be divorced from his low-born wife, Josephine, requested from Alexander the tsar's sister's hand in marriage. Alexander balked, and Napoleon soon married the Archduchess Marie-Louise of Austria. Perhaps it was this personal rebuff, as much as issues of state, that broke the precarious friendship between France and Russia and led to the 1812 invasion of Russia by Napoleon's Grand Army. The truth is that Alexander himself was probably in love with his own sister, Catherine, with whom he may have had an incestuous relationship—psychologically significant given Alexander's separation from his mother and his narcissistic personality.

So the fate of the world may have turned on this personal drama. Napoleon, however, would have been happy with another of Alexander's sister, the youngest, Ann. It was aristocratic snobbishness that led the Romanovs to spurn attachment to this upstart Corsican heading a country that had executed its rightful king and proclaimed a revolutionary republic. In any case there were other points of conflict. Napoleon demanded that Russia embargo British goods, in line with his strategy of striking at British economic power by imposing a counterblockade. This economic warfare caught even the far-off United States of America in its toils and pushed her eventually into the War of 1812 with Great Britain. The embargo hurt Russia, dependent on British trade, and she did not fully apply it. "Napoleon's true reason for attacking Russia was that he feared her and resented her rivalry; his declared reason was that she refused to cooperate fully in his strategy to starve and bankrupt Britain into submission," wrote the historian Nigel Nicolson.

ALEXANDER AND THE WAR FOR THE WORLD

Napoleon's Grand Army of half a million men, the largest fighting force ever assembled in Europe to that time, confronted a Russian army of less than half that number; Napoleon, the greatest military genius of his or perhaps any other time, faced in Alexander a commander of little experience. The tsar was not in fact by temperament or ability a soldier. Nor were most of his generals very competent. Napoleon had thrashed the Russians just about every time he met them. No wonder he expected victory.

But Alexander had formed a stubborn conviction, first, that Russia had been designated by Providence to bring the tyrant-usurper low and rescue Europe from his grip; and, second, that in the end the Russian weather and the Russian ability to endure suffering would outwear the French and their allies, who included quite a few Germans, Italians, and Poles. Once the invasion began, the holy soil of Russia would have been profaned and there could be no compromise: "Never will I sign a peace with Bonaparte so long as a single French soldier remains on the soil of Russia," Alexander vowed.

The French ambassador at Moscow, Caulaincourt, warned Napoleon that while some thought Alexander weak, this was an error; there is a core of integrity Alexander will not breach, the ambassador believed. A mixture of abstract idealism, stubbornness, and a sense of his own destiny mingled in Alexander's mind to produce an unshakable resolve never to give in to the invaders.

And so the frightful ordeal began. Making a virtue of necessity, the Russians seemingly had no plan except to retreat, though public opinion forced them to stand and fight several times. The great distances over almost impassable roads in weather that first featured heat and rainstorms, later the intense cold of a Russian winter, exhausted French supplies and killed their horses; the Russians destroyed food and poisoned wells in a scorched earth strategy. When the Russian forces gave battle briefly at Smolensk in August 1812 and later at Borodino they suffered terrible casualties. But after victory at Borodino Napoleon's Grand Army seemed more depressed than the losers; its losses had also been heavy. Napoleon captured Moscow, and the Russians set it afire—"uncivilized behavior," Napoleon complained. He offered peace, and Alexander replied, "We have not even begun to fight."

Napoleon, he said, would have to make peace in Kamchatka, (east of Siberia). The bulk of the Russian Army had evacuated Moscow and remained intact. All this showed extraordinary courage on Alexander's part; some suspected staggering stupidity. At times public and court opinion, even Alexander's own family, bitterly reproached him for cowardly retreat and sacrificing so much of Russia including Moscow. At one moment at least he faltered, replacing the first commander of the armies with General Kutuzov before the battle at Borodino; but then he defended Kutuzov's decision not to defend Moscow.

Not many more than 100,000 men of the French Grand Army began the retreat from Moscow in October 1812. Short of food and fodder, harried by Cossacks and partisans, they and their horses died of exhaustion, hunger, and then cold amid terrible scenes of cannibalism and death. On December 6 the temperature fell to 36° below zero (Fahrenheit) and men froze to death in their tracks. Stendhal, later a famous novelist, observed men drinking their own blood and eating their own severed fingers. Only a few thousand survived the long march out of Russia. It was the most terrible and fascinating ordeal in all the annals of warfare.

All this has been described in many a book, not least by Leo Tolstoy in the epic *War and Peace*. The Russian campaign has been endlessly analyzed and debated. Franz Kafka, whom few would associate with military affairs, compiled a list of Napoleon's fifteen major mistakes, beginning with his unclear objectives in the beginning, and including a host of minor lapses uncharacteristic of Bonaparte, who was by then perhaps over the hill. In any case it was a setback from which Bonaparte never recovered, although he rallied to win other victories and stave off total collapse until 1814/15.

Some have thought "nationalism" was the force that defeated him. Bonaparte stood for an Enlightenment internationalism that believed a rational social order was the same everywhere, and would be welcomed by all reasonable people. The revolutionary principles of equality of citizens under the law, an end to "feudalism" and monarchy, should be exported to all of Europe. Why should the Russian or the Spanish peasants fight against their liberator and for their oppressor? But they did. Blood and custom proved stronger than abstract reason.

THE TSAR AND THE LATVIAN SYBIL

Alexander's turn to a biblical religion began in the shattering experience of 1812, amid "so many commotions, so many sacrifices." There were nights without sleep, bloodshed, unhappiness, misery; then suddenly the mercy of God. It was a startling conversion. Child of the Enlightenment, Alexander had never read the Bible before 1812, he said. Laharpe had told him that Jesus Christ was: "a Jew from whom the Christian sect took its name." Before 1812 Alexander adhered to an Enlightenment deism in which religion was rational morality, and religious "enthusiasm" as well as dogmatism was to be avoided.

In April 1813, while the war was still going on and finding himself near Herrnhut in Saxony, Alexander paid a visit to the Moravian Brothers. The victorious Russians had pursued Napoleon's shattered army into Germany and renewed the alliance with Prussia. Napoleon, though, was not quite finished. Alexander journeyed to London in 1814 for an international meeting of France's foes; there the tsar did not spend all his time at balls and festivals; curiously, it must have seemed to aristocratic society, he sought out Quakers and Methodists. He visited a Quaker meeting and talked at length with William Allen and Stephen Grellet, who later visited Alexander in Russia. The tsar was drawn to this subjectivist, unceremonial Christianity because it was so very unlike the Russian Orthodoxy whose interminable rituals had tortured his childhood. To Allen he remarked that "the adoration of God does not consist in external ceremonies or in repetitions of words, which sinners and hypocrites readily adopt, but in having the true spirit prostrated before God." Alexander had embarked on an extraordinary obsession with prayer, with kneelings, prostrations, and adorations of the Heavenly Father not in church but in private. He wore calluses on his knees, according to his doctor.

This obvious search for a surrogate father brought relief from the terrible burden of his public responsibilities; Alexander could put everything off onto the Divine Will: "It is the Supreme Being alone who has guided all, and to whom we owe this great success. The All-Powerful has granted me a brilliant victory." Or, perhaps, in His inscrutable wisdom, a setback.

Returning from London in 1814, Alexander went to the estate of his parents-in-law at Bruchsal in Baden, the summer home of the court of the Grand Duchy of Baden. There he met a romantic mystic calling himself Jung-Stilling, an ex-tailor who had become a medical doctor, then (of all things) a professor of political economy at Marburg and Heidelberg; adviser, too, to the Grand Duke of Baden, who of course happened to be Alexander's father-in-law. Jung-Stilling had known the great writer Goethe, who mentions him at some length in his autobiography. The Munich mystic philosopher Franz von Baader was a close friend. Jung-Stilling had filled the years between 1795 and 1810 writing books bearing such titles as *Theory of the Knowledge of Spirits* and issuing predictions on the end of the world. He and the tsar hit it off immediately.

Beginning in 1808, Jung-Stilling had known the remarkable Julie de Krüdener. Krüdener was about fifty when Tsar Alexander I met her in 1814, yet she was still attractive. Born in Riga of an aristocratic Latvian family, she was the widow of a baron who had served the Russian state as diplomat. Born Barbara Juliane von Vietinghoff, she converted to Julie in honor of the most famous literary heroine of her age, who was also the daughter of a baron. Julie had experienced the usual upper-class marriage of convenience, to a man eighteen years her senior, and likewise the almost expected liaisons with other men. She made the infatuation of a young embassy secretary in Venice, to which place her husband was posted in 1784/86, the theme of her novel *Valérie*, published in 1803. In Paris in 1789, she attached herself to the large collection of amorous ladies deeply smitten by the author of *Paul et Virginie*,

Bernardin de Saint-Pierre, successor to Rousseau as master of "sensibility." All her life she was to be drawn to literary and intellectual men.

There were few signs in her first decades of the passionate religious seer and seeker she later became—more of a would-be literary lioness mixed with sex symbol, aspiring like Germaine de Staël of Switzerland to be mistress to an age. After separating from her husband for good in 1801 (he died a year later) Julie for a time lived a truly dissipated life, first in Munich (1798) and then in the notoriously wicked high society of Berlin. She had an affair with the novelist Jean Paul Richter, the German Rousseau. For a time Julie lived with her daughter in rural Switzerland à la Rousseau. This pastoral existence soon lost its allure, and she returned to Paris, where in 1804 she blossomed as a writer herself.

Valérie was a success. The little novel was called a minor masterpiece by no less a critic than the celebrated Sainte-Beuve, dean of all nineteenth-century French arbiters of literary taste. It went through a number of printings and is indeed a charming period piece. But it was the only thing she ever wrote. Julie soon fled from Paris. Religion was taking hold of her; it had never been entirely absent from her thoughts, but now she began to take it more seriously. She may have met the celebrated "unknown philosopher," Claude Saint-Martin, source of so much of the new religious consciousness at that time. Perhaps more to the point, she had turned forty, that famous moment of midlife crisis. We might recall that Rousseau's Julie turned to God in the end as her last and greatest love, having gone through both romantic and married stages.

Between 1804 and 1814 when she burst into Alexander's life and world history, Julie lived mostly with a motley crew of religious enthusiasts, some of whom bordered on the bizarre. Tsar Alexander's semiabolition of serfdom in her native land caught her attention and appealed to her newly aroused social conscience. She also stumbled onto the Moravian Brothers, the same source of religion that Tsar Alexander found, and experienced a profound religious conversion.

The war for the world that now swept over Europe created a fertile ground for fervid religiosity. In London the hysterical prophetess Joanna Southcott gathered a small army of supporters; her chiliastic predictions fed on fears of a Napoleonic invasion. Under the impact of violent change, the old region of radical Protestantism in Germany spawned a new crop of millenarians. Bonaparte, who did away with the Holy Roman Empire in 1806, was surely a good candidate for the part of Antichrist.

The reborn Mme. Krüdener performed heroically in 1807 when the bloody battle of Eylau left wounded and refugees all over the Königsberg area, where she found herself at that time. Soon she drew close to those southern German visionaries among whom was the previously mentioned Jung-Stilling. Julie's religious visions included the not unusual one of a reunited

Christianity: A religion of the spirit must transcend all doctrinal differences to forge a new Church Invisible.

The Latvian sybil had reached a peak of either madness or divine inspiration by 1814, pouring forth eloquent prophetic utterances to all and sundry. The poet E.M. Arndt, who met her at about this time, wrote, "This woman, although aging, still exhibited strong evidences of beauty, and was suffused with the magical radiance of a yearning and penitent Magdalene." Julie's younger friend, Roxandre de Stourdza, a beautiful Greek girl of aristocratic family who was a maid of honor of Empress Elizabeth, had known Tsar Alexander for several years. Jung-Stilling joined with the two women, Stourdza and Krüdener, in a mystical experience; together they conceived an adoration of Alexander. When they met him at Bruchsal in March 1814, Alexander asked to join this spiritual circle in "a bond of love and charity which is indissolvable."

It is by no means certain that this love was entirely spiritual. Swedenborgian doctrines of the flesh and spirit, William Blake's "Marriage of Heaven and Hell," were around for Alexander to absorb. Roxandre's very good friend, the Munich theosophist Franz von Baader (an important figure in the history of thought, influencing such later thinkers as Kierkegaard and Berdyaev), was probably the most impressive spokesman in Alexander's immediate circle for this view of carnal love as a gateway to the spiritual. The tsar was later to invite Baader to Russia as an honored guest. The Bavarian sage, who wrote much about the Philosophy of the Erotic, thought that in the Christian era sexual love takes on a religious character. The union of the sexes is the first step toward union of humankind with God in the ultimate mystical marriage. Men and women lose their selfish individuality in this sexual merger, lose even their male or female qualities in a restoration of androgynous nature. The ecstasy of physical love is or can be a foreshadowing of the mystic's ecstasy of Divine love.

In Vienna, whither Roxandre Stourdza followed him from Baden, Tsar Alexander spent much time alone with her. Amid the glitter of the Viennese peace conference, Alexander closeted himself with this enchantress. She wrote that the Emperor "dedicated to me sometimes some hours in the evening, and we chatted in my little apartment, as at Bruchsal." She added that she resisted his entreaties "*les plus obligeantes*"; we may suspect she did not always do so. She wrote to Julie that Alexander's wife could never understand him! Secluding himself with Roxandre and a few others including Roxandre's brother, and his adviser Capo d'Istria, Alexander ignored invitations to most of the elaborate balls Metternich and Talleyrand hosted as a part of their diplomacy; he openly showed scorn for the wicked realists and thus helped widen the rift that developed between the Allies during the peace negotiations, one that came to the brink of actual war between the victorious powers, with France joining Austria and Great Britain in a cabal aimed at Russia. There seems to have been a good deal of both social and sexual diplomacy involved in these memorable negotiations.

Alexander and Julie Krüdener met in Heilbronn when the Emperor, hastening together with other Allied leaders to again confront Napoleon who had returned to France from his short-lived exile on the island of Elba, paused there in early June of 1815 en route from Vienna. He listened to her for three hours almost hypnotized, tears streaming down his cheeks, as with matchless eloquence she urged him to repent of his sins and redeem himself through his mission to redeem the world. Basically masochistic, desiring submission to the Divine Will, Alexander put himself under Mme. Krüdener's control. The appearance of this incredible creature was surely a sign from on high! At their first meeting he enjoyed it when she lectured him severely. Soon he was following her advice "like a child." She became a kind of psychoanalyst for him; she wanted Alexander to confess his sins and he was delighted to do so. He was able to tell her "the griefs and the passions which had troubled his life." (The witness is Mme. Stourdza.) Alexander's turbulent childhood, the murder of his father, his sexless marriage, his dissipations and mistresses; his sister Catherine; he could confess all and then find solace on the bosom of this substitute mother, so saintly yet ardent.

They spent some idyllic days together near Heidelberg. Then, as the final great battle loomed with Bonaparte, she followed Alexander to Paris. Together they created one of history's most remarkable political documents, the treaty of the Holy Alliance.

THE HOLY ALLIANCE

After Napoleon had been defeated again, had abdicated, and been shipped off to the remote island of St. Helena, Alexander was a hero in France, for he insisted upon the lenient treatment of the defeated nation. Distinguishing between the people of France and their diabolic dictator, he found the former essentially blameless, at least forgiveable. "I love all French people except him [Napoleon]! I respect the glorious courage of all those brave men whom I have fought against. . . . I am ready to render them justice and honor; they have earned it. . . . Tell the Parisians that I do not enter their city as an enemy. . . . If they will let me I will be their friend." It was a rare and remarkable attitude on the part of a victor in war—one of the longest and bitterest wars in history.[1] Alexander prepared a great military pageant held on September 19, 1815, on a hillside near Epernay, some seventy-five miles east of Paris—followed the next day by an equally enormous spectacle of piety. Some 120,000

---

[1]Talleyrand, the French diplomatic genius who much influenced Alexander, had told him, "The French people are civilized but their sovereign is not. The Sovereign of Russia is civilized, his people are not. Therefore the Sovereign of Russia must be the ally of the people of France."

of those assembled knelt in a solemn mass; it was a day of countless priests rather than generals. "The most beautiful day of my life," Alexander said of this *fête*. "My heart was filled with love for my enemies," he told Mme. Krüdener. "I wept at the foot of the Cross as I asked for the safety of France." The spectacle climaxed an amazing chapter in the saga of the Russian ruler, now nearing his thirty-eighth birthday.

The Prussian statesmen Friedrich Gentz reported that, during his Paris sojourn, Alexander "existed only for affairs of state and for Mme. de Krüdener. His usual gallantry seemed to have totally abandoned him; the most beautiful women seemed to have no appeal for him. He spent every moment when not with his cabinet in secret talks, theological discussions, and acts of devotion and prayer with her." The result was the "Holy Alliance." With the help of Alexandre Stourdza, who was Roxandre's brother, Alexander and Mme. de Krüdener wrote out this most famous and controversial of political treaties in late September 1815. The French statesman-author Chateaubriand, who was there, attributed the text to her.

"The reign of the Savior will come!" she told Tsar Alexander. "Form a holy alliance of all those who are loyal to the faith. Let them swear to fight with a common accord all those who wish to tear down religion, and you will triumph with it!" Alexander was to be the arm of the Almighty. Now at the peak of his fame and power, he must stride on to become nothing less than a divine savior. In one of Julie's images the kings of Prussia, Austria, and Russia were the Three Magi, presiding over the birth of the Millennium.

The practical politicians, of course, never liked or even understood the *Sainte Alliance* (Holy Alliance). The other sovereigns greeted Alexander's "treaty" with as much embarrassment as astonishment. "A philanthropic aspiration disguised under the cloak of religion," Austria's Prince Metternich muttered. Neither philanthropy nor religion had anything to do with world politics. The British representative, Lord Castlereagh, who thought the Holy Alliance emanated from "an old female fanatic," called it "a monument of sublime mysticism and nonsense." If issued at all, the statesmen thought, it should be as one of those edifying and normally ignored "manifestos" that heads of state hand to the press at the conclusion of a conference. But Alexander intended to make this "grand aspiration" the actual law of nations. The old order of international relations must be "absolutely changed" and replaced by one "uniquely founded on the sublime truths which the eternal religion of God the Savior teaches us." And, as Julie's next few years proved, at least in her mind this revolution was supposed to include a new social order based on real concern for the needy, the oppressed, the hungry.

Some editing of the treatise by Prince Metternich took a sharp edge or two off Alexander's megalomania. "The precepts of this holy religion," the Krüdener-Alexander draft ran, "far from being applicable only to private life, *as has always previously been thought*, must on the contrary directly influence the decisions of princes and guide all their endeavors. . . ." The italicized words above, so redolent of millenarianism, were omitted in the final draft. Also, the phrase "absolutely changed" (see above) fell by the wayside. The official version leaves a more anodyne impression, that Their Majesties proposed to go on being Christian as usual, rather than making a dramatic new start. It left "subjects" out of the partnership of virtue, including only "sovereigns," and the Metternich version also got rid of an insinuation in Alexander's version that there would be only one European army, a sort of United Nations peacekeeping force replacing the separate armies of individual nations.

But Alexander on his return to Russia defiantly published his original version of the Holy Alliance in a mighty proclamation addressed to the Russian people, and he issued it on Christmas Day 1815.

Forty-eight states were invited to adhere to the watered-down version of the Holy Alliance; only the Papacy refused. How the Holy Alliance was transformed from a hoped-for purifying revolution into a repressive agency opposed to change and freedom, as it was widely perceived to be by 1821, is a long chapter in the history of international relations. Like its successors the League of Nations and the United Nations, the Holy Alliance deserved a better fate. In May 1821, when Austrian troops entered Naples to suppress a revolt, Alexander's old tutor and longtime friend, the Swiss Laharpe, finally gave up on his idol: "My task is done!" the old *philosophe* wrote. "I have done all I can. Hereafter I have nothing more to say to the tsar of all the Russias. We no longer speak the same language; my principles are not his. I believed him the benefactor of his people and of humanity; I loved him for that and for himself; hereafter, he no longer exists for his old and faithful friend."

The Holy Alliance's very inception was ill-starred in that having delivered themselves of it in a moment of ecstatic union, the tsar and Mme. Krüdener soon parted for good. Within a few days of the Holy Alliance's completion, Julie was distressed to learn that Alexander was spending a great deal of time now with another lady. By September 28, 1815, just two days after the finalization of the Holy Alliance treaty, Alexander had left, declaring in a letter to his sister, Catherine (October 1 from Brussels), that he was glad to be out of "this accursed Paris." Always subject to violent attacks of jealousy, as he had also been, for example, with his sister Catherine, Alexander may have been aroused by the appearance in Paris of one of Julie's former mystical roommates; perhaps he simply wearied of the aging enchantress and broke the spell. Julie and Tsar Alexander met again only twice, briefly on both occasions, in 1819 and 1821.

Alexander did little to assist Julie when, in 1817 and 1818, she found herself the victim of persecution throughout the Continent. Leading a strange band of prophets and Christian revolutionaries, she was expelled from region after region in Switzerland, Austria, and Germany, until finally compelled to return, exhausted, to her Latvian home. She had taken the Holy Alliance seriously and this was the consequence. Metternich regarded Mme. Krüdener as a dangerous revolutionary because "her prophecies have the goal of exciting the indigent classes against the proprietors." Little help came from Alexander, although some German peasants were allowed to migrate to southern Russia, and Alexander did rebuke the Governor-General of the Baltic provinces who actually wanted to prevent Julie from entering her homeland. The episode greatly enhances one's respect for Mme. Krüdener, and it does the tsar little credit. Perhaps her radicalism that so alarmed Metternich and virtually every police agency in Central Europe repelled the tsar; yet his own retreat from liberalism had not yet begun. He was to let all kinds of unconventional preachers into Russia in the next few years, as he continued to believe in a new spiritual, international religion rising on the ruins of existing establishments. And in fact he continued to see mystic ladies under questionable circumstances. It was not until 1820 that Alexander recanted his revolutionary faith, at which time he told the Comtesse Sollub that Mme. Krüdener's actions "while well intended had brought about great harm."

It is obvious Alexander did not want to see her any more. He even avoided a meeting when, near the end of her life—she died on Christmas Eve, 1824—she journeyed to the Caucasus with the Princess Golitzin. But Alexander was to go there and visit her tomb just before his own death (or disappearance) a year later. She felt betrayed and abandoned by the one she had worshipped as a god: "He had not even a single flower for me, not even a cup of water. . . ," she declared (1821).

Alexander followed her to the grave before long. Was it because he after all needed this strange and marvelous woman to sustain his life? He was only forty-eight. There is the alternate version, romantic enough to be true, that he faked his own death in order to withdraw from public life. The story goes thus: After visiting Julie's grave in the Crimea and consulting with the monks, he made use of his passion for charades to contrive his own death, paying his debt to Julie by thereafter humbly serving the poor. According to this legend, Alexander reappeared in Siberia as the monk Fyodor Kusmich, an extraordinary holy man, living on for many years. Leo Tolstoy believed this story. It is almost as unlikely as many other tales through the ages (from Jesus to Elvis, we might say) about the mysterious survival of some charismatic figure after his presumed death.

It is more plausible in Alexander's case because he had so many times longed to live a simple life, away from the Russian court, yet found this impossible to do. Much is sometimes made of the fact that when Alexander's tomb was finally opened decades later, it was empty. What is important is less whether the story was true or not than that people wanted to believe it.

In any case, by 1824 all of Alexander's hopes and illusions had faded. He had not reformed Russia; for some time it had been governed repressively by those acting in his name, especially the brutal Arakcheev. The tsar broke with all his old liberal friends, imposed censorship, banned societies such as the Freemasons. In their disappointment the so-called Decembrists were already preparing the attempted revolutionary coup that occurred soon after Alexander's death (or disappearance). He had not done anything about serfdom.[2] He had not saved Europe; Metternich and the cynical realists had converted the tsar's dream of a new order of peace and brotherhood into a system for the repression of popular movements. Like Byron, who died at about the same time and at an even younger age than the tsar (who was not yet fifty in 1825), Alexander could have said that "the flowers and fruits of love are gone."[3] He had enough insight to know and regret his failures, his lost opportunities, his weaknesses and sins. These were many; and yet in the end we feel that Alexander's flawed grandeur shines through. The conqueror of Napoleon remains one of history's most attractive and enigmatic figures.

It should be added that the tumultous years of the amazing era he shared with his enemy Napoleon transformed all Europe and began the transformation of Russia. "The events of our time are more surprising and improbable than anything that has ever taken place," one of the leaders of the Decembrist rebellion wrote. "How will posterity be able to believe what has happened under our very eyes?" The Russian poet Ryleev had gone with Alexander's forces to Germany and France; he had been in Paris in 1815. "I was infected by freethinking during the campaigns in France in 1814 and 1815," he later told an investigating commission. Hardly less than Napoleon and the French Revolution, Alexander I had awakened forces in Russia that would never afterward be destroyed, however much later rulers struggled to contain them.

[2]At the beginning of his reign Alexander I introduced a plan by which with the consent of the proprietors, and funded by the government, a class of free peasants was gradually to be created—the state buying them back, in effect, little by little. But by 1824, in all his reign, no more than 40,000 peasants had been freed in this way. In Poland, Estonia, Courland, and Livonia, between 1807 and 1819, Alexander did secure an end to servitude.

[3]The analogy between Alexander and the great English poet Byron is more than casual; in 1814, when Alexander visited London, Byron had just awakened to find himself famous, and he and the tsar were the two heroes of the hour. Byron too tried in his way to mix a literary and a political life, dying in the campaign for Greek independence of which he was a leader. He too was a Rousseauist. Russian literature, via Pushkin, would be strongly influenced by Byron. But Byron disparaged Alexander as "the autocrat of waltzes and of war, with no objections to true liberty/Except that it would make men free." This was after Alexander refused to help the Greek revolution in 1821.

6

Karl Marx and the Appeal of Marxism

MARX'S EARLY DEVELOPMENT

For one who was destined to be forever associated with capitalism and the Industrial Revolution, Karl Marx was born in a remarkably inappropriate place. He came from no factory town or urban financial center, but rather a small, very ancient city on the Mosel River devoted then as now mainly to the cultivation of the grape. Every citizen of Trier worth his salt wanted to have a vineyard on the hillsides overhanging the town, and Karl's father, Heinrich, achieved this goal. The elder Marx was no proletarian; neither was he an exploiter of labor, but a lawyer and government official, in effect the local district attorney. He had enough means to give Karl a good education, sending him on from *Gymnasium* (secondary school) to the university at a time when only a tiny fraction of the populace achieved this goal; but he was not rich, and he had occasion to complain about his son's extravagant habits at the university.

Although the Marx family was Jewish, with a long string of rabbis in its lineage on both father's and mother's side, it was becoming assimilated. Heinrich Marx had once been Herschel but changed his name at the same time he changed his religion, less than a year before Karl's birth on May 5, 1818, in order to keep his job by complying with the Prussian government's restrictions on Jews holding public office. This cannot have cost Heinrich Marx much pain, for his outlook was thoroughly secular; admirer of Voltaire and Rousseau, he had absorbed Enlightenment deistic ideas. By all accounts he was an excellent public servant—able, judicious, and honest. He was also modest and deferential, with a personality as different from that of his tempestuous and revolutionary son as it is possible to imagine.

Heinrich's letters to his only surviving son betray literary skill and sensitivity. He died before Karl finished his education and began his career. Of nine children born to Heinrich and Henrietta Marx, five died in infancy. Karl Marx's own children were to suffer an almost comparable decimation. The main killer was tuberculosis, a scourge of this era.

The psychological effect on Karl Marx of his Jewishness, or of his father's abandonment of it, is speculative. Marx does not seem to have experienced much if any anti-Semitic discrimination during his formative years in the Rhineland. He was popular in school and later married the daughter of the local grandee, Baron Ludwig von Westfalen, formerly an administrator in the short-lived kingdom of Westphalia created by Napoleon. The baron, a liberal and a lover of literature, had a significant influence on young Karl. It is true that the Westfalens and the Marxes got on less well after the deaths of the two patriarchs (1838, 1842); but then Karl quarreled seriously with his own mother, too. The cause seems to have been less religious or racial than economic, involving Karl Marx's predilection for a career in left-wing journalism that promised doubtful material benefits. His mother once expressed a wish that Karl would earn some capital instead of writing about it.

In general, Karl Marx regarded the "Jewish question" as secondary and irrelevant; ideological and economic class factors were for him the important cards of identity. He found his friends and collaborators among Christians as well as Jews (Friedrich Engels is a good example) and thought that in the coming socialist era ethnic and religious issues would vanish. Like Franz Kafka later, he could sound anti-Semitic when he wrote (privately) about certain traditional Jewish characteristics and beliefs. Marx's university friend Moses Hess eventually became a pioneer of Zionism, but this was well after his early period with Marx as a "Young Hegelian."

Some have discerned Jewish features in the deep structure of Marx's thought. The apocalyptic and messianic strains in Judaism seem echoed in Marx's vision of a journey through history toward a final great climax followed by the resolution of all problems. But this can just as easily be tied to Christianity or to Romanticism. It came to young Marx directly from Hegel and the socialists.

In his youth, introduced to it by Baron von Westfalen, Romantic literature bowled Karl over, as well it might in this age of Byron and Goethe. Passion, excitement, and strenuous individual goals of achievement permeated the social atmosphere. Byronic heroes, moody rebels who defied conventions to love passionately and seek adventure, were the role models for strongminded young men. It was this romantic strain in the young, fiery, handsome, would-be poet that won Jenny Westfalen's heart and led her to call him "my dark little savage." Unfortunately, Marx's poems (1836/37) did not stamp him as destined to succeed Byron or rival his friend Heinrich Heine. They had more than enough romantic feeling but insufficient literary subtlety.

By temperament, Marx was a strong, even arrogant person; some childhood stories from his sisters picture him lording it over them as the confident older male, a point of similarity with another great Jewish intellectual, Sigmund Freud. These two strong personalities seethed with ambition to seize the world and leave their mark on it. To a remarkable degree they did just that. But Freud, as medical doctor and professor, was to achieve a position of respectability from which to launch his intellectual revolution. Marx never did. He earned his Ph.D. in 1841, with a dissertation on the ancient materialist philosophers, but he lost his chance for an academic appointment because of his radical writings. It was unlucky for him that at just that time a new Prussian king, an ultra-conservative, assumed the throne. Becoming editor of a Cologne newspaper, Marx fell afoul of the censorship laws there.

Karl's fortune took a turn for the better when he made the friendship of young Friedrich Engels. Later, Marx leaned heavily on the financial support of this friend and collaborator, who was the son of a partner in a prominent German textile company with a branch in Manchester, England. Here was a more direct contact with the new industrialism. Engels became interested in socialism before Marx did. In the early 1840s he studied a number of socialist writers. In the aftermath of the French Revolution a throng of such theories appeared in France as well as in England and Scotland where the factory system of production, especially in textiles, began to flourish early in the nineteenth century. In 1844 Engels wrote a much-admired account of the Manchester working class, drawing both on a parliamentary inquiry into scandalous conditions in the textile mills and on his own observations.

An urgently felt need to formulate a new structure for society, in the aftermath of the French Revolution's destructive turn, provided the chief impetus to socialism. The Old Regime was gone; Bonaparte had effectively ripped it apart all over Europe. But what would take its place was less clear. An ordered society based on a hierarchy of unequal estates (status groups) had given way to "equal rights under the law." This equality of opportunity sounded good, but in practice turned out to mean a highly competitive situation in which only the luckier and more aggressive individuals flourished. Socialists rejected the liberal idea of pure individual freedom as a cruel disappointment if not a fraud. It frees the middle class, they argued, but leaves the workers in chains, even heavier chains than before. For the Old Order, at least in principle, conceded a duty to look after the lower classes, who had a place in society, albeit a modest one. The New Order seemed to grant the downtrodden only a right to make it on their own or perish. "One law for the lion and the lamb is tyranny," cried William Blake. The law, Anatole France added, with fine impartiality prohibits rich and poor alike from sleeping in the streets.

Marx's interest in socialism came after an earlier interest in pure philosophy, and in some ways was a result of that interest. Germany was aglow with philosophy in the early years of the nineteenth century, a consequence largely of the work of one of the greatest of all philosophers, Immanuel Kant, whose epochal writings appeared in the latter part of the eighteenth century. Few thinkers of such depth and difficulty have had so much general impact. When Marx transferred from the University of Bonn to the University of Berlin in 1836, he fell into the ambience of Kant's leading successor, G.W.F. Hegel, usually regarded as the greatest of nineteenth-century philosophers. Although Hegel had died of cholera in 1831 at the age of sixty, his pervasive reputation lingered on.

In Berlin in 1836, a great many people wondered who or what would come after Hegel. Conservatives, liberals, and radicals competed for Hegel's legacy, each faction finding something in the master's thought to support its own position. Marx joined a group of "Young Hegelians" in Berlin who stood on the political left. This meant chiefly that they were atheists. Small wonder the Prussian dynasts took a dim view of this group's leadership role in teaching German youth at the university.

Hegel had taught the ongoing dialectical interpenetration of mind and matter, as Absolute Spirit projects and realizes itself in the real world, most especially in human historical development. From Hegel, Marx viewed this dialectical principle of change as coming about via the clash of opposites, as a social order engenders its own "contradictions," and (as Shakespeare had put it) is "consumed with that which it was nourished by." Marx usually assumed, too, the forward motion in all this; the economic-social order known as "capitalism," which supplants "feudalism," marks an advance, just as socialism or communism, the next destined phase, will improve upon capitalism. Hegel's vision of a meaningful overall progression in human history, which to him represented the providential growth of Spirit or God toward fuller and fuller self-realization, left its impression on Marx even though he came to criticize Hegel for mistakenly putting the Idea first rather than physical reality.

Though many found German philosophy mystifying, certain of its key ideas were appealing—not least this vision of meaning in history, the unfolding of life toward a purposeful end. Marx wedded to it not only socialist ideas, chiefly French, but also British political economy. Adam Smith influenced him as much as did Hegel. In the end Marx thought his own chief contribution was his critique of political economy in its "classical" form, contained primarily in the writings of Adam Smith and David Ricardo, whose 1817 *Principles of Political Economy and Taxation* was a landmark of economic theory. Marx's criticism accepted much of Smith and Ricardo but claimed to have corrected them in crucial ways. They had supposed their "laws" of economic behavior timeless and absolute; he would show that these laws were valid only within an institutional framework destined to crumble and be replaced by a new order of things, marked by social and not private ownership of capital. In terms of social classes, which to Marx were the dynamic agents in history, a single working class or proletariat would replace the bourgeoisie or capitalists.

All this, of course, did not materialize overnight. Marx worked his way forward laboriously. In 1844, in Paris, he extruded a massive and ill-organized manuscript that was not published until a century later, when scholars studied the roots of his thought. He wrote several books jointly with Engels, but one was obscure and the other abandoned, as he said wryly, to the criticism of the mice. Meanwhile, he had married Jenny von Westfalen and had begun a family; she had borne him three children by late 1846. After he lost his Cologne newspaper job Marx lived precariously on publishers' advances, first in France and then in Belgium, where he moved after having also overstayed his welcome in France. France was alive with revolutionary ideas, and an uprising in Lyon had produced official panic a few years earlier.

Marx's vast ambitions encompassed more than a literary or social-scientific career. His philosophical views led him to believe that thought must be applied to real life and in turn modified by practical experience in a continuing dialectical relationship. This was a remarkable if not exactly original conviction, and he tried to carry it out, with indifferent success. His first encounters with workers (artisans, for the most part, not the new factory hands) found him appalled at their stupidity while they were offended by his arrogance. This was in Belgium. Later, in London, where he lived from 1849 on, he played a considerable role in the International Workingmen's Association, founded in 1864, and devoted countless hours to administrative drudgery. But the (First) International perished of schisms and feuds within a decade, being revived as a more successful institution only in 1889, after Marx's death.

It was in Belgium where Marx joined a Communist League that he, along with Engels, wrote for this organization the celebrated *Communist Manifesto*, widely read as a short and accessible statement of Marx's views. In it he predicted the coming workers' revolt: "let the ruling classes tremble at a communistic revolution." In 1848, revolutions did erupt all over Europe, although they were scarcely communistic. Marx returned from Belgium to edit the newspaper in Cologne where he had worked five years earlier. The ruling classes may have trembled, but they quickly regained their courage and profited from confusion and contradictions among the revolutionaries to regain control. By the middle of 1849 Karl and Jenny, who had another child on the way, pawned the family jewels and fled to London, the refuge of many other continental rebels in that year of political reaction. They would live in England the remainder of their lives.

Marx had become marginalized; he would never have a position in the respectable world, as a professor or a recognized, successful writer. He would be forever associated with the idea of a total revolution of which he was the prophet—a position bearing the risk, especially in Victorian England, of seeming crazily eccentric. He would have to overcome that impression by solid intellectual achievement, as in time he did. It was not an easy task. As an alien among a crowd of refugees in London, jobless and with several small children, Marx experienced some hard times, although his penury has been exaggerated. Engels and others provided subsidies that later became almost lavish. (Not at first, however, when Marx and his family lived in miserably poor quarters.) Three of Marx's six (legitimate) children were to die between 1850 and 1855. There was another, born in 1851, whose mother was the lifelong family servant, Helene Demuth. This departure from bourgeois morality was long kept secret. It somewhat marred a marriage relationship between the devoted Jenny and Karl, a union that many considered to be almost idyllic. In general, Karl was a good family man, adored by the three daughters.

We know a good deal about Karl Marx's life from childhood on mostly because of the strange fate of his reputation. He became the prophet and idol of an organized political movement that more than thirty years after his death managed, for rather accidental reasons, to gain control of Russia, which then lavishly subsidized research into Marx's life. This fame was mostly posthumous. Marx was reasonably well-known in his last years, but chiefly among the German socialists. He published a goodly number of books and pamphlets, but few were calculated to reach a large audience, nor did they have much standing in academic circles. Outside of socialist sectarians, Marx's appeal was to a coterie of primarily Jewish intellectuals but including increasing numbers of others who might be described as the new intellectual class.

The affairs of post-1848 France supplied Marx with material for some brilliant current history, and in 1852 he began a ten-year career as foreign correspondent for the New York *Tribune*. Engels wrote some of these pieces for him. Many of them were outstandingly good. Marx had a literary flair, although his style might tend toward the ponderous. He was a keen student not only of world politics but also of world literature. Marx knew the classics as well as he did his contemporaries such as Balzac and Dickens. We might especially note that, according to Marx's daughter Eleanor, Shakespeare was "the Bible of our house."

Marx aspired to be more than a journalist, and in 1857/58 he outlined an ambitious program for his inquiries into political economy. The spectacular success of Charles Darwin's *Origin of Species* in 1859 encouraged Marx in his ambition to become the founder of "the science of society," doing for humanity what Darwin had done for the lower forms of life. Like Darwin's, his would be an evolutionary scheme. It would show how humankind's struggles to wrest a living from nature had led through several stages marked by changing social relations that were reflective of material conditions. Such a scheme of history had occurred to others before him, notably Scottish writers like Adam Smith and Adam Ferguson. But Marx would greatly extend and sharpen their primitive views of social revolution.

MARX AND THE LAWS OF CAPITALISM

The long-deferred first volume of *Das Kapital*, Marx's magnum opus, came from the press in 1867. Projected to cover a vast terrain of historical, social, and economic analysis, the work was never finished. Volume I of *Das Kapital* gained him some fame in his lifetime but the remaining volumes appeared only after his death, edited from miscellaneous fragments by friends and disciples. Within a few years the first volume was translated into Russian and then French, while a second German edition also came out, even though it had taken four years to sell a thousand copies of the original work. Aimed at showing to the industrial workers—the modern "proletariat"—their path to self-liberation, it was not pitched at the level of working-class understanding; one worker to whom Marx sent a copy said he felt like he had been handed an elephant. In his preface to *Das Kapital*, Marx indicated rather scornfully that he was not writing for nincompoops. Though at times deeply eloquent, the book was too abstruse and technical for all but a handful of experts.

As George Bernard Shaw noted in his notable review of *Das Kapital*'s first English-language edition in 1887, Marx's epic also radiated a superb self-confidence, conveying a contagious feeling that here was a momentous discovery superseding all previous accounts of human history and destiny.

That there was no English translation until 1887, four years after Marx's death, may have been because of the competition. The rich mid-Victorian harvest of literature and ideas was at its peak. Not many in an England, where serious readers were absorbed in John Stuart Mill, John Ruskin, and Matthew Arnold, paid heed to the often indigestible tome of a German refugee. Its socialist audience was intensely committed but small and culturally isolated. And even among socialists, Marx had many rivals. In time, the weight of *Das Kapital* was to overcome most of them.

The 1860s was indeed a dramatic decade, embracing as it did such decisive events as the American Civil War, emancipation at long last of the Russian serfs, unification of Italy as well as Germany, and in Britain a crucial political reform extending the vote to the urban working class. *Das Kapital* appeared at about the same time as such landmarks of serious Victoriana as Walter Bagehot's *English Constitution*, Matthew Arnold's *Culture and Anarchy*, and John Ruskin's *Unto This Last*, the latter actually a greater influence on English socialism than Marx.

In 1871, following an astonishing French defeat at the hands of Prussia (a war that Engels, the supposed military expert, failed to predict the outcome of), the new German Empire came into existence. Paris rebelled against the government that had lost the war and signed the humiliating peace, seeking to form an independent Commune—an event Marx mistakenly hailed as the beginning of the long-awaited proletarian revolution. These were extraordinary times, and in retrospect Marx's great book ranks along with these other events as a leading statement from a remarkable era.

The message of *Das Kapital* was, in fact, somewhat ambivalent. Running through Marx's writings about the existing social order of "capitalism," from the 1840s down through the 1870s, is a vacillation between the view that a contemptible system will soon be overthrown by a violent revolution of the oppressed, and the view that a progressive, productive system will peacefully die when it has given all that it has to give. This sets forth the two extremes somewhat too sharply; Marx is usually more nuanced, but these were the opposing tendencies. In either case, of course, capitalism dies, to be replaced by socialism and communism. (At times Marx used the term "socialism" to designate a kind of in-between stage before humanity is quite ready for the ideal condition of communism.) In both cases, the assumption is the historicist one that human society passes through successive stages, each dominated by a specific "mode of production." But there are significant differences within Marx about the durability and the value of capitalism, as well as the way in which it will be replaced.

The two views were affected by changing conditions and moods in Europe over the decades. In the 1840s Marx came of age amid an acutely felt sense of crisis. It was not just or even chiefly the advent of large factories employing machine-tenders, a new "mode of production"; such methods as yet accounted for but a small percentage of the goods produced. This was also the time of the Irish famine, caused by failure of the potato crop, and of a cholera epidemic, as London and other large cities confronted a health crisis. A good many writers called attention to a general crisis of society, Thomas Carlyle's 1843 *Past and Present* being a notable example. It might even be said that the discovery of the urban poor belongs to this decade. Eugene Sue's *Mysteries of Paris* found an echo in the widely read reportage of Henry Mayhew in London's *Morning Chronicle*. Charles Dickens had already published *Oliver Twist*, his tale of orphanage, poverty, and crime in London that reached and moved a far larger audience than any socialist tract.

Leading up to the revolutions of 1848 was a feeling that some apocalyptic climax was about to happen. But in the aftermath of the 1848/49 revolutionary failures the mood changed sharply as conditions improved noticeably. The Hungry Forties gave way to a mid-Victorian era of prosperity. During the next two decades cities met the threat to public health by constructing new water and sanitation systems. Karl Marx's first year in London saw preparations for the great Crystal Palace Exhibition of 1851, widely regarded as a landmark in the development of capitalist self-confidence; on display to the gaping masses were products of the new technology. In France, a man Marx detested and scorned, Napoleon III, assumed control of France and presided over nearly two decades of political stability and economic progress, until his dismal downfall in 1870.

In the 1850s Marx lost most of his illusions about a speedy and successful social revolution, and he resigned himself to a long wait. Left-wing causes were in sad decline; the Communist League to which Marx had belonged ceased to exist. In the 1860s a certain revival of revolutionary activity drew him back to politics; we have already mentioned his work for the International from 1864 to 1874. But after the Paris Commune of 1871 disappointed him, Marx in his last years, beset by illness and flagging energies, seems to have lost hope in revolution again—except perhaps in a place as little suitable for his theories as Russia.

Das Kapital at times seethes with indignation at the iniquities and hypocrisies of capitalism. Yet as he grew more scientific, Marx wished to separate himself from the sentimental moralists. They, including the earlier socialists he designated "utopian," drew his withering scorn for a lack of clarity and realism. In his analysis of capitalism Marx tried to show that it was doomed, but not because it was wicked or unjust. By what objective standards could a social order be so judged? Capitalism had performed many useful services in accumulating capital, enlarging the market, creating large-scale enterprises, bringing workers together. It would die only when it no longer was a force for progress, as once it had been, but when it became "a fetter on production." It would perish of its own operations, not from some revolutionary uprising. Its demise was inevitable, but it might take a long time. The mills of the gods grind slowly. . . .

Marx's main argument for the self-inflicted death of capitalism sought to show that the capitalist decreases his profits as he uses more and more machinery and less human labor power. (To Marx, the capitalist was the manufacturer, the employer of labor and producer of commodities. Other economists have distinguished between the capitalist as one who supplies money for investment, and the entrepreneur who borrows this capital, rents land, and hires labor to create a production facility.) Marx held that profits come only from the exploitation of human labor, as a "surplus value" representing the difference between the value created by labor and its market price, the price the employer pays in money wages. As the proportion of human labor in the factors of production diminishes, owing to the ever greater use of machinery, so must profits.

This "falling rate of profit" analysis was to be severely criticized; in saying that machinery cannot produce profits it flew in the face of empirical evidence. Marx tied it to other arguments, less strictly economic, designed to show that capitalism as private ownership of the means of production could not last. As the masses of hired workers gain class consciousness they will inevitably unite to socialize a system that deprives them of both the psychological and the material rewards of their labor. Moreover, capitalism is prone to breakdowns marked by business failures and unemployment. It has, in fact, already almost socialized itself, as huge corporatively owned enterprises replace the old family workshops.

Das Kapital failed to convince professional economists. The art or science that Smith and Ricardo had created had found other devotees, among the best brains of the age. The "labor theory of value" on which Marx leaned was soon to be challenged; indeed, William Stanley Jevons's theory of utility was published only four years after *Das Kapital*. The marginal utility school, represented by Jevons and Alfred Marshall, abroad by Karl Menger and Leon Walras, undermined the foundations of Marx's theory of value. No metaphysical "value" consisting of labor power inheres in a commodity; value is just exchange value, and this is determined by how much people desire a certain commodity and how painful it is to produce it: It is a psychological equation more than a social one.

Marx was surely mistaken insofar as he claimed, which he did at times, that the condition of the working class was steadily growing worse—subject to ever greater exploitation, as capitalists strove to counteract the decline of profits. Most economic historians today believe that, although living standards may have fallen in the early part of the nineteenth century, they began to rise at least by 1850 and continued to do so. Similarly, economic inequality increased at first and then began to diminish. The thesis of impoverishment may have been valid for the 1840s, but in the long run capitalism was a material success, providing a higher standard of living on the average for a population that, in Great Britain, increased eightfold during the nineteenth century. Marx's belief that workers grew ever more impoverished under capitalism wavered, in fact, in the second edition of *Das Kapital*, where he preferred to put more emphasis on psychological alienation as a factor in the failure of capitalism.

It is important to note that economic theory was not for Marx truly basic. In his most impressive book he tried to nail down the economic details, but his larger view of capitalism's inevitable transition to socialism was rooted in Hegelian historicism. The dialectic of change decreed the movement of humanity through different stages en route to some final destination. At bottom this was a kind of cosmic—ultimately mystical—process. Marx tried to transform this idealistic or religious vision into concrete, material terms; but it seems clear that the model came prior to his empirical investigations. The popularity of a somewhat vulgarized Marxism owed much to this quasi-religious structure. It was an eschatology of hope, a vision of the poor and oppressed finally inheriting the earth after millennia of painful struggle upward. They were first slaves, then serfs, then exploited wage workers before finally becoming free men, expropriating their expropriators in the last act of history, which considerably resembled the Christian millennium or Second Coming.

That Marx cast his thought in an apparently more up-to-date form did not of course hamper its appeal. A scientific age needed a scientific faith. Traditional Christianity and Judaism were now obsolete, many "higher critics" of this period believed. Marxism took their place as a religion. Marx's faith in a socialist future transcended the economic details. He had remarkably little to say about exactly how a socialist economic system would work; he simply assumed that somehow it would. That could safely be left to experience. The laws of economics were not absolute; the New Order would create new laws.

That they were certain to be better than the old laws was basically because a classless and therefore nonexploitative society would replace a class-dominated one. The future would expose serious flaws in this quasi-Hegelian logic.

Did Marx in his mature years have in mind a sudden great revolution, or a gradual and peaceful evolution? He said that some countries might be able to achieve socialism by democratic processes. All his life he rejected almost scornfully romantic revolutionaries like the French insurrectionist Blanqui, and then the great Russian anarchist Bakunin, who went about trying to stir up revolts without regard to social conditions. Revolution would come when the time was ripe; and when the time was ripe it would come naturally, like childbirth at the end of pregnancy. Capitalism had first to finish its term, fully preparing the field for its socialist offspring. Nevertheless, the two systems were separate and could not mix; socialism coming little by little, as the British Fabian Socialists favored, was foreign to the Marxist spirit. On the metaphor of childbirth, that would be like the new offspring coming into existence without the traumatic moment of birth.

There seemed, however, to be contradictions in the Marx-Engels thesis of a great proletarian revolution that was the product of an advanced capitalism. For one thing, the most advanced industrial-capitalist country, Great Britain, was the least revolutionary. In the year that *Das Kapital* was published the second Reform Act extended the vote to urban workers. Despite some gloomy predictions, the British constitution survived this influx of propertyless citizens, who did not proceed to vote in socialism but rather to acclaim the liberal democrat William Gladstone. Socialism virtually disappeared from the British scene for half a century. The fact was that revolution was a possibility only in lands extremely backward by Marxian standards, places like Russia and Spain, which had hardly even begun to industrialize. This paradox persisted to haunt the future of Marxism.

MARX'S INFLUENCE ON THE SOCIALIST MOVEMENT

What strange intellectual children Marx was to have! In 1991, more than a century after Marx's death, newspapers carried stories about a "Marxist" regime—in Ethiopia, where a murderous tyrant finally fled for his life. Marx would have been amazed to learn that his name was attached to this and other such governments. Apart from the fact that Marx knew and cared little about non-European peoples, lumping most of them together as a stagnant "Asiatic mode of production," he believed in social democracy, including freedom of speech and other civil liberties. Marx believed that the working class in a fully developed industrial-capitalist society would inherit the liberal institutions of the bourgeoisie and improve upon them. In Ethiopia there was neither a bourgeoisie nor a proletariat. Even terrorists have been labeled "Marxist," although all his life Marx opposed such actions.

In popular or at least journalistic parlance, "Marxist" has come to mean what Stalin said that Lenin said Marx said—a double distortion in which the thought of the master became twisted beyond all recognition. This happened because the Russian Revolution of October 1917, the product of defeat and breakdown in the world war of 1914–1918, fell into the hands of a faction labeling itself Marxist. Led by the man who called himself Lenin, these Russian Bolsheviks had departed considerably from orthodox Marxism as it was taught from about 1889 to 1914.

In 1869 a Social Democratic party was founded in Germany, just then in the throes of being united into one political nation by Bismarck's forceful Prussian diplomacy. The German Social Democrats were deeply influenced by Marx, although not by him exclusively; his friendly rival Ferdinand Lassalle was for a time better known than Marx. In 1874 Marx offered some sharp criticisms of their program. The Social Democrats suffered persecution in the new Germany, were for a time outlawed, and did not gain much strength until after Bismarck's departure seventeen years later, by which time Marx was dead. But after 1889 with a return to legality the Social Democrats flourished, gaining a large membership and publishing numerous newspapers and journals. By 1912 the Social Democrats had become Germany's largest political party. The German socialists dominated the revived (Second) International, which held impressive quadrennial meetings.

This did not mean they had much real power. The elected German Reichstag (Parliament) had limited ability to control the chancellor, a powerful post, appointed by the emperor, which Bismarck had fashioned for himself. Beyond that, the German Social Democrats were far from revolutionary. Accepting the democratic order, they held firm to the Marxist belief that capitalism and socialism did not mix; one could make the transition from one system to the other peacefully and democratically, but not gradually. There was a great party debate on this point when Marx's old friend Eduard Bernstein argued for total abandonment of the Hegelian mysticism in favor of a pragmatic approach, but the party decided against Bernstein. People did not want to give up the eschatological hope in an eagerly awaited Great Day when revolution would usher in an idyllic society. The party refused to accept a role in any "bourgeois" government, on the grounds that such collaboration undermined socialist solidarity. The majority of the Social Democrats found themselves locked into a peculiarly passive attitude of waiting quietly until the gods of history had done their work. Lenin called it "requiem socialism."

It was against this quietism that a few of the German socialists and Lenin's faction of the Russian Social Democratic party rebelled. Marx himself, replying to a letter from Russian comrades in his later years, thought that Russia might possibly be able to bypass or condense the bourgeois-capitalist stage, jumping directly from feudalism to socialism, because of the survival of communal institutions among the Russian peasants. A whole school of *mir* (communal) socialists had arisen in Russia. This not very well known letter by Marx was heresy from the high priest himself. Almost all Marxists, including the leading ones in Russia, held that Russia must first march through the bourgeois stage before she could enter into the promised land of socialism; to attempt socialism prematurely could only lead to tyranny. Lenin was to suggest that a highly trained elite party, schooled to seize power and exercise a dictatorship in the name of the proletariat, could preside over an accelerated passage to socialism. Lenin found the phrase "dictatorship of the proletariat" in Marx; but as the words plainly indicate, Marx was not talking about the forcible rule of a small group claiming to speak in the name of the proletariat. Nor did he mean a permanent regime. He had suggested only a short period after the revolution during which liquidation of the remnants of capitalism might require emergency powers.

But Lenin assumed that the theater of history was international, not national; if the revolution began in Russia it would soon spread to other places until it encompassed the globe. No reason why it should not begin in a backward and exposed salient of the long front in the class war.

Marx himself might have been pleased at Lenin's cheekiness. He retained to the end traces of his rebellious personality, rejoicing in the next to last year of his life that today's children "have before them the most revolutionary period with which men were ever confronted." He sometimes scoffed at his disciples, once bursting out, "Thank God I am not a Marxist!"

Marx's long-time rival Bakunin, an anarchist, argued that in approving use of the state even for a short time Marx was sanctioning a potentially oppressive government. The state was the state regardless of its declared purposes; in attempting to use it rather than destroy it Marxists would fall prey to the evil beast and end by becoming oppressors in the time-worn mold. Bakunin was a good prophet. After Lenin's small Bolshevik faction gained power in war-ravaged Russia in 1917 they proceeded to outlaw all other political parties and to organize a secret police system to terrorize opponents. Lenin's legacy of rule by a few men subsequently passed into Stalin's one-man dictatorship with intensification of the terror and perfection of its apparatus. This power was used to install a centrally planned economy, ultimately entailing an enormous bureaucracy making the major economic decisions. Though described as socialism, with the promise of ultimate communism, this regime of bureaucracy backed by terror had little if any foundation in Marx's thought. It is true that Marx expected the economy of the future somehow to run without a market and with some central planning. But he also believed that coercion would be unnecessary and the state as such would cease to exist. Even Lenin said this in 1917 just before the Bolshevik Revolution (*The State and Revolution*).

Of course, the immense paradox remained: Marxism meant the coming of socialism to an advanced capitalist, liberal society, amid conditions of developed political and social institutions; it was not the forcible imposition of socialism on an industrially undeveloped country with virtually no bourgeoisie or proletariat, no democratic political institutions, little tradition of individual liberties protected by an independent legal order. Where Marx (and Lenin) expected socialist revolution, it did not happen. Remember that Lenin thought the revolution would soon spread from Russia to the more advanced societies; Russia was only a trigger for the expected world revolution. It was not merely that capitalism proved economically more durable and successful than Marx predicted; it was, even more, that what Marx sometimes called its "superstructure" of political and social institutions made it resilient enough to absorb protests and enact reforms. Trade unions and the welfare state mitigated the hardships of the working class under capitalism.

Whether by force of example or simply force, Marxism-Leninism spread to other places from the great and powerful (at the time) Union of Soviet Socialist Republics, the product of Lenin and Stalin's Russian revolutions. As a result of World War II other countries of Eastern Europe were compelled to accept Communist governments. In 1948 the largest territorial state in the world (the USSR) was joined by the most populous one, China, later by Vietnam, Cuba, and other not inconsiderable nations. It looked for a moment, about a century after the *Communist Manifesto*, that the world might belong to Karl Marx, or what Lenin and Stalin said was Marx. A series of some thirty volumes on "Marxist" regimes published by Columbia University Press between 1985 and 1989 identified twenty-six such regimes. But even as this testimony to Marx's influence was being written, a wild flight from communism was taking place.

The crisis in the Soviet Union and the East European Communist countries from about 1987 on, which sent them desperately looking for new answers amid the wreckage of the old Communist economic system, tended to sweep Marx aside along with Stalin and Lenin—false prophets all. But occasionally it was noted that the real Marx was not a dogmatist but a believer in experimentation and change. He had written of the need to revise ideas constantly under the influence of real conditions. Since the 1930s, there had been a major effort among some non-Soviet scholars and philosophers to rescue Marx from the Kremlin by rereading all his texts and rethinking their meaning. The Marx that emerged from the ruminations of the Frankfurt School and other neo-Marxologists was usually less deterministic, less dogmatic, above all much subtler than the one that Communist propaganda had stamped on the mind of a generation. Marx was also seen as more humanistic and more democratic. The Leninists and Stalinists had gravely distorted his message by selecting only what they wanted to find. Much as the French revolutionaries used Rousseau, arming their power lust with a few phrases taken out of context, so the Russian revolutionaries plundered Marx without really understanding him. (One of Stalin's innumerable victims was the director of the Marxism-Leninism Institute in Moscow who dared to publish all of Marx.) The Russian revolutionaries had misused Marx above all in justifying the dictatorship of a small group, in suppressing criticism and dissent, and in establishing a narrow thought-control that outlawed experimentation in the arts and literature.

There is some question whether Marx would ever have been considered so important a thinker but for the Russian Revolution of 1917, which was largely a historic accident. An interesting thinker, surely, but there were many other nineteenth-century social theorists and sociologists. A Russian anthology of sociology published in 1905 included Marx along with about a dozen others, most of whose names are now known only to specialists. Some were disciples of Auguste Comte, the French contemporary of Marx who coined the word "sociology," and also proposed a succession of historical stages. "Social Darwinists" like Herbert Spencer and Benjamin Kidd took their cue from Darwin's principle of natural selection or "survival of the fittest." A sweeping interpretation of world history in terms of races came from the Comte de Gobineau in the 1850s. Another historian in Marx's England, the widely read Henry Buckle, offered a scheme of determinism, supposedly making history "scientific." What if young Vladimir Ilich Ulyanov (Lenin) had happened on the writing of these theorists, instead of Marx, and found them to his taste?

But to ask this question is to suggest reasons why an activist like Lenin would choose Marx above other social theorists. Marx alone combined acute theory and scholarly knowledge with a thoroughly revolutionary perspective. He linked the toiling masses to the deepest philosophy. Philosophy had up to then only understood the world; now it would have to change it: The statement may have come first from another of the "Young Hegelians," but Marx took it over. Those whose embittered spirits burned to change the world, with themselves at the controls, found Marx uniquely exciting.

MARX AND THE WESTERN INTELLECTUALS

The working class to whom Marx claimed to appeal was an abstraction; it never actually existed except as an ideal. Obviously his major theoretical works were not addressed to such an audience. There were many different kinds and levels of "workers," and they never felt themselves a single community. Insofar as some workers found unity it was within specific crafts or trades, at best within an industry. A recent carefully researched study finds that in Victorian England, "class" played an insignificant role in the lives of working people.[1] Trade unionism, "the capitalism of the proletariat" as Lenin called it disgustedly, was the most the real working class could attain. In turn, union leaders frequently regarded the Marxists with disdain, calling Marxism an ideology of the intellectual class. Socialism was almost always

---

[1]Patrick Joyce, *Visions of the People: Industrial England and the Question of Class, 1840–1914* (Cambridge: Cambridge University Press, 1991).

a thing of the intellectuals, seldom of the rank and file of industrial workers. "Yes I fear my socialism is purely cerebral; I do not like the masses in the flesh," Harold Nicolson confided in a letter to his wife, in terms applicable quite generally to his generation of English intellectual socialists and Marxists.

Never was the peculiar appeal of Marxism to the intellectuals more dramatically shown than in the 1930s, among the elite university youth of Europe. At Cambridge, where a remarkable story of Moscow's recruitment of future top-level spies was unfolding, Marxism became *de rigueur* among the brightest students, almost as much so as homosexuality with which it was incongruously linked. Marxists usually of the Stalinist variety virtually took over the ancient and distinguished Apostles club. Anthony Blunt declared, possibly with some exaggeration, that between about 1933 and 1937 "almost every intelligent undergraduate who came up to Cambridge joined the Communist party some time during his first year." (See further in Chapter 12.)

Already there had been many examples of the capitalists themselves becoming flaming radicals, perhaps from a sense of guilt. The leading American Communist intellectual of the 1930s was an offshoot of the Wall Street banking house of Lamont. One of the Cambridge group of young Stalinists was the son of the Morgan Bank partner Willard Straight, who had founded the left-liberal American journal *New Republic*. Another was a Rothschild, while Nancy Cunard of the steamship tycoon family entertained the young comrades lavishly as they vacationed on the Riviera. Scions of the highest society in Britain, whether at Cambridge or Oxford, flocked to the Communist party. Well might Soviet leader Karl Radek boast that "in the heart of bourgeois England, in Oxford, where the sons of the bourgeoisie receive their final polish, we observe the crystallization of a group which sees salvation only with the proletariat." Cambridge was even redder. The young radicals were not just the children of English businessmen; there were aristocratic scions as well. Among the Cambridge crowd were two sons of a baron who later became Lord Chief Justice and a high-ranking diplomat in the British government.

If it seemed that Marx's fate was to convert not the proletariat but the wealthy to communism, this was partly an illusion; it was to the intellectuals that he appealed. It was simply that the chances of children of the upper bourgeoisie becoming intellectuals were much greater than that of those less well born. Not only did they have the wealth and the leisure, but they often reacted negatively against the values of their status-obsessed parents. The intellectual was marked by alienation from mainstream society, which he (or she) hated with a peculiar ferocity. Intellectuals accused society of fostering injustice, but the animosity came much more from their boredom with the life of "business."

The intellectual sought a more heroic and esthetically shaped life. Marx presented a picture of drastic social renewal coming after a great revolution in which the masters of Marxian theory would play a vital role. In the early 1930s, Anthony Blunt set off on a holiday carrying with him the works of Shakespeare and Karl Marx. The combination suggests the essentially dramatic nature of undergraduate Marxism.

Probably the greatest source of Marx's appeal was the totality of his teachings. The assiduous student who mastered or came close to mastering Marxian theory was in possession of a unifying system of thought offering explanations for almost everything. He or she had a picture of the entire world. It is true that this model was made up of abstractions; each fact or event in the real world had to be decoded, sometimes painfully, to make it fit into the structure of ideas. Its real meaning then became some symbol that had its place in the Marxist framework. Almost nothing, to the Marxist, was as it seemed. There was a perfectly logical explanation for this: The dominant class in an exploitative system excretes an ideological smokescreen to mask its infamy, a "false consciousness" that disguises the truth. Only when the Marxist strips away this cloud does truth appear clearly. Marx joined Freud as a "master of deceit" who taught their acolytes to mistrust every outward appearance, looking behind it for some shameful secret. The poet W.H. Auden, recalling his undergraduate Marxism of the 1930s, said that, "We were interested in Marx in the same way we were interested in Freud, as a technique of unmasking middle class ideologies." Once decoded, the world ceases to be a jumble of confusing events and takes on a perfectly rational character. Everything can be made to take its place in a harmonious totality.

There was something inhuman about this world of abstractions. Living in a realm of ideas rather than human beings, Marxists could be led into extreme Machiavellianism. As Louis MacNeice, the brilliant young poet who never quite bought his friends' dogmatic Marxism, put it, "The great danger of Marxist doctrine is that it allows and even encourages opportunism." Communists notoriously were so sure of their ends that they allowed themselves any kind of means, including lying and murder. What matter a few deaths now, of those on the wrong side of history, if it brings closer the final Great Day followed by eternal bliss? Stalin's millions of victims were only an extreme case of a tendency in all dogmatic faiths such as Marxism. Any card-carrying comrade would lie on principle; if the Communist party ordered it, it must be good for the human race. The issue became an urgent one when Stalin began systematically to wipe out all his foes in the great party purge of the mid-1930s in the USSR, charging his old comrades with crimes no rational person could believe they committed. The loyal Communist had to defend the purge trials and deny that the huge prison camps existed. Marxism's dance of categories could become wildly and weirdly divorced fom reality; the world it hypothesized was quite different from the actual one.

The odyssey of bright young people in and usually out of the party in the 1930s was found all over the world. French novelist André Malraux, who later recanted entirely, was said to have converted more people to communism than did Marx. Most of the intellectual Communists like Malraux sooner or later became severely disenchanted with the Soviet Union—not difficult to do—and with Communist duplicity. They might then hang on to Marx, deciding that Stalin's grim dictatorship and stodgy culture was a travesty of all the founding father had believed in. But most of those who saw betrayal of their hopes by "The God That Failed" (the title of a notable 1948 anticommunist anthology) left all left-wing views behind them. It remained for the next generation to rescue Marxism from Stalin and even Lenin by careful study of the entire corpus of Marx and Engels's writings. The extent to which we may rightly attribute to Karl Marx world communism's spectacular rise and fall, an immense saga around which much twentieth-century history has revolved, is still an open question.

7

Giuseppe Mazzini and Democratic Nationalism

MAZZINI AND "YOUNG ITALY"

Among the numerous political refugees who joined Karl Marx in London was the Italian Giuseppe Mazzini. The son of a distinguished Genoese doctor, he conforms to the rather general rule that revolutionaries came from well-off bourgeois families richly nourished with ideas. Like Marx, and later Lenin, Mazzini was a brilliant university student, emerging with a law degree at the age of twenty-one, but abandoning the law to become, in effect, a professional revolutionary. He came from the richly cultured and commercially important city of Genoa, Columbus's city.

Northern Italy strongly felt the influence of Rousseau and the French Revolution. Not a few Italians contributed to the Enlightenment, a good example being the criminologist Cesare Beccaria, and the revolutionary society that preceded Mazzini's "Young Italy" had its roots in the Masonic lodges so widespread in the eighteenth century. Napoleon Bonaparte, born in Corsica, was more Italian than French in ancestry, and his thorough reorganization of Italy around the Code Napoleon, abolishing feudal privileges, found strong support there. At Milan in 1805 he had crowned himself King of Italy, and he soon compelled Austria not only to recognize his predominance over the entire Italian peninsula but also to cede him Venice. With his brother Joseph named King of Naples and Sicily (later replaced by brother-in-law Murat), this was something close to a unification of Italy—all in one family, as it were.

Napoleon intimidated and even imprisoned the pope! But in the south the British navy, which had dealt the French a smashing defeat at Trafalgar near the Straits of Gibraltar, stood in the way of Napoleon's control of the Italian peninsula.

With Napoleon's final defeat in 1815 all this disappeared, replaced by a substantial return to the old order under Austrian control. The Congress of Vienna, at which the victors over Napoleon dictated a general territorial re-arrangement of Europe in 1814/15, adopted the principle of "legitimacy" and restored most of the old rulers to their thrones; this included the House of Savoy in northern Italy. The Grand Duke of Tuscany relied on Austrian power to keep him in power, while the Austrians governed directly in Venice and Lombardy. Nowhere was there more discontent with this reactionary peace settlement than among the young idealists of Italy. Nationalism, which in Germany dates from the humiliating Prussian defeat at Jena, thrived in Italy on hatred of an alien ruler.

Nationalism can hardly be said ever to have existed in Italy, and it was now pretty much an invention of the poets, at first. The first revolts against the Vienna settlement were in the name of Enlightenment equal rights without regard to nationality. The spiny, much-divided Italian peninsula has less geographical unity than appears at a glance at the map; and ever since the days of the Roman Empire it had never come under a single government. The spectacular Renaissance culture of the fourteenth and fifteenth centuries intensified this localism, for it became associated with the Italian city-states; Milan, Florence, and Venice were rivals in art and often enemies in war. The latter city at one time created a mini-empire of its own, looking overseas to Asia Minor. Sicily in the south had a far different culture from the north; it was more a part of North Africa and the Middle East than Europe; while in-between lay the Papal States, ruled by the Supreme Pontiffs of Christendom as the temporal base of their international spiritual empire.

The popes wanted nothing to do with Italian nationalism, which implied secular rule over Rome. Among the factors that had prevented Italy from unifying, the presence of the popes in Rome was one of the chief. The papacy by its very nature was the enemy of Italian unification; it wanted Rome and the region around it as the headquarters of its international activities, not the capital of an Italian state.

The peoples of the Italian peninsula, soaked in the history of proud regional cultures, felt scarcely any sense of "Italianness." Since the great revolution in trade that followed the post-Columbus opening of the westward oceanic routes, Italy as a whole, suffering economic decline, had been rather somnolent. The French Revolution and Napoleon awakened her, at least in the north. Now the "Metternich system" proposed to subject her to native tyrants backed by foreign power.

The Kingdom of Sardinia, usually known as Piedmont, with its capital at Turino and ruled by the House of Savoy, was somewhat more independent than were the other small political units of northern Italy, but its ruler wanted no part of constitutions and liberalism, much less revolution and democracy. Piedmont was moreover a fairly small and not well integrated state, embracing regions quite different from each other and speaking different dialects. By the 1814 peace settlement it acquired the city of Genoa in which Mazzini was born. It is not surprising that spirited youth in this proud commercial city, which had been an independent republic until 1797, rebelled against the illiberal autocracy in Turino that was now its legal sovereign. Yet in the end the Piedmont kingdom was to be the nucleus around which Italy united.

That day lay far ahead in 1821, when as Mazzini turned sixteen he watched refugees fleeing through Genoa from an insurrection that the Austrian army had brutally suppressed. (Nothing, incidentally, did more to destroy the reputation among liberals of Tsar Alexander I's Holy Alliance than this episode.) Here was the beginning of a remarkable career as revolutionary that was to span almost a half century. Giuseppe Mazzini was a dreamy, intellectual, yet passionate young man of upper-class stock. His work as a revolutionary proved rather more dangerous than that of Marx, who never went to prison (his wife, Jenny, once spent a day in a Brussels jail, but it cost the police commisioner his job). As a young man Mazzini languished in the fortress of Savona for six months, then was forced into exile.

In southern France he organized the "Young Italy" association. *Lo Giovana Italia* was built on the foundations of the *Carbonari*, a revolutionary movement crushed in 1831 after an ill-planned insurrection. Young Italy has been called the first modern revolutionary organization. Mazzini anticipated Lenin's elite party of highly trained and motivated professional revolutionaries. "Revolutions must be made by the people and for the people," the Young Italy manifesto proclaimed. But apparently they must be directed by a small group of dedicated enthusiasts. Members were sworn to secrecy and no one over forty could join! American college students of the 1960s who refused to trust anyone over thirty were echoing the 1830s. And in other ways too: Taking drugs, burning the flag, and wearing their hair long were habits of the "bohemian" youth of that era. There is little new under the sun.

Mazzini, though, was no bohemian, even if he lived a highly un-bourgeois life in the revolutionary underground. The apprehensive authorities, who mistrusted Italian nationalism as much as democracy, took seriously this Young Italy movement led by the intense and eloquent young Genoese. The Piedmont government executed some of Mazzini's followers in Genoa and persuaded the French government to crack down on Mazzini's group of conspirators, who were issuing revolutionary manifestoes from nearby Marseilles. Mazzini then fled to Switzerland. There the incorrigible idealist organized a Young Europe as well as a Young Switzerland association; after he tried to lead a march on Italy the Swiss also banished him.

His relentless foe was the crown prince of reaction, Metternich, who as Austrian foreign minister dominated European affairs between 1815 and 1848 and sought to root out revolutionary movements. Metternich thought Mazzini, like others among the revolutionary agitators and writers of Europe, a menace to public order. Metternich once called the Breton priest Lamennais, who had turned socialist, an "abject being." Mazzini was even worse. All manner of unconventional people had come forward in the unsettling atmosphere that followed 1815. This was the heyday of Romanticism, which became a revolt against all authority.

Mazzini did indeed have an amazing capacity for fomenting conspiracies, allied to a soaring romantic eloquence—a strange and potent combination of talents.

MAZZINI'S IDEOLOGY OF NATIONALISM

Mazzini came to London as a refugee some twelve years before Marx and the others who fled from the post-1848 reaction. It is a tribute to the spirit of the times as well as to Mazzini's ability that a foreigner who knew no English and wrote abstract treatises on politics should have made his way to considerable literary renown in England. Mazzini indignantly rejected a suggestion that he earn money by writing something more amusing.

Thomas Carlyle was the writer of the hour. He had just published his much-read history of the French Revolution; *Chartism* (1839) prepared the way for the notable *Past and Present*, a work that influenced Engels and Marx. In an eccentrically romantic, highly charged, and enormously effective prose style, Carlyle announced the coming of the "social question," thundering against "the gospel of Mammon," the economics of irresponsibility, the substitution of a "cash nexus" for real human ties. Though Carlyle was a defector from Scottish Presbyterianism and Mazzini from Catholicism, they were in many ways kindred spirits, and Carlyle helped the Italian get literary work. Calling for new heroes, Carlyle saw qualities of heroic leadership in Mazzini. Jane Welsh Carlyle, whose marriage to Thomas Carlyle was notably turbulent, found the dark, brooding Italian appealing.

The Carlyles and Mazzini shared what has been called "social romanticism." On its politico-economic side Romanticism sometimes glorified the free spirit, the rebel; it also showed a Rousseauist tendency to deplore urbanism and industrialism. Few friends were found among the Romantics of the "dark Satanic mills" or their capitalist owners, one of whom Carlyle caricatured as "Plugson of Undershot." Organic human communities crumbled under the impact of this inhuman system of production, they thought. The young Marx was under Carlyle's sway when he wrote that bourgeois society "dissolves the human world into a world of atomized and mutually hostile individuals."

The world needed a renewal of faith, the faith that binds people together in a common cause. The old faith of Christianity was dying, mortally

wounded by the Enlightenment. But that "chilled age," with its cold rationalism, had been able only to destroy, not to create. The task of their age, Carlyle and Mazzini thought, was to rescue humanity from Enlightenment materialism by producing a new religion, one appropriate to the post-Revolution
era. "Life without a noble goal, life not devoted to the pursuit of a great idea,
is not life but vegetation," Mazzini pronounced. The French socialist prophet
Henri Saint-Simon, a strong influence on both Carlyle and Mazzini, had written of a *Nouveau Christianisme*. Carlyle's religion was hero worship, the inspiration that comes from imitating the best examples of human achievement.

Mazzini's religion was nationalism. He wrote of his Damascene moment in terms of a religious inspiration:

> There flashed upon me, as a star in my soul, an immense hope: Italy reborn as
> the missionary to humanity of a faith in progress and in fraternity more vast
> than that of former times. . . . Why should there not arise from a third Rome, the
> Rome of the Italian People, a third and higher unity which, harmonizing earth
> and heaven, right and duty, should speak, not to individuals, but to peoples, the
> word of Association, teaching to the free and equal their mission here below?

"Association," always one of Mazzini's favorite words, was a term of the
1830s meaning socialism: Mazzini was part socialist. This element lurked in
Rousseau, we know. Mazzini's socialism was quite different from Marx's, and
though some Mazzinians took part in the First International they did not stay
long. Marx called Mazzini "the Pope of the Democratic Church in exile" and
sneered that he was a mere phrase-maker who knew nothing of the real problems of the Italian peasantry. Mazzini described Marx as "a man of acute but
dissolvent genius," a materialist devoid of religious belief, preaching hatred
rather than cooperation.

Mere economic details scarcely interested Mazzini. His socialism was a
function of that selfless devotion to the whole national community which the
religion of popular nationalism was supposed to inspire. Marx's class warfare was anathema to Mazzini, whose watchwords were harmony and cooperation. His objection to the *Carbonari* was that they based themselves on an
Enlightenment idea of cosmopolitanism. Equal rights for all is a worthy goal;
but rights need to be rooted in a specific human family not a vague universality of humankind.

Mazzini's democracy, too, was subordinate to and dependent on his key
idea of nationalism. Democracy and nationalism accompanied each other, at
least up to a point. The French Revolution had abolished inequality, in the
sense of assailing privileged status groups such as the nobility. All people, at
least, are equal. Equal as what? As *enfants de la patrie*, the revolutionary hymn
declared; children of the Fatherland. They are equal as citizens of the state.
"*Freies Reich! Alles gleich!*" sang the German nationalists of the *Turnerschaften*.
Formerly, people took their legal identity from being members of an estate or
order, that is, peasant, clergyman, noble. Now it was through the national

state, a nation of equals whose rights were guaranteed by the state. The state belonged to the people, enforced their will, drew its authority from their sovereignty.

"The larger the fatherland becomes, the less one loves it," Voltaire had thought. "It is impossible to love tenderly an overly large family that one scarcely knows." That is why the eighteenth-century philosophers doubted that democracy could exist beyond the village level. But now it was becoming possible to think of a nation as a single family because improved transportation and communications were breaking down provincialism; administrative systems could operate over larger areas because of these technological advances. The age of Mazzini and Marx was also the age of the railroad. And with the weakening of traditional, localistic communities, the need for community became attached to the nation. In Old Regime France few people would have identified themselves primarily as Frenchmen; provincial identity was greater (Bretons or Provençards or Gascons). That social order belonged to the past; the movement of history, involving technological and economic factors, was toward centralization. People discovered the nation for the first time. Not least was this true in the swelling cities of the age of urbanization; uprooted from secure local communities and thrown into the confusion of urban life, the masses eagerly sought some new kind of solidarity with accompanying symbols and rituals.

It was not a movement everyone welcomed; Pierre Proudhon, the French decentralizing socialist, declared that "Civilization progressses, and services are rendered to the world, in inverse proportion to the immensity of empires"; small, not big, is beautiful. But Proudhon was out of step with the times.

Nationalism, as discussed by such German philosophers as Fichte, produced its own *mystique*, which assigned to national peoples a special mission in God's plan for the progressive development of the human race. According to the Romantic nationalists, the nation is an organic growth that flowers in history and expresses the deepest potentialities of a people. The free individual realizes himself or herself through this membership in an expanding group consciousness. As Mazzini explained, "Nationality is the role assigned by God to each people in the work of humanity; the mission and the task which it ought to fulfill on earth so that the divine purpose may be attained in the world." Thus conceived, nationalism was not opposed to either individual fulfillment or internationalism. The eventual goal of a universal brotherhood of man will come after each nation has been liberated and has flowered culturally. People must first find membership in their own national community. "He who wants humanity wants a fatherland." Just as individuals are fulfilled in finding a community, so the nations will blend together to form collective humanity. The popular French historian Jules Michelet declared that each people has its special part to play in the great unfolding drama of history, the symphony of humankind.

Nationalism blended with other ideas of the first half of the nineteenth century. The rise of historical studies to a position of dignity and importance is a remarkable feature of this period. Historians like Karamzin in Russia, Macaulay in England, Michelet in France are only examples of writers whose passion and eloquence combined with scholarship earned them great popularity. They were prophets as well as scholars, bearers of an urgent social message in their exciting stories of the birth and growth of nations. This was their principle subject: how the French people, or the English, fashioned themselves over the centuries, little by little, into the nation of today; how they won their liberty from foreigners, emancipated themselves from domestic tyrants, fought valiant battles and revolutions in the name of popular rights and national liberation.

"The idea of progress" has been called the great nineteenth-century idea, but so have the ideas of Democracy, Freedom, and Nationalism. In fact they all went together. The people struggle forward slowly but relentlessly through history to arrive at full emancipation; they do so within the framework of their natural community, the nation. Each of the slogans implied the other. Full progress demands democracy, in that obviously the perfect condition of humanity sees *everyone* happy, not just a few. Nationalism demands democracy in the sense that all members of the sacred community, all blood-brothers as it were, have equal rights. And the growth of the nation provided a splendid example of progressive development.

These heady ideas were much in the air in the first half of the nineteenth century. Mazzini was not their only spokesman, the Italian *risorgimento* not the only democratic-nationalist movement. Usually led by intellectuals but finding some measure of popular response, such movements flourished all over Europe. The Slavophiles were the heroes of the 1840s in Russia. Nationalism can be found in virtually every significant German writer and thinker of the times; a galaxy ranging from serious philosophers to popular organizers shared it. In 1848, when nationalism was the key component in the political explosions, possibly the most outstanding European figure was the Hungarian nationalist leader Louis Kossuth. Polish nationalism flared up in 1830 and 1863.

But Mazzini was the master spokesman. "Eloquent, repetitive, diffuse," the Italian was a prize example of rhetorical excess such as Romanticism produced at its high tide. He combined this verbal art with a considerable passion for organization; when not writing or orating he spent his time creating "associations" and fomenting conspiracies. Thus he resembled Marx in wanting to combine "thought and action." The difference lay in Marx's attempt to let experience guide theory in an ongoing dialectical relationship. Mazzini, whom Marx rightly accused of having little interest in mere experience, preferred to enunciate ringing ideals and then organize and exhort his forces to carry them out. Though it seems a poor charge to level against a man with so much social conscience, one might accuse him of a basic egoism. What mattered to him at bottom, as he frequently said, was for people to choose a heroic mission and stick to it. Mazzini had chosen to unite the Italian people; this was what gave his life meaning and excitement. It was his religion.

MAZZINI AND THE REVOLUTIONS OF 1848

When the revolutions of 1848 erupted in Europe, Mazzini, like Marx, was ready to return from exile to his native land. Earlier, in 1843, overworked and underfed, Mazzini had been seriously ill in London. His ascetic life became legendary; the only luxury was his cigars, a taste he shared with Marx; his only amusement, apart from evenings with the Carlyles or Ashursts, was playing his guitar. But he made many friends in London, including Charles Dickens and Robert Browning, top Victorian literary stars. He played chess—recklessly, of course—at a well-bred London club. Something of a quaint lion in London literary society, his earnestness and innocence charmed many, not least the ladies. A visitor left a description of Mazzini's study, reminiscent of a similar one of Marx's, as a confusion of piled-up books and papers, the air filled with the odor of cheap cigars, not evidently impairing the health of his pet canaries and house plants. Mazzini continued to create organizations and maintain a huge correspondence. He wrote rather prolifically. From Genoa occasionally came helpful funds his adoring mother pried from a grumbling but not hostile father. Gradually the Italian refugee acquired a reputation, totally at odds with his gentle personality, of being, like Byron, though for somewhat different reasons, mad, bad, and dangerous to know. Foreign governments pressured the British government to keep an eye on him.

This last situation added to Mazzini's spreading fame in 1844 by creating a scandal that shook the British government. It became known that Mazzini's letters were being secretly opened before delivery! Lord Peel's administration was embarrassed, and there were indignant speeches in Parliament and a public outcry. Such practices disgraced foreign despotisms but not free Britain, according to popular belief. The British government first denied the charge, then had to admit it. The unhappy Home Secretary, Sir James Graham, was the least popular man in England. Carlyle wrote a stunning letter to *The* (London) *Times* testifying to Mazzini's noble character. The publicity about the opened letters drew attention to Mazzini and the cause of Italy as nothing else had done, and he did not miss the opportunity to launch eloquent pleas for aid to the suffering Italian people.

From this not unpleasant literary life the revolutions of 1848 awakened him. The first rumblings of the eruptions of that year came in fact from Italy—not so much the north as, rather surprisingly, the south. In 1846 a new pope, Pius IX, seemed to be a liberal who would not oppose Italian unification, although in the end this turned out to be a misunderstanding. Then came an uprising of the subjects of the benighted kingdom of Sicily, which the British liberal leader Gladstone once described as "the negation of God erected into a system of government." Much as Mazzini had predicted might happen, and been thought mad for doing so, the spark of revolution set off fires all over Europe, usually in the cities—Paris, Naples, Dresden, Budapest, Vienna itself. In Italy, the flame spread to the cities of the north, and to Rome too, when "Pio Nono" (Pius IX) reneged on his alleged promise to allow self-government in Rome.

The revolutions of 1848 were notable for having started out favorably and ending in confusion and defeat. A number of reasons accounted for the failure; perhaps the foremost was that the revolutions were an affair of an urban activist minority, to whom the great bulk of rural folk, still a considerable majority, were indifferent or hostile. Yet the revolutionaries, evidently unaware they were a small minority, insisted upon universal suffrage. Intoxicated with the slogans of democracy, they invoked "the People" as a kind of mystic talisman, but they actually knew very little about the real "people." This was true of Mazzini, by and large. Though he could occasionally charm Italian workers and peasants, basically he was an urban intellectual living in a totally different mental world than ordinary people.

One of the great scenes of 1848, following soon after riots in Paris that forced the abdication of King Louis Philippe, was the Five Days of Milan in March when that city's citizens rose up and drove out the Austrian garrison. Venice followed suit; then King Charles Albert of Piedmont miraculously granted a constitution and declared war on Austria, which seemed to be falling apart. Mazzini hastened to Paris to be received as a guest of honor by the poet Lamartine, leader of the newly proclaimed French Republic. He crossed the Alps on foot, arriving at Milan on April 7 to receive a roaring welcome, such as only the Italians could produce. The great composer Giuseppe Verdi arrived at about the same time, and Mazzini commissioned him to write a battle hymn. What a revolution of the artists and intellectuals!

Already, however, there were seeds of dissent within the ranks of the revolutionaries, for the more moderate ones feared Mazzini, who in turn mistrusted them; they wanted constitutional government, the rule of law, protection for property, but definitely not socialism or even democracy. Moreover, the various Italian states were going their own way, aiming at enlarging their own boundaries, jealous of each other. Little national consciousness yet existed.

From the king of Piedmont, Mazzini received the offer of a prominent place in its government if he agreed to Piedmont's annexation of Lombardy. But Mazzini refused it, demanding that King Charles Albert boldly come out for national unity. Mazzini's writings were then publicly burned in Genoa, and when Garibaldi and his little army arrived from South America they received a cold welcome. Meanwhile in Rome Pope Pius IX was also losing his enthusiasm for Italian unification, while in Naples King Ferdinand had recovered his nerve and withdrawn the constitution he had granted under popular pressure. To make matters worse, Mazzini and Garibaldi, the twin heroes of the Risorgimento, had already begun to quarrel.

Giuseppe Garibaldi was born in Nice, that lovely city on the coast of Provence, today in France, but a part of Piedmont when he was born. (Its streets still bear the names of Paganini, Rossini, and many another Italian culture hero.) Like Mazzini, Garibaldi had been deported as undesirable and had spent twenty years in exile. Fate led this soldier of fortune not to London but to South America; he learned guerrilla warfare in Brazil and Uruguay. In understanding something of the art of warfare he had an advantage over Mazzini. But the regular Piedmontese army officers resented this upstart rival who wanted to horn in on all the battles with his motley crew of adventurers. Garibaldi almost had to fight the government of Piedmont as well as the Austrians. In the end he proved an even greater hero than Mazzini, though less of a philosopher. The two were something less than compatible personally—two oversized egos, if you like.

Not knowing quite where to establish his base, Mazzini lingered in Milan, though he wrote to the Ashursts that he was "disliked, dreaded, calumniated, threatened." But in July Charles Albert paid the price of his military incompetence, and suffered severe defeats at the hands of Austria. Milan called on Mazzini to rally the people for a defense of the city, and he responded magnificently—only to see the blundering Piedmont king return to depose Mazzini's committee of defense. The hated Austrian (mostly Croatian) forces then took Milan, and Mazzini fled. It was small consolation that a disgraced Charles Albert would soon abdicate. The people, Mazzini lamented, had thrown the national flag not at the feet of a principle, but a wretch. Mazzini spent a few days with Garibaldi, but was soon off for Rome, where more of the Italian plot was unwinding.

There, after all, was the heart of Italy, and unification might yet succeed if Rome could be won to the cause. On November 15 a mob stormed the Capitol and assassinated the reactionary papal adviser Count Rossi. Within a week the pope fled from Rome in disguise! A revolutionary junta announced democratic elections to a constitutional assembly and proclaimed, in the pope's absence, a "Roman Republic." Elected a deputy along with Garibaldi, Mazzini hastened to Rome early in 1849. Soon he was to become the virtual ruler, for three months, of the Roman Republic.

It was a little late in the day; almost everywhere the revolutionary flame had burnt itself out, the revolutionaries were at each other's throats, the forces of order were gaining the upper hand. The French Second Republic had ended by electing another Bonaparte as its president. The Frankfurt Assembly went home after finding no one to install the long German constitution it had so laboriously written. The tsar of Russia, Nicholas I, younger brother of Tsar Alexander but no liberal, was more than eager to lend support to the reaction. There had been no revolution in St. Petersburg. Nor in London, despite a major Chartist rally. British opinion was largely sympathetic to the cause of Italy, thanks in good part to Mazzini, but all the British sent was sympathy.

Amid the confusion in the Eternal City from which the pope had fled, a mixture of poets, preachers, and adventurers attempted to bring order out of chaos. Suddenly they saw Mazzini as the figure around whom everyone could cluster; he exerted at this hectic moment a remarkable charisma. The American writer Margaret Fuller, married to an Italian and living in Rome at this time, wrote to her friend Ralph Waldo Emerson, always on the lookout for great men, that Mazzini assuredly was one: "a great poetic statesman, in heart a lover, in action decisive and full of resource." Technically a triumvirate ruled, but the others conceded Mazzini's superiority. He continued to live as he always had—simply, giving his small salary to charity, and receiving anyone who wanted to see him in his modest quarters. More remarkable, everyone agrees that he governed with great skill, attempting some reforms while trying not to alienate the religious faithful. It was a virtuoso performance. And yet the odds were all against the Italian Republic. As revolutionary regimes fell in city after city, the international Roman Catholic community clamored to have the pope restored to his rightful place.

A key to the situation was the second Bonaparte to rule France. Louis Napoleon was perhaps a pale imitation of his uncle, but in the elections of late 1848, based on universal suffrage—a sudden leap from the very restricted suffrage of the July Monarchy—he won the presidency by a wide margin. The French peasants, disgusted with the strife of socialists and liberals in Paris, turned to a name they remembered favorably. Owing his office to conservatives and Catholics, Louis Napoleon helped restore Rome to the pope; it was French troops who defeated Garibaldi's gallant little army and forced the hero to flee through the marshes of Ravenna, thus ending Mazzini's short-lived Roman Republic.

"It is a far better thing to die in a supreme glorious battle, fought under the eye of God with our national banner unfurled, than to see our land fall under the axe of the executioner," Mazzini wrote a few years later. But in 1849 he failed to find death in battle. Garibaldi was more of a hero, leading his valiant band on a long retreat to San Marino in which his beautiful wife, Anita, died; he survived to reach Staten Island, New York. Mazzini escaped in disguise on a French steamer bound for Marseilles, eventually to reach London again where he joined the rest of the 1848 refugees, including Karl Marx and Louis Kossuth. He left behind many friends and followers who died on the ramparts or were executed in a terrible vengeance the pope himself enthusiastically supported.

The year 1848 has been called the revolution of the intellectuals; certainly it was remarkable for the participation of poets, artists, political theorists, and for their seeming failure in this role. Lamartine was political leader of France before retiring from politics in high disgust at the human race, exclaiming "the more I see of people the more I like my dogs." Richard Wagner was one of a triumvirate ruling Dresden, until forced to flee to Switzerland. High-minded lawyers and professors filled the Frankfurt Assembly. The experience had a devastating effect on confidence in visionaries and dreamers to act effectively in politics. They largely retreated, after 1848, to the ivory tower; "give me the highest one possible," cried Gustave Flaubert. That Wagner took to operatic composition may have been a victory for art, but it reflected his bitter disenchantment with politics. The same can be said for Charles Baudelaire and many another refugee from the camp of practical affairs. Verdi's operas take on a less romantic flavor after 1848. That year was, in fact, the terminus of Romanticism.

THE UNIFICATION OF ITALY

Italy and Germany were to be unified within two decades by other means, not by heroic revolt but by devious diplomacy; by the masters of Machiavellian diplomacy—Cavour and Bismarck—not revolutionary idealists like Mazzini—indeed, by those who were his enemies in 1849. He did not like this process at all, though it achieved the result at which he had aimed in that it unified Italy.

Again, Louis Napoleon Bonaparte of France played a key role. Within three years Louis Napoleon had converted the Second Republic into the Second Empire, an event Karl Marx described with great eclat in his pamphlet *The Eighteenth Brumaire of Louis Napoleon* on the coup d'etat of December 1–2, 1851. Napoleon III's regime was to last nearly twenty years and achieve many good things for France. Despite the bitter hostility of some who saw him as the assassin of liberty, Louis Napoleon's coup d'etat, like that of his uncle had been, was confirmed by a popular plebescite; France, someone said, was less the victim than the accomplice of this crime.

Foreign affairs were not Louis Napoleon's strong point, and he was to succumb to this weakness in the end. But as a Bonaparte he was not unsympathetic to Italian nationalism. He had indeed joined the *Carbonari* in his youth. Early in 1858 an Italian patriot named Orsini tried to assassinate the emperor, whose reaction was typically unpredictable: while executing the would-be regicide, Bonaparte responded to Orsini's plea that he do something for Italy. Count Camillo Cavour, meanwhile, had begun his career as the wiliest of diplomats, working as foreign secretary for a new Piedmont king. Victor Emanuel III was more liberal than his predecessor. Cavour, who had helped bring down Mazzini's republic in 1849, worked to secure the unification of Italy, or some of it, not by revolutionary societies and flaming slogans but by patient maneuvering amid the power rivalries of Europe. He won a claim on France's gratitude by bringing Piedmont into the Crimean War of 1854–1856 on France's side against Russia. In 1858 he persuaded Louis Napoleon to aid him in a war against Austria if Austria could be made to appear the aggressor. For a diplomat of Cavour's talents this was child's play; he baited the Austrians into striking the first blow.

This was not pure charity on Napoleon's part; France was to get Nice and Savoy. Piedmont in recompense was to absorb Lombardy, Venetia, and the other small states of Italy north of the Papal States. France did come to Piedmont's aid and fought two bloody battles with the Austrians, at Magenta and Solferino. Unfortunately, Napoleon III had little of his uncle's relish or talent for battle; appalled by the slaughter at Solferino, to Cavour's consternation he withdrew from the war, taking care, however, to keep the two Mediterranean provinces. Despite the French backing out, the Piedmontese were able to press ahead and secure the unification of much of Italy, as a wave of nationalist sentiment swept over the Italian peninsula.

But the main prophet of that sentiment did not approve of this unification process. Garibaldi stole the hour; returning with a small army, he marched them down to Sicily in an operation that captured the world's imagination and made him one of the century's chief heroes. His thousand Red Shirts touched off rebellions in Sicily and Naples, the much-criticized Bourbon king of Naples being forced to flee. Sardinians advancing from the north and Garibaldi's army from the south defeated the Papal States, where rebellion again broke out. But again French troops intervened to defend the city of Rome and assure the pope's independence. With this exception, and that of Venetia which remained in Austrian hands, the whole of Italy voted by plebescite to join a new Kingdom of Italy, under the king of Piedmont with its 1848 liberal constitution.

Garibaldi's enormous public reception in London in 1864, said to be the largest one of all time in that city, indicated his great appeal. He upstaged even Abraham Lincoln and the tsar of Russia in 1861, a memorable year of liberations. British opinion had been stirred by the Italian cause, and Lord Palmerston, the British prime minister, lent the aid of the British navy to Garibaldi's crossing from Sicily. The French Emperor, who had started the whole thing, incurred Italian ill-will by his withdrawal and his defense of Rome, while alienating the British with his seizure of Nice and Savoy. He got the worst of both worlds with a vengeance. He was soon to maintain his reputation for ineptitude in foreign policy, first with his Mexican adventure, which Gladstone called the greatest political blunder of his time, then as Bismarck outwitted him and secured the unification of Germany.

Cavour died in 1861, anathematized by the Pope as well as Mazzini; his successors in the government of Victor Emmanuel completed his plan for the unification of Italy by gaining Prussia's goodwill, which enabled them to add Venetia in 1866 and Rome in 1871, thus crowning an amazing achievement in just a little over a decade.

Most of this, sadly, passed our hero by. Mazzini did not give up after his 1849 defeat; he spent the 1850s in vain attempts to stir up popular revolutions in Italy, which Cavour opposed and thwarted. In 1858 Mazzini wrote in an open letter to the Piedmont minister, "Between ourselves and you . . . yawns an abyss." (A favorite phrase of his; he had used it with regard to the papacy ten years earlier.) Based on monarchy rather than republicanism, on government diplomacy rather than popular power, above all on opportunism rather than principle, Cavour's policies, Mazzini persuaded himself, were the very opposite of his. There were no "solemn moral principles" or great ideas in this unification, he complained. The thought of accepting aid from the tyrant Napoleon III nauseated Mazzini; when the French proved treacherous he thought his suspicions were vindicated. He returned to Italy spouting manifestoes, but had little influence this time on the course of events. His old rival Garibaldi stole the show. While all London lined the streets to cheer Garibaldi, few even recognized Mazzini. No wonder this tried the patience even of a saint, if such Mazzini was.

The weakness of the moralist in politics, demanding all or nothing, refusing compromise, seems evident here; most Italians were ready to bend their principles a little if it promised success in unifying their country. All over Europe, the post-1848 word was *Realpolitik*. Romantic sloganizers had failed, and the time had come to try other methods, more aware of the ways of real people in a real world. Romanticism as a style in life and literature gave way to Realism.

But Mazzini would not be reconciled. "The Italy that I have preached, the Italy of our dreams, the great, the beautiful Italy of my heart," the old idealist wrote in the late 1860s, had fallen victim to "this combination of opportunists and cowards and little Machiavellis. . . . I see only its corpse." Agitating for a republic and universal suffrage, he managed to get himself arrested by the government of the united Italy he had yearned for. One is left wondering whether to admire this heroic intransigence or lose patience with a sterile politics of purism. Were the mass of Italians to refuse unification just to placate Mazzini's tender conscience? The stubborn egoism of Mazzini's personality seems revealed in his refusal to accept amnesty from the government; he had to be a martyr; he would not play ordinary politics. He had to continue in his role of revolutionary conspirator. Does the high-minded idealist often mask a petulant child demanding the center of the stage?

This *delusione* may be compared to the disappointment of antislavery idealists in the United States after the Civil War: Corruption, materialism, and greed seemed the legacy of that victory of which they had expected so much. All very well to have ended the curse of slavery, but it had been done in the wrong way, for the wrong reasons. The "Gilded Age" atmosphere in the United States had its counterpart in England, as a novel like Trollope's *The Way We Live Now* suggests, and in the glittering cynicism of Second Empire France. Everywhere, it seemed, the romantic dreams of the first half of the century had turned to capitalist ashes.

Mazzini continued writing and preaching and proselytizing to the end of his life in 1872. He wandered around Italy like a lost soul, refusing all consolation yet trying in some way to reclaim his lost mission. Education was a persistent impulse; in exile in London he had founded an evening school for the Italian workers living in London, and in his last years he tried to propagandize the working class in Italy in behalf of his religion of republicanism and democracy. It was a strange scenario, the father of Italian independence going around the country with a price on his head, rather as if George Washington, instead of being elected president, had become a plaintive outlaw. But Mazzini had been in opposition all his life, and he was not about to join the Establishment. He felt deserted, betrayed by the Italian people for not having, as he saw it, remained faithful to his ideals. "I am as one awakening from a long dream; all my Italian pride has gone, leaving within me a blank which nothing can fill." This despite the fact that many Italians adored him and made him welcome.

MAZZINI'S PERSONAL LIFE

Mazzini's lifelong crusade was an impressive record of energy dedicated with remarkable consistency to a towering vision of humanity purified and restored to wholeness, with a new faith and a new society. He "sublimated" almost his entire emotional drive to the public level. He had little private life. He never married. Significantly, he spoke often of loving Italy, or Rome: "love of country . . . is life, religion, fever for me." He felt "caressed" by an idea. The language of eroticism creeps into his passionate eloquence about the cause he held dear. In the place of a person, as the object of his libidinal desires, Mazzini put "Italy," or "the people of Italy." This "People," one of his critics correctly perceived, "is nothing but the great soul of Mazzini"; he formulated it out of his own ego as an object and related to it as a lover. In place of the wife and family he lacked, Mazzini substituted the family of Italians, marrying himself to them.

He did not achieve this strenuous sublimation without a cost. In his early years Mazzini had attacks of convulsive sobbing. After the failure of his attempt to liberate Italy and his expulsion from Switzerland in 1837, he experienced what he called in his autobiography a "moral tempest" during which he momentarily doubted his mission and was racked by feelings of guilt. But faith returned.

It is not true, however, that Mazzini never had a love affair. The companionship of women was indeed essential to him. He was very close to his mother, writing to her constantly all through his life until her death, reuniting emotionally with her in 1848. Maria Mazzini was in fact a widely revered Madonna-like figure to Italians, and one must surely credit her with supplying much of Giuseppe's intense spirituality.

During his youthful exile in Marseilles, Mazzini fell deeply in love with a beautiful Lombard woman named Giuditta (Bellerio) Sidoli, the widow of a Carbonarist by whom she had had four children. She may have borne another to Mazzini. But for revolutionaries, always in hiding or on the move, marriage was out of the question. Giuditta went back to Italy in search of her children; she met Mazzini sixteen years later when he returned to Milan during the revolutions of 1848. One of her sons fought for his republican forces in Rome. This was a romantic interlude, in this most romantic of lives, and there were others, though in a sense Mazzini's heart always belonged to Giuditta. Jane Carlyle was doubtless no more than a good friend; yet she had a locket made of her hair and his, intertwined around Young Italy's motto "Now and Forever." Later Mazzini grew intimate with the family of William Ashurst, a London lawyer whose four emancipated daughters, like George Sand, smoked cigars.

Mazzini never lacked friends, was indeed surrounded by a host of people at most times. Yet he also was a lonely person, going his own inner-directed way. Carl Jung would have classified him as an intuitive introvert, a type that includes the great spiritual prophets of humanity. He had a vision of what he must do and be, and he never swerved from this vision. It was the source of both his strength and weakness—his loyalty to high principle and his refusal to compromise.

The psychoanalyst may have his day with Mazzini, but in the end we must come back to the climate of opinion and feeling in his time, to Romanticism, as the chief key to Mazzini's life. Perhaps we can take him back to Shakespeare, certainly a Mazzini favorite.[1] Or to Dante, about whom he wrote one of his main literary essays: "Both as a man and as a poet, Dante stands the first in modern times . . . ; he is at the head of that series of great men which, numbering in its ranks Michelangelo, has been concluded in our day by Byron; while another parallel series . . . numbering in its ranks Shakespeare, was concluded by Goethe."

The mention of Byron and Goethe, about whom Mazzini wrote an essay, shows how important the great Romantics were to him. The essential Romantic idea was that individual human beings share in the spirit that moves the world, and must use this spark of divinity to the utmost of its potential:

Strong is the soul, and wise, and beautiful;
The seeds of godlike power are in us still;
Gods are we, Bards, Saints, Heroes if we will!

[1]When Ugo Bassi, the revolutionary friar, one of Mazzini's associates, rode into Rome in 1849 he carried in his saddle only Shakespeare, Byron, and a manuscript of his own unfinished poem.

So wrote Matthew Arnold, paraphrasing Emerson. *"Ernst ist das Leben,"* said Schiller; "life is real, life is earnest." To do something memorable with one's life was a Romantic obsession, surely a noble one.

MAZZINI'S HERITAGE

In seizing upon nationalism as the religion for modern humanity, Mazzini was no bad prophet. Before long there were national anthems, national holidays, national ceremonies, flags, saints—all the panoply of sectarian religion. World War I showed how much loyalties to nation exceeded any others. And even today, it has been remarked that "No political movement . . . seems likely to succeed unless it allies itself to national sentiment." We have seen the stubborn revival of nationalisms long thought dead, from Scotland to Slovakia, from the Basques of Spain to the Kurds of Iraq and Turkey. It remains the strongest and most basic political force.

It is often noticed as a slightly puzzling phenomenon that nationalism was associated with the political left through most of the nineteenth century, certainly in Mazzini's time, but that thereafter the political right took it over and it grew distasteful to liberals and radicals. In Mazzini's youth arch-conservatives like the great Metternich, "crown prince of reaction," feared and persecuted nationalist movements such as the one led by our hero. They seemed subversive of the ancestral political order and dangerously democratic. As we have seen, Italian princes and their ministers, even a Cavour, only gradually overcame their deep suspicions of Italian nationalism. The turning point came about the time of the Boulanger and Dreyfus affairs in France—that is, the last decade or so of the century, when liberals began intermittently to question something that seemed to look toward intolerance and war. It is true that World War I temporarily changed that; but after the war, fascism and nazism arose to espouse a particularly virulent form of nationalistic intolerance of minorities. And so today our ideas about it are likely to be rather ambivalent. The left occasionally tries to reclaim the nationalist cause; a conference of radical British historians not long ago undertook the task of showing that the national heritage rightly belongs to the working class.

We may feel that, despite all the Mazzinian protestations to the contrary, nationalism does conflict with individual liberty and with internationalism. Nationalism, said Canada's Pierre Trudeau, as he struggled with two national cultures trying to live in a single political house, is "by nature intolerant, discriminatory, and when all is said and done, totalitarian." It allows no decent place for those who do not belong by blood and culture to the national community. It conflicts with economic welfare, which is best when trade and competition are global. It tends to breed wars between rival nations. Some historians have singled it out for the unenviable role of chief villain in the modern world: To Arnold Toynbee, it bespoke a disintegration of Western civilization's ancient unity that is a sign of decay.

Mazzini writing enthusiastically about war may give us pause. "I hail the glorious emancipating battles of humanity, from Marathon down to our own Legnano."[2] War, Mazzini added, is a great crime "when not sanctified by a *principle*." But when it is so sanctified it is sacred. And, of course, each country is likely to consider its cause a just one.

Certainly Mazzini had no doubts about the justice of any war that contributed to throwing out the Austrians, or French, and unifying Italy; or any war fought against tyrants on behalf of "the people." "The people armed in a holy cause" is the most inspiring spectacle known to humanity, he avowed; it "awakens to a kind of inspired life and exalts to enthusiasm capacities for struggle and sacrifice." To the Italian nationalist Mazzini as to Marx the prophet of "class struggle," struggle was an operative word. All life is a struggle, as Charles Darwin was then explaining from a naturalist perspective.

Combine the lofty idealism of Romanticism and the religion of nationalism with this view of life as combat, and one has something near the recipe for the ghastly war of 1914–1918. It was not what Mazzini intended, but it may have resulted from his principles. There was also an ambivalent place for the Mazzini tradition in Mussolini's Fascism, the post-1919 movement of fanatical nationalism combined with authoritarian leadership that influenced Adolf Hitler and helped push the world toward another devastating war. It was certainly possible for the fascists to draw on aspects of Mazzini's thought.

For better or worse, this passionate idealist, who devoted his life and his considerable talents unwaveringly to a cause he thought just, took his place among the foremost luminaries in the nineteenth-century gallery of moral leaders.

[2]Verdi's opera of 1848 was *The Battle of Legnano*, celebrating the 1176 defeat of the German Emperor Frederick I by the Lombard League.

8

Max Weber and the Disenchantments of Progress

As we will recall from the chapter on Karl Marx, the decade of the 1860s was a decisive one for the modern world. Throughout the West, at least, decisions were taken that registered the crumbling of an old society and the birth of a new one. These decisive actions included the American Civil War, the abolition of serfdom in Russia, and the unifications of Germany and Italy. One could add such other landmarks as the 1867 vote extension in Great Britain, the publication of Marx's *Das Kapital*, James Clerk Maxwell's formulation of the laws of electromagnetism. The decade saw the modernization of Paris (new streets as well as water and sanitation systems) and similar improvements in other cities; in London, victory over a serious health threat from cholera and typhus resulted from water and sanitary modernization. The list could be much extended.

Victory of the North and the central government over an agrarian slave society in the South set American feet on a path toward urbanization and industrialization. Emancipation of the serfs, accomplished without a bloody war, was equally decisive for the future of Russia. Both issues had been debated and shelved for decades, and now they finally were resolved. So too the long-deferred unifications of Italy and of Germany occurred. In a series of brilliant diplomatic and military maneuvers between 1865 and 1870, Prussia under the guidance of Otto von Bismarck surprised the world by isolating and then defeating France. Crowning the Prussian king as Emperor of Germany in Versailles was a humiliation that left France reeling and fuming. Europe had found a new master.

Appropriately, the new Germany became a leader in technological and industrial progress, the leading feature of the era into which the Western world now entered. A series of discoveries in science and in related areas of technology brought a sense of amazement. It would be difficult to enumerate them all. The Atlantic cable, finished in 1866, was a well-publicized communications wonder, followed within a decade by Alexander Graham Bell's telephone. The Bessemer, Siemens, and Gilchrist-Thomas processes between 1856 and 1870 made possible mass production of steel. Railroads, which the Germans used effectively in the Franco-Prussian War, continued to link countries together as never before; the last third of the century saw the basic railway grid completed, and by the end of the century the iron horses were advancing on Asia via the trans-Siberian and Berlin-to-Baghdad railways.

Steam-driven ships further revolutionized the transportation of goods across great distances, as did the Suez Canal, completed in 1869, among other maritime improvements. Even the age of internal combustion transport could be discerned by the late 1880s, time of the first practical automobiles (the German firm of Daimler probably got there first, in 1887); the Wright Brothers' first airplane flight, inspired by earlier German attempts, was not far off (1903). Above all, electrical power, developing gradually out of Michael Faraday's 1831 discovery that the motion of a conductor in a magnetic field can produce an electric current, had reached the stage of Edison's electric light by 1879. Electric light was flooding the cities and electric power was being used to run street cars in the 1880s; Berlin had an elevated electrical railway in 1900, Budapest an underground one by 1896.

Science and, in fact, nearly all branches of pure and applied knowledge were being professionalized at this same time. Max Weber was to name this curious feature of modernization "bureaucracy." Things formerly done casually or capriciously—humanly, one might say—now had to be regulated by written rules. The practice of medicine, for instance, once was the privilege of almost anyone who wanted to hang out a sign; now a "physician" had to have a degree, pass an examination, get a license, join a professional society. An unprecedented international organization by means of societies, conferences, and journals accompanied the great advance of science in the late nineteenth century and may even have caused that advance. This was Adam Smith's "division of labor" applied to the work of the brain.

As Carlyle and Marx had already glimpsed, this new society gave rise to alienation, in the sense that bureaucratic ties replaced personal ones, especially in economic production. In 1865 the law of employers and employees replaced the law of masters and servants in Great Britain. "Master and servant" might suggest what indeed was the case, a degree of inequality and deference; but it referred to the practice by which a youth was introduced into the productive world though service as an apprentice to a master craftsman—living with him, working closely with him in a small shop. Now more typically the owners (perhaps a corporation) of a large factory had little or no direct acquaintance with their employees, their "hands." Again, rules formerly understood tacitly now would be spelled out in written agreements negotiated between employers and employees, the latter perhaps represented by the officials of their trade union. "Contract" replaced custom as the regulator of social relations.

Trade unions grew rapidly from the 1880s on in industrialized countries like Great Britain and Germany not only as a means of wresting some material gains from employers in a market economy, but as a form of human fellowship in the bleak atmosphere of mass-production factories and factory neighborhoods. "The concentration of population in cities," a British student of urbanization remarked in 1889, was "the most remarkable social phenomenon" of the nineteenth century. Between 1801 and 1891 the percentage of Britain's population living in cities of 20,000 or more inhabitants increased from 17 percent to 54 percent. Most of this increase came after mid-century, when Germany also experienced a surge of urbanization. Taken together with the general increase in population (Europe's population just about doubled during the nineteenth century), this meant an enormously greater number of people living in cities compared to any previous epoch, and living in cities of vast size by previous standards. Something like 15 percent of the total population resided in cities larger than 100,000 inhabitants (twice that percentage in Great Britain). This was truly a social revolution, with all kinds of consequences. One of the first sociologists, the German Georg Simmel, set himself the task of studying the different mentality of city dwellers, their life-style and values.

Throughout human history the vast majority of people had lived in small communities and developed cultures appropriate to such a milieu. What was to be the condition now of these masses of people uprooted from their villages and thrown together in the confusion and anonymity of large cities? The leading French novelist of this era, Maurice Barrès, wrote about the *deracinés*, the uprooted ones. Another pioneer German sociologist, Friedrich Tönnies, drew a famous distinction between *Gemeinschaft* and *Gesellschaft*: community and society, meaning the traditional tightly knit folk community contrasted with the impersonal relationships of the large city, the "great society." "The deepest problems of modern life," Simmel wrote, "derive from the struggle of the individual to preserve his autonomy and individuality in the teeth of overwhelming social forces." A similar theme can be found in the great French sociologist Emile Durkheim. "Profound changes have occurred in the structure of our societies in a very short time," Durkheim observed. "Our faith has been troubled; tradition has lost its sway; individual judgment has been freed from collective judgment. . . . The new life that has emerged so suddenly has not yet been completely organized."

THE RISE OF SOCIOLOGY

Changes in society assisted the birth of "sociology." Conditions forced attention to the problem of individuals' relationships to their social group. For perhaps the first time there was widespread awareness that there existed different types of society; the group is not just "given" and natural. Growing knowledge of other peoples throughout the globe, people with very different customs, beliefs, and institutions, studied by sociology's companion discipline of anthropology, reenforced this feeling. A question about society cannot arise until people realize that there *is* a society, which can only come from seeing it change or observing other societies.

A sense of alienation, enabling the student of society to stand off from it and view it as a foreign object, was necessary for sociology. Sociologists of this era such as Durkheim and Tönnies experienced in their own lives the cultural shock of being plunged into the vastness and anonymity of a large city after having been raised in a cohesive community—a small town, a closely integrated family. Among other major figures of social theory, Werner Sombart came from a small village to Berlin; the American sociologist Thorstein Veblen was a real outsider.

Professionalization, secularization, and scientific division of labor also contributed to the emergence of a new "discipline." These sociologists were products of the social order they sought to analyze. At one time the village priest or vicar had served as psychologist or sociologist, without knowing such terms. (There is a recent biography of an Elizabethan curate who developed quite a practice dealing with people's emotional problems such as "mopishness"—a reasonable equivalent of today's "depression.") The decline of traditional religion, the growth of scientific thought and methods, the rise of the professions, ever greater division of labor in knowledge—all these factors helped create modern specialists in areas once handled informally if they were handled at all; the professional psychologist and the sociologist replaced the priest or the innkeeper.

The period from about 1880 to 1920 was the golden age of sociology. A second generation refined the cruder generalizations of Marx and Comte without getting lost in particulars as happened later. Of all these masters of a new science of society, the most impressive was Max Weber, a native of Berlin who became professor at Heidelberg and died in 1920 at the age of only fifty-six, leaving behind a body of writing of both enormous range and penetrating depth. Weber also participated to some extent in his country's political affairs. He was at the Versailles peace conference representing defeated Germany after World War I, and he helped write the new constitution that replaced the old kaiserdom at that time. Some thought he was on his way to becoming a national leader and a rare example of the intellectual in politics, when the terrible influenza epidemic cut him down in the prime of life.

Germany seemed to lead the way in sociology. It is true that this new discipline appeared almost everywhere, from the United States to Russia, featuring names such as Giddings, Baldwin, Gumplowicz, Ratzenhofer, Vaccaro, Ammon, Lapouge, and Kidd. The Italian economist and sociologist Vilfredo Pareto was an outstanding thinker who drew on a native tradition that reached back to Machiavelli. Auguste Comte, who coined the term "sociology," had as his chief successor, in end-of-the-century France, Emile Durkheim, generally considered one of sociology's founding fathers. The once quite well-known Benjamin Kidd was one of a number of "social Darwinists" who attempted to apply to human society Charles Darwin's theory of biological evolution.

Yet it was east of the Rhine that sociology flourished most. That so many notable sociologists emerged in Germany was doubtless because that land entered the modern industrial era so abruptly. Nowhere was the contrast so sharp between modern cities and villages unchanged since medieval times. But a contributing factor was also the mood of disillusionment that followed the failure of romantic idealism in politics; nowhere was this felt more keenly than in Germany, where the realistic diplomacy of Bismarck achieved what the revolutionaries of 1848 could not.

Sociology is a natural refuge for the disillusioned. Historian Fritz Ringer called it "a heroic ideal of rational clarification in the face of tragedy." One can ruthlessly dissect and implicitly criticize society, exposing its myths and shams, without descending to the soap box or pulpit; this is done in the guise of scientific objectivity. Someone said sociology was the village atheist studying the village idiot. Weber wrote of "the cool calm harbor of resignation, in which I have lain at anchor for many years." Some sociologists mixed their allegedly scientific approach with a good deal of ideology, whether socialist or (as with some Social Darwinists) capitalist. But Weber was foremost among those who insisted on drawing a sharp distinction between science and ideology. The former is value-free, a neutral inquiry. Scientific reason cannot discover ends, it is only about means, and the social scientist *qua* scientist does not serve any cause except that of knowledge. This person's realm is that of fact and not value.

This Weberian position is sometimes associated with neo-Kantianism, which was indeed a prominent school in Weber's Germany. But it was found also among the British political economists, who claimed to be establishing economic truths available for use by those of any political persuasion. Men of action ignored this knowledge at their peril, of course.

The chief theoretical framework for most sociologists was that of Charles Darwin's evolutionary naturalism, applied to human development. Darwin had created the main sensation of the nineteenth century by arguing in *The Origin of Species* that present species of plants and animals have evolved from an original simple organism over a long period of time largely through the mechanism of "natural selection," in which organisms better adapted to (a changing) environment flourish while others die out; given small differ-

ences within species, those characteristics with better survival value are preserved. More than a little shocking in its argument for the creation of life
forms by natural rather than divine agency, as well as its assumption of a
blind, amoral, and often cruel process in nature, Darwin's powerful work
soon came to dominate biological science and suggested applications to human social evolution. Could not existing social institutions (or peoples, races,
ideas) be explained in the same way, as products of a contest between com-
peting units in which the least efficient, the worst adapted to external conditions, went under? A shocking implication might be that if we believe in God
or have the monogamous family, this is because these things provided an advantage in the struggle for survival. Whether or not one believed in "natural
selection," one could accept Darwin's challenge to study social institutions
and beliefs as a natural process, comprehensible by means of historical research and analysis.

MAX WEBER'S LIFE AND CAREER

Max Weber's parents resembled Marx's and Mazzini's parents, only more so,
in being affluent, upper-middle-class people. Weber's father, with a family
background of bourgeois wealth, was a prominent politician, sitting in both
the German Reichstag and the Prussian legislature. Not only government figures but professors, such as the famous historians Treitschke and Mommsen,
visited the Weber home. Weber's mother came from a distinguished intellectual family. Altogether, it would be hard to find people who better represented the fine flower of Germany's political and intellectual elite.

Prussia's defeat of France and creation of the new Reich happened when
Max Weber, Jr., was a child; he grew up in the shadow of the great Bismarck,
whom his father supported. For Germany and for Weber, the overpowering
presence of the "Iron Chancellor," inhibiting the growth of representative
democracy, was a problem. The Weber family scenario resembled Mazzini's
and that of many others who became writers or intellectuals: a sensitive, artistic mother somewhat estranged from a worldly, practical father.[1] In Weber's
case politics entered the equation, for one parent was anti- and the other pro-
Bismarck. There was also a geographic symbolism. His mother's roots were
in the university town of Heidelberg, and for Max Weber the dualism of
Berlin-Heidelberg stood for the two Germanys of political authority, patriarchal strength, Bismarckism, as opposed to learning, humanism, culture.

The young Weber unhesitatingly chose mother and Heidelberg. But in
his maturity he was ambivalent. Weber's thought was marked by a stern realism, aware of the constraints that circumstances place on our thought and

[1]W.H. Auden observed that "whenever we have information about the childhood of an
artist, it reveals a closer bond with his mother than with his father."

action. To behave "responsibly" is to be "free of illusions," to recognize realities, not flee from them into utopian fantasy. The most basic of these realities he found in Darwinism: "the eternal struggle of men with one another." And from Friedrich Nietzsche he learned the importance of the "will to power," which means each essence entering into the arena of life to fight for its own distinctive qualities.

Yet Weber acquired from his mother a sensitivity that ill fitted him for public life, which part of him longed to enter. He was a problem child, nervous and fearsome; later in his life he suffered a nervous breakdown. He described himself as "lonely and uncommunicative." This is misleading: Weber went through the motions of conviviality, joining a university fraternity with its drinking and dueling (he got his scar). But an interior self always distanced itself from the outer web of social relations.

Weber's emotional collapse in 1897 came after a stormy domestic scene; his hostility toward his father, whom he accused of unkindness to his mother—Berlin against Heidelberg—burst out when he was in his early thirties. (Compare Franz Kafka, in Chapter 10 below.) Soon after this quarrel the elder Max Weber died, leaving his eldest son with a burden of guilt that may explain the famous breakdown. This rendered him unable to perform his duties as a teacher at Heidelberg for a number of years. In 1897 Max Weber suffered from insomnia, exhaustion, fits of weeping and rage, deep depression. Yet in later years he was a powerful lecturer.

Eventually Weber became an institution at Heidelberg. The body of his writing grew to encompass an incredible range of subjects. From him emerged ideas and phrases that entered the vocabulary of social and political studies, and profoundly shaped our understanding not only of the modern world but also of history in general. For like any good historian (his sociology was more historical than structural), Weber found that the social world is a seamless web; to understand any particular subject you have to understand the whole. And so with enormous energy and a razor-sharp mind he created an empire of knowledge, cut short unhappily by his premature death—but not before he had won fame to the extent that led some to call him the greatest German of his generation. Just before his death he achieved in some measure his ambition to become a man of action as well as thought, a political as well as an intellectual leader.

Of this more later. Weber's private life was not uninteresting. It was marked by an encounter with the "erotic revolution" of the early years of the twentieth century. In one form or another a rebellion against Victorian morality may be found at this time from England to Russia. Closely related to the esthetes and artists of the Modernist revolt, this defiance of traditional restraints also touched Sigmund Freud and the psychoanalytic movement. In Germany, the physical center of this impulse was the Schwabing sector of Munich, a place of unconventional living, the Greenwich Village or the Left Bank of Germany. Munich was then a center of artistic modernism second only to

Paris, if not (as Paul Klee thought) surpassing even Paris. It housed painters as distinguished as Kandinsky and Klee. Even today Schwabing is recognizably bohemian, if more for tourists than for starving geniuses.

From the ranks of Schwabing's bohemia by way of Freud's circle in Vienna came a priest of sensuality named Otto Gross, the son of a well-known Austrian criminologist, who en route to drug addiction and an early grave flashed through a number of important lives. The Psychoanalytic Association rejected him as too disreputable: "the extreme attitude [to sexuality] represented by Gross is decidedly wrong and dangerous to the whole movement," wrote Carl Jung. This did not prevent Gross from preaching and practicing the doctrine of therapy by means of sexual liberation. The Freudian disciple Ernest Jones wrote that Gross was "the nearest approach to the romantic idea of a genius I have ever met." Freud himself once thought (1908) that Gross ranked with Carl Jung as his two most gifted and original followers. Later, after Gross had become a scandal, Freud and Jung edited all references to him out of their works, rather like Stalinists making Trotsky a nonperson in Russia—and Freud biographers went along with this.

Though in almost all respects the complete opposite of this anarchical temperament, Weber was to fall in love with a (married) woman who had born a child by Gross. This was Else Jaffe, *nee* Else von Richthofen, sister of the woman who was to marry D.H. Lawrence. Else also had an affair with Otto Gross while married to her first husband. Soap opera seems pallid compared to the intimate lives of these distinguished Germans.

Weber had married Marianne Schnitzer in 1903, a marriage that was to endure; she eventually wrote the leading biography of her husband, a work of loving care. Six years younger than Max, Marianne had enormous respect for him mixed with not a little awe; she came to feel that she did not meet all his needs and was generously prepared to grant Else Jaffe a place in her husband Max's life.

Else, a schoolteacher at seventeen, earned her own way through university to a doctorate in economics, one of the first women in Germany to do so. In 1900, she became an inspector of factories in Baden—the first woman in that German state to serve as protector of women factory workers. Her chief teacher was Max Weber, though she also encountered Simmel in Berlin along with the celebrated academic socialist Gustav Schmoller. She was clearly a remarkable woman, intellectually above Marianne's level—but Weber's wife was Else's friend and deeply influenced her. A beautiful woman as well, Else somewhat resembled a more famous figure in England at about the same time—Beatrice Potter Webb, pioneer Fabian Socialist, advocate of workers' rights, author, along with her physically unprepossessing husband, of influential social histories and tracts.[2]

---

[2]The political creed of Heidelberg, by and large, was similar to British Fabian Socialism (influenced by the German university "Socialists of the Chair," Schmoller and Adolf Wagner), and Else in fact translated some Fabian pamphlets.

Beatrice Potter had fallen in love with the rising star of British politics, Joseph Chamberlain, but refused to subordinate her career to his and, avoiding the enticements of eroticism, joined Sidney Webb in a marriage of which it was said that they had books rather than children. In 1902 Else also married a scholar, the retiring economist Edgar Jaffe, from a wealthy Jewish family. "It seems to have been generally agreed that Else never loved him," Martin Green remarks in his book *The von Richthofen Sisters.* But Jaffe built his wife a villa on the picturesque hill leading up to the Castle in Heidelberg, surely one of the most enticing spots in all Europe, and Else became the wonderful little city's chief *saloniste.* Heidelberg University, graced by many other distinguished names in philosophy, religion, psychology, and literature, was possibly the world's most notable university in the humanities. After 1911 Else also exercised her talents as salonist in Munich, in a circle headed by the charismatic poet Stefan George. Jaffe also bought a journal for Max Weber (very nice for a scholar to have his own!)—the *Archiv für Sozialwissenschaften und Sozialpolitik,* which came to be closely associated with Weber's teachings.

Else then largely abandoned her professional career, unlike Beatrice Webb. But her other affairs were far from over. Her involvement with Otto Gross in 1907 has been mentioned; she met Gross through his marriage to an old school friend of Else's, Frieda Schloffer from Graz, Austria. Years later, when Gross had hopelessly ruined himself, Else wrote in effect (to Gross's wife) that Otto Gross was the only one who had ever given her happiness; but if even Else's sister, Frieda, altogether a wilder spirit, believed that Otto Gross "did not have his feet on the ground of reality," Else, however regretfully, had to bid him goodbye.

Max Weber strongly disapproved of Gross and of the affairs with the two von Richthofen sisters. His own romance with Else, whom he had known for some years, seems to have blossomed briefly in 1910, but Else's friendship with Marianne, Max's wife, stood in the way. Else then, doubtless to Max's chagrin, entered into a liaison with his brother, Alfred, whom Max did not like—a sociologist and economist of some ability destined to spend his life overshadowed by Max. Else and Max were to resume their close relationship seven years later. In the meantime, Weber's salvation was through work. He set about creating an impressive body of writing that combined wide and deep factual knowledge with cogent analysis.

During the Great War of 1914–1918, Weber emerged as a figure of national prominence. Like most intellectuals, he greeted the war's coming in 1914 with enthusiasm, calling it "great and wonderful." The war brought a regeneration of national spirit, of *Gemeinschaft.* But Weber became a critic of German leadership in the conflict and a proponent of democratic reforms. He opposed German annexations of foreign terrritory (for example, in Belgium and Poland), and in 1917 he joined those who thought the decision to resume submarine warfare a blunder. His articles on this subject in the Frankfurt *Zeitung* were so bold that they incurred official censorship, being a direct attack on the German Emperor and the high military leaders who dominated policy. A crisis of political leadership, he thought, was leading Germany to disaster. In the long, bitter test of will that the cruel war imposed, Germany was proving the weaker, because she had no effective political system. The democracies were stronger; against the pitiful Kaiser and some politically inept generals the democracies offered leaders like David Lloyd George, leaders who were able to appeal to the masses.

During the war, as a result of his response to the challenge of Germany's need for political leadership, Max Weber attained his highest powers and his greatest prominence. He taught brilliantly to crowds of students in the spring and summer of 1918 in Vienna. On his return he found himself a national figure. Weber was surprised and disillusioned by the vindictive peace settlement the victorious Allies dictated, which he saw as shortsighted and irresponsible. He had his choice of prestigious academic posts in 1920 when he decided to replace Lujo Brentano at Munich, writing his own ticket with regard to terms. His sudden death in the early summer of 1920 may have been due in part to overwork.

WEBER'S SOCIAL AND POLITICAL IDEAS

Sociology was only just becoming recognized as a scholarly discipline; the German Sociological Society was founded in 1909, and Weber held a chair specifically called Sociology only in the last months of his life. His first published work, his doctoral dissertation, was on the history of medieval trading companies, followed by a study of ancient Roman agriculture in its relation to law. He then undertook a survey of rural farm workers in contemporary eastern Germany, which was published as part of a series on "Social Politics" (1892). Then in his mature years he turned to a massive synthesis of *Wirtschaft und Gesellschaft*, which is comparable to Marx's *Kapital* in its scope—and like that book, never finished, being edited for publication after his death from a miscellany of fragments.

History, law, economics, social history, "Social Politics": Weber did not much worry about categories. He has been described as a historical sociologist, or a comparative historian ("an interdisciplinary historical—comparative scientist," says Weber expert Vatro Murvar). His range of inquiry was amazingly wide; in terms of subject matter, periods, and places, it included ancient Judaism, ancient Greco-Roman society, China, India, cities in general. Weber did not define his subject matter in terms of places or eras; he was interested in themes. He followed Lord Acton's advice to historians to "study problems, not periods." The comparative method was his favorite, but he used many methods. He had some favorite themes, among them the relation between religion and society, the modes of political authority, the development of Western capitalist economic society. But "an intricate web of related themes" (Reinhold Bendix) runs through his work. All of it is marked by an extraordinary combination of exact knowledge and penetrating analysis. The best way to be introduced to Weber is via an edited selection of his writings.

Weber had a good deal to say about "capitalism," adopting Karl Marx's favorite term. He was keenly interested in tracing the origins of modern Western economic society, which he thought the unique product of a special historical experience. Capitalism, he explained, is not new or unique in the sense of greed, acquisitiveness, desire for gain, or a desire to trade, Adam Smith's "propensity to truck and barter." These have existed always and everywhere. But "The Occident has developed capitalism both to a quantitative extent and in types, forms, and directions which have never existed elsewhere." Weber differed from Marx in thinking this came about not in a series of revolutions but as a long continuous process, and in finding the key in a kind of psychology of efficiency rather than in technological change per se: a subjective more than an objective factor.

"Rationality" is the key word. Western civilization has become ever more "rationalized" in the sense of becoming more efficient; we might say more cost-conscious; it has produced the "economic man" who carefully calculates every act for maximum advantage. It has also produced a corps of "technically, commercially, and above all legally trained government officials." It is in some sense the fate of the world to get organized, and in the process disenchanted. "Everything begins in *mystique* and ends in *politique*," said the noted French writer Charles Péguy. But the Western world has shown a peculiar drive toward rational organization of life—rational not in the chosen end, for values do not lie within reason's orbit, but in the means toward that end.

Weber traced the origin of this peculiar European ethos back to ancient Judaism, transported into Christianity. His conviction that religion and economics are closely bound up together was expressed in probably his best known essay, on "Protestantism and the Spirit of Capitalism," in which he provocatively suggested that the Protestant religion furthered or was compatible with capitalism by its stress on success in an earthly vocation as proof of one's eligibility for eternal salvation—a "this-worldly asceticism." No social theory has ever inspired more debate.

Weber's conclusions were less optimistic than were Marx's. Marx always clung to a belief that the socialist revolution would make possible a technologically advanced society in which human relations were restored to harmony and community. Weber, at times close to moderate German socialists, came to see socialism as likely not to end alienation but even to increase it. The huge factory, the great city, the organization of production through elaborate division of labor, economic efficiency in general—the socialists wanted to keep all these. They thought the problem would be solved by nationalizing property. But would it matter much that the state rather than some giant private corporation was the owner? The bigness, the bureaucracy, the mechanization would remain, and these were what counted.

Weber was at times deeply pessimistic about this irreversible process of rationalization. He saw it driving out religion, art, poetry, beauty, or removing these nonrational qualities into the margin of existence. Weber's term *Entzauberung* literally means *taking out the magic*, as one might say "the magic has gone out of our marriage." Mankind loses all that is really most valuable in life, and is confined within an "iron cage" of workday efficiency. We pay a high price for our vaunted material comforts and power over nature. The technical expert, a narrow and dehumanized creature, replaces the well-rounded personality, the "cultivated man or woman," as the leading type. On this theme Weber was hauntingly eloquent; the more so in that he saw it as an unavoidable tragedy. We cannot escape the fate of our times by retreat into some imagined utopia. Like Freud, whom in some ways he resembled, Weber believed science—disabused, objective—was our only hope, and we must do the best we can, but we should have no illusions about the difficulties. "It would be nice," Weber said in his 1918 speech on "Politics as a Profession," "if matters turned out in such a way that Shakespeare's Sonnet 102 should hold true . . . .[3] But such is not the case. Not summer's bloom lies ahead of us, but rather a polar night of icy darkness and hardness." This, it is true, was at the moment when his country had suffered defeat in a terrible war.

Weber's realistic pessimism extended to democracy. An insight he shared with a few others at this time was that "Everywhere, whether within or outside democracies, politics is made *by the few*." Democracy in actuality is only another kind of oligarchy. Thomas Hobbes, in the seventeenth century, had suggested that democracy amounts to an oligarchy of orators. (Today we might say PR people.) In the early nineteenth century Benjamin Disraeli noticed that "Whatever form a government may assume, power must be exercised by a minority of numbers. . . . Self-government is a contradiction in terms." The principle of representation was itself an obvious demonstration of this. "The strongest man in some form or other will always rule," James Fitzjames Stephen had written. In different circumstances and epochs the essential qualification has altered: The sword, the tongue, the bank account, the ability to organize might variously define political strength. But the point remains that a small number of the ablest will govern, and this threatens any moral superiority that democracy might claim over other modes of dominance. In post-Mazzinian Italy, where disenchantment with the hopes of the Risorgimento was acute, elitist theory was particularly strong, represented by the great Vilfredo Pareto and by Gaetano Mosca. Pareto said of one Italian head of government that he was "the leader of a syndicate of speculators ruling the country and robbing the state."

---

[3]Our love was new and then but in the spring
When I was wont to greet it with my lays. . . .

The more voters, the more party organization, controlled by a small minority; oligarchy advances apace with democracy. The paradox was worthy to rank with Marx's alleged discovery that in the process of making profits capitalism destroys private property. Democracy creates oligarchy through the operations of its own instrument, the mass political party. "Children of democracy," the direct product of a mass electorate, necessary in order to mediate between the voters and the electoral process, great political parties found their very size forcing them into an elitist structure. A new phenomenon, the mass political party had more than anything else to do with this era's discovery of the "iron law of oligarchy." Max Weber's friend Robert Michels, in a study bearing that same title, used the great German Social Democratic Party to prove his point that oligarchy is "a preordained form of the common life of great social aggregates." The mass institution becomes too big for self-government, and falls into the hands of insiders skilled at organization. In the United States of America, the home of democracy, an "invisible government" of professional politicians or "bosses" made the real decisions behind closed doors through their control of the party "machine."

Among Weber's other insights, especially celebrated was his classification of the modes of political authority. This taxonomy of power has deeply influenced modern thought on the subject. The terms *patriarchalism, patrimonialism, bureaucracy, charisma* have entered the vocabulary of political theory. The modern mode is of course bureaucracy, corresponding to our age of rational organization; authority derives from written rules, enforced impersonally by official, licensed judicial and administrative bodies that keep elaborate records. Of course, the other sources of authority may still be found lurking here and there in the corners of life. Patriarchy still pervades the family, "charismatic" figures arise, especially in times of crisis (with which bureaucracy, bound to unalterable procedures, cannot cope); feudalism or patrimonialism[4] can still be found in politics as well as business, as the loyalty of retainers to their chief. Weber intended these models as "ideal types"—that is, they are useful for analysis even if seldom found in their pure state in the real world.

In his wartime political writings Weber seemed to favor a parliamentary government, not because of any notions about the people's sovereignty but because it provides a school for leadership. Producing capable leaders was the most important thing to Weber, and in the British system he saw a valuable training that sent politicians out to meet the people and win elections, then into Parliament to debate the issues. A mature political people will know how to evaluate the performance of politicians. A sound system will grant sweeping powers to an able leader while reserving through Parliament the

---

[4]Weber used the term "patrimonial" to describe the early modern kingdoms, a phase of preparation for the modern state. The king was seen as the father of his people, endowed with an aura of power based chiefly on the patriarchal. Shakespeare provides many examples.

power to throw the leader out if he (or she) fails. Weber thought Germany had lost the war because of poor leadership stemming from a defective political system.

The mere charisma of Adolf Hitler, Germany's next attempt at a political leader, would not have impressed Weber; Hitler lacked political experience, hence judgment, and he proved a disaster. In following him the German people again showed their lack of political maturity.

But it must be admitted that the problem of leadership in a democratic system remains a formidable one. Democratic, parliamentary politics seldom produces leaders of both decisiveness and mass appeal; it grinds out mediocrity. When leaders are needed they usually come from outside that system, like Lenin, Hitler, Peron, de Gaulle—or maybe a Jimmy Carter, a Ronald Reagan— hence they lack political experience. Strong leadership is needed to counteract the powerful thrust of bureaucracy (the bureaucrat is necessary in his place, as a servant of politics, but he cannot lead). But unless linked to the people through democratic institutions the charismatic or military dictator will prove disastrous. Something like this was the structure of Weber's political thought; his premature death tragically prevented him from completing it.

WEBERIAN INFLUENCES

Max Weber's influence has continued in many ways. As with any great thinker, his terms and ideas have entered the general civilized vocabulary. Neither bureaucracy nor rationalization nor disenchantment were new words, but Weber gave them the meaning they have taken on for us. "Charisma" was even more startlingly his own word. "The iron cage" is frequently cited as a metaphor for a twentieth-century state of existence that numerous others have described. Emile Durkheim, Weber's French counterpart, wrote of "anomie," a condition of being deprived of norms by the decay of religion and social solidarity, the dissolution of values. Neo-Marxists stressed "alienation"; in fact, Weber exerted no little influence on this concept as found in such "critical theorists" as Georg Lukacs (once his student) and later Jürgen Habermas, despite their quarrels with him on some grounds.

The encounter between Marx and Weber has given rise to a considerable literature, both polemical and scholarly. Careful students tend to find that at bottom, if we take Marx himself and not vulgar Marxism as the basis of comparison with Weber, there is not all that much difference between the two German giants. What Marx meant by an abstract entity, "the bourgeoisie," is similar to what Weber meant by a process, "rationalization." Marx retreated from his early belief that capitalism reduces the workers' standard of living, to stress the psychological damage it does in alienating them from their labor and making them machines.

Existentialism, with its vision of the self groping for identity in a society that objectifies it, also acknowledged a debt to Weber among others. The existentialist philosopher Karl Jaspers was a student and long-time admirer of Weber. All the legion of complainers about "dehumanization," or the conversion of the human personality into a collection of social functions—the "double bind" or the "other-directed" personality—owed something to Weber's haunting vision of humanity being squeezed by "rationalization" into an iron cage of "disenchanted" life.

Weber longed to be a man of action as well as a thinker, an ambition increasingly elusive in the modern age. In this role, like Marx or Mazzini, he had limited success. His neurotic paralysis for many years in the prime of his life stemmed from this divided will. He left some imprint on the Weimar constitution that post-1918 Germany lived with uneasily for fifteen years until a charismatic but undisciplined personality (Hitler) subverted it—hardly the fault of the constitution. Charles de Gaulle's Fifth Republic in France, which still survives, owed something to Weberian ideas: the strong president, able to appeal directly to the people via plebiscites, with parliament not interfering in his day-to-day leadership, are recognizably Weberian.

Weber's effort to be an activist found its greatest foe in himself, for he had taught that the scientist should not try to be a politician. He once told a distinguished gathering of German academics not to advise rulers what to do, but to stick to their role of providing politicians with options and their consequences; the politician should then make the choice. He entertained scorn for pseudo-prophets in the halls of learning; science is an austere mistress who forbids efforts to market some nostrum or creed. Science "is not a gift of grace that entitles seers and prophets to dispense sacred values and revelations, nor does it partake of the contemplation of sages and philosophers about the meaning of the universe," he warned. To his students he remarked tartly that they ought not look to their professors for guidance: "Ninety-nine of a hundred professors do not and must not claim to be masters in the vital problems of life, or even to be leaders in matters of conduct." It is not their *métier*. In brief, the intellectual and the preacher ought to stay out of politics, Weber suggested, a proposition in support of which one might muster much evidence.

Those looking for a faith, instead of inventing a new one ("humbug and self-deception") should go back to the old Church, still there and waiting. As Weber stated:

> To the person who cannot bear the fate of our times like a man, one must say: may he return silently, without the usual publicity build-up, but simply and plainly. The arms of the old churches are opened widely and compassionately for him.

A dusty answer, no doubt, to those searching for a cause. Weber accepted the national state as the arena of modern politics, but unlike Mazzini he did not invest it with the qualities of religion. And if he was a socialist, his was the severely factual and analytical kind: Only insofar as social ownership or control could prove itself to be more efficient than private capitalism, in specific instances, was it entitled to respect.

Obviously Weber thought it worthier to "bear the fate of our times like a man" than seek refuge in a fantasy. In this regard he was much like Sigmund Freud, whose widely read tracts of the 1920s, *The Future of an Illusion* and *Civilization and Its Discontents,* radiate a similar pessimistic view of the human predicament along with scorn for the illusions of religion, and a faint hope in (human) science.

Mention of Freud along with Marx reminds us that Weber's fame rested less than theirs on one great key idea. He did not found a school or establish a doctrine, as Freud did of psychoanalysis. It is true that some of his ideas have proved mightily influential for our understanding of social, economic, and political phenomena, but he never claimed exclusive validity for any of them. They have functioned as hypotheses to be criticized and tested.

Zygmunt Baumann wrote several years ago that "the `protestant ethic' debate . . . has long reached the stage when the sheer volume of facts and views it has produced makes it no less moot and bottomless than the subject matter it purports to clarify." The problem almost became not the growth of capitalism but the growth of Weber's thesis about it. In its earlier years the Weber thesis produced echoes that were themselves minor masterpieces, like R.H. Tawney's *Religion and the Rise of Capitalism.* Later it produced critiques, reinterpretations, scores of arguments about factual details; collections of articles about it graced the "Problems in European History"-type of textbook.

One can only admire a theory that has had such vitality, so much resonance; but eventually all provocative historical "theses" (compare the Frederick Jackson Turner "frontier thesis" in American studies) fall prey to sheer exhaustion. We may come to think, with the aid of linguistic philosophers like Wittgenstein, that in the end it is a matter of defining terms. When we have defined them thoroughly enough the problem tends to go away. At any rate the so-called Weber thesis (actually contained in one essay that is a small percentage of Weber's total output, though the relation between religion and economics was one of his major interests)[5] no longer has the power to stir the imagination that it once had. But then, what ninety-year-old theory does? Even the Relativity theory of his great German compatriot, Albert Einstein, would finally cease to amaze. Weber would have been happy to know that his attempts at clarification of an important question passed into the main-

[5]Weber first published what later became known in English as *The Protestant Ethic and the Spirit of Capitalism* as a series of journal essays in 1904–05. He never in fact completed it. These writings were included in vol. I of his *Gesammelte Aufsätze zur Religionssoziologie* in 1920, under the title "The Protestant Sects and the Spirit of Capitalism" (Die Protestantischen Sekte und der Geist des Kapitalismus). Only when this was translated into English in 1930 and published as a book did it become "The Protestant Ethic. . . ."

stream of thought for further refinement. In fact, the absorption of Weber's ideas, contained in the extensive body of writing he left unpublished at his death, is still going on. Because he illuminated whatever he touched, his contributions to our understanding of the human sciences are likely to continue.

In regard to the methods of the social or human sciences, Weber insisted upon a sharp distinction between the natural or physical sciences and the human or "spiritual" (*Geistes*) ones. A wide-ranging debate about this, a *Methodenstreit* or "methodological controversy," broke out in Germany during Weber's time, in the late nineteenth century; philosophers and psychologists as well as historians and sociologists joined in. Weber was one of those who became identified with the view that there is a radical distinction between the two types of science. Social studies can and should be scientific in the sense of finding exact knowledge by careful and critical research, knowledge that enables us to understand human affairs better. The difference lies in the nature of its results. Most natural sciences seek to frame general laws. Social science, on the other hand, is a science of the particular, aiming not at lawlike generalizations—which, since human minds are not primarily physical objects, seldom are valid in this domain—but rather at an "understanding" of a unique situation. We cannot frame a law to explain the appearance of the Renaissance or, say, a Richard Wagner. We can only bring enough information and insight to bear on a topic so that the student finally "understands" in the sense of grasping the situation intuitively within one's mind—much as one "understands" a person or a personal problem. Much damage had been done to social science by a failure to realize this, leading to vain attempts to mimic the law-finding sciences. There is more than one kind of science. The human ones must declare their independence and seek truth in their own way.

Weber has also been compared to Emile Durkheim in a remarkably persistent methodological debate among sociologists, about whether the researcher should begin with the individual or the group. It is rather a chicken-and-egg question, seemingly irresolvable but fun to argue about. Weber, who was dismayed by the growth of academic specialization (he once lamented over "specialists without spirit and hedonists without heart"), might or might not be pleased at the present state of the art. But he continues to loom large in its affairs. It is a tribute to him that he seems far more than a sociologist or a professor; he was one of the major seers of the twentieth century.

9

Marie Curie: A Woman in Science

EARLY LIFE

Maria Sklodowska, born in Warsaw three years after Max Weber, did not have a prominent businessman-politician for a father but a rather improvident schoolteacher, who far from standing in the way of his children having an intellectual career constantly encouraged them to do so. Maria was the youngest of five children, one of whom died of typhus not long before their mother succumbed to tuberculosis, leaving the father to raise four youngsters. In material terms the elder Sklodowski was far from successful, losing most of the family money in a bad investment and being fired from a supervisory position he once held in the *Gymnasium* (secondary school). In a human sense he seems to have succeeded magnificently.

The Sklodowskas were not powerful people nor were they citizens of a powerful country like Weber's; in fact, Poland was not a country at all, politically. Twice since 1815 the Poles had rebelled against Russian rule, the most oppressive of the three foreign governments that shared control of their homeland. The Russians held the lion's share, but other pieces of Poland belonged to Prussia and to Austria, the latter a rather less brutal administration. In 1863 when the Poles rose up in rebellion against Russian rule, it was the signal for the founding of Karl Marx's First International. The revolt was crushed, Prussia lending full support to Russia. The Sklodowska children grew up in an atmosphere of forcible Russianization, which included attempted suppression of the Polish language and religion, deportations, and the forced induction of young men into both the Russian and the Prussian armies. The tsar who liberated the Russian serfs felt no such mercy toward the Poles. He was to be assassinated in 1881, but his successor proved no more liberal, although he was more dedicated to the sciences. Among notable victims of this repression, the great Polish-English writer Josef Conrad grew up in Russia where his father had been exiled.

This persecution made the Polish family even more close-knit and mutually supportive. The somewhat bleak picture sketched above did not prevent much happiness in the Sklodowski family, including pleasant holidays with relatives in the country, and evenings of family members reading together such as marked the benighted days before television. The children were all bright and ambitious. There was some kind of special genetic chemistry at work here. Maria's brother and her older sister, Bronia, both got into medical school. In order to pay for the latter's years in Paris, Maria took a job as governess for an upper-class family in the country some ways from Warsaw, spending the best part of the four years before her twenty-second birthday there. She survived the boredom and a romance with the family son, whose desire to marry her met with firm resistance from the boy's status-conscious parents—who, however, treated and paid the vivacious Maria well. Maria wrote endless letters, sometimes deploring the lack of enough money for stamps.

At times Maria despaired about her own career; but her unselfish investment in her sister Bronia in the end turned out to be a wise one. Bronia married another Polish medical student, and upon completion of their degrees they invited Maria to come to Paris and live with them while she attended the Sorbonne. Moreover, Papa Sklodowski had retrieved his fortunes somewhat by gaining a position as director of a prison. Meanwhile, Maria had fallen in love with the chemistry laboratory of a cousin in Warsaw, who had studied in Russia under the great Mendeleyev.

This was a time for the scientist as role model. Politically, Maria and her young friends embraced the then fashionable credo of *positivism*, regarded by the tsar's police as dangerously radical. It came from France, where the disciples of Auguste Comte became famous scientists, like Claude Bernard and Louis Pasteur. In the role as culture hero the scientist threw aside religion and superstition to bore relentlessly for the truth, defined as demonstrable fact. The scientist put aside all other interests in concentrating on the great task of overthrowing old errors and leading humanity toward the fair haven of a better tomorrow. He (or she) disdained everything except what could be experimentally verified. Romantic poetry normally interested the scientific positivist as little as Shakespeare had interested Newton. Religion was an enemy, the embodiment of the "superstition" that had to be rooted out.

The ideal was very close to Max Weber's idea of the purity of social science: value-free, "disinterested," divorced from all considerations of practical use, which Pasteur regarded as inconsistent with pure science; austerely dedicated to exact knowledge for its own sake. One can call this cult *scientism*; it flourished as science began to be more and more professionalized, and it grew on the soil of success. It even became a kind of substitute religion, as art was for others. Charles Darwin and Louis Pasteur were chief among the heroes who had defied the idols of the tribe to find their way by arduous toil to exciting new truths. Any bright young person coming of age in the late nineteenth century might well be attracted by the persona of the scientist-hero, and might resolve to dedicate his or her life to the high ideals of the scientist—the more so as new discoveries seemed to arrive almost daily from about 1880 on.

Science was becoming professionalized and organized; an international network of specialized journals and conferences drew scientists together and collated and reported on their findings. It was an exciting moment in the history of science that Maria chose for her debut, as in 1893 the twenty-six-year-old Polish woman took first place in the final exams for the physics degree at the Sorbonne, then went on to study mathematics in which she achieved second place the following year.

Arguably, Maria would have been better served in Berlin or in Cambridge; more than Paris, these places were to function as centers of the new scientific revolution from 1880 on. Louis Pasteur was already in a sense passé. But Maria's general outlook drew the Polish girl to Paris. Polish ties to France were historically and culturally much stronger than to Germany (one of the hated conquerors) or to England. And the relaxed though metropolitan atmosphere of the most charming of all cities proved better for Maria than any other place. This was true in relation to her almost epochal role as feminine invader of a masculine society. For Paris was more tolerant than most places in this regard. Maria's French was good, although she had to improve it to follow the scientific lectures. She made herself a nearly perfect French speaker. The foothold established by her sister Bronia and Bronia's husband, Casimir Dlusbki, was an enormous help to Maria.

It must be admitted that there were very few women scientists at the time. Before Madame Curie, a major scientific career was largely closed to women. Darwin held views about women's creative ability that today would get him consigned to the deepest circles of sexist chauvinism. Some have claimed that Albert Einstein's first wife, Mileva Maric, another Slavic woman science student, whom Einstein divorced after a few years, really contributed more to the famous Relativity theory than she got credit for. As Mme. Marie Curie, the petite Polish girl Maria Sklodowska was to become one of the very few towering female figures in the burgeoning scientific renaissance of the late nineteenth and early twentieth century—at first, the only one. Probably only Lise Meitner, and Maria's own daughter, Irene, can compare to her. It was the age of Heinrich Hertz and Max Planck and then Albert Einstein in Germany; of J.J. Thomson and Ernest Rutherford in England, of H.H. Lorentz of the Netherlands, and a host of others, all males. There is a 1911 photo of the first Solvay Congress (an annual meeting of top scientific brains, endowed by a Belgian industrialist) that shows twenty-four men, among them Planck, Rutherford, Einstein, Lorentz, Poincaré, and one woman—M. Curie.

She herself took on something of a masculine air. The far from unattractive Maria was so reserved, so totally businesslike (and, it must be added, indifferent to her appearance), that would-be suitors seldom came close. She was so hard-working and so obviously competent that her teachers respected her. A neglect of life's amenities gave rise to stories about her similar to those about Newton; she often forgot to eat and dress properly. But her sister and brother-in-law, the Dlusbkis, were there to keep an eye on her. A model of total commitment, in her way as single-minded as Mazzini, Maria flourished. Assisting her in her student years was a grant from the Russian government which a friend, Mme. Dydynska, helped her win. The Cossacks were not always the enemy!

Pierre Curie was a scientist working on his doctorate at the University. He had a special interest in the field of electromagnetism, and was thirty-five, eight years older than Maria, when they met there in 1894. To say it was love at first sight might underestimate the constraint of these serious people. But it did not take them long to begin a marriage that, if it was made more in the laboratory than in heaven, was marked by deep affection on both sides. They complemented each other nicely. Pierre, the son of a doctor, was reclusive, had some mystical qualities, and totally lacked the energetic competitive spirit of Marie. He was languishing in a poorly paid position while fiddling with a drawn-out doctoral research project when he met Marie and, having never before known an attractive woman with a scientific brain, immediately fell in love with her. If she took a little longer to decide to marry him it was probably because of a reluctance to abandon her beloved Poland for France. There was in fact another suitor; but Pierre had many attractive qualities. He was an experimental scientist of genius, as well as a gentle and sensitive person, and his amiable, moderately well-off parents adored Marie. She came to love Pierre deeply and to depend on him for her emotional security.

Within a couple of years the first of two children was born. Irene was destined to become a scientist almost as famous as her mother—together making up probably the most outstanding mother-daughter team in the history of science.

SCIENCE

At first, Pierre advanced more rapidly than did Marie. He gained promotion to professorial rank through work on electricity, and was acclaimed by Lord Kelvin, the British master of this domain. With his brother, Jacques, Pierre constructed instruments capable of measuring extremely small electrical charges.

Marie was lucky in advancing on her major research project a little later. For a number of astonishing things happened at that time. Early in 1896 the German scientist Wilhelm Roentgen's discovery of X-rays, immediately caught both the scientific and the public imagination, as well they might, these mysterious rays with the power to pass right through solid objects and make pictures of internal body parts. A month later the French physicist Henri Becquerel accidentally discovered that the salts of uranimum emit rays that penetrate matter like X-rays. Becquerel had stumbled upon what would be called "radioactivity."

A crowd of rays or "waves" emerged, predicted by James Clerk Maxwell's equations. Heinrich Hertz, the brilliant German scientist who died young, had found radio waves in 1885. In 1897 J.J. Thomson was repeating a Hertz experiment at Cambridge University when, after devising a cathode-ray tube, he discovered "electrons," or negative units of electricity. A few years later Ernest Rutherford was to show that electronic particles can pass right through atoms, an astonishing thing because atoms had always been thought to be the smallest units of matter (the Greek word itself means that). Like Newton's particles, they were supposed to be "solid, massy, hard, impenetrable." As such, they had formed the solid basis of chemistry ever since John Dalton reinstated them early in the nineteenth century. Now it seemed that, far from being solid, atoms were largely hollow shells, containing a nucleus (responsible for most of the weight, but small in size) surrounded by negative electrical charges. Ernst Mach began to doubt that they existed at all—perhaps they were a linguistic illusion.

Rutherford used "alpha particles" obtained from radioactivity, and thus from Marie Curie, who had coined this term. Using the quartz instruments her husband had invented, she worked in a university laboratory measuring the electricity discharged by uranium. (The quartz watches that have widely replaced the old mechanical ones in recent decades stem from Pierre Curie's work in the 1890s.) Marie tested other metals for such discharges, and found them in thorium. Only a few metals show this phemomenon; she thought it consisted of rays coming somehow from inside the atoms, and named it "radioactivity." And she also came to believe there was at least one element as yet unknown, not found in the famous Mendeleyev table of elements, which was more radiocative than any other. She published a note on this hypothesis in April 1898, meeting with the usual skepticism. But on July 18 she found a new element that she named "polonium"; by the end of the year she had identifed another more radiocative element, which she called "radium." The Curies' method for measuring radiation was a notable contribution to chemical analysis; it involved spreading the product to be measured on one of the two plates of a condenser, spaced about an inch apart, and measuring the conductability of the air between them by means of Pierre's electrical measurement instruments. From this the amount of radioactivity could be calculated.

What lay ahead was long and arduous work extracting from huge quantities of the ore pitchblende the tiny percentage of radium it contained; this was necessary to get enough pure radium to establish its atomic weight. Marie bore the brunt of the labor, for Pierre had his classes to teach. She did this in an abandoned shed or barn with poor ventilation, under conditions that later seemed almost unbelievable; no shining modern lab with all the latest equipment, more like the kitchen sink in a hovel. Only the excitement of the hunt, and anticipation of what lay ahead—a contribution to humanity of incalculable value, and with it world fame—could have kept them at the task. In fact, the place was a shrine to the Curies and the few chemists who were privileged to assist them.

In the autumn of 1898 Mme. Curie applied for a vacant chair of physical chemistry at the Sorbonne but failed to get it. She was then thirty, and the mother of a three-year-old child. She and Pierre began to suffer from minor illnesses, which would later be attributed to the radiation they were absorbing. But they drove ahead with the arduous work. The adventure did not end until March 1902, when Marie was able to state exactly the atomic weight of radium. Nor did it quite end there, for the task still remained of getting an absolutely pure specimen of radium.

Meanwhile, the world gradually began to notice. The quite disgraceful treatment France had meted out to the Curies—partly the result of their unconventional status, Marie a woman and a foreigner, Pierre an odd and prickly personality—came somewhat to an end after the University of Geneva tried to lure them away with a handsome offer in 1900. Even so, Marie as well as her husband had to teach difficult courses at remote locations, assignments that today would be thought extremely strange for people whose research almost monopolized the attention of international physics meetings. It soon became known that radium's radiation could destroy cancerous cells, thus offering the possibility of one of history's most remarkable cures for disease—a fact about radium that tended to dwarf all others in the public mind and make the Curies probably the best-known scientists in the world. Naturally, radium, which glowed in the dark, was soon being smeared on the hands of wrist watches and the costumes of chorus girls, among other uses.

The Curies had in fact stumbled onto something more than they realized. They knew that for some reason a few elements, one especially, had the power to exude powerful rays. Where these rays came from and why was another matter. Today we know that they represent the spontaneous disintegration of atoms—something never before thought possible, almost a contradiction in terms. Some of the atoms of some of the heavier elements are unstable, and gradually break up—very slowly indeed, as human time is measured, but steadily. The particles that make up their atomic structure escape. The brilliant New Zealand-born scientist Ernest Rutherford was quick to notice that in fact these rays consist of two kinds, which he named *alpha* and *beta*. *Gamma* rays were subsequently added to the list.

Gradually it became evident that atoms, if they exist at all, consist of a small, heavy nucleus made up of protons (later, neutrons were found to be there too), balanced by the negatively charged electrons in a relationship that puzzled physicists until the 1920s and to some extent still does. The Newtonian laws of motion and gravity, always assumed to be absolute, did not work inside the atom at all, and a new mechanics had to be found. Inside what had once been thought irreducible was a whole new world of complex forces. Holding atoms together was a force so powerful that to disintegrate atoms could unleash a source of energy far beyond anything previously known.

All this the Curies did not at first know. They tended to think that somehow the radioactive atoms had the power to transform rays from the sun into energy. But they did not really develop a precise theory; Rutherford remarked that the Curies held "only a very general idea of the phenomenon of radioactivity." It was enough for them to have established its existence and noted its powers. They were capable of coming up with this answer had they had the time; Rutherford simply beat them to it, being able to take up fresh where these weary workers had left off.

"The discovery of radioactivity," Mme. Curie said later, in a lecture at the Residencia de Estudiantes in Madrid in 1931, "marks an epoch in the history of science." No one had ever before thought that atoms had an internal structure. Now this unsuspected dimension became the new frontier of scientific research, destined to dominate science for the rest of the century and radically influence all human thought.

AFTER RADIUM

Marie and Pierre Curie had indeed worked themselves to exhaustion, while exposing themselves to dangerous radiation. Friends worried about their health. "I would long since have been stretched out in my grave if I had abused my body as both of you abuse yours," one of their friends wrote to Pierre in 1903. A certain masochism seemed at times to afflict the Curies; overworked and underpaid, Pierre turned down decorations and medals while Marie refused to accept royalties from the commercial development of radium. The price of radium was to reach $100,000 a gram by 1920. Yet all kinds of intellectual honors came their way, the kind they appreciated; the climax was reached in 1903 when they were jointly awarded the Nobel Prize for physics, just recently established by the Swedish government and rapidly becoming the ultimate standard of excellence. This honor, a genuine recognition by a jury of the foremost international scientists, they did not refuse. It meant both financial independence and world fame.

No Nobel award ever exceeded this one in glamor and glory; indeed, in some measure it made the reputation of the Swedish prize. The Curie story dripped with fairy-tale qualities. The achievement by a woman galvanized the feminist movement. Radium, the miracle cure as many thought, added a touch of magic. The story greatly moved the world. With the Boer War just over and the Russo-Japanese one just ahead, 1903 was perhaps a year with something of a news vacuum, though it also saw the Wright brothers' Kitty Hawk flight, but the Curie story under any circumstances would have stolen the headlines. News was now being transmitted quickly by the magic of another wave. Guglielmo Marconi sent the first long-distance radio signal from England to Newfoundland on December 12, 1901. The Curies' Nobel Prize was one of the first big news stories to be flashed around the world via this more rapid means of communication.

Marie wrote that their sudden fame was "a disaster" for Pierre and her. On principle he despised adulation; she suffered from a nearly pathological fear of crowds. Virtually no one even among her close friends ever called Mme. Curie by her first name. Now they were besieged by sightseers and journalists, invited everywhere and misquoted in the press. Marie, moreover, was pregnant with her second child, after an earlier miscarriage. Pierre argued with the French government about the conditions of a chair being created for him at the Sorbonne; he grumbled about scattering his time and energy. In fact, he published nothing after receiving the Nobel Prize.

He had only a short while to live. There is no doubt he was ill as well as distracted by all the fame. The accident that claimed his life on a rainy afternoon in late April 1906 may well have resulted from his agitated state of mind. Pierre was hurrying on foot along a little street near the Pont Neuf and Boulevard Saint-Germain, where so many tourists stroll every day, when, his umbrella in front of his face, he did not see a massive horse-drawn truck, or perhaps he slipped on the muddy street trying to avoid it. The driver of the wagon claimed that Pierre virtually threw himself in front of the wheel that smashed his skull. Death was instantaneous. Pierre was in his forty-seventh year. He and Marie had been married eleven years. During that time they had changed world history and made each other happy, though just possibly they were less happy at the end. Now Marie would have to carry on alone.

She was awarded a chair in physics, in Pierre's name, at the Sorbonne— the first woman ever to occupy one. Among other outpourings of sympathy and aid the most important, perhaps, came from the Scottish-American steel tycoon Andrew Carnegie, the Mæcenas of his age, who generously endowed a research foundation for her. There Marie and her assistants were able to pursue the quest for pure radium; in finding it at last she disposed of a few remaining skeptics, including the aged Lord Kelvin.

These bitter quarrels among great scientists, jealous of their prerogatives, should be familiar to us from having met them before in the case of Isaac Newton. Rutherford, Marie's perennial rival but good friend (he charmed her and melted her fierce reserve as few others outside her own little circle could do), thought that she tried a little too hard to claim all the credit for radioactivity; this was a small fault when one knew how much she had contributed. Others often found her difficult.

In 1910 she put herself forward as a candidate for election to the chair of the French Academy of Sciences, one of five in the Institut de France, an institution hard to find an equivalent for in the Anglo-Saxon world; it was a kind of national, official super-university. Like all academies, it was stuffy and had frequently in the past preferred pretentious mediocrity to real genius; French writers and artists made jokes about it, which did not prevent them from trying to get elected to it. Mme. Curie's chief rival was Edouard Branly, known for his work on radio (wireless telegraphy) where, many thought, he stood second only to Marconi. He had shared the prestigious Osiris award with her in 1903. If radium was a useful and popular invention, radio was even more so. Branly was more than twenty years Marie's elder. He was also a good Catholic, decorated by the pope, whereas the free-thinking Marie scarcely excelled in piety. The "war of the sexes" thus became also a war of ideologies, which in France always included the conflict between the Church and anticlericalism, dating back to the French Revolution and notably revived in the period between 1895–1910. And Marie, lest we forget, was not even a native-born Frenchwoman, a fact of some significance at a time of fervent nationalism.

In the end, after strenuous campaigning, she was defeated by a vote of 30 to 28. She showed her bitterness by severing all connections with the French Academy of Sciences. But a consolation appeared from Sweden in the form of another Nobel Prize (1911), in chemistry, this time without sharing it. Only one other person in the history of the Nobel Prize has ever received it twice.

A TOUCH OF SCANDAL

The personal lives of scientists are usually ignored, presumably because they are uninteresting as well as irrelevant. In a novel written a few years after Marie Curie won the Nobel Prize, Robert Musil mused that

> Scarcely anyone remembers even the name of the man who gave mankind the untold blessing of anaesthetics; nobody probes into the lives of Gauss, Euler, or Maxwell in the hope of finding a Frau von Stein; and hardly a soul cares where Lavoisier and Cardanus were born and died. Instead, one learns about how their ideas and inventions were further developed by the ideas and inventions of other, equally uninteresting people, and one concentrates exclusively on their achievements, which live on in others long after the short-lived fire of the personality has burnt out.[1]

This may be less true today, when historians of science sometimes regard the life and times of their subjects as important, but it is still largely so. If the life

[1]*The Man without Qualities*, vol. 1, p. 356. Translated from the German by Eithne Williams and Ernst Kaiser. Picador Classics (Pan Books), 1988. First published London: Secker & Warburg, 1954.

of a scientist is studied it is in the hope of casting light on the roots of "creativity," or the processes of scientific discovery, not for its own sake.

Mme. Curie's life, however, was not without its inherent interest. Raised in a household where all the muses were at home, she did not entirely confine herself to scientific circles, dedicated a scientist though she was. Her acquaintances included people as diverse as the American-born dancer Loie Fuller, a hit in Paris before Isadora Duncan or Josephine Baker; and Ignace Paderewski, the great Polish pianist, a friend from the early Paris days. She enjoyed opera and ballet. The little "Curie clan," her circle of carefully chosen close friends, did not entirely exclude people from the arts and humanities, though its pillars were other notable chemists, physicists, and mathematicians—Paul Langevin, Jean Perrin, Emile Borel, and the rather glamorous wives of the last two.

Langevin had long been a close friend. Professor at the Collège de France, he was a theoretical physicist of great distinction, close to Einstein's level, a future Nobelist himself; in fact, he was only a step behind the Swiss genius in Relativity, of which he was a brilliant expounder. He arrived at the $E = mc^2$ formula in 1906 without knowing that Einstein had already figured it out. He more than anyone else called Marie's attention to Einstein, whom she greatly admired and defended when his photon theory of light was as controversial as her radioactivity theory had been. Langevin, unlike the Borels, Perrins, and Curies, did not usually include his wife in the social circle; of working class origin like Langevin himself, she did not share his intellectual interests but stayed home to take care of their four children. After Pierre Curie's death it was rather natural for the now unattached Marie to pair off with the handsome (and slightly younger) Langevin when the salon gathered. This did not escape Mme. Langevin's attention. She separated from her husband in the summer of 1911.

Some suspected that Marie had a relationship, prior to Pierre's death, with the chemist André Debierne, an associate during the heroic days in the shed working on radium; Debierne now became violently jealous of Langevin. Soon after the opening of the celebrated first Solvay congress in Brussels in October 1911, which Langevin and Mme. Curie both attended, the popular press blazoned stories of an affair between the two—*une histoire d'amour*. Both Langevin and Curie indignantly denied it. Unfortunately, there was proof of it in letters stolen from Paul Langevin by Mme. Langevin's brother-in-law.

Frantic efforts to suppress the scandal followed. For at this very moment the news broke of Mme. Curie being awarded her second Nobel Prize! But of course some newspaper was bound to leap at so juicy a morsel. The damning letters appeared on November 23, 1911, in a journal called *L'Oeuvre*. It was the signal for a season of pandemonium, climaxed by a duel between Langevin and the editor of *L'Oeuvre*; fortunately for science, at the last moment they refused to fire their pistols. Today we might smile at the furor over a case of sexual attraction. Scientists are human, after all. Still, we could recall that as late as 1988 adultery detected *in flagrante* was enough to blight the career of an American presidential candidate. In 1911 it had recently ruined that of the great Irish political leader Charles Parnell.

Feminists cried that a double standard was in evidence in the Curie affair; French males notoriously carried on amorous dalliances without fear of adverse publicity. It was almost a reproach to one's manhood not to have a mistress in the France of that era. But a woman was different. A latent hostility to Marie as a foreigner as well as a woman also surfaced. The Dreyfus affair had earlier inflamed political passions. The war with Germany lay just around the corner, rehearsed for in a series of incidents from 1905 to 1913; the landing of a German gunboat at Agadir in Morocco precipitated an international crisis in 1911 just as the Curie scandal was about to break. The liveliest political movement of the day was the *Action Française*, preaching "integral nationalism." There was a measure of nationalist hysteria in the pre-1914 air, and some of it spilled onto the foreign lady who was outshining all the French, of either sex.

The scandal blew over, as scandals do. Marie sank out of sight for a time, clearly stunned by the affair's impact. An English friend, the feminist scientist Hertha Ayrton, invited Marie to rural England for a quiet rest. Though she maintained her friendship with Langevin, Marie never afterward resumed intimate relations, with him or any other man. Langevin eventually returned to his wife, though not exactly as a model husband. He was to continue a brilliant scientific career. After 1919 he drifted into politics as a man of the far left; his career as a Communist further testified to his turbulent and unconventional personality, sometimes capable of atrocious judgment.

THE GREAT WAR AND AFTER

The outbreak of war in Europe in 1914 awakened Mme. Curie and her friends from a rather routine if not somnolent life, as it did so many other European writers, artists, scientists. She took charge of a program to provide X-ray facilities to medical units serving the French army's wounded. Her chemist friends worked on answers to the German use of poison gas. Langevin signally helped in the development of an ultrasound device to detect the presence of submarines, after the Germans decided to go all-out with the U-boat weapon in 1917. They all threw themselves into the war effort with enormous energy and a sense of highly charged excitement.

The war confronted Poles with a tragic dilemma. Germany and Austria-Hungary, the Central Powers, fought against the alliance of France, Britain, and Russia. Ought Poles to support the oppressor enemy, Russia? Austria-Hungary (the Dual Monarchy) treated her Poles much better. But the defeat and dismemberment of the Dual Monarchy, plus Allied pressure on Russia, might lead to the restoration of an independent Poland. The issue caused a bitter rift between the Polish-born British historian Lewis Namier and his father. But neither Marie nor her sister, now again living in Poland, seem to have had any doubt about where their loyalties lay. Any doubts her enemies might have entertained about Mme. Curie's patriotism were certainly quenched; she was a tornado of energy as she rushed about the front supervising a small army of improvised nurses, doubtless in some cases at the risk of their health. Marie herself was storing up an amount of radiation in her system that increasingly affected her health and ultimately killed her. For she still was reluctant to admit the dangers involved in handling radioactive materials.

In her last decade or so Mme. Curie may have overstayed her time. Honors were now heaped on her, and money flowed in, from the Rothschilds as well as the Rockefellers, even from the French government. She could have used it better when she was working her fingers off in a barn back in 1898. She was now not so much too old as too sick to do much with it.

Her supply of energy, nevertheless, seemed boundless. In 1921 she visited the United States for a taxing round of interviews, honorary degrees, and visitations, including one to the White House. Her trip was crowned by presentation to her of a precious gram of radium from American women. The enterprising American woman journalist who master-minded this stunt became a bosom crony of Marie's, whose predilections in friendships were unpredictable. (Seven years later Mme. Curie returned to visit President Herbert Hoover and receive another gram of radium from the American people.)

But in 1921 she returned to a France much more interested in the Dempsey-Carpentier heavyweight boxing match than in radium. The new kind of news market that shot up in the 1920s occasionally embraced high science as well as sports and scandal, but in 1919 it was Einstein who seized the headlines. Mme. Curie did not play a prominent role in the exciting debates of the 1920s about ultimate physical properties that featured Einstein and Bohr, Broglie and Heisenberg, Dirac and Schrödinger. Much more involved was her old paramour Langevin, who exchanged visits with Einstein in the early 1920s chiefly as a gesture of reconciliation between France and the new German Republic. The mathematical physicists had stolen some of the thunder from experimentalists like Curie and Rutherford.

Langevin was prominent among those French intellectuals who sympathized with Russian communism in the 1920s. Though her son-in-law was to follow this path with a vengeance, Mme. Curie, while vaguely leftist, was not militantly political. What energies she had left she preferred not to squander on politics. She underwent an operation for cataracts, in those days considered major surgery. She presided over the Radium Institute in Paris, on a street named for Pierre Curie, where she watched and encouraged her daughter, Irene, heir to the Curie scientific dynasty.

In 1919 her friendly rival, the New Zealand-born genius Ernest Rutherford, who worked at Manchester University before moving to Cambridge in

1919, split the atom. In 1914 he had pointed out in a popular lecture that the potential energy stored inside atoms was now, after Einstein, known to be incredibly great: "many million times greater than for an equal weight of the most powerful explosive." Already the science-fiction writer H.G. Wells had foreseen its use. But the possibility of tapping this source by "causing a substance like uranium or thorium to give out its energy in the course of a few hours or days, instead of over a period of many thousands or millions of years," in other words, to greatly speed up radioactivity, "does not at present seem at all promising," Rutherford believed. Interrupted by the war, during which he too worked on submarine detection, this greatest of experimental physicists pecked away in odd moments until he finally succeeded in making alpha particles (which were helium atoms) break up nitrogen atoms, resulting in hydrogen and oxygen.

"If I have disintegrated the nucleus of the atom," Rutherford wrote in June 1919, "this is of greater significance than the war." But Rutherford's achievement led to no immediately sensational results. Another scientific event overshadowed the Paris Peace Conference, just then delivering itself of the debatable Versaille Treaty. This was the observation, during an eclipse of the sun, that appeared to vindicate Albert Einstein's new principle of gravity, his second or General Theory of Relativity. Newton was at last dethroned!

Thirteen years later Rutherford's student and colleague James Chadwick discovered the neutron, a particle within the atom having neither positive nor negative charge, something Rutherford had earlier predicted. This was to lead to atomic energy, because the neutron—as heavy as a proton—is able to approach the nuclei of larger atoms without being repelled, and thus be used to split them. But European physicists—Otto Hahn, Lise Meitner, Leo Szilard, Enrico Fermi—took the lead in developing controllable uranium fission, the source of atomic energy. The Hungarian Szilard filed for a patent on a chain reaction in 1934, the same year as Fermi caused a uranium atom to split by bombarding it with neutrons. Fermi, "the Italian explorer," was to join Einstein and Szilard in the United States where he supervised the creation of the first atomic reactor under the football stadium at the University of Chicago. Lise Meitner, another pioneer who, along with Einstein's old friend Hahn and Meitner's nephew, Otto Frisch, had perfected Fermi's experiment in 1938/39, also fled Nazi intolerance in Germany to settle in the United States.

Irene Curie and Frederic Joliot, whom Irene married in 1926, came close to finding the neutron. The Joliot-Curies, as they called themselves, performed much the same experiment as did Chadwick, but they failed to deduce from it what he did. A few years later, the Joliot-Curies also narrowly missed discovering the way to nuclear fission, arriving just behind Fermi, Hahn, and Meitner. Frederic Joliot demonstrated the possibility of a chain reaction almost as soon as did Fermi, but after the spring of 1940 French scientists were caught in a German trap.

During the war, Frederic Joliot-Curie became a Communist. The Joliot-Curies did not emigrate, though they had a chance; they stayed in France to protect their laboratory and, as Frederic wrote, "to remain in Paris near my colleagues who are unable to leave France." He was building a cyclotron, in which the Germans showed a great deal of interest, thinking it relevant to atomic weaponry, although Joliot-Curie did not intend it for that. He submitted to a degree of Nazi supervision in order to continue his work, and, it seems, he discreetly sabotaged the military aspects. He smuggled information to England about the Germans' interest in his work. A pioneer in "heavy water," the kind containing a rare isotope of hydrogen needed for a successful atomic explosion, the French helped to keep a supply of this from the Germans. Later, with the aid of their intelligence network, the British sank a crucial shipment of heavy water, a key factor in slowing the pace of German progress toward building an atomic bomb.

Increasingly, Joliot-Curie was drawn into the Resistance movement, as he attempted to defend friends and colleagues. Langevin was imprisoned, then placed under house arrest. It was dangerous work, against a ruthless foe who was ever more desperate as the war turned badly for Hitler's regime. Frederic carried it out while Irene became increasingly sick. Toward the end of the war the family escaped to Switzerland before returning to France when the Americans, British, and Free French finally liberated Paris. Frederic had conducted himself heroically.

By 1943 he had come to believe that the Communists were the best leaders of the Resistance movement. He was by no means the only Frenchman in the Resistance movement who drew close to them. Unfortunately, he became a quite uncritical and obsesssive believer in Stalin's Soviet Union. There is no evidence that Joliot-Curie helped the USSR build its nuclear weapons, first the fission "atomic" bomb in 1949 and then the much more powerful fusion "H-bomb" a few years later. One of his former colleagues at the Radium Institute did. Bruno Pontecorvo, long a dedicated Communist, headed for the United States after the fall of France. In 1943 the Italian scientist took his atomic expertise to Canada where he worked on heavy-water research along with another Communist, the Cambridge-trained Alan Nunn May. Pontecorvo later went to England to work on the British atomic bomb at Harwell; then in 1951 he defected to the Soviet Union to give valuable aid to the USSR's H-bomb project. Nunn May and another European scientist, the German Klaus Fuchs, had meanwhile been arrested, tried, and sentenced for passing nuclear secrets to Russia—Nunn May in 1946, Fuchs in 1950; both confessed. Both had had abundant access to the Manhattan Project where the first atomic bomb was assembled during World War II. The surprisingly rapid Soviet development of nuclear weapons owed much to the plentiful supply of information they received from devoted European and American Communists.

Frederic Joliot-Curie's communism doubtless reflected the naivete often exhibited by scientists in politics, but it was about par for the course in his generation. Being pro-Communist, even becoming a Soviet agent, was evaluated differently in Western Europe than in the United States, a fact reflected in the different punishments meted out to the "traitors." Nunn May and Fuchs received fairly short prison terms from British courts; the latter not many years later was back in East Germany unrepentantly helping its Communist government. But in 1951 an American judge condemned Ethel and Julius Rosenberg to death for similar spying activities, a sentence duly carried out.

After the war Frederic became high commissioner of the French Atomic Energy Commission, building the first French nuclear reactor. He said he would never help build an atomic bomb for France, and he was one of those Frenchmen who implied that he would not fight for France in a war against the Soviet Union. His enthusiastic pro-Soviet position led him to visit the USSR to accept the Stalin Prize, accompanied by Irene, who never joined the Communist party, and to attend the world peace conferences the Soviets sponsored in the postwar years as they attempted to slow the pace of Western armament while building their nuclear weapons. As the Cold War heightened, Frederic's outspoken communism got him into trouble. The Communist party was driven into isolation after 1948 as it opposed the Marshall Plan, the NATO alliance, the Yugoslav revolt against Kremlin domination, the defense of West Berlin, and other actions denounced by Stalin's regime as "capitalist imperialism" but seen by most French citizens as a necessary reply to the Soviet Union's aggressive assault on free institutions. Frederic was forced out of his government post in 1950; so was Irene a little later. They both continued their careers as professors at the University of Paris. Their counterparts in the USSR under Stalin would probably have been shot or sent to early death in an Arctic labor camp.

THE CURIE LEGEND

By this time, of course, Marie Curie was dead, a victim of leukemia in 1934 at the age of sixty-six. Her daughter, Irene, was to die of the same disease in 1956, and Irene's husband, Frederic, two years later at age fifty-eight. The other Curie daughter, Eve, who had no interest whatsoever in science or radioactivity, became an eminent journalist and married a prominent diplomat; she lived to a ripe old age.

What features of Marie Curie's story are the most important for posterity to remember? It was a good story; the world applauded; multitudes were still entranced when Greer Garson and Walter Pidgeon portrayed Marie and Pierre on the silver screen in 1943. The Curie legend grew; Marie Curie's life struck a response all over the world largely because it conformed to the model of a fairy tale. According to the Russian Vladimir Propp, in his *Morphology of the Folktale* (1928), the standard hero story features a low-born person who goes on a journey, receives crucial help from a benevolent assistant, is tested, transformed, and finally raised to a higher state to achieve a marvelous triumph. Almost all great novels contain some version of the trial, test, or ordeal of hero or heroine. The poor Polish girl who survived persecution as well as penury in Paris to crash the male citadels of science and make a miraculous discovery fitted the ideal to perfection, not least in her marrying the prince who had helped her.

Inevitably, something of the human interest faded with time, as did radium itself, no longer so much used in radiation treatment for cancer. The Curies took their place in the history of modern science, but they were part of a large crowd. Max Planck and Albert Einstein, Werner Heisenberg and Niels Bohr replaced them in the forefront in the 1920s and 1930s; later, the molecular biologists came to the center of the stage. There are now so many frontiers, and so many scientists, that it is hard to keep track of them all.

One issue Marie Curie raised, that of women in science, is still a relevant one. It would be comforting to say that after her pioneering breakthrough the barriers went down and women rushed in to share the laboratory with men ever after. This has not quite happened. For whatever reason, women are still in a distinct minority in the ranks of distinguished scientists. There are many of them, because there are a great many more scientists today, but the proportion is still small. Some would argue that the scientific culture is still a masculine one and a woman confronts most of the old familiar obstacles. If she is married to a scientist, he is likely to gain most of the accolades. If she stays single, deciding—as many women have—that this is the price she must pay for scientific success, she will perhaps be harassed or made to feel unwelcome in the male-dominated scientific culture; she may suffer guilt feelings about her desertion of the traditional commitment to motherhood and family. She will indignantly reject the thought that women can never equal men in the professional sphere, whether from genetic or social causes; but she knows that many men believe this. Concern has been expressed about the small percentage of women entering scientific careers even today. These questions are still relevant ones.

Mme. Curie managed without a great deal of fuss, if with superhuman energy and discipline, to be successful wife and mother as well as great scientist. She stood about halfway between being traditional and modern. Cautiously, not militantly, feminist, she held to many ancestral values, which, feminists would stress, were created by males. The mild radicalism of her youth, rooted in Polish positivism, contained some hostility to conventional religion, seen as the enemy of scientific progress. But she never pushed this very far. Despite her one adventure, sexual permissiveness horrified her, and she did not even like her daughter, Eve, using makeup. One feels that despite her total devotion to Irene she would not have joined the Joliot-Curies in their choice of Russian communism over Western democratic values. Irene herself, in an imitation of her mother's fierce independence, never actually joined the Communist party or submitted to its discipline.

The defection of the intellectuals to communism grew out of a total alienation that the generation growing up during and right after World War I felt, a feeling to which Marie was a stranger. She might criticize aspects of her society, but she never gave up on it to opt for its total destruction and radical replacement. One is reminded of a remark by Bertrand Russell, a man of Marie's generation, that his criticism of society differed from that of the young men of the post-1919 generation; in George Orwell's formulation of the same thought, he did it as a member of the family while they wanted to leave the family:

> We believed in ordered progress by means of politics and free discussion. The more self-confident among us may have wished to be leaders of the multitude, but none of us wished to be divorced from it. The generation of Keynes and Strachey did not wish to preserve any kinship with the Philistines. They aimed rather at a life of retirement among fine shades and nice feelings, and conceived of the good as consisting in the passionate mutual admiration of a clique of the elite. (Bertrand Russell, *Autobiography*, I, 85–86)

Marie Curie's faith was the religion of science. It was characteristic of people whose minds were formed in roughly the last half of the nineteenth century. And indeed it has been pervasive ever since. A noted philosopher recently remarked that the whole thrust of intellectual history since the Enlightenment "has made it second nature" to "accept the authority of science rather than that of religion or philosophy in fixing belief concerning what is and might become the case."[2] What this philosopher calls "the steady demystification of the world," and what Max Weber termed "disenchantment," has been an irresistible, steady trend. Today, even in human, personal matters, the "authority" turned to is likely to be someone with a claim on science—the psychologist, rather than the parson or the poet—when the media want a comment on some extraordinary action like a murder. Even the Roman Catholic Church sends its deficient priests to a psychiatrist.

The hold of science, and of the scientist as culture hero, is, however, less strong today than it was in Marie Curie's time. For one thing, science has become too complicated. Only a few can do it. One of Curie's contemporaries, the English scientist C.T.R. Wilson, inventor of the "cloud chamber" (in which to Rutherford's delight one might view the trail of electrons), expressed his belief that science could be made intelligible even to a barmaid. Planck and Einstein and Bohr, if not Curie and Rutherford and Chadwick, brought that illusion to an abrupt end. A 1983 study by John Miller of Northern Illinois University found that 93 percent of American adults are scientifically illiterate.

Science seemed to give up its claim to superior knowledge, in the time of "uncertainty principles" and "probability waves." We "weep for the lost

[2]Kai Nielsen, in *Dalhousie Review*, 67:4 (1987/88), p.11.

ages," the poet W.H. Auden wrote, "before Because became As If, or rigid certainty/The Chances Are. . . ." Nineteenth-century science, "positivist" and materialistic, had tended to claim a monopoly of true knowledge, dismissing art and especially religion as relics of barbarism. The new science turned out to be more mysterious than any poet could imagine or any priest proclaim. Science seemed to be returning to the mysticism from which it had emerged in the sixteenth century.Science had stood for steady and certain progress: No truth was ever lost, as a ladder of ascertained fact gradually stretched upward toward the "Truth." But today scientific truth changes almost hourly, and very little is immune from being overthrown. Writing in 1925 in his *Science and the Modern World*, Alfred North Whitehead already could say that

> The eighteenth century opened with a quiet confidence that at last nonsense had been got rid of. Today we are at the opposite pole of thought. Heaven knows what seeming nonsense may not tomorrow be demonstrated truth.

From the beginning, a minority of artists and humanists resisted the claim of "science" to be the only reputable kind of knowledge. We will remember Max Weber's caveat that if social and historical research is scientific, it is science of a quite different sort from the phsyicist's. Some of the artists went much further. Leo Tolstoy, for example, probably the world's most revered seer of Mme. Curie's time, castigated the uncritical belief in science as a new god, which he thought quite analogous to dogmatic religion. "The two most terrible plagues of our time," the Russian sage reflected, are Church Christianity, the official religion of the state—of which Tolstoy himself was often the adversary—and "materialism," the crude dogma of the scientists (including Darwinists and historical materialists). And humanity for want of any real spiritual guidance falls into a last and terrible crisis. Around the turn of the century a crowd of poets and philosophers and sociologists—Nietzsche, Bergson, poets like Stefan George and William Butler Yeats, novelists like the great Leo Tolstoy, Robert Musil, and D.H. Lawrence—projected this sense of a gigantic crisis of civilization, the chief cause of which, as they saw it, was a shriveling of the religious and esthetic sense, or of the integrated human personality, under the impact of excessive scientific materialism.

Modern scientists themselves gave up scientific imperialism, in the age of Bohr and Heisenberg, to welcome the insights of seers and poets. Nothing, after all, could be more mystical than the universe revealed by Einstein and by—yes—the Curies. It is difficult to imagine Mme. Curie abandoning her old-fashioned faith in scientific positivism, however. In her tribute to her husband, she had cited Louis Pasteur: "I believe invincibly that science and peace will triumph over ignorance and war." This belief that science represented progress, and ignorance was its opposite, had captivated her early and she never departed from it.

Marie Curie's vision of science was not corrupted by materialism in the sense of valuing only practical benefits. Einstein called her "the last uncorrupted person," and her actions throughout her life in scorning personal gain tell their own story. Some critics blamed post-Galilean science for deserting the quest for deep truth in favor of an ignoble pursuit of the mechanically useful.[3] This was not the Curie spirit. Both she and her husband held a generous vision of pure, disinterested science, followed for its own sake, without thought of any other reward. Marie wrote of her husband, Pierre, that he was

> a man who, inflexibly devoted to the service of his ideal, honored humanity by an existence lived in silence, in the simple grandeur of his genius and his character. . . . Believing only in the pacific might of science and of reason, he lived for the search for truth.

The epitaph serves for her as well.

In one of her last lectures, delivered in Madrid in 1931, Mme. Curie listed some of the novelties that had emerged from what she said "marks an epoch in the history of science," the discovery of radioactivity. Apart from the sheer wonder of discovering that something previously thought indivisible and infinitely small, the atom, in fact contained within itself a complex structure and incredible energy, there was the potential harnessing of this energy, which she could then barely foresee; likewise, there was the use of radioactivity to establish the age of minerals, by measuring how far they had disintegrated, something destined to have all kinds of applications, from archaeology to criminology and the realization that our sun is burning up its atomic fuel and will someday follow other suns into extinction.

The isotope phenomenon, meaning that atoms of the same element can vary in their structure, was another startling new perspective. "Finally, it is likely that radioactive elements can intervene in biological evolution on the surface of the earth," she added.

Stranger things than even Mme. Curie knew about were going to be unveiled. At about that very moment, while James Chadwick was discovering the neutron, a Belgian priest proposed that the universe itself began as an atom, which has been exploding ever since at nearly the speed of light. Mme. Curie had been a vital part of the beginning of all this.

---

[3]See, for example, Robert Musil, *The Man without Qualities*, ch. 72.

10

Franz Kafka and the Terrors of Modernity

KAFKA'S LIFE

A few years before Mme. Curie came to Paris, Franz Kafka was born in Prague, later (as Praha) the capital of Czechoslovakia,[1] then a part of the Austro-Hungarian Dual Monarchy—the large multinational state, heir of the medieval Holy Roman Empire, which was destined to be dismembered by World War I. Encyclopedias and other source books often categorize Kafka as a "Czech" writer, but although he knew the Czech tongue he was a member of the German-speaking community there and wrote in that language. He was also Jewish. He died of tuberculosis in 1924, little more than forty years old and far from famous. An obituary written by a one-time intimate, Milena Jesenska, declared that "he wrote the most significant works of modern German literature"; some discriminating connoisseurs would have agreed, but few outside his native city were aware of his work—much of which, indeed, remained to be published. This included his two major masterpieces, *The Trial* and *The Castle*.

Though the Nazis burnt his books in 1933, and the Gestapo destroyed a number of his manuscripts, Kafka's reputation spread in the 1930s and has continued to grow, until today few would question the judgment that he

---

[1]Which in 1992 agreed to divide into separate Czech and Slovakian republics. Czechoslovakia was created after the dissolution of the Austro-Hungarian Empire in 1918.

wrote among the most significant works, not just of modern German literature but of all literature. He joins James Joyce, Marcel Proust, Virginia Woolf, D.H. Lawrence, Thomas Mann, and a handful of others among the acknowledged masters of twentieth-century European literature. They were all of about the same generation, the quintessentially "modernist" one.

The excuse for presenting him here as a figure of European history goes beyond his literary achievement. For one thing, though a relatively obscure person in his lifetime, Kafka touched a number of significant events and movements. His three sisters were victims of the Nazi Holocaust; had Franz lived he would probably have shared their fate. Toward his Jewishness he had a most ambivalent attitude, but he became deeply interested in Zionism. His enigmatic masterpiece *The Trial* has been read as a commentary on the tragic predicament of European Jewry in the age of Nazism.

He also stands for the dilemma of the modern alienated intellectual-writer. No one more poignantly felt the condition of that marginal being. The world of literature he yearned to make his home stood in glaring contrast to the "real" world of business and bureaucracy. Son of a businessman, Kafka became a government official, a job he performed well enough yet privately hated with every fiber of his being. Part of him wanted to get married, have a family, join the community as a "normal" being; his deeper soul could not endure such a prospect. His early death may have been caused by this tragic split. His stories and novels uncannily reflect and express this uniquely modern conflict, which we can glimpse through his life as revealed in a diary and some marvelous letters. It is the dilemma of the sensitive "civilized consciousness," steeped in the heritage of Western art and literature, trying to find a home in the bureaucratic, rationalized, capitalistic society, and the democratic, mass-culture one.

All of Kafka's writings have a kind of mythic or allegorical quality, presenting in symbolic form issues of great philosophical depth. Like Shakespeare he had the ability to encapsulate universal themes in concrete situations. His admiration for the English Bard was indeed great—Kafka belonged to a circle in Prague deeply interested in English literature—but the chief model for a metaphysically significant kind of fiction probably came to him from the great nineteenth-century Russian, Fyodor Dostoyevsky. But Kafka, like James Joyce, read delightedly in virtually the whole of the Western literary tradition. To name writers who inspired him at one time or another is to risk compiling an endless catalogue. One critical study deals with his relationship to Charles Dickens. The French novelist Gustave Flaubert was another nineteenth-century giant he greatly admired. Kafka, whose native tongue was German, naturally knew the imposing German literary tradition intimately: His heroes included Grillparzer, Schiller, Kleist, Heine, and Goethe, the latter virtually a father figure to whose home in Weimar, a famous shrine, Kafka made a pilgrimage in the summer of 1912 with his friend Max

Brod. But he eagerly read or saw the plays of a galaxy of more recent writers; he was acquainted with Freud, just then rising to fame, with Nietzsche, so powerful an influence on Kafka's entire generation, and with the Danish precursor of Existentialism, Søren Kierkegaard.

Why go on? One of Kafka's contemporaries in the avant-garde artistic movement of his generation wrote a chapter of some fifty pages that consisted simply of naming all the artists and writers down the centuries whom he hailed as kindred spirits. There was indeed a long list of them, starting with the ancient Greeks and Jews. How was one to deal with this rich inheritance? The young writer wanted to make his own statement, find his own voice, joining this illustrious company as an equal; but learning to do this entailed a long apprenticeship. Kafka fell in love with literature and wanted to do nothing else but write. "Simply rush through the nights forever writing, that is what I want."

An intellectual, he once remarked, is one who, given a choice between experiencing paradise and reading about it, would choose the latter! "They say life's the thing but I'd rather read," as Logan Pearsall Smith remarked. Kafka was an intellectual from the start. Yet the shy youngster was an indifferent student at his *Gymnasium* (the European secondary school). He claimed a total disinterest in the school, regarded as one of the best in Prague. Precocious and alienated young people of Kafka's generation seldom remembered their school experiences with anything but horror—witness the accounts of any number of other writers in England as well as on the European continent. Like theirs, Kafka's adolescent years saw an interest in "radical" ideas, a means of expressing a vague discontent with the incomprehensible adult world and with an education that to his generation seemed irrelevant. In Kafka's case this attachment to the left was never very strong, but many of his friends professed socialism.

Under parental pressure he went on to study law at Prague University and scraped through to his law degree although the courses drove him twice to seek rest cures. He had no interest in the subject. He had little talent for abstract thought; he could not, he said, "toss big words around like giant boulders." His only interest was in literature.

The real world would hardly permit such a career. His father, a selfmade businessman, hardly breathed the same moral air as his educated and literary son. A dominating and demanding figure, unable or unwilling to see in Franz's literary interests anything but a waste of time and a recipe for (economic) failure, and not tactful enough to disguise this contempt, the elder Kafka was destined to engage in a hopeless and mutually destructive struggle with his son. It was a classic scenario, repeated countless times in the modern world. Kafka's mother was not a strong enough person to rescue her son from the terrible Herrmann, who wanted Franz to manage an asbestos factory. The conflict between the world of his art and of his father almost tore Franz apart, and erupted in a "Letter to His Father," which he finally wrote at age thirty-six—a long and bitter indictment, rehashing incident after incident from childhood on. The irony is that Herrmann Kafka could not possibly have understood it; the mental and cultural gap between the introverted, sensitive artist-intellectual and the businessman employer was too great. One might note that the elder Kafka had known bitter poverty in his youth, something Franz never really experienced. Eventually Herrmann did try as best he knew how to be kind to his strange son, and Franz said some nice things about his father. But in the formative years they were like silent enemies. The two were condemned to live in the same house for most of Franz's life.

The father-son conflict was of course the major interest of another Jewish genius, Sigmund Freud, probably the most significant humanistic thinker of the generation just preceding Kafka's and well known to him. But Freud's postulate of a basic sexual jealousy revolving around the mother does not seem to apply in Kafka's case. The conflict was simply one of temperaments and life-styles. Kafka's generation marked the debut of the "intellectual" and the antisocial avant-garde artist, not indeed for the first time in European history—the young bohemians of the 1830s often sound remarkably like those of fifty or sixty years later—but with a new intensity. This esthetic revolt against the norms of a rationalized, materialistic, business-dominated civilization found its chief spokesman in the French Symbolist poets and in Friedrich Nietzsche, but its prophets were legion. It sent the educated youth of Europe into offbeat cafés to create a revolutionary art and literature. Kafka was by no means the only young person in this generation to rebel against the elders of the tribe, their morals and their manners, their values and their taste—most especially the last. It is a constant theme, from Edwardian England to revolutionary Russia.

Compared to this powerful "modernist" movement of the spirit, Kafka's family and even his Jewishness seem of less importance. But it is interesting that like another Jewish genius of about his age, Albert Einstein, whom Kafka probably met when Einstein was in Prague in 1911/12, Kafka attached himself closely to a sister. Indeed, he was fond of all three of his (younger) sisters, but especially of Ottla. With other women, to put it mildly, he was to have his problems.

As many testify, Franz Kafka could be a person of engaging appeal, radiating a high seriousness mixed with boyish charm that deeply impressed most people who knew him well. His uneasiness with people, especially with women, was a defense against something that "threatened his very existence." He felt overwhelmed and depersonalized in a crowd; he felt that fear of being objectified by the "other" that Jean-Paul Sartre was to describe so notably just a few years later. Above all he felt unable, as a different one, a writer, an intellectual, to participate in the common life of his time; yet he yearned to do so too. "What a fate!" Kafka thought, to be set apart, different. Like Thomas Mann's Tonio Kröger he longed for "the bliss of the commonplace." With the English poet A.E. Housman he could have pleaded

Grant me the ease that is granted so free,
The birthright of multitudes, give it to me,
That relish their victuals and rest on their bed
With flint in their bosom and guts in their head.

Kafka seldom relished his victuals, suffering digestive problems through many diets; he also suffered frequently from insomnia. His bosom was all too soft and his head was filled with gossamer not guts. He knew and resented this quality. There is a degree of self-hatred in many European intellectuals of Kafka's generation—one may find it, for example, in James Joyce. These intellectuals experienced a revulsion from morbid egoism even as they explored the frontiers of deep subjectivity. They both loathed and were fascinated by "decadence," the state of modern society marked by dissolution of social and spiritual unity. Their distaste for the everyday world of philistine vulgarity went along with real agony at being thus separated from a human community.

Kafka all his life labored under a sense of inferiority, disparaging himself, hiding his light, fearing sometimes even to publish his writings. This fundamental ego insecurity probably owed much to a lack of support from his parents. Self-hatred was involved: Franz Kafka partly despised his own weakly body, his incapacity for the real world. In this pattern of self-hatred his Jewishness perhaps played some part. The situation of Prague Jews was a complex one, and that of someone like Kafka, estranged from his own partly assimilated parents, even more so. We will consider this point later, in discussing the tragic intertwining of the Kafkas with Hitler's anti-Semitism.

Though often identified with the message that red tape is strangling mankind, Kafka became, ironically, a successful bureaucrat. Faced with family pressure for gainful employment he found a rather humble government post and, more surprisingly, moved up in the ranks of the Workmen's Accident Insurance Institute to Senior Secretary before ill-health forced his retirement in 1922. Highly esteemed by his colleagues, his work could be seen as reasonably important, concerned with reducing industrial accidents and, during World War I, helping disabled soldiers. He was something more than a cog in a pointless machine, monstrous though all bureaucracies in many ways are. It was not what Kafka wanted to do, which was of course to write, and he referred in February 1911 to "a horrible double life, from which madness probably offers the only way out." On one occasion he jeopardized his employment by bursting into uncontrollable laughter at some solemn ceremonial occasion in the office.

But since literary genius seldom is lucky enough to get its apprenticeship subsidized, a six-hour-a-day job with reasonable salary and security was not the worst fate for a fledgling writer. Kafka did manage to write, with time left over for an ample social life. The image of a painfully shy loner does not fare any better than that of a Kafka miserably caught in the toils of bureaucracy. His diaries and correspondence provide evidence that he went to plays and also films, missing none of these fascinating novelties; he attended lectures and discussion groups, dined with friends, went on holidays to an extent that seems at times almost frivolous. He was or could be a gregarious person. This activity included visits to brothels, evidently a fairly normal ritual of budding manhood in Prague as in other European cities.

No one, however, has ever suggested that Kafka's premature death at age forty was, like the great Russian poet Alexander Blok's about the same time, or Guy de Maupassant's, Oscar Wilde's, and so many others of this era, the result of syphilis. The disease of which Kafka fell ill was diagnosed in 1917 as tuberculosis of the lungs, later spreading to his larynx. Tuberculosis was the plague of the nineteenth century, thriving in decaying areas of big cities such as Kafka had lived in. It flared up during World War I with special virulence. It was thought to be spread by raw milk such as Kafka had drank in copious quantities. It flourished in weakened and run-down bodies. Kafka almost constantly suffered from headaches and insomnia, brought on by his nervous intensity and by overwork; "I have for years been asking for a major illness," he said. Many another intense writer suffered from TB; D.H. Lawrence and George Orwell, among his near contemporaries, were to die from it in their forties. Marcel Proust succumbed to asthma at fifty. A much stronger person physically than Kafka, Max Weber, died of overwork and influenza in 1920 at the age of fifty-six.

Kafka's vacillation between the real world and the literary one, between his alienation from human society and his yearning to be a part of it, found classic expression in his hopeless ambivalence toward marriage. The chief victim of this indecision was the daughter of a Berlin insurance agent, a perfectly normal young woman with a normal job. After she emerged from a scathing experience with Kafka, stretching over several years, during which he alternately proposed marriage and broke off the engagement, Felice Bauer married a Berlin banker and had a pleasant, normal marriage—except for the intervention of politics, which forced the family to flee to the United States in 1936. That she kept almost all his letters to her, numbering several hundred, was a priceless contribution to the world which she made without any thought of fame—she had no way of knowing that Kafka would become an immortal. He courted her chiefly by mail, a strange romance; they were awkward and embarrassed when they actually met.

Franz's yearning for companionship was as keen as his fear of a commitment to life. He wanted desperately in a way to join a community, to be as other men; yet when it came to it he could not face this awful surrender of his selfhood to conventionality, this desertion of the artist's lonely mission. He proposed marriage, then found reasons to back out: he was ill, he was impotent, he was a miserably incompetent creature. "Marriage, our union . . . will doom me . . . also my wife." Poor Felice waited patiently for her lover to grow up, but he never could. After breaking off the engagement in October 1913, Kafka met Felice later for a consummation, but a brief one. In July

1916 at Marienbad "we attained a human closeness such as I have never known. . . . " Again he planned marriage, after the war. The TB was a final excuse; he himself called it a weapon indispensable to him. When Felice finally gave up and married her businessman, Franz felt relief, though he was overcome with grief after their final meeting.

Kafka's letters to Felice are memorable simply as literature. Her letters to him did not survive. There is little indication that she shared much of his intellectual life, fine and good woman (and competent person) as she was. Felice's superb normality makes her a classic counterpoint to Franz's classic neurasthenia. D.H. Lawrence married, and fought with, an intellectual woman. Einstein's second wife was simply a caretaker. Kafka's Felice was neither; with an infallible instinct he chose a marvelous being from the "real" world, and then could not face the reality.

But despite all his protestations of inadequacy, Kafka knew quite an assortment of women. He may have fathered a child born to a friend of Felice's, Grete Bloch, in 1914; he never knew this and the child died at the age of seven. This was according to Grete's story, told much later, and some scholars question it. But in October 1913, Franz and Grete did meet and were attracted to each other. Kafka repeated the Felice scenario in miniature with a Prague girl, Julie Wohryzek, declaring his intention of marrying her, to his father's astonished rage (Julie's family didn't have much money) and then reversing himself to the accompaniment of a long and incredible letter to Julie's sister. This was in 1919.

Among other romances especially notable was one with Milena Jesenska. A free spirit, the attractive wife of a rather unappealing man, she understood Kafka deeply and played an important role in transmitting his manuscripts. The daughter of a professor of dentistry, Milena in her youth had rebelled against her own father and indeed did violent and spectacular battle with him; he once had her confined to a mental hospital, a scenario resembling that of Hans and Otto Gross. Not herself Jewish, Milena frequented the mainly Jewish intellectual and artistic circles of Prague and became a legendary figure of beauty and mystery among them. When she met Kafka she was married, albeit unhappily, and Franz was dying; their romance was not the less deep for being aborted, and he entrusted his diaries and some manuscripts to her. She is Frieda in *The Castle*. Translator of some of his stories into Czech, she was a talented writer herself.

Meanwhile, the Great War had come and gone, bringing with it the ruin of the Dual Monarchy. Rather astonishingly, as it appeared to a later generation, the writers and artists of Europe almost unanimously embraced the war, usually with enormous enthusiasm and idealism. Kafka certainly did not oppose it. He expressed a hope that he might be called to military service. That he did not serve is explained by the importance of his civilian war work at the Insurance Institute, which secured him an exemption, and later by the state of his health. Thus a part of him responded to the surge of solidarity feeling that the war brought, and which for many intellectuals was its most appealing feature.[2] On the other hand he did not participate in the often frenetic prowar rhetoric of the day, and in fact almost ignored the war in his diaries, letters, and other writings. He began *The Trial* in August 1914, but it is hard to see what relation it had to the war though a few have sought to discern a message. There is nothing in his diaries or letters that suggest any intention of making the novel a commentary on contemporary society. In general, his reaction to the war, which forced some changes in his living arrangements, was: "In spite of all this I am going to write, absolutely" (July 31, 1914). It rather reminds one of Virginia Woolf's annoyance with World War II for spoiling the reception of her latest novel.

Franz's tuberculosis was diagnosed in August 1917. It was not an automatic death sentence. Many people show evidence of having had the TB infection at some time without ever developing a serious problem. But 30 percent of deaths in Prague at that time were from TB. Kafka firmly believed he would never recover, even claimed to welcome the news: It saved him from marriage! This evident death wish was suspended as he spent eight happy months at the home of his sister, Ottla, resting and eating. But he then caught the influenza that was beginning its devastating spread through a war-ravaged world, destined to kill probably as many people as died on the battlefields. With this serious illness Kafka's recovery from tuberculosis, until then evidently going well, received a fatal setback.

He did return to work in the fall of 1918, just as the war was ending amid the breakup of the Austro-Hungarian Empire. As Czechoslovakia became independent, Kafka survived a purge of the old civil servants, but he quickly proved too sick to perform his duties. He sought rest in a Bohemian mountain village, Ottla now being away at school. She was about to marry a non-Jewish Czech of modest means, which sent the elder Kafka into another tantrum. All these convulsions, political and domestic, cannot have helped Franz's path of recovery.

But even more, he worked very hard at writing. Rest was supposed to be the best cure for TB, but Kafka under the threat of death intensified his literary activity. To his last years belong *The Castle* and a number of stories; he resumed work on *The Trial*, which he had laid aside, and on the book eventually published as *Amerika* (his title was *The Missing Person*, or *The Man Who Disappeared, Der Verschollene*). Nor did he entirely give up keeping the diary, which constitutes one of his chief literary achievements. He also engaged in the semi-romance with Milena Jesenska. Another attempt to return to his job in the summer of 1921 lasted only a month or so, and after that the path was steadily downward.

Kafka's last and best love came in the last year of his life, with Dora Dia-

---

[2]See Roland N. Stromberg, *Redemption by War: The Intellectuals and 1914* (Lawrence, Kansas: University of Kansas Press, 1982).

mant, an intense, deeply idealistic young Polish-Jewish girl who loved him totally and cared for him during his last painful illness—one of the century's most touching romances. She was nineteen when they met.

Milena Jesenska said that Kafka as a person was more astonishing than his works. His rather pathetic and foreshortened life ran its course to the accompaniment of a constant strain of self-depreciation; threats of suicide or hopes for death abound; few of his writings satisfied him, and he could not finish the longer of them (neither *The Trial* nor *The Castle* nor *Amerika* was ever completed). Despite that, Kafka was a vibrant person who left a deep impression on almost everyone who knew him, and who had a fairly wide circle of friends. In him spiritual greatness and intellectual clarity combined with absolute integrity, searching for truth without compromise, to create an effect some found almost Christ-like. There is much about his persona that reminds us of another German of Jewish background from Austria-Hungary, of about his same age, the philosopher Ludwig Wittgenstein. But their minds were utterly different; Kafka had absolutely no talent for mathematics or abstract science. His genius was for the human and the concrete.

KAFKA'S WRITINGS

In his lifetime Kafka published comparatively little. Between the two world wars James Joyce finished his two great novels, seeing the second into print a year before he died in the turmoil of World War II's beginning. In the 1930s *The Trial* and *The Castle* joined *Ulysses* as classic statements of the artist in a tormented world, but Kafka had been dead for some years. His novels did indeed appear in German within a couple of years of his death; he had loyal and dedicated friends who took charge of his literary remains. But unlike the instantly famous *Ulysses*, or T.S. Eliot's *Waste Land*, Kafka's masterpieces took several years to receive international recognition.

The Leipzig publisher Kurt Wolff took a keen interest in Kafka in his lifetime, printing some of his stories and fragments, even though as Wolff tells us, they sold very few copies. Kafka had been writing stories at least since 1903. His debut in print in 1908 was in one of those little magazines that dotted the early twentieth-century literary landscape, usually destined for a short life—this one called *Hyperion*. His first book, *Meditations*, was published in 1913. This was a memorable year in modern literature, with Joyce, D.H. Lawrence, and Marcel Proust debuting, but Kafka's little book, obscurely published in central Europe, cast a pale light compared to theirs. Kurt Wolff also published the first chapter of *Amerika*, called *The Stoker* (*Der Heizer*), in 1913, and in 1918, eighteen Kafka stories appeared under the title *A Country Doctor*.

Also printed in his lifetime, and the chief source of his reputation, was the best known of all Kafka stories, translated as *The Metamorphosis* (*Die Verwandlung*—"The Transformation" is a more exact rendering). In fact, Kafka himself thought it good, a rare case of self-approval. That it was an account of how poor Gregor Samsa, a minor bureaucrat, turned into an insect was significant. Published in 1915, a second edition in 1918 testified to its success, but it was the only one in Kafka's lifetime. As he lay dying in 1924 another collection of stories came out under the title of *A Hunger Artist*. Kafka never quite straightened out *The Trial* (*Der Prozess*: "The Action" or "The Legal Proceedings" would be a more exact translation than the customary one), leaving a problem for his editors to establish even the correct order of the chapters. Nor did he live to finish *The Castle*. He left behind also the so-called diaries, actually a litter of notes, and numerous letters preserved by his friends, which are still being edited.[3]

The Trial has become the most widely known of Kafka symbols. Several years ago an American nominated for a cabinet post and who was subjected to the usual inquisition by the U.S. Senate, and ultimately rejected, said that what happened to him was "Kafkaesque." He meant that he had been confronted with vague charges, with innuendoes and slanders. John Tower's problem was far less sinister than procedures in the totalitarian regimes of Hitler and Stalin, where the Gestapo and the GPU were beyond the law, able to arrest and execute without any sort of formal charges, just on suspicion, or because of guilt by association. Such brutal actions, which marked the years just after publication of Kafka's book, made him seem prophetic. But Josef K's problem in the novel *The Trial* was slightly different. He could not find out exactly what he was being charged with. He could not put his finger on an enemy that was everywhere and nowhere, a miasmic cloud of guilt and suspicion surrounding his every move, impossible to dispel.

The Trial has been construed in many ways—as the outcome of a personal crisis, as a religious-philosophical tract on human estrangement from God, as an anticipation of the totalitarian state, as a commentary on dehumanized mass-man. In some sense it is all of these; as the medieval philosophers knew, there are several levels of meaning in any work of art or thought. *The Trial* is a modern allegory whose meaning each of us is free to decide. What is beyond doubt is the compulsive readability of its clinically exact prose.

The same fascinating air of lucid bewilderment hangs over *The Castle*. The stranger who comes to the village thinks he has a confirmed appointment as surveyor, but he can never get through to the bigwigs in the castle just outside the village to verify his claim; indeed, he cannot even get to it—the roads turn and bend back, he loses his way. The villagers are sometimes less than friendly. Writing in 1944 Hannah Arendt thought the alien, the outsider, the pariah in *The Castle* was the Jew: "You are not of the castle, you are not of the

[3]Max Brod, invaluable though his labors were, left behind many problems for the Kafka editor by arbitrarily omitting some passages and arranging others according to his own notions of what Kafka meant. Particularly does this apply to the diaries; also to the order of chapters in *The Trial*.

village, you are nothing at all." More likely, however, Kafka meant the artist, the intellectual. In a deeper sense the anonymous K stood for all mankind, condemned to be estranged from itself, from God, from Being. All of these interpretations are possible. A bow to Max Weber: Certainly no one can miss the bureaucratic features of the impenetrable hierarchy that hands down its faceless edicts from the Castle. Some features remind us of Dickens' Circumlocution Office in *Little Dorrit*. But it could just as well be Heaven.

K's encounters with women in the village bear a fascinating resemblance to Kafka's in real life. In the end, the haunting question that runs through the novel concerns the individual's membership in a community. Increasingly, Kafka was preoccupied with community, including identity. (Who am I? is essentially what group do I belong to, who are my people, what is my place with them?). That is why he speaks so much for humanity in our century, when primordial ties of family and tribe have slowly dissolved into the impersonality and anomie of the Great Society.

Kafka's parables are often Aesopian, using animals as their characters (compare George Orwell's *Animal Farm*, perhaps influenced by Kafka). The beetle in *Metamorphosis* is not the only example. There is the remarkable account by an ape of how he managed to adapt to human society ("A Report to an Academy"), as well as "The Investigations of a Dog," and the ruminations of a fox in his burrow, among others. All of these, of course, are devices for saying something about human characteristics.

The last story that Kafka wrote was called "Josephine the Mouse-Singer." Josephine is very vain about her singing, thinking herself a great artist because all the mice come to hear her. What she doesn't know, fortunately for her vanity, is that the mice really think she is a terrible singer; they can hardly stand her. Why then do they come? Because they want to be together; they value the ceremony as a ritual. They like to "relax and stretch themselves in the great, warm bed of the community." Art is a social need, not an esthetic one. The moral would seem to bear closely on contemporary popular entertainments.

In most of these allegories there is an ominous note. It is the more so for not being quite identifiable. It is like the *angst* that Kierkegaard spoke of: a nameless dread that springs from the very nature of existence. Of what is Josef K accused, and who are his persecutors? What keeps K from establishing his secure identity and membership in the village? We do not quite know, yet the foe is remorseless and invincible. In "The Burrow" the animal who contemplates with satisfaction his intricate passageways and his ample stores of food hears the sound of some other animal, he thinks, burrowing nearby, and is panic-stricken.

There is a dreamlike quality about almost all of Kafka's stories. It is difficult to believe he did not get them from his dreams, unless, as seems possible, he was one of those rare people who dream waking, whose very life takes on the features of a dream, as Milena Jasenska's attempt to describe Kafka's "astonishing" personality seems to suggest. His characters act and talk in that bizarre yet strangely pseudo-rational way that people do in dreams. Situations of being lost and unable to find the way out, or of being haunted by some vague apprehension, are characteristic of many dreams. Another great novelist of the earlier twentieth century, James Joyce, also wrote his *magnum opus* in the form of a dream, though what came out in *Finnegans Wake* is very different from Kafka's literature. The purpose of using the dream form was to rekindle the dead imagination of a prosaic age by making contact with primeval symbols, a counterworld of the night and dark where we are nearer to the unconscious mind with its mythic images and archetypes. In dreams we rediscover the lost mentality of early humanity when words were magic and poetry was natural, before the rational and the useful drove religion and art into the margins of existence.

Or, we may explain the retreat to a dream world as flight from an intolerable real world. Of the Symbolist poets who flourished just before Kafka and Joyce and who strongly influenced them—Maeterlinck, Mallarmé, Hofmannsthal—it was said that they could neither accept nor transform reality. The utopian dreams of the socialists seemed to them boring as well as naive. And so they invented a wholly different world of the imagination. With Oscar Wilde they declared "reality" wholly boring, and suggested that nature would do better to imitate art. The classic gesture of the Symbolists, in Joris Huysmans' 1884 *Against the Grain (A Rebours)*, was withdrawal to a refuge of art after cutting all ties with the existing society.

The suggestion in "Josephine" is that Kafka would like, if he could, to have been a popular writer, appealing to everyone. It was not his fault that the times were out of joint. The strange thing is that so desperately maladjusted a writer did in the end become amazingly popular. Millions have read *The Trial* and *The Castle*. The man who turned into a bug is as well known as any character in literature. Films were made of *The Trial* and *The Castle*. *Metamorphosis* was transformed into a popular ballet.

Yet Kafka's major writings might never have survived but for the dedicated efforts of a few of his friends. Playing the role John Heming and Henry Condell performed for Shakespeare was above all Max Brod, an extraordinary personality who in addition to being the voluminous author of novels, plays, essays, criticism, and biographies was also a Zionist who sat in the Czech parliament. A tornado of energy despite a malformed body, Brod was distinguished above all by his selfless work in promoting the cause of other writers and musicians. His eighty-three books, many of them decidedly ephemeral, and his outgoing, genial personality stand in such contrast to the secretive and gnostic Kafka that their long and close friendship can only be explained as the attraction of opposites. In the end Brod earned most fame by writing Kafka's biography and becoming known as the man who saved Franz's writings from destruction. Brod's own autobiography, *Streitbares Leben (A Life in Conflict)*, never translated into English, is a memorable document of the first half of the twentieth century. He survived the Holocaust to die in Tel Aviv in 1968, much honored there.

"Chances are," writes Kafka's later biographer Ernst Pawel, "that without Brod the bulk of Kafka's work would have been lost to the Night and Fog that settled over his world." But Milena Jesenska also helped preserve Kafka's manuscripts as did Felice Bauer. The latter kept all his letters. In 1955, now widowed and ill in New York City, she reluctantly sold them to a publisher for $5,000. Some twenty years later when they were sold again the price had soared to many times that. The obscure Prague misfit had become a cult figure.

Kafka has kept his standing as one of the major figures in twentieth-century literature. Franz's enemies only added to his stature. Not only did the German Nazis condemn and burn his works, destroying those Kafka manuscripts the Gestapo was able to lay its hands on, but Stalin's Communists made him a symbol of the "formalism" it condemned, calling it "bourgeois decadence." The enormous irony of this appears when we think of how totally Kafka rejected "bourgeois" values if by that much-abused term one means the business-success outlook of his father, or the mechanical rationality of a society oriented toward economic efficiency at the expense of freedom and creativity.

Writing in the 1930s, Walter Benjamin declared that "Kafka's world . . . is the exact complement of his era which is preparing to do away with the inhabitants of this planet on a considerable scale." To many others in the troubled 1930s, Kafka had caught the flavor of a "nightmare world" of economic depression, fascism, communism, and the drift toward World War II; or perhaps people read this mood into his cryptic fables. Walter Benjamin could have had no idea of how many of earth's inhabitants would perish from Hitler's Holocaust, Stalin's terror, the immense battles and aerial blastings of 1940–1945. Kafka's writings seemed to expose the grotesque logic that made such things possible. Indeed, one of his stories, "In the Penal Colony," was about the sadistic yet impersonal torture of prisoners.

KAFKA AND JUDAISM

In these horrors the lives of Kafka's own kinfolk and friends came to be tragically involved. Numbers of them were to be fed into Hitler's gas chambers. As background for this incredible explosion of racial genocide, happening of course years after Kafka's death, a review of his relationship to Judaism is pertinent.

Kafka was estranged from the Judaism of his own people. He identified with German culture. Between Germans and Jews in Prague, both a minority in a sea of Czechs, there was evidently little animosity, though some nuances of social segregation. For the Western, "emancipated" Jew, represented by his own father, Kafka felt something like revulsion. At moments he could almost sound like Adolf Hitler: They all ought to be wiped out! "Sometimes I'd like to stuff them all into the drawer of my laundry-chest, wait a while, then open the drawer a little to see if they'd all been suffocated," he once wrote to Milena Jesenska. A people alienated from their inheritance, half-converted to European culture, they produced either sickly intellectuals or crude and materialistic businessmen, like Herrmann Kafka.

Hours spent in the synagogue in his youth bored Franz to death. As first-generation assimilates, Kafka's parents retained what his biographer Ernest Pawel calls "a tenuous and largely sentimental attachment" to Jewish religious tradition. But Franz Kafka was deeply interested in aspects of Judaism—not his own emancipated, semi-assimilated type, but Eastern European Judaism, quite different from Western European. He became keenly interested in the Yiddish theater, forming a personal friendship with some wandering players from Poland who were bizarre creatures in the eyes of Kafka's parents and probably most of his friends. Kafka's interest in this Judaism of the ghetto was a part of his search for community and for restored belief; as such it was a critique of the disintegrating, overly rationalized, and intellectualized urban capitalist society of his day—a viewpoint found widely among artists and intellectuals of his time.

Like Anne Frank later, Franz chose Eastern Judaism against his own family's assimilated, skeptical Western style, as a gesture of revolt, but also of hope for a regeneration of real community in which the intellectual could find a home. These Eastern European Jews were completely alien to Western ones such as Kafka's father, who regarded them with embarrassed disdain. They were poverty-stricken, strangely dressed, and clung to queer and ancient ways—but they had a culture, and they belonged to a living community. These were the people, of course, who were to supply Hitler with the vast majority of his Jewish victims. Brought up in Austria, Hitler encountered Eastern Jews in Vienna and, unlike Kafka, reacted violently against them.

Kafka was also somewhat attracted to Prague Zionism. As purveyed in the journal *Selbstwehr* and the Bar Kochba Society, this was an ideology of cultural Zionism; migration and a political Jewish state were not its goal but rather a spiritual renewal based on development of Jewish consciousness within the present political situation. The prophet of Prague Zionism was not Theodor Herzl but one Ahad Ha'am. It stemmed from a society formed in Prague in 1899 by Jewish students at Prague University, and it became a significant movement although Herzl's more dramatic Vienna-based Zionism eventually overshadowed it. Kafka's best friend, Max Brod, became attracted to Herzl's Zionism in 1909, and he attempted to draw Kafka into it, with little success at the time. But after 1915 Kafka showed more interest, and in his last year as he studied Hebrew with Dora Diamant, they planned to migrate to Palestine. He was strongly attracted by Hasidism, once traveling some distance to visit a rabbi prominent in this mystical and communitarian tradition.

He shared this interest with Martin Buber, subsequently a famous religious philosopher.

It has been argued that Kafka's alienation and identity doubts were the result of his conflicting attitudes toward his Jewishness. He had a sense of guilt for having rejected Judaism and adopted German culture. But the thesis has not convinced many; the reverse seems more plausible. That is, Kafka adopted the attitudes he did toward Judaism because of his alienated personality as an intellectual. He could not endure his father's religion because he could not endure the vulgarity of his father's culture. He turned toward the despised Judaism of the Warsaw ghetto because he needed a community he could tolerate.

Certainly there was anti-Semitism in Prague. Popular, highly irrational anti-Jewish outbursts occurred in 1899 and again in 1920; relics of the medieval pogrom, they featured mob attacks on Jewish stores. Kafka was virtually the only Jew in his government department, and he thought it all but impossible there would ever be another.

Adolf Hitler was born in Austria a few years after Kafka, his father a member of the same civil service Kafka worked for; Hitler imbibed his anti-Semitism from some Viennese ideologists of the era with whom Franz would have been familiar. Hitler's use of these ideas between 1941 and 1944 to murder several million Jews in the gas chambers of Auschwitz, Majdanek, Treblinka, Belzek and Sobibor nevertheless seemed beyond understanding; not even Western European Jews believed stories about extermination camps at first. Germany, where a comparatively tiny Jewish minority had been well assimilated, was an unlikely source of such genocidal anti-Semitism. The historian of the Holocaust, Raul Hilberg, remarks that while the Jews were prepared for pogroms, or sporadic acts of violence against them in the Slavic world, such as, for example, occurred in Prague and Hungary in 1920 and in Romania in 1941, "they were not prepared for the death blow from the nation of Goethe and Schiller that struck them in 1942 and 1943"—organized with German efficiency. Bureaucracy as much as ideological fanaticism was at work in this ghastly business. "Hitler was only one part of a complex, polycentric, governmental system which allowed policy impulses to start from many different origins and meant that Nazi policy and the Nazi government were far from being Hitler's personal creation," historian Alan Milward comments.

Kafka's three sisters perished in the Holocaust. Ottla, because she had married a Gentile, might have escaped but insisted upon being deported along with her sisters, formally divorcing her husband. The Kafka parents by then were dead.

Kafka's friend Milena Jesenska also perished in a prison camp. After Kafka's death her life had became increasingly tragic, with problems of health and drug addiction, but she partly recovered to speak out against the Nazis even after Hitler took control of Czechoslovakia following the surrender of the

Western powers to him at the Munich conference of October 1938. She sewed a yellow Star of David on her jacket in sympathy with the Jews persecuted by the Nazis, and she even helped some of them to escape. She soon found herself in Ravensbrück concentration camp where she became close friends with a German woman named Margarete Buber-Neumann, with whom she planned to write a book on the camps. But Jesenska died in the camp in 1944. Buber-Neumann survived to write a remarkable autobiography and a biography of Milena. Milena's daughter, Jana Cerna, also published a book about her mother.

FRANZ KAFKA AS A FIGURE OF THE TWENTIETH CENTURY

Kafka was one of a number of Jewish writers and intellectuals who, taken together, have almost dominated the Western mind in the twentieth century. A list of them could begin with Karl Marx,[4] move on to Sigmund Freud, Albert Einstein, and Ludwig Wittgenstein, and include creative artists such as, in addition to Kafka, Gustav Mahler, and (half-Jewish) Marcel Proust in France. The leading philosopher in France, Henri Bergson, had a Polish Jewish father. Significantly also, the lapsed Irish Catholic James Joyce made his Everyman hero of *Ulysses*, Leopold Bloom, a Jew; Bloom was perhaps modeled after the German Jew that Joyce had known in Trieste, who published under the name of Italo Svevo.

It must be noted immediately that all these figures were in some measure emancipated or alienated from their Jewish heritage; some were even converts to Christianity; others like Marx and Freud were totally secularized, quite without feeling for any religious position—they were scientific atheists or agnostics. After rejecting their own Western European Judaism, Einstein and Kafka eventually embraced Zionism, a movement emanating from the Jews of Eastern Europe that was a rebuke to the ideology of assimilation prevalent in Western Judaism ever since the Enlightenment. Modern thought has lain heavily under the influence of Jews seeking to escape from their Jewishness, one might say. In so doing they sublimated the Judaic tradition that treasured the pursuit of knowledge, extending it into non-Judaic directions. They created powerful fables for the modern secularized mind.

If Kafka can be placed among the intellectual Jewish group, he can also be seen as a modern intellectual, of whatever ethnic background—a recognizable and important community in the twentieth century. He was typical of this group in many ways. One might compare another great modern nov-

---

[4]Lenin and Stalin, who more than anyone else made Marx relevant to the twentieth century, were not Jewish. But the German Social Democrats were heavily so, as were the Russian Mensheviks and Leon Trotsky, prominent in the Russian Revolution. The neo-Marxist "critical theorists" of the celebrated Frankfurt School were chiefly Jews.

elist of Kafka's generation, Virginia Woolf. Woolf's powerful ability to create memorable literature, with vividly realized individuals engaged in situations fraught with meaning, was bought in great measure at the cost of an unsuccessful personal life. As John Halperin remarks,[5] she was "unable to organize a personal life outside of her study," and she cared less about real people than about the characters in her books. "The sensibility which was present in her writing was not present in her daily life." She suffered periodic nervous breakdowns and finally committed suicide. Like Kafka she was a voluminous and noted writer of letters and of a diary, which served largely as a substitute for direct personal relationships; she was not happy except when writing, making literature out of life. Her fascinating novels are usually poised somewhere tantalizingly between a dream world and the real world. In her case as in Kafka's, we do not find simply an unfitness for social life, owing to some basic personality defect or physical handicap. Virginia Woolf was a beautiful woman, as Kafka was a handsome man; she had many friends and in some ways lived an active social life. But the literary imagination possessed her so completely that she did not function effectively in "real" life.

This schizophrenic split between the inner mind and the outer world has been a feature of modern times. It gave rise to the masterpieces of modern art and literature, which astonished and sometimes shocked the post-1900 world. A general feature of this modernism was a rejection of conventional naturalism or realism, in which the artist tried mimetically to reproduce a real object in the external world. "Objects hinder our meaning," painters like Matisse and Kandinsky declared. "Away from the Thing, away from Matter!" cried Cubists and Expressionists, Acmeists and Supremacists, among a horde of revolutionary "movements" in art that sprang up just after the turn of the century. They wanted to express a subjective reality, representing spirit or some inherent form to be disengaged from its external appearance.

The Nazis feared and hated all these drastic experimentations in the arts because the Nazis rejected the whole process of modernization; in theory at least, they wanted to restore a primitive rural folk community. The irony is that modernist artists like Kafka and Joyce themselves wanted somehow to restore a community; but to most others they seemed strangely marginal figures.

The Communists, supposedly at the complete opposite end of the political spectrum from the Nazis or Fascists, also rejected artistic modernism. While the Nazis regarded the new art, music, and literature as communistic, the Communists said in effect that such art was Fascist. Neither side understood this artistic modernism. This was also true of the general public, who were bewildered and often outraged at pictures of things they couldn't identify, music that sounded strange, poetry that seemed incomprehensi-

---

[5]"Bloomsbury and Virginia Woolf, " *Dalhousie Review* (Autumn 1979). Virginia Stephen Woolf was not Jewish but married a Jew, the writer Leonard Woolf.

ble. It took a generation, at least, to domesticate most of the modernist classics.

Stalinism in the Soviet Union officially condemned and suppressed the new esthetic, branding as reactionary Kafka, Joyce, the modern painters and architects, even Einstein's physics, as we know. The only approved artistic expression was "socialist realism," in reality propaganda glorifying the great achievements of the workers' state in old-fashioned style. This line laid down by politicians for the compulsory guidance of artists increasingly became ridiculous but persisted even after the death of Stalin in 1953. During the Czechoslovakian protest of 1968 against Soviet repression, orthodox Communists declared that the source of this subversion lay in Kafka. The Czech opposition movement of 1963–1968 had made defense of Kafka a key issue. The veteran Hungarian Marxist Gyorgy Lukacs, who had once opposed Kafka and modernism, changed his mind after the Hungarian revolution of 1956. Observing the strange maneuvers of the Soviet bureaucrats, he said this proved Kafka was a realist after all!

Kafka in this way entered deeply, as a symbol, into the politics of Eastern European anticommunism in the dramatic events of 1956, 1968, and finally 1989 when Communist authority crumbled in country after country of Eastern Europe. In Czechoslovakia, headed after 1989 by one of his disciples, Franz Kafka was again honored as a national hero.

Franz Kafka's life, and his afterlife through the influence of his books, was deeply interwoven with the wars and massacres of this tragic era of history, but even more so with the psychic problems of sensitive people trying to live in a society organized around the production and consumption of material goods. His uncanny literary skill focused on the theme of dehumanization. In recent decades, the rates of suicide, mental illness, drug abuse, and crime among young people have reached alarming levels, testifying grimly to the human costs of social adjustment. There has been discussion of the "double bind" in which individuals are caught: Their consciousness enriched beyond anything previously known, they are free to choose from a bewildering number of options, but the economic system demands that they conform to a hyperspecialized, extremely complex organism—to be cogs in an immense machine. And this professional specialization invades even the realm of knowledge, which becomes fragmented into a horde of almost unrelated divisions and is treated like a commodity.

Those who have spoken to this condition in the twentieth century have been, more than anyone else, the great imaginative artists. It is a paradox that we keep our sanity by reading those great novelists and poets who trembled on the brink of insanity themselves, in their personal lives, but perhaps for that very reason were able to express lucidly and elegantly the important truths about the modern world. "In our world today, serious literature has taken the place of religion," as James Joyce's brother Stanislaus observed. Deserting a career in science for the novel, the Viennese writer Robert Musil pointed out that the novel can depict an inwardness that eludes science. Oscar Wilde put it more flippantly, as was his wont: Science cannot deal with the irrational, that is why it has no future. The intellect must deal in superficial things; the thing-in-itself yields only to the flashes of inspiration coming from prophet or poet. And in our age it has been through imaginative literature and art that these great truths, with the power to move us, have been revealed.

11

The Life and Crimes
of Adolf Hitler

THE YOUNG HITLER

It is a curiosity of history that Austrians Ludwig Wittgenstein and Adolf
Hitler were classmates in 1904 in a Linz grammar school. Both were distinctly
outsiders, maladjusted to their world at the turn of the century; but in other
respects they seem complete opposites. Wittgenstein went on to study aero-
nautical engineering and then logic, before becoming possibly the twentieth
century's greatest philosopher; his was an analytical brain of the highest
power. Yet he was always a driven person, an eccentric who never married
and had few friends; and there was something charismatic about the Wittgenstein personality that has made him along with Albert Einstein one of the legendary thinkers of modern times. This charisma he shared with Hitler, who
sought unsuccessfully to be an artist before embarking on the twentieth century's most extraordinary political career.

The Vienna Academy of Fine Arts turned down young Adolf's application for admission in 1907, surely in retrospect the most unfortunate academic decision in history, if more understandable than Bern University's rejection of Albert Einstein as a faculty member at about the same time. The son
of a middle-level Austrian government employee, Hitler really wanted to be
an architect. He daydreamed about redesigning his hometown of Linz; later
he would imagine building a new Berlin to be the capital of the world. But

he had had a miserable educational record, flunking out of one school after another. Wittgenstein's school performance, to be frank, was not a whole lot better.

Adolf Hitler's relationship with his father was comparable to that of Franz Kafka with his father, except that it was briefer. The elder Hitler died when Adolf was an adolescent, the only surviving child by his father's third and last wife; there was one surviving sister, in a family almost as decimated by infant deaths as Karl Marx's family. By all accounts Alois Hitler was a good citizen and bureaucrat whose cheerful, unimaginative Austrian peasant nature must have driven his moody offspring up the wall. The scenario is reminiscent of the Webers, though at a lower social level, as well as of the Kafkas, Marxes, and Mazzinis—the perennial battle of rebellious youth against complacent and manipulative adults. For Alois Hitler evidently would have liked his son, Adolf, to become a civil servant too, a fate that Adolf regarded as worse than death. Like the senior Kafka, Hitler's father had himself risen from considerable poverty. But, in his fifties when Adolf was born, he did not live long enough to have any epic battles with his wayward son.

Young Adolf was left to face adolescence without any guidance. For his mother also died, soon after the young man received the crushing news that his drawings, in the judgment of the Vienna Academy, were "unsatisfactory." With a small pension and a little inheritance money, he lived a marginal existence in Vienna, then possibly the most civilized city in Europe, until 1913. He moved into a home for men, in American terms somewhere between the YMCA and a "flophouse." He later recalled these years as the worst of his life, having only the redeeming virtue of testing his soul. He claimed that he suffered from hunger and cold. He worked at odd jobs and took to postcard painting, but most of the time he spent in idleness—visiting museums, reading, going to the opera (he was a Wagner addict). He tried many kinds of writing and drew up architectural plans. He raged against the world and developed paranoid feelings. He tried again to get admitted to the Vienna Academy and again failed. He had few friends. In brief, he followed the course of many a reasonably bright, socially not very adroit, undisciplined, unguided young man trying to find his way in the confusion of the modern world in a large city. We should not accept Hitler's own version and see him as a particularly extraordinary person.

More extraordinary was the harvest of ideas in this end-of-the-century era. Freud was making a name for himself in Vienna when Hitler was there, although there was evidently no contact between them. Socialism and Marxism flourished in Austria; Social Democrat Victor Adler is credited with inventing the May Day parade of the workers, perhaps a model for National Socialist pageantry later. Recent fashions in the arts appeared in Vienna at this time in the music of Mahler and Schönberg, the paintings of Klimt and Kokoschka, the architecture of Loos and Hoffman, the poetry and drama of

Hofmannsthal. Young Vienna gathered in its favorite cafés to talk and write and try to create an esthetic "movement," as young people were doing in other European cities at the time.

The university, where Freud received his M.D. degree and later taught, had a distinguished faculty in physics and philosophy, which were on the cutting edge of the new scientific revolution represented by Albert Einstein. One of the strongest influences on Einstein came from the philosopher and scientist Ernst Mach, associated in his later years with the University of Vienna. This hardly exhausts the list of exciting new ideas in *fin de siècle* Vienna. But young Adolf did not respond to this esoteric modernism. To many people this explosion of novelties and dissent was not comforting. The conservative temperament—found among all classes, not just the rich—reacted with hostility to cultural subversion. An important line of thought all through the nineteenth century located the source of modern humanity's disease in the destruction of order, the erosion of secure foundations of values, stemming from the French Revolution, urbanization, industrialism—perhaps even from modern scientific skepticism, the decline of religion, or the subjective individualism that Rousseau and Kant had introduced. Some associated this "degeneration" with the intermingling of cultures and "races."

Anti-Semitic thought could be found on the left as well as the right. A man of the left, the radical journalist Edouard Drumont, led an outcry against Jews in France during the celebrated *affaire Dreyfus*. The leading figure in Viennese anti-Semitism, and the idol of young Hitler, was the son of an industrial baron, virtually the Andrew Carnegie of Austria. But Georg von Schoenerer (1842–1921) turned against his father and attacked capitalism, becoming a militant spokesmen for the agrarian class; in terms of American politics at about this same time, he was a Populist, a sort of Austrian William Jennings Bryan. Though mutterings about Jewish financiers were not entirely absent from American Populism, Schoenerer added a great deal more of this to his ideological brew. In "international Jewish bankers" such as the Rothschilds he saw the "vampire that knocks at the narrow-windowed house of the German farmer." The other leading Viennese anti-Semite, who also influenced young Hitler, was Karl Lueger (1844–1910), briefly mayor of the city in the late 1890s. Lueger inveighed rhetorically against "financial cliques" and monopolies. This anti-Semitism of the left associated Jews with rich bankers and manipulative speculators. Lueger's Christian Social party owed something to the influence of the new pope, Leo XIII, who attacked greed and materialism in a famous 1891 encyclical, *De rerum novarum*.

There were always demagogues willing to play on anti-Jewish prejudices lurking in the popular mind, a relic of the Middle Ages. But anti-Semitism usually played only a small part in Austrian politics, and in fact after flaring up in the 1890s it receded after 1900. By later standards of the Nazis the Luegerites were moderate, their chief proposal being a limitation on Jewish immigration, on the model of the Chinese Exclusion Act passed in the United States.

Hitler's musical idol, the great Richard Wagner, had assailed Jewish cultural influence, which to him and other cultural anti-Semites was a symbol of the destruction of an organic culture by forces of social disintegration. The leading exponent of racialist theory around the turn of the century was a Wagner disciple, the Englishman Houston Stewart Chamberlain, who in search of a prophet had migrated to Wagner's shrine at Bayreuth and married Wagner's daughter. Chamberlain's widely read *Foundations of the Nineteenth Century* (1901) offered to some Germans a flattering portrait of themselves as the most creative people because they were the least racially corrupted, most nearly descended from the only creative race, the Aryans. This historical concoction can be traced back to the French aristocrat the Comte de Gobineau, "father of racist thought," who in the 1850s produced a huge tract on the inequality of races largely as a result of his dislike of the French Revolution. Gobineau in his old age also became a Wagnerian. In most of this racialist ideology, Jews figured as a cause and example of racial impurity, symptomizing a degenerate society of mixed races and cultures.

In the slums of Vienna lived many Jews who recently arrived from the East, strange people who fascinated Franz Kafka but clearly repelled Adolf Hitler. Three waves of Jewish migration came into Vienna during the nineteenth century, first from the Czech regions (Moravia, Bohemia), then from Hungary, and finally from Poland. The first was the most assimilated to German society and in fact produced many of the great figures of Viennese culture, among them Freud, Gustav Mahler, and Karl Kraus. The Polish immigrants were the least adapted to the dominant German culture, looking and acting to the Viennese like a strange race.

Stories circulated of a great Jewish plot to take over the world; the curious and fraudulent document *Protocols of the Elders of Zion*, originally written by a French author as a satire, migrated from Russia to Vienna. Of course, this mythical Jew became a scapegoat to serve as an excuse and explanation for other people's own failures and frustrations: The deck had been stacked by Jewish conspirators, the theory went.

Hitler absorbed a great deal of all this, dragging home loads of books from the public library as he pieced together what he would call his *Weltanschauung*, his worldview—an attempt to make sense of a puzzling world. Some of its elements came from more reputable sources than popular anti-Semitism. There was the legendary Friedrich Nietzsche, whose writings of the 1870s and 1880s reached a peak of influence in the first decade of the twentieth century; he appealed greatly to restless young rebels and artists. Hitler probably did not fully understand Nietzsche—who did?—but culled from his electrifying writings a sense of the West's degeneration, the need for heroic commitment and action to save it, the possibility of creating a new kind of humanity by "living dangerously." Perhaps most of the present contemptible human specimens would have to perish in order to produce a race of supermen, Nietzsche suggested. Hitler was to make Nietzsche the official philosopher of the Third Reich. He apparently did not realize that Nietzsche hated anti-Semitism as well as German nationalism.

HITLER AND THE WAR

Twenty-four-year-old Adolf Hitler moved to Munich in 1913, mainly, it seems, to escape military service in Austria. The Austrian authorities tracked him down in Munich and took him to Salzburg where he failed the physical examination, being pronounced "too weak to bear arms." Another reason for the move to Germany may have been Hitler's growing dislike of Vienna and Austria. Politically, he felt more at home in the Second Reich of Kaiser Wilhelm than in the polyglot, multinational empire of the last Hapsburg. Germany was the land of his idol Richard Wagner, as well as the home of Germanic nationalism. Yet significantly, Adolf did not go to Berlin but to the more relaxed Bavarian capital, where artists were welcomed and conversation along with beer flowed freely in the taverns. Hitler was still at heart a would-be bohemian.

The Great War of 1914–1918 was about to break out. Initially the war swept up everyone—left, right, center—in a mystical experience that can only be understood in religious and psychic terms. It was an in-gathering of the divided community that discovered a single common purpose—to defend the Fatherland, to defeat the foe. Many who later repented of their actions rallied to the flag with fervent patriotism in 1914. Socialists who had vowed never to fight a capitalist war flocked to bear arms. Alienated intellectuals saw in the war a cleansing fire or flood that would wash away corruptions and lead to an apocalyptic revolution.

Certainly Adolf Hitler was not one to resist this wave of communal emotion. "My heart, like that of a million others, overflowed with a proud joy," he wrote of the first days of the war. He promptly volunteered to serve in the Bavarian army. One reason for the war's popularity was that, as Hitler said, "In the army a corporation director was no more important than a dog barber." Military service was a great equalizer. It also resolved questions of identity and role in society; the goal was clear, duties were laid out, each man had his assigned function. But in addition, Hitler believed in the cause of German nationalism. And he had already learned the "crude Darwinism" that marked his political thinking: Life is a dog-eat-dog struggle, and the only rule is sink or swim. The better presumably survive. (Some deviant Darwinists had denied this, pointing out that the worst is what usually survives.) War seemed to Hitler the natural state of man, and he threw himself into it with a will.

He was by most accounts a brave soldier. But his superiors "could discover no leadership qualities" in the future Führer! He spent the war serving as a courier, impressing his fellow soldiers as something of a harmless lunatic. Nevertheless, he obviously gained in confidence during his time in the trenches. Wittgenstein, also a brave soldier, who also preferred to serve only as a private, sustained himself by reading Tolstoy's exposition of Christianity; Hitler said he read Homer and Schopenhauer as well as the Gospels. That both of them survived this bloody holocaust that cost Europe half its educated class was not due to cowardice. Hitler was decorated three times. His fellow soldiers regarded him as lucky. Wounded rather lightly in 1916, at war's end he was in the hospital as the result of being gassed. (The use of several kinds of poison gas was one of the war's many shocking creativities.)

The end of the war came as a shock to Hitler as it did to most Germans, and this experience probably influenced him—and them—more deeply than any other. Few Germans had realized they were so close to defeat, and few could easily accept the fact that they had been wholly defeated. German propaganda, which Hitler soon accused of terrible failures, had certainly not prepared the public for the collapse that came suddenly in the late summer of 1918. There was no taste of defeat via invasion; during the entire war German troops stood on enemy soil. Now suddenly the government was suing for peace, then accepting stern conditions for an armistice; the kaiser abdicated, and within months the Germans found themselves forced to accept what seemed a Carthaginian peace treaty, amid humiliations the victors inflicted on them. Meanwhile, a strange new government, a republic with a Social Democrat at its head, replaced the kaiser's regime; revolution broke out in a number of German cities, including Hitler's adopted hometown of Munich. The fatherless Hitler came back to a fatherless Germany. The kaiser had failed his people.

As soldiers returned home, confusion and chaos reigned. Hitler's lament, as subsequently recorded in his autobiographical *Mein Kampf*, found an echo in many hearts (not only in Germany): The war had all been futile. The years of hardship and heroism, the two million dead, the countless wounded—"it had all been in vain." Only a few years before, a powerful and prosperous Germany had dominated Europe. Now there was hunger and civil strife, as a defeated and leaderless people contended with bolshevism and mutiny. The future seemed bleak. It was tempting to look for a scapegoat, a great betrayal. Some of the revolutionaries took as their model Lenin's Russian Bolshevik Revolution of 1917. The tsar's abdication in Russia had opened the way for the Bolsheviks. Would this also be Germany's fate?

Hitler shared the confusion for a year after the November 1918 armistice; for a time after returning to Munich he evidently accepted the authority of the Communist regime temporarily in power there. He certainly had come to view the old government with disgust. He believed the kaiser's regime had failed on the moral front, losing the propaganda battle to the Allies. Then its strategic blunders had cost Germany victory. But he gradually formed the opinion that a crucial stab in the back had come from within Germany. It was a far-fetched theory, confusing cause and effect, for the abdication, the republic, the mutinies, the local leftist revolutions were all results of military defeat, not its cause. And, indeed, a subsequent extensive investigation into the famous naval mutiny at Kiel near the end of the war concluded that socialist agitation had very little to do with it.

But confused people were looking for scapegoats, and Hitler found one in his old obsession with the Jews. At this time he became an effective public speaker, by most accounts rather suddenly. At a political meeting one night, he intervened with an eloquence that impressed everyone, and soon after that, on October 16, 1919, he electrified a crowd of a little over a hundred people. He never afterward doubted his oratorical powers. Adolf Hitler's success as a speaker stemmed from his obvious sincerity, a consistent if simplistic set of ideas, and a command of language that on the printed page sounded bombastic and trite but in the charged atmosphere of a political meeting, attended largely by those basically sympathetic to his viewpoint, touched deep chords of response in his unsophisticated but concerned listeners. Enlivened with invective, his rhetoric was far from dull.

Hitler would never have found a political career in normal times, going through the usual boring channels; but he could fish in the troubled waters of postwar Germany, where the old order had fallen and everyone was groping for a new one. After a short time it became clear that the new order would not be Russian-style bolshevism; there was a general reaction against it. When returning "Free Corps" soldiers overthrew the soviet government that more or less ruled Munich for a few months in 1919, Hitler helped them. From the East came horrifying stories of the atrocities committed by Lenin's gang, often grotesquely exaggerated yet with a certain basis of fact as civil war raged in Russia with barbarities on both sides. The leading socialist revolutionary in Germany, Rosa Luxemburg, had rejected a Lenin-style revolution; yet Free Corps soldiers murdered her and fellow left-socialist Karl Liebknecht. With a fine impartiality they were also to assassinate (1922) the Jewish industrialist who had helped Kaiser Wilhelm's government try to win the war, the brilliant Walter Rathenau. Such mindless violence reflected the hysteria of a bewildered people.

During World War I soldiers found some compensation for the horrors of battle in a feeling of solidarity as they fought side by side and depended on each other. Hitler was not the only ex-soldier who missed this community of the battlefield, which was celebrated in postwar literature by writers such as Ernst Jünger. Hitler would name his political followers Storm Troopers, and organize his political party like an army. That meant absolute obedience to the leader. As the price of his heading the National Socialist party (NSDAP), Hitler demanded complete power to be the boss, with no party member allowed to question his decisions. The messenger lad of World War I was to fulfill his fantasies and become commander-in-chief. From the start the NSDAP was less a political party in the ordinary sense than a church organized like an army. "Our purpose must be to create not an army of politicians but an army of soldiers of the new philosophy," Hitler wrote.

THE RISE OF NATIONAL SOCIALISM

The little group of tavern-frequenters who adopted Hitler as their leader was only one of dozens of such gatherings of the malcontented in Munich after the war. Next door, Italy was already falling into the hands of a new movement, calling itself fascism, which stressed restoring order and regaining national strength by eliminating the weakening forces. The people must rally around a strong leader who embodies the national will and who acts ruthlessly to destroy the poisons that corrupt peoples. Benito Mussolini was less certain than Hitler than this poison was the Jew; Italian fascism displayed little anti-Semitism. But Hitler could agree with the Italian *Duce* that not only Marxism and class war but parliamentary democracy, a degenerate system crippling the government for decisive action, had to be purged from the body politic.

Parliamentary democracy had shallow roots in Germany. Before the war there was an elected Reichstag, but it had little power or prestige. By far the largest of the states comprising the German Empire, Prussia, did not even have a democratic suffrage. The 1918 constitution, associated with defeat as it was, lacked widespread acceptance. But dissatisfaction with parliamentary government in the 1920s was by no means confined to Germany. H.G. Wells called for a new class of samurai leaders; H.L. Mencken in the United States made fun of the boobs who elected corrupt members of Congress. Was this the way to a government by the best? Even before the war, the French writer Gustave Le Bon, whose work on crowd psychology deeply influenced Hitler, declared that parliamentary democracy had become a mortal danger; "the basest interests of the multitude" rule the elected representatives who dream only of reelection and do not consult the national interest. Such complaints against a system that, as George Bernard Shaw put it, substitutes government by the incompetent many for rule by the corrupt few were legion in the postwar years. The war, it is true, was thought to have been a victory for the democracies; France, Great Britain, the United States had stuck it out while the autocracies in the end collapsed. But Hitler thought this was because the former produced better leaders. All that mattered was the leadership principle.

Fascism had a democratic side. It was a response to the collapse of order and authority and integral community, which the masses felt as deeply as anyone, perhaps more so than the classes. Movements such as Mussolini's and Hitler's drew for the most part on "little people"; they emerged from outside the established channels; they were revolts of the losers and rebels. Much ink has been spilled on the question of just who the Nazis were, especially the early ones, the hard core of true believers who joined the movement before it became a success. The great German writer Thomas Mann said they were "truants from school," the natural bad boys. Konrad Heiden called them "the armed intellectuals." Attempts to fit Nazis into "class" categories often found them more "lower middle class" than anything else, yet in fact they came from all classes—surprisingly, in view of Nazi propaganda about the virtues of rural life, least from the ranks of farmers. Some Marxists tried to make them out to be capitalists, but this collides violently with an almost manic hostility to bankers and financiers in Nazi ideology. "Storm the banks! Set the money on fire! Hang the white and black Jews!" shrieked Nazi handouts. Early discussion topics were about how to eliminate "capitalism."

A study by Peter Merkl of 581 early Nazis found "a childhood of poverty and frustrated upward mobility in the city" to be a significant common denominator. Jean Baechler declared that all the early Nazis had "experienced a major setback that prevented them from realizing their life ambition." The little circle of pioneer members of the National Socialist German Workers Party (NSDAP in German), as Hitler's Nazi band titled itself early in 1920, included an engineer and amateur economist, a folklorist and poet, a would-be artist and writer, a pharmacist, an industrial chemist, and a machinist. Most were far from wealthy, though not desperately poor, but the ex-airplane fighter ace Hermann Goering had money. To attempt to generalize about such a group in terms of class, profession, status, or any other objective factor seems fruitless; what drew them together were common ideas and perhaps a similar temperament. A study of British fascists found they were brighter than the average person. They were undoubtedly more ornery.

But for a number of years the NSDAP met with little success. With a growing reputation as a rabble-rouser, Hitler could attract large crowds to his harangues; but actual Nazi party affiliation did not exceed a few thousand members by 1922. Then came the celebrated episode of Hitler's unsuccessful "Beer Hall Putsch." On the evening of November 8, 1923, at a meeting in Munich attended by leaders of the Bavarian government, Hitler with the help of General von Ludendorff attempted to seize the leaders and force them to join him in a march on Berlin, "that sinful Babylon," to overthrow the German Republic. The insurrection continued into the following day, but it failed ignominiously, and Hitler was arrested and later tried for high treason. He allegedly behaved with anything but high courage in the course of the skirmishing on November 9. True, with the aid of a friendly judge and prosecutor he turned the courtroom proceedings of February 1924, into something of a propaganda success. A great deal of sympathy for Hitler's position in Bavaria led to a general feeling that he was guilty of little more than an excess of patriotic zeal. He escaped the deportation he might have faced as an alien, and was sentenced to only a short prison term. But the Nazi party was banned, and with its leader in prison it was in danger of falling apart.

Worse for the Nazis, a period of grave postwar crisis, climaxed by the terrible inflation of 1922/23, ended in 1924 as the Weimar Republic began to show signs of stabilizing. With the aid of American loans, Germany ended the monstrous inflation, which had accompanied a quasi-renewal of war with France over German reparations payments, and began an economic rally that lasted for several years. The doomsayers and crisis-mongers looked foolish, temporarily. In the Reichstag at Berlin, Social Democrats, Catholic Centrists, and two small liberal parties joined together to form a coalition with a precarious majority. As president of the German Republic, former war leader von Hindenburg provided a stabilizing influence. The leading ministerial figure, the People's Party leader Gustav Stresemann, before his untimely death in 1929, presided over an able foreign policy that was based chiefly on reconciling Germany with her Western foes of World War I, namely France and Britain.

With a good deal of courage and persistence Hitler stuck with the cause, which had now become his life. The NSDAP had dug its roots in deeply enough to survive the drought. Funds, after 1923, even began to improve—whether the result of donations from wealthy patrons or a spreading network of small contributors has never been entirely clear. Nevertheless, Hitler's Nazi party—which was not the only one seeking to appropriate the "National Socialist" label—received very little national support. For one thing, it was marred by a certain southern German provincialism. "Hillbilly" would be a rough American equivalent; Dixie demagogues inveighing against blacks had something in common with Hitler's style. Most conservatives gave their votes to the more respectable German Nationalist party. In the 1928 elections Hitler's Nazis got 2.8 percent of the vote, winning 2.5 percent of the Reichstag seats.

While cooling his heels in Landsberg prison in 1924, Hitler had busied himself penning an account of his career, titled *Mein Kampf* (My Struggle), but this subsequently famous work did little then to enhance his reputation; it was verbose, poorly written, and seemed pompously conceited. Only after Hitler had become master of Germany did people look at it to judge how far Hitler had adhered to a master plan laid out at the start. Of course, millions of German students also had to read it then, though even its author admitted stylistic flaws. It did radiate the fanaticism of a true believer who would never deviate from the philosophy he had found. Along with the conviction that Jews and Bolsheviks were leading an assault on the foundations of order ran a persistent emphasis that life is a brutal struggle for survival, nature teaches that we must eat or be eaten, and in the last deadly fight that is at hand, victory will go to those with the strongest will. Germany could restore herself to health if only her masses willed it ardently enough. "Nature . . . confers the master's right on her favorite child, the strongest in courage and industry. . . . Mankind has grown great in eternal struggle, and only in eternal peace does it perish." Thus spoke Adolf Hitler.

Fascist movements appeared in countries other than Germany and Italy. The intellectual roots of fascism, it might be argued, were more French than anything else, considering the importance of Le Bon, Georges Sorel, Maurice Barrès, and Charles Maurras; Benito Mussolini found most of his doctrine there. In February 1934, French fascist groups sent 200,000 demonstrators into the streets of Paris to create a bloody affray hard to match in all that city's stormy history of revolutions. Belgian Rexists, Romanian Iron Guards, Spanish Falangists, the Austrian *Heimwehr*, and others featured ideas and symbols similar to Hitler's. They all rejected parliamentary democracy, waged war on communism, called for national unity under dictatorial rule, and organized militant paramilitary forces. Most of them were anti-Semitic, the Romanians violently so. But only in Germany and Italy did a fascist movement manage to seize and hold power.[1] More important, no other fascist movement as fanatical and brutal as Hitler's gained power; Mussolini's dictatorship in comparison with Hitler's was mild. Only Stalin's Russia witnessed as much bloody persecution.

HITLER'S TRIUMPH

Why did the Nazis succeed in winning control of a country often regarded as the best educated and most enlightened in Europe? For all their will power, Hitler and his followers might have languished to the end in obscurity had the Western world kept on its course toward international prosperity. The Great Depression, which hit Germany harder perhaps than any other country, began by breaking up the fragile Weimar coalition as the Social Democrats, whose clients were the trade unionist workers, refused to go along with cuts in the government budget that included unemployment benefits. With no combination of parties able to muster a parliamentary majority, a perpetual political crisis led to government by presidential decree under emergency powers. A natural tendency to blame all members of the coalition for the economic disaster helped the parties outside the coalition; the Communists increased their vote along with the Nazis. In the election of September 1930, Hitler's party shot all the way up to 18 percent, as the Communists gained 13 percent of the vote. Nearly two years later, another election found a startling 37 percent of Germans voting for the Nazis, an almost unprecedented increase that made the Hitlerites easily the largest single political party in Germany.

Analysis of the vote reveals that the Nazis took ballots from all the other parties except the Communists and the Catholics, and probably profited from many new voters drawn into the process (in July 1932, 84 percent of those eligible to vote did so). Except for the Catholic (*Zentrum*) party, the middle was virtually wiped out, while more than half of the old conservative party, the DNP, deserted to Hitler. But he obviously also stole some working-class votes from the Social Democrats. Losing 8 to 9 percent of the electorate between

---

[1]The frequent description of General Francisco Franco's Spain as "fascist" is an error; Franco suppressed the small Falangist group and ruled as a military dictator of a traditional sort; to call every nondemocratic government "fascist" is confused thinking. Franco's government was not anti-Semitic. To be sure, neither was Mussolini's.

1928 and 1932, the Social Democrats evidently gave only about half of these to the Communists. The Nazis at this time pretended to be socialistic.

A great deal of evidence indicates that most of those who voted for Hitler knew or cared little about his ideology but were registering a protest against the mainstream parties or against the entire parliamentary system, a system that seemed to have failed so badly. Hitler's talent for publicity had given him a good deal of national exposure by this time. The Nazi leader, who soaked up ideas from so many sources, acknowledged a debt to American advertising as well as to grand opera. Yet the first of the great Nazi party rallies at Nuremberg, which became famous for their elaborate pageantry, did not occur until after the party had begun its upward ascent, and hence was able to attract money from wealthy donors. Earlier, in 1926, a rally in Weimar at which Hitler wore his leather-belted raincoat and army boots, while saluting his uniformed followers in the manner of Mussolini, impressed most observers as a dreary affair.

Doctrinal disputes among the Nazi leadership, especially between Hitler and the brothers Strasser, who stood closer to orthodox socialism, had at times troubled the party. But in this crisis, of a sort that typically occurs in growing political movements, Hitler showed unexpected political skill and secured a reaffirmation of his absolute control. By 1929, just in time for the Great Depression, Hitler had solidified his little band and stamped it with an unmistakeable quality of zeal and color. One of his tactics was the creation of an army of streetfighters who baited the Communists into violent confrontations in Berlin. The Nazis in some ways resembled the youth gangs of a later epoch.

Their very vagueness on specific issues could be an advantage. "Those to whom Nazism chiefly appealed were people with a strong but directionless craving for morality," Hitler's biographer Joachim Fest remarks. We are familiar with the "down with all the politicians" mood that occasionally strikes the public today. Democratic politics with its inevitable compromises and evasions as well as occasional corruption can often induce such a reaction. The mood usually passes, and organizations based on angry "get rid of them all" feelings prove ephemeral. But the yearning for "one still strong man in a blatant land" (Tennyson), a wise and pure Leader above the disgraceful factions, has appeared intermittently in all modern democratic states. Hitler established his party as the representative par excellence of this position—not just another political faction but a foe on principle of the entire system.

The fact remains that the Nazis had become easily the largest party in Germany, and under the normal rules of democratic politics could not be excluded from a role in government. What is perhaps most surprising is that Hitler proved a skillful politician as he maneuvered his party into the government and exploited all his enemies' weaknesses. The thundering orator and prophet who liked to compare himself to Martin Luther became a shrewd Machiavellian schemer. Somewhere along the line, perhaps in dealing with intraparty disputes among the temperamental Nazi hierarchy, Hitler had picked up the art of wily manipulation. Of course he had the advantage of being absolutely unscrupulous. In waging war on the hated system he respected no moral restraints about lying and deceiving and if necessary killing; as much as the Communists, from whom tactically and organizationally he claimed to have learned much, he believed that the end justifies any means.

After long negotiations failed to break the parliamentary deadlock, so did another election, though the Nazi vote declined slightly. Hitler then took the chancellorship with a mainly non-Nazi cabinet on January 30, 1933. The other politicians thought the realities of power would tame Hitler. They had mistaken their man. Hitler forced fresh elections while stepping up the Brown Shirts' terror attacks on rivals. Someone set fire to the Reichstag on February 27; Hitler accused the Communists and persuaded aging President Hindenburg, not heretofore an admirer of his, to suspend normal civil liberties. It was the last of a series of blunders by Hitler's opponents. The evidence suggests that the Nazis themselves set the fire while contriving to pin it on a Dutch Communist.

Conducted in an atmosphere of intimidation, the new election (March 5, 1933) yielded 44 percent of the vote for the Nazis, 25 points better than their nearest rival. To make things easier for Hitler, the Communists blundered by refusing to join a coalition in the Reichstag against the Nazis, thus helping to bring down the German Republic. Hitler then persuaded Nationalists and Centrists to join the Nazis in voting to outlaw the Communist party; next came an Enabling Act, supported by everyone except the Social Democrats, that granted dictatorial powers to Hitler's government for four years. He had thoroughly outwitted his foes and now had his hands firmly on the machinery of power. It had all been done in a way that was technically legal.

In itself this may not have been so extraordinary. The times were not ordinary. (At about this same date, the American Congress granted unprecedented emergency powers to the newly elected president, Franklin D. Roosevelt, to deal with the devastating economic crisis.) Hitler had shown a capacity to change, people thought, and perhaps he would grow into his role as a true national leader. Unfortunately, there were some ways in which he never changed. He adhered with incredible rigidity to the set of simple dogmas he had held to ever since adolescence. These included a determination to do away with the liberal, democratic state and substitute for it a "racial community" led by one party and one man, with no place for minorities or dissent: *ein Reich, ein Volk, ein Führer!*

HITLER PREPARES FOR WAR

In Hitler's mind foreign policy was only an aspect of his domestic policy, that is, of the total revolution in values his worldview demanded. His withdrawal of Germany from the League of Nations in 1933, approved by a huge majority of Germans in a subsequent plebescite, was a nose-thumbing gesture at the arrogant victors of World War I, and also a rejection of the entire "world of opinions" that the League of Nations represented: pacifism, democracy, internationalism. Likewise, it signaled a German intention to break the "fetters of Versailles" and rearm.

In the next half dozen years as Hitler successfully defied the Versailles system by rearming, marching troops into the supposedly demilitarized Rhineland, absorbing Austria, and then dismembering Czechoslovakia, one of the successor states created in 1919, he drew on a good deal of sneaking sympathy in the Western democracies. Their leading lights partly accepted Hitler's claim that the Versailles treaty had been unjust, and the entire 1919 peace settlement indefensible. British Prime Minister Neville Chamberlain argued in defense of his surrender to Hitler's demands that these could be justified "on account of racial affinity or of just claims." In any case these Depression-harried countries did not feel like going to war. The United States had reverted to "isolationism," wishing to have little to do with the politics of the Old World. Moreover, the World War I alliance of France and Britain with Russia no longer existed. Relations between the Soviet Union and the Western democracies vacillated between hostile and suspicious; Russian policy had tended to see the "Versailles powers" as the USSR's worst enemy, and the attempted shift after 1934 to a "popular front" with them against Nazi Germany struggled against deep mutual suspicions. At the beginning of World War II Hitler was to pull off his greatest coup by making a pact with Stalin.

Hitler assumed that Germany must expand or die. Had she not lost World War I when she had even more than her present territory? This expansion, he thought, must direct itself to the east, breaking with "the colonial and commercial policy of the prewar period" and instead securing a great land empire. Here the geopolitical ideas of Professor Karl Haushofer, derived in part from the British geographer Halford Mackinder, taught Hitler to find the key to world power in control of the Eurasian heartland. This agreed nicely with his anticommunist, anti-Semitic, and racialist ideas: The Jewish Bolsheviks in Russia ruled over Slavic "submen," who could rightly be exterminated or enslaved to make way for the superior Germans. For in the ruthless struggle for world domination that is the key to history, "might makes right." Hitler said in 1934, "I have a right to remove millions of an inferior race that breeds like vermin."

If his ultimate goal was always an invasion of Russia, Hitler first found easier targets, which would strengthen Germany's position. After absorbing Austria, he used the presence of a German minority in the new state of Czechoslovakia, formerly part of Austria-Hungary, as a reason to make demands on that country, which then found itself deserted by its supposed allies, Great Britain and France. At the celebrated Munich conference of September 1938 (actually the last of three international meetings at which Hitler confronted the British and French leaders), Western leaders allowed Hitler to dismember Czechoslovakia. Yet rather illogically the democratic leaders reversed themselves when Hitler, confident they would not act ("I have seen these miserable worms at Munich"), turned next to Poland, demanding the return of German territory ceded to that country in 1919. It had dawned on them that they were confronting more a power-crazed maniac than a normal statesman, and that he would soon have too much power. "Is this not, in fact, a step in the direction of an attempt to dominate the world by force?" Chamberlain now wondered. In a belated effort to slow Hitler's drive, the British prime minister joined with France in guaranteeing Poland's independence (March 1939).

But no defense of Poland against Germany was possible without Soviet Russian help. On August 23, 1939, Hitler signed a pact with his mortal enemy, the USSR, a protocol of which granted Germany a free hand in most of Poland in return for Soviet control of the Baltic states. Hitler ordered preparations for a military campaign against Poland the day the Nazi-Soviet pact was signed. (The Russians soon moved into Poland from the east to claim their share of the unfortunate country, which became partitioned for the fourth time since 1772.) Stalin was buying time, and Hitler was positioning himself to attack Russia later. For the moment, the spectacle of Communists and Nazis clasping hands astonished the world. But people did not have long to relish the irony; on September 1, 1939, German troops crossed the Polish frontier, thus beginning the greatest war in history—a war that opened with spectacular successes for Hitler's armies but would end almost six years later with his defeat and death, after the death of tens of millions of others.

In London a restive British Parliament repudiated Neville Chamberlain's "appeasement" and demanded an ultimatum to Hitler to call back his troops or face war with Britain. France followed this lead. But there was nothing France and Britain could do to help the Poles, except launch an offensive against Germany from the west, and this they were unprepared to do. They declared war on Germany, but the Germans quickly overran Poland, and the war lapsed until the following spring, when Hitler unleashed his panzer divisions against France and the Low Countries.

HITLER'S PERSONALITY

In a way Hitler had no private life. He had no real friends. At the Nuremberg trials, Albert Speer testified that "if Hitler had had a friend, I would have been it." Joseph Goebbels' wife, who surely knew Hitler if anyone did—she died with him in Hitler's Berlin bunker—said, "In a sense Hitler is simply not human." He had sublimated everything to the Cause, the Movement, the Party, the Fatherland, making himself completely a public not a private personality.

He endlessly rehearsed his speeches and the effects that went with them, the costumery and choreography, cultivating his "image." Extremely theatrical, Hitler saw all this as a drama, with himself in the leading part. For the rest, he surrounded himself with individuals at whom he talked but to whom he did not listen. They were simply his audience, his props. There were no conversations with Hitler, only scenes. As chief of state he issued orders to subordinates who were functions, not persons. Hitler was instinctively aware that a leader must stand apart. In the words of Charles de Gaulle, "A leader of this quality is inevitably aloof, for there can be no authority without prestige, nor prestige unless he keeps his distance."

Hitler was capable of being tender and charming, and many women were strongly attracted to him. We may be reasonably sure that all the fashionable ladies who claimed to have had an affair with the Führer were not telling the truth, yet an impressive number of verified cases remain. These conquests were not all made after he had become powerful. Evidently a good part of the Nazi party's income in the early days in Munich came from rich women who donated their jewelry or art after falling under Hitler's spell. There were a number of cases of women committing suicide, or attempting it, because of Hitler; these included his niece, Geli Raubal, who was his mistress for several years; Eva Braun, who attempted suicide at least twice; there were attempts at suicide apparently by Unity Mitford, of a celebrated English literary family, and by Martha Dodd, daughter of the anti-Nazi American ambassador at Berlin. There were others as well.

This in spite of—or because of?—the fact that Hitler held women in low regard. As Eva Braun complained, "He needs me only for certain purposes." Yet Eva stayed with him the last decade of his life and he married her just before their joint suicide at the end of the war—perhaps another theatrical gesture on his part. It is clear that Hitler never gave himself fully to women, which was the reason for their frustration; he simply made use of them. He did have quite an active heterosexual interest in beautiful women. He was not a homosexual, though it is possible to suspect a slight ambivalence; he did not number homosexuals among his objects of persecution and hate, like Jews, Communists, Americans, modern art, etc., as much as one might have expected in view of his animus against all "decadent" phenomena. After coming to power, in 1934 he wiped out the SA (*Sturmabteilung*, a quasi-military arm of the Party) followers of Captain Ernst Röhm, notable for their homosexuality, but this was primarily because they represented a rival source of power within the Nazi party. Some homosexuals remained in Hitler's service and his good graces.

Hitler exercised virtually a hypnotic effect on almost everyone who stayed with him. Even quite sophisticated foreign witnesses were deeply impressed with the pageantry of the famous party rallies at Nuremberg, which rivaled Hollywood or the Ballet Russe. All this, of course, was part of a personality notable for its rigidity; once Hitler had created his worldview and established the agency for carrying it out, he never deviated from his goal. The politicians we are familiar with in a pluralistic society adapt with the times and issues, sometimes to a degree that leads to charges of cynicism, opportunism, or corruption, but which if they are successful marks them as truly creative—that is, able to respond to the challenge of changed conditions. Hitler never changed.

Hitler had some qualities normally thought of as praiseworthy. He had genius, which he devoted quite selflessly to the cause of rebuilding and reviving the morale of his country after defeat in war. No one ever questioned his motives; he was neither corrupt nor self-serving in any personal sense. In two wars, one as private and one as commander-in-chief, he fought with courage, tenacity, and considerable ability. Likewise with great energy, sleeping only a few hours each night during his last years, he ruined his health by taking drugs to keep him going.

For a time as leader of a revived Germany, Hitler attained a popularity probably not equaled by any national leader in Europe in this century. Up to that point, his career conformed closely to the classic hero story. But instead of a final triumph Hitler faced a ghastly final failure. In the end he committed an enormous evil, undoubtedly the greatest evil in European history.

Until near the end, Hitler's celebrated luck continued. A number of assassination attempts just missed him, the most notable one being that of July 20, 1944, when a bomb in a briefcase under a table at his East Prussian headquarters exploded, killing several people but managing only to wound the *Führer* slightly—a miscarriage that condemned Germany to almost another year of hideous and futile struggle. Earlier a bomb placed on his plane failed to explode, another went off prematurely, while abrupt cancellation of a visit to a Berlin arsenal foiled another plot. In his Berlin bunker at the end of the war, as Russian troops bombarded the city, Hitler kept waiting for another miracle to save him, but this time it did not occur.

We do not have space here to tell the epic story of World War II. It was much larger than Hitler; he cannot have had any idea when he began it with a quick overrunning of Poland that it would spread over the entire globe and encompass changes too vast to be described. In it he showed both brilliance and committed some frightful errors. In the beginning he had the insight to back those young German officers who favored a new way of using tanks and motorized vehicles and planes in a war of rapid movement (*Blitzkrieg*), tactics that worked with spectacular success in the stunning defeat of France within six weeks in May–June 1940. But Hitler misread Britain, which he thought would make peace and join him in the crusade against the Soviet Union. He misread the United States, doubting its will to fight. In the air battle of Britain he and Hermann Goering appeared to misunderstand the new device of radar, which enabled the British to intercept the bombers. In the air war the Germans had inferior fighter planes as well as bombers. Meanwhile, the Allies had deciphered the German code, and throughout the war were able to read German military messages; the Nazis never seemed to have caught on to this. Along with the superior Allied intelligence system this proved a decisive factor in most of the great engagements of the war. German intelligence was riddled with incompetence and treason.

The Germans also lost the race for a superbomb; in the last year of the conflict they launched some V-2 rockets at London, but these weapons that Hitler counted on to win the war did relatively little damage, whereas the much more devastating atomic bomb, soon to be completed in the United States, lagged far behind in Germany. The Germans made Allied bombers pay heavily for their attacks on German cities but could not prevent widespread damage. Meanwhile, Hitler's massive invasion of Russia, the mightiest battle in all history, had gone wrong after brilliant initial successes with the panzer type of offense. Here Hitler's inflexibility proved fatal. Taking over personal command of the armed forces he insisted on grandiose plans for total conquest and refused to draw back to more defensible lines even after he lost an army at the great battle of Stalingrad far inside the Russian interior. The pattern was repeated in the Italian campaign, and of course in the defiant rejection of all surrender terms at the end—though to be sure the Allies made this decision easier by in effect offering no terms, demanding "unconditional surrender." Hitler was incapable of compromise and adaptability in war as well as in politics.

The Holocaust or mass extermination of European Jews, the most hideously evil of all Hitler's actions, was related to his stubbornness and rigidity. He had never deviated from his youthful conviction that the world's chief evil was Judaism. In 1939 he warned that if war came it would lead to "the annihilation of the Jewish race in Europe." It is true that he allowed German Jews to escape, for a price, and toyed with ideas of resettling the Jews in Madagascar, off the coast of Africa. But the fateful "Final Solution" of mass killings of Jews evidently sprang from Hitler, although the actual order has never been found. (A directive from Goering to SD head Reinhard Tristan Heydrich on July 31, 1941, is the first extant authorization.)[2] Hitler probably did not want to know the frightful details, and did not want himself personally identified with the monstrous action. It has been thought curious that in his voluminous private conversations, which were abundantly preserved, he never mentioned the Final Solution. While some have tried to blame the extermination of the Jews on Heinrich Himmler, the fact that Hitler vetoed biological warfare when Himmler wanted to use it clearly indicates that Hitler could have done the same to the Final Solution had he wished to.

---

[2]A man after Hitler's own heart, Heydrich was the son of an operatic family and bore a Wagnerian middle name. A handsome naval officer who excelled in languages, music, aviation, fencing—an extraordinary personality, in many ways the arch-Nazi—he became head of the party's secret intelligence organization, the *Sicherheitdienst* (Security Service). Heydrich was such an effective intelligence chief, in an area where most of Hitler's officials did not shine, that British Intelligence conspired to have him assassinated in Czechoslovakia. In retaliation the Germans wiped out the entire Czech village of Lidice, which had sheltered the assassins.

Yet the Gestapo and the SS (elite Nazi troops) pursued Jews all over Europe, where there were few and where there were many, as in the Warsaw ghetto. For a considerable time no one, not even Jewish leaders in the West, would believe the stories about murder camps where Jews were systematically exterminated. The whole gruesome truth was not fully appreciated until well into 1944, at least publicly. Beginning after the war and extending to the present, a huge controversy over whether the Allies might have done more to halt or slow the Holocaust has not reached a definitive conclusion. Would it have helped, or was it possible, to bomb the extermination camps? Probably not.

So the world was finally left with only the memory of a hysterical little man who had managed, with the aid of much stupidity and cowardice among his enemies, to convulse the world for five years and cause the death of millions of people. The consequences lived on to shape the contours of world history for decades. The total defeat, destruction, and invasion of Germany brought about a situation conducive to the Cold War as Soviet and Western powers competed to fill the vacuum. Shaken to the roots of their being, the small remnants of European Jewry fled the Continent to establish their own state in Palestine, with momentous consequences.

As for Hitler, he lived on in the public imagination. Myths about his survival flourished for decades, despite overwhelming evidence that he and Eva Braun committed suicide in Hitler's bunker in Berlin on April 30, 1945. Apart from the vast body of scholarship about his regime and the war, there are numerous books about Hitler that can only be described as demonological. Some of them attribute to him occult qualities. Although a small minority admired him, for the overwhelming majority of people Hitler became the incarnation of pure evil. Hitler had projected onto a mythical Jew the satanic forces of evil in the world. Now he himself became such a figure for the twentieth century, and beyond.

There have always been controversies among historians about Hitler, including one about the degree of his responsibility for causing World War II, also about his place in German history: Was he an unaccountable aberration or a logical end product? More recently, the chief debate has focused on the Holocaust, with a tendency to see it as more complex than simply Hitler's will. In 1986 the prominent German philosopher Jürgen Habermas accused several leading historians of modern Germany, including Ernst Nolte, Klaus Hildebrand, Andreas Hillgruber, and Michel Stürmer, of being soft on nazism and the Holocaust, playing down Hitler's crimes. They denied this. What they had really done was intimate that others also were guilty.

It is indeed ironic that many of the people who strenuously declared Hitler's nazism to be the greatest evil in human history enthusiastically supported Stalin's communism, which was guilty probably of an even greater number of deaths by execution, torture, and lethal imprisonment, running certainly into many millions. At the end of the war the democracies, Great

Britain and the United States, forcibly returned two million people to face certain death at Stalin's hands; these were in many cases only refugees, not enemies of the Soviet regime, whom the tide of war had left stranded in Europe. (The Nazis had taken millions of people out of Russia to work as slave laborers in Germany.)

On this view Hitler rather than being the unique case might take his place in a long list of horrors perpetrated in the twentieth century. Cambodia's Pol Pot committed genocide against his people on a scale almost comparable to the Nazi Holocaust in numbers, and yet he survived to be treated as a respectable politician. Other cases of genocide could be cited—more recently the "ethnic cleansing" in Bosnia, Iraq's effort to destroy the Kurds, tribal massacres in Rwanda-Burundi in Africa, and the extermination of native peoples in New Guinea and Brazil. The melancholy fact may be that Hitler's evil survives intact in some elements of the human race.

12

Anthony Blunt
and
the Cambridge Moles

SPIALLS AND MOLES

Human history, unfortunately, is filled with cases of deceit and treachery. Rulers since time immemorial have spied not only on enemy states but on their own people.[1] They have tried to subvert their foes both internal and external by penetrating their organizations, or misleading them with false information. In turn, revolutionary organizations tried to do the same thing to their enemy—the established order. In his history of the reign of Henry VII, Shakespeare's contemporary Francis Bacon noted that the king employed "spialls" both at home and abroad "to discover what practices and conspiracies were against him. . . . He had such Moles perpetually working and casting to undermine him." Someone writing about the group of Soviet agents en-

---

[1]According to *The Oxford History of India* (3rd ed., 1958, p. 112), in the ancient Mauryan kingdom "the king employed hosts of spies or detectives, masquerading in disguises of all kinds, who were controlled by an espionage bureau. Cipher writing was used. . . . The doctrine of the necessity for constant espionage in every branch of the administration pervades the whole of the *Arthasastra* [widely used Indian treatise on statecraft], which treats every form of villainy as legitimate when employed in the business of the state."

We might add, referring to our Shakespeare chapter, that an important factor in the defeat of the Spanish Armada in 1588 was information obtained from spies. If not Will himself, his ill-fated friend and fellow dramatist Christopher Marlowe evidently was employed as a government spy.

listed from among Britain's elite young men at Cambridge University in the 1930s picked up the term "mole" and applied it to them.

In May 1951, on a Friday evening, two veteran, highly placed British intelligence officers, Guy Burgess and Donald Maclean, drove to Southampton from Maclean's home in the south London suburbs and from there took a boat across the English Channel to St. Malo, France. Though Maclean was now under surveillance, and the Southampton immigration officer picked this up from Maclean's passport and relayed the information back to MI5 (British Intelligence) headquarters, the French police did not receive an alert for forty-eight hours, time enough for the fugitives to get through to Czechoslovakia from where they were taken to the Soviet Union.

The two spies had been passing on important information to the Soviets for some years, doing considerable damage to Anglo-American Cold War projects. News of their flight did not leak out for some days but then hit the headlines with an enormous impact. Nothing quite like this had happened before in British history. Ensuing inquiries and polemics about the flight of Burgess and Maclean, and that of their cohort "Kim" Philby twelve years later, strongly suggested that British authorities were lax, perhaps deliberately so; they had preferred to let the spies go quietly rather than arrest and try them at the cost of much scandal. They were, after all, as Cambridge graduates, members of the tightly in-bred British ruling class—personal friends of top officials in British Intelligence and the diplomatic service. Guy Burgess prided himself on a personal tie to none less than Winston Churchill. The "fourth man" of the spy group remained in England but was never arrested; he was distinguished art historian Anthony Blunt, curator of the queen's art collection and personal friend, and a distant relative, of the royal family; he continued to hold the position long after being granted immunity in return for a secret confession in 1964. Queen Elizabeth II granted him a knighthood in 1975.

Spy cases had been sensational news events many times before in history. The celebrated Dreyfus affair, which shook France and, in some degree, the entire world at the end of the nineteenth century, turned on a case of espionage. The French army captain Alfred Dreyfus, a Jew, was accused and convicted—falsely, as it later turned out—of passing important information about long-range artillery to the Germans. The facts were so confusing that they have never been entirely clarified. It is commonly said that the real culprit was a Major Esterhazy, but this is not certain; Esterhazy may have been a double agent—that is, pretending to spy for the Germans while actually trying to penetrate their intelligence service on behalf of his own country. Two branches of the French secret police evidently failed to communicate with each other—far from an uncommon occurrence in espionage matters, shrouded in deep secrecy as they have to be. (In Soviet Russia, the KGB and the GRU each had its own secrets.) The Dreyfus case got involved with politics and became a touchstone in a way that Arthur Koestler described in connection with a later *cause célèbre*: "symbols in a Punch-and-Judy show or dream fantasy, where guilt is attributed, not on the strength of evidence, but according to the dream-logic of the unconscious." More simply put, according to political prejudices.

Prior to World War I, books in England such as William Le Queux's *Spies of the Kaiser* (1909) helped inflame national rivalries. Spies were common enough in World War I, during which the execution of a British nurse accused of spying by the Germans provided the Allies with a propaganda victory. An Allied deception that convinced the Germans there were far more Americans in France than there actually were helped bring on the end of the war in 1918.

After the Bolshevik Revolution of October–November 1917, the new Russian regime devoted an extraordinary amount of attention to secret police methods, espionage, and subversion. The reasons for this included the dramatic and somewhat paranoid mentality of Lenin and his cohorts, who saw themselves as soldiers in a final great war, surrounded by enemies desperate to do them in. They viewed this as a struggle not of nations but of classes within each nation. Because the working class everywhere was supposed to be on their side, it was the duty of the Bolshevik rulers of Russia to help the workers subvert their capitalist bosses. And no one believed more strongly than Lenin that the end justifies any means. "The Terror and the Cheka [secret political police] are indispensable," he declared, in order to win the merciless war with the old order.

The Soviet Union worked up espionage via ideology into a fine art. The chief founder of the Soviet state, perhaps, was the Polish aristocrat Felix Dzerzhinski, who created Lenin's secret police system, and later by throwing his support to Josef Stalin probably ensured the latter's victory in the struggle to be Lenin's successor. The Cheka became what was called the State Political Administration (GPU in Russian), an indication of its importance. Its job was to keep a watchful eye on any domestic opposition to the Communist party's monopoly of power. But it also was supposed to fend off subversive efforts from outside. In the early 1920s when the British tried to help anticommunist underground groups in Russia, the Cheka countered with its own agents who penetrated the opposition groups.[2]

The GPU eventually evolved into the NKVD before becoming the KGB. The extraordinary care and zeal with which Soviet intelligence agencies organized their program to recruit spies or "moles" in Western countries triggered amazement when its scope finally became known. This program involved a lengthy process of spotting, approaching, and testing potential agents. Then they would be carefully disguised. After becoming a Soviet agent, Kim Philby covered the Spanish Civil War as correspondent for a conservative British newspaper, writing pro-Franco stories in order to establish

---

[2]Anyone who watched the absorbing television series "Reilly, Ace of Spies" a few years ago knows something of this grim game.

an identity the very opposite of what one would have expected from a Communist. Secrecy was so great that often an agent's closest relatives did not suspect the truth about his espionage activities. Because it was easy to watch over official diplomatic channels, agents were "run" by illegals, whose identity was carefully disguised. Of course messages were sent in code, of a sort thought to be unbreakable. An agent had to submit himself (or herself) to an incredible discipline. The spy Klaus Fuchs, a German scientist working in England, whose information helped the Soviets build an atomic bomb before he was caught in 1950, spoke of a "controlled schizophrenia," by which the agent lived two totally different lives.

Two questions suggest themselves: Why did the Soviets lavish so much energy on this program? And why did highly capable, well-educated young Americans and Europeans join it? The questions are intertwined. One reason the Russians did it was because they saw a golden opportunity to put their friends into the highest offices of enemy nations, thus either taking over those countries the easy way, or forestalling attempts to harm the USSR. The opportunity existed because Soviet ideology appealed to these Western youths. They were more than eager to betray their own society, which they despised.

Britain offered special opportunities because of a tradition of recruiting top government officials through an informal process based on the public schools and the two great universities. These educational institutions provided the training ground for future civil servants. Anyone who was anyone had gone to Eton and Oxford, or Harrow and Cambridge; they were all acquainted, they came from a fairly small body of aristocratic families, and many of them were destined for political, administrative, or diplomatic careers. Capture the Oxbridge students and in effect you captured tomorrow's British government. This system was peculiarly British—far less egalitarian than the French, less professional than the German, ingrained in Britain because in the past it had been so successful. Not that Moscow did not try ideological subversion elsewhere, sometimes with notable success, for communism appealed widely to European and American intellectuals in the 1930s. But in England the prospects of using this undergraduate idealism as a direct stepping stone to political power were brighter.[3]

CAMBRIDGE AND COMMUNISM

The story began at Cambridge University in the 1930s among a group of bright and alienated students who were attracted to Marxism and were supporters of the Soviet Union; some of them became Soviet agents. They then

---

[3]There was a trace of Marxist theory in making Britain a special target, for not only had Marx spent much of his life there but he had thought of Britain as the most advanced capitalist country, pioneer of the Industrial Revolution; therefore, Britain was likely to lead the way toward socialism and communism.

moved into high offices in the British Intelligence Service and diplomacy, where they faithfully served the interests of the USSR for a dozen years, most of them never wavering in their loyalty to Stalin's government even though their illegal activities involved them in a devious and dangerous game. Some spies, of course, at the lower levels, were simply bought with money, but these university people acted from principle, were therefore more loyal, and occupied higher positions in government.

From 1941 to 1945, Soviet Russia was the ally of Great Britain and the United States. After that, the situation changed sharply. During the Cold War years after 1945 the Soviet Union was seen as a challenge and a threat to the Western powers allied in the North Atlantic Treaty Organization. According to some, the Western fears were all anticommunist hysteria, "McCarthyism," named after the particularly paranoid American senator; to most people in the West, however, Stalin's state appeared as a vicious tyranny, responsible for millions of deaths in the USSR and unrelentingly hostile to other societies.

In the 1930s sympathy for the USSR and interest in Marxism had been commonplace among the intellectuals. Nathaniel Weyl, who participated in this experience in the United States, has written that "During the popular-front and war-alliance years, 1935–1939 and 1941–1945, many New Dealers regarded communists as heroes, members of a dedicated elite of uncompromising social revolutionaries. . . . During my brief period in the Washington underground, at least one government official, a man with access to the White House, pleaded to be allowed to join the C.P. [Communist party]. But he was told he was unworthy of Party membership." Kim Philby said that he regarded it as a great honor to be selected by the Communist party. Distinguished British historian Hugh Trevor-Roper in his book on *The Philby Affair* (1968) remarked that "it would never have occurred to me, at that time, to hold Philby's communist past against him." For one may say with little exaggeration that an entire generation of inquiring young people at the universities had undergone the Communist experience either during the 1920s or, more frequently, the Depression-ridden 1930s.

It began in the letdown that followed the Great Crusade of 1914–1918. The world war that claimed such an astounding toll of human life ended not in a brave new world but in a fog of disappointment. The Great War dissolved the Austro-Hungarian monarchy and replaced it with a confusion of small new states with uncertain boundaries. The great peace conference at Paris in 1919, to which the president of the United States came, left the defeated Germans with a sense of keen injustice and left the victorious Allies divided. Most people saw the peace conference as having failed to provide a morally exhausted world with a new sense of purpose. The only gleam of hope seemed to come from the Russian Revolution of November, 1917, whose leaders during the "ten days that shook the world" swept aside the old ruling class, denounced the entire international political order as well as the reigning economic system, and called for world revolution.

The Bolsheviks did not favorably impress everyone, even among the intellectuals, as we know from the case of Bertrand Russell. But the word went out that the system based on public not private enterprise worked; moreover, it respected and promoted science more than in the West. Why did the capitalist countries seek to overthrow the Bolshevik regime by blockade and armed intervention if they did not fear for their profits? Here was the planned production for abundance not scarcity that represented the economy of the future. Led in France by Marie Curie's friend Paul Langevin, Western intellectuals signed up to protest anti-Bolshevism and hail its martyrs.

Then in 1931 came the Great Depression. In Great Britain that year, which Arnold Toynbee dubbed *annus terribilis*, brought the collapse of a Labour government, and with it apparently the failure of gradualist, "Fabian" socialism. The Fabian intellectual leaders Sidney and Beatrice Webb and George Bernard Shaw visited the USSR to lavish praise on Stalin, the Webbs in 1935 publishing an influential study of the Soviet system that accepted all the Communist claims at face value. (They virtually let Stalin's government write it.) The onset of the first Soviet Five-Year Plan, raising hopes about a new attack on poverty and backwardness, coincided with the rise of National Socialism in Germany. Nazism (fascism) or communism: One must choose. The bankruptcy of Western civilization left nothing in-between. So held young poets as well as veteran socialists.

At Cambridge a Communist economics professor, Maurice Dobb, demonstrated to admiring students the superiority of the "planned" Soviet economic system.(Perhaps students were more eager to study economics under Dobb because by this time mainstream economic theory had been thoroughly immersed in mathematics. Alfred Marshall and his students had professionalized the subject at Cambridge.) Why were students so ready to believe that the Soviet system was superior to their own? It was by no means self-evident; amid much bloodshed and disorder the Soviet economic system never really worked, and to make it viable at all Stalin had to resort to incredible violence. Economists other than Dobb argued that planned—that is, bureaucratic-decision making on economic matters—was inherently irrational, unable to do effectively what the free market did in determining what goods should be produced at what prices. But the reigning passion of the hour was a fierce rejection of Western capitalism with its "corrupt and degenerate" social values and an uncritical acceptance of communism as the hope of humanity.

So there was a moment in the earlier 1930s when to be young and intellectually alive was almost by definition to have fallen under the influence of Marx and Lenin. The spirit evaporated, leaving behind an ugly deposit of Stalinist malignity and moral corruption. Most of those who underwent this experience could confess their mistake without much damage, or somewhat uneasily consign it to the buried debris of memory. But some were trapped by having gone too far into the Communist party. To leave it after having been an agent was even more dangerous. First, the party did not think twice about murdering those who betrayed it, as a long list of mysterious deaths testified. Then, a promising career could be ruined by revelations of treason to one's country, even if due repentance was expressed. Moreover, it took courage to break with one's liberal friends, who were likely to accuse you of selling out to the Establishment. There were some striking examples, such as Goronwy Rees in England, of the complete ruin that might face a man who incurred the displeasure of the intellectual community by "ratting" on a left-wing luminary.

One other notable feature of the Cambridge spy story must be noted. To be young and bright at Cambridge in the interwar years was to label oneself not only Marxist but probably also homosexual or bisexual. Guy Burgess, Anthony Blunt, Kim Philby, and Donald Maclean all fell more or less into these categories. Burgess was the most strongly and openly "gay," shocking conventional East European Communists by appearing after work dressed in women's attire for the evening's entertainment. Philby, married five times and with many mistresses, was much more heterosexual but on occasions evidently demonstrated his versatility. The hard-drinking Maclean was quite at home with either sex. Blunt was an active and adventurous homosexual, but he did not always spurn women.

Homosexuality was a gesture of dissent, a badge of nonconformity. Associated with intellectuality, estheticism, and civilized wickedness, its vogue primarily came from Oscar Wilde's generation of the 1890s, carried on at Cambridge before the war by the Bloomsbury esthetes, among whom was the great economist John Maynard Keynes. Goronwy Rees wrote (in 1968) that at both Oxford and Cambridge in the 1920s and 1930s, "among undergraduates and dons with pretensions to culture and a taste for the arts," homosexuality was "at once a fashion, a doctrine, and a way of life." The universities were still overwhelmingly a masculine society, whose social and sexual habits grew out of the all-male public schools. Cambridge, Rosamond Lehmann remarked in her 1927 novel about it, "disliked and distrusted all females."

One could argue that in their permissive personal habits as well as their thirst for spy adventures these young men were children who never grew up—Peter Pans of politics. At any rate the Cambridge radicals were promiscuous, alcoholic, sometimes boisterous and bawdy—habits that the leading "moles" continued for the rest of their lives. Their unusual life-style formed a hidden bond between them and their classmates that explains much about subsequent handling of their cases.

THE MOLES IN ACTION

Espionage and counterespionage played an important part in World War II, as is well known—a story that would take volumes to tell. Called one of the all-time great spies, the German Communist Richard Sorge, a journalist working in Tokyo, was able to give the Russians valuable information about Japanese intentions in 1940/41. Breaking the Japanese code provided the Americans with an advantage in the war with Japan. The biggest story, however, was the British cracking of the German code, "Enigma," with Polish and French help,[4] which enabled the Allies to read Nazi communications throughout the war, a significant factor in their victory over Hitler. The British also succeeded in virtually taking over the German spy network in England, the famous "double cross" operation that ranks as perhaps the greatest *tour de force* in intelligence history. This advantage allowed the Allies to mislead the Germans about invasion sites, disrupt their atomic weapons program, and in other ways achieve military success. This secret war of cryptology, espionage, and disinformation was more decisive a factor than anyone except a few then suspected, though it could backfire; information had to be evaluated. The Allies repeatedly warned Stalin about the impending German attack on Russia in 1941, but he ignored them and was caught totally by surprise. Presumably he thought the British were trying to trick him. Having the ULTRA (code name for reading the German cipher) advantage did not save the British from defeat in the German conquest of Crete early in the war.

The Soviet Union was an ally in the conflict against Hitler, but far from a close and trusting one. The Russians and the Anglo-Americans treated each other more like enemies than allies, though to be sure there were times in 1944/45 when the Americans seemed to trust the Russians more than they did the British. But the Americans did not share with the USSR the atomic bomb project that went forward in the United States and Canada during the war (after the war they did not share it with the British either). So Stalin relied on information from his spy network. Only later, after they had begun to crack the Russian code used during the war, did American and British intelligence officers realize how much had been passed on to the Soviets from the various places where atomic bomb construction had occurred. These "Venona" decrypts, which could not be revealed in court, began to point an accusing finger at various spies by 1949.[5] Moreover, incriminating evidence

---

[4]Polish cryptologists accidentally came into possession of a German cipher machine in 1929; then a German gave information to the French in 1931, which was passed on to the British at the beginning of World War II. Many thousands of people worked during the war at Bletchley Park near London deciphering intercepted German radio material. Another Cambridge homosexual, Alan Turing, invented one of the first computers to help process this flood of material.

[5]Peter Wright, in *Spycatcher*, called Venona "the greatest counterintelligence secret in the Western world." The charred remains of a Russian codebook found on a battlefield in Finland provided the basis for painfully slow deciphering of the wartime Washington–Moscow cables. This revealed that there was an immense amount of espionage, with literally hundreds of spies and agents seemingly involved. The information they had transmitted included private telegrams from Roosevelt and Truman to Churchill, data from the atomic bomb program, countless other supposedly secret documents. Fuchs, the Rosenbergs, also Alger Hiss and Maclean were eventually identified, but most of the other sources never were.

came from Soviet defectors, especially a cipher clerk in the Soviet Embassy in Canada, Igor Gouzenko, who defected in 1945.

The scientist who supplied the most important atomic secrets to the Soviets was a German named Klaus Fuchs. Earlier, the Cambridge physicist Alan Nunn May, working in Canada, had passed critical materials to the Russians. Dr. Fuchs was a German Communist who emigrated to Britain and then to Canada and later to the Manhattan Project (America's atomic bomb program) as a British representative from 1944 to 1946, the crucial years; he returned to England to work at the British nuclear weapons site at Harwell in 1949. In 1950 Fuchs confessed to having passed secrets to the Soviets since 1941. It was Fuchs' confession that led to the arrest of Julius and Ethel Rosenberg in the United States; their trial and subsequent execution was one of the Cold War's most startling and controversial episodes. Soviet achievement of an atomic bomb by 1949 totally shocked President Harry Truman, who had supposed the Russians lacked the capacity to build one. There followed the race to develop the much more powerful H-bomb.

Fuchs was a top physicist, but he was not the only scientist in Britain to supply the Russians with information; another who did so was the distinguished biologist J.B.S. Haldane, long an avowed Communist. The difference in attitudes may be seen in the different ways the British and Americans treated the spies; while the Rosenbergs went to the electric chair, having defiantly refused to save themselves by revealing other agents, Fuchs spent only a few years in prison after which he went to East Germany and resumed his services to the Soviet weapons program.

In 1951 the sensational Alger Hiss case also came to a head. The second trial of this top-level American State Department officer, who had sat at President Roosevelt's side during the 1945 Yalta Conference when the Americans and British divided up the world with the Soviets, resulted in his conviction for perjury (January 1950); the Supreme Court denied his final appeal in March 1951 and he entered prison for a 3½-year term. The perjury charge grew out of Hiss's denial of Whittaker Chambers' allegation that Hiss had turned over to him, when Chambers was a Soviet spymaster, copies of numerous confidential State Department documents for transmittal to the Soviet Union. The case aroused immense interest, serving as a catalyst of left-right ideological differences much as the Dreyfus affair had done in France a half century earlier. Chambers had joined the Communist party as early as 1925, but he fought his way out of it by 1938, after which he became a writer and editor for *Time* magazine; a repentant Communist, the able Chambers had all the fury of the disenchanted believer.

But unlike all the major Cambridge moles, Alger Hiss never admitted his guilt, and in the eyes of some liberals he was a martyr to the anticommunist hysteria then sweeping America under the leadership of Senator Joseph McCarthy. But the case against Hiss was very strong.

To return to the Cambridge moles: "The network's services to Stalin were many, large, and lethal," Stephen Koch remarks. Douglas Maclean had been British representative to the Combined Policy Committee that shared information on atomic research between 1945 and 1947, and he was privy to the highest atomic secrets. As the MI6[6] officer in Washington, Kim Philby suppressed a report on the Communist affiliations of the Italian nuclear physicist Bruno Pontecorvo, who had worked with the Communist Pierre Joliot-Curie. Pontecorvo, who joined the British atomic energy team in Canada during World War II, went back to England in 1949 to receive British citizenship and continue work for their nuclear effort; in 1951 he defected to the Soviet Union and helped the Soviets build the H-bomb.

Philby also did what he could to block connections to the anti-Nazi groups in Germany during the war, to prevent any compromise short of Germany's total destruction. After the war he was in charge of MI6's anti-Soviet operations for several years! In 1949 he betrayed an attempt by British and American counterintelligence agencies to contact anticommunist underground groups in East Europe and subvert the Communist regimes there. Marshal Tito had just led Yugoslavia out of the Soviet camp. Nearby Albania seemed to offer prospects for leaving. Philby was in Washington, directly participating in planning this covert action! By alerting Moscow he saw to it that the operation failed; the agents that landed or parachuted into Albania were "like lambs to the slaughter," Enver Hoxha boasted, as the Albanian Communist leader intensified the most oppressive dictatorship in Europe. Which soon, it might be added, deserted the Kremlin camp. There were other occasions on which Philby caused the death of British agents and of Russians attempting to defect. Maclean obligingly kept Moscow thoroughly informed about plans for NATO, as well as for the Korean War.

By late 1949 the Venona decoding revealed that the source of a 1944 leak at the British Embassy was a spy named "Homer" who made weekly trips to New York where he met his Soviet contact. This pointed a finger directly at Maclean. He was sent to Cairo where he began to drink heavily again; after he wrecked a woman's apartment in May 1950, the British Foreign Office brought him back to London and put him on sick leave. But before long he was named head of the American department at the British Foreign Office. From there he sent valuable data to the Soviets about the Korean War. Military intelligence reports from General MacArthur's headquarters in Tokyo found their way to Moscow. The Chinese Communists may have invaded North Korea because they were certain this action would not lead to any bombing of Chinese soil, a fact they had learned via espionage.

Guy Burgess in the Far Eastern division of the British Foreign Office had done what he could to assist Mao Tse-tung's Communist takeover in China.

---

[6]The MI5 is the British Home Office's internal security bureau, equivalent to the FBI in the United States; MI6 is the Foreign Office overseas Secret Intelligence Service, roughly the CIA in American terms. Both British organizations have always been highly secret, so much so that MI6 was until quite recently not officially recognized as even existing.

Burgess also passed to Moscow an important British policy study on Southeast Asia in 1949, relevant of course to the Vietnam situation, soon to be so significant. In August 1950 he was posted to Washington as second secretary at the British Embassy. Though still drinking heavily and frequenting homosexual bars, he was able to continue supplying information to Russia about the Korean War. The moles indeed were able to send sensitive material to the Russians to the end—that is, early 1951 for Burgess and Maclean.

Apart from this, and speeding up the date at which the Soviets acquired atomic weapons by as much as several years, the damage done to the West by Burgesss, Maclean, Philby, and the other moles is hard to assess; but it is hardly comforting to reflect that, in historian John Lewis Gaddis's words, between 1945 and 1949 the Soviets knew all about "planning with respect to the British withdrawal from Greece and Turkey, the creation of the Marshall Plan, the discussion of options for dealing with the Berlin blockade, the formation of the North Atlantic Treaty Organization, and . . . virtually all aspects of American, British, and Canadian cooperation on atomic energy matters." At least it sheds new light on these historic policies. A further by-product was the deterioration in Anglo-American relations that resulted from American disgust with lax British security.

THIRD, FOURTH, AND FIFTH MEN

After the Burgess-Maclean defections there was no serious doubt of the guilt of their close companion Kim Philby. He scarcely denied it in the in-house interrogations, but he made no confession sufficient to bring him to trial. The trouble with putting spies on trial, of course, is that the evidence against them is too sensitive to be made public, involving as it does ongoing espionage and counterespionage. The MI6 bureau fired Philby, giving him a cash payment in lieu of a pension. For the next few years he worked intermittently as a journalist, supported by his friend and fellow Communist Tomas Harris, a wealthy painter and art dealer, whose wealth evidently came in part from works of art stolen by Soviet agents in Spain during that country's civil war. Harris, who during World War II had served brilliantly in misleading the Germans about Allied invasion plans, died somewhat mysteriously in an auto crash in Majorca not long after Philby's defection. But in 1955 Foreign Secretary Harold Macmillan, soon to be British prime minister, rose in answer to a question in the House of Commons to state that: "I have no reason to conclude that Mr. Philby has at any time betrayed the interest of this country." The next year brought Anthony Blunt's knighthood.

The somewhat rehabilitated Philby now went off to the Middle East where his father had once made a great reputation as an explorer. Ironically, the politics of that region proved troublesome. Kim's journalistic writings for the prominent London newspaper *The Observer* were pro-Arab, which had become the Soviet line in the growingly bitter Arab-Israeli conflict. This was too much for one of Philby's old friends, Flora Solomon, who had not minded him betraying his own country but could not stomach Philby's hostility to the Jewish state. In Flora Solomon's scale of loyalties Israel now outranked the USSR, and she turned bitterly on Philby, about whose past she knew a good deal. A friend of Victor Rothschild, and possibly Philby's lover at one time, Flora was prominent in wealthy London Zionist circles. International politics had caused the Jewish connection to turn sour for the Communists, with considerable repercussions. Also at this time several Soviet defectors brought information that helped close the net around Philby; in particular Anatole Golitsyn, who had worked for six years at KGB headquarters in Moscow, defected in Helsinki late in 1961 bringing with him much interesting information (which had of course to be evaluated; perhaps it was Soviet disinformation).

Even with this new evidence, the intelligence chiefs decided not to arrest Philby but to promise him immunity from prosecution if he would cooperate fully. This was less strange than it might seem, for if Philby could be "turned" or even just made to divulge all he knew, the rewards in the intelligence game could be great. But while admitting guilt in a general way Philby stalled long enough to contact the Russians and arrange an escape from Beirut on January 23, 1963. He spent the rest of his quarter century of life in Moscow basking in the role of retired master KGB secret agent. He had again outwitted the British service he had fooled for so many years. He managed, additionally, to inform Blunt about the offer of immunity, so that the latter knew this in all probability would be an option for him too.

Anthony Blunt was "the principal Cambridge recruiter" of the young Communists who became spies, some careful students of the espionage ring such as John Costello (*Mask of Treachery*) have concluded. Blunt was certainly the most complex and interesting. That this distinguished art historian and connoisseur was also a long-time Soviet agent remained unknown for many years, except to a few insiders. In 1963, not long after Philby's flight, the net had also closed in on Blunt. The American liberal journalist Michael Straight, an intimate of Blunt's at Cambridge long ago, decided to come clean and tell all he knew, which was much.

British Intelligence director Roger Hollis and his MI5 advisers favored an offer of immunity to Blunt in exchange for his full cooperation in identifying past and present spies. Blunt seems to have won his bout with the intelligence agency even more brilliantly than Philby. He did not flee to Russia. He had no desire to leave his posts at the Courtauld Institute and Buckingham Palace, his worldwide reputation as an art historian, his lecture tours, and art collecting. He admitted guilt, but when asked to identify spies, according to Peter Wright who interviewed him, he came up only with those "who were either dead, long since retired, or else comfortably out of secret access and danger." He did name a few minor figures; two of them, one a senior member of Parliament, committed suicide soon after being questioned.

This was in the aftermath of a Profumo affair suicide, that of Stephen Ward, after his conviction for procuring Christine Keeler and Mandy Rice-Davies, two young women who had shared their favors with British cabinet minister John Profumo and a Russian intelligence officer. This famous scandal embarrassed the government and eventually caused the fall of Prime Minister Macmillan. No wonder a shell-shocked British government thought it unwise to hit the public with the truth about Anthony Blunt at this time.

MI5 had treated Blunt more gently than it did Philby back in 1951. Top officers dismissed as unreliable charges brought against Blunt by his one-time friend Goronwy Rees, though the distinguished novelist Rosamond Lehmann supported the accusation. The MI5 officers who investigated Blunt thought that he was a spy, but was there enough proof to convict the queen's friend and art adviser? It was easier to sweep the matter under the rug for the time being.[7] The result was that Blunt, who had talked the Soviets out of their wish to have him leave with the other two spies in 1951, stayed on for years doing further services for his Russian masters. In 1963 he escaped disclosure again, at the price of a confession. Then for sixteen years after confessing to having been a Soviet agent, Blunt continued on as an art adviser to the queen. The revelation of this in 1979 caused a considerable public outcry.

In November 1979, Prime Minister Margaret Thatcher, no member of the Oxbridge old boy set, revealed in Parliament the secret that Anthony Blunt had been a Soviet agent. The queen followed suit by stripping Blunt of his knighthood, though she had known about his spying activities when she granted it. (Philby had also been stripped of his O.B.E [Officer of the Order of the British Empire] in 1964.) After the bald announcement about Blunt the British government again imposed an embargo on information, refusing to name a parliamentary commission of inquiry.[8] Blunt invoked the Official Secrets Act to refuse to answer questions. In fact, the authorities' hands had been forced. Historians and others seeking to rescue the truth about the spy network from the deep obscurity in which British Intelligence held it captive (the Americans were less secretive) had come to the conclusion that there had been not only a "third man" (Philby) but also a fourth. In 1979 Andrew Boyle, long a pursuer of the fourth man, in his book *The Climate of Treason* (American title, *The Fourth Man*) did not explicitly name Blunt but left it easy to read between the lines.

Blunt possessed an acute intelligence and an amazing capacity for di-

---

[7]A persistent story never yet verified has it that the secret hold that Blunt and Philby had over the authorities was knowledge of the close connection between the Duke of Windsor (King Edward VIII in 1936 before his abdication on the issue of his marriage to an American divorcee) and Adolf Hitler. That the duke had been pro-Nazi was well known, but correspondence discovered in the German files after the war allegedly proved actual treason during World War II. The correspondence was supposedly destroyed with only a few people having seen it.

[8]In her memoirs, published in 1993 (*The Downing Street Years*), Lady Thatcher says nothing about either Blunt or the *Spycatcher* case. Mum still seems to be the word.

versifying his life. His multileveled career, in which he evidently gloried, might in a single day include escorting the president of France around the queen's gallery, then meeting his Russian contact, then picking up a soldier in a homosexual bar. He drank heavily. Cold, aloof, detached, Blunt preferred lower-class men as lovers, the "rough trade," and lived with an Irish ex-guardsman in his later years—a man who attempted suicide after Blunt's 1979 exposure. Blunt's favorite art history subject was the great seventeenth-century French neoclassicist artist Nicolas Poussin, whose paintings are severely rational in their attention to form, yet often seething with passion. Blunt was the proud owner of one Poussin, which hangs appropriately today in the Fitzwilliams Museum in Cambridge.

What drove Blunt to this strange life? Like all the intellectual Communists, he believed that his own society was diseased and doomed, and that communism was the wave of the future. But Blunt's obvious reluctance to live in the Soviet paradise suggests a more subjective motivation for his subversive activity: a deep-seated grudge against his own society based on some damage to his soul in early years. His extreme intellectuality, making even esthetics a matter of reason, along with his homosexuality, could provide Freudians with material for an analysis. Blunt was different from the other moles. They all seemed to harbor an inner insecurity, expressed in their alcoholism and violence. They were socially more marginal. "I never felt I belonged," Philby said. But Blunt unquestionably belonged, and he had more control of his life. He stands apart from the others, and is in many ways the more frightening case.

Was there still another major mole, a Fifth Man never detected? The evidence for there having been another spy very high up in MI5 seemed strong to some keen students of this complex story. It included a long series of intelligence failures that could be explained in no other way, and also testimony both from defectors and deciphered material that there was indeed another spy, code-named "Elli," who had worked for GRU (Soviet military intelligence) for many years. The identity of this fifth man preoccupied Peter Wright, the now retired MI5 assistant director, whose absorbing book *Spycatcher* became a bestseller in 1987, not least because the British government tried to suppress it.[9] Wright suspected no less a person than former director (1956–1965) Sir Roger Hollis. But this was disputed. John Costello (*Mask of Treachery*, 1988) preferred to pin the label of grand mole on Guy Liddell, who had preceded Hollis as a major figure in MI5, for which he had worked since 1931. Hollis was his protegé. Liddell, of a noted British family (descendant of the Duke of Wellington, and related to Alice Liddell, for whom *Alice in Wonderland* was written), had been a close friend of Philby and Blunt; he was a

---

[9]Wright was living in retirement in Australia when he wrote the book. The British government tried to stop Wright's book in Australia, New Zealand, and Hong Kong as well as at home, and evidently succeeded in intimidating other ex-spycatchers in Britain. The book became a bestseller in the United States.

musician and art connoisseur. Guy Liddell's personal story of growing up under a stern military father and a doting, artistic mother reminds us of Mazzini and Weber and Kafka. It was a recipe for an alienated intellectual. Liddell certainly brought Blunt and Tomas Harris into the Intelligence Service, knowing of their Communist sympathies. But the case against him as a Soviet agent failed to convince many.

Nigel West, author of *Molehunt*, nominated Graham Mitchell, object of an intensive investigation by M15 at one time, and author of a devious 1955 White Paper on Burgess-Maclean. Wright, however, thought Mitchell innocent. And in 1991 John Cairncross, an exile in France for many years, declared that he was the "fifth man." It was no secret that Cairncross had been a Soviet agent; he had confessed in 1964, at the same time as Blunt, being then granted immunity in return for living outside Britain. Cairncross had worked for MI6 for many years. A Soviet defector, Oleg Gordyevsky, as well as a former KGB colonel writing in a post-Gorbachev Moscow magazine, now named Cairncross as the "fifth man" of the spy team. Gordyevsky co-authored with British historian Christopher Andrew a book that stressed Cairncross's importance, claiming that it was he who first notified the Soviets of the Anglo-American decision to build the atomic bomb. But could Cairncross have been the "Elli" Peter Wright and others searched for? Elli was in MI5, not MI6. Gordyevsky later asserted that "Elli" was a man named Leo Long. But this has been disputed.[10]

These issues may yet be resolved if in the atmosphere of the post-Communist Soviet Union, secret intelligence files are opened up. It may not matter much exactly how many "moles" there were. There were certainly enough. One Venona decrypt mentioned eight in MI5 and MI6.

EPILOGUE TO THE CAMBRIDGE TRAITORS

The morose Scotsman Donald Maclean lived in the USSR until 1983, clearly not very happily. He died a few weeks before Anthony Blunt succumbed to a heart attack in London. Guy Burgess, the most irrepressible and outrageous of the Cambridge band, predictably died rather young, of liver disease, in 1963, some months after Kim Philby joined him in Moscow. Maclean paid tribute to Burgess as "a gifted and courageous man," but Philby subsequently referred to Burgess disparagingly ("that bloody man"). After Philby's affair with Maclean's wife, Melinda (like Eleanor Philby an American) in 1964, those two men no longer spoke to each other. Maclean was still prone to drunken violence. Eleanor Philby left Moscow to return to California in 1965, and Kim Philby then married (his fifth wife) a younger Russian woman, while the hapless Melinda Maclean moved back in with Donald for want of any-

---

[10]See Anthony Glees' letter in the *Times Literary Supplement*, December 14–20, 1990.

where else to go; the Maclean children were soon also looking for that most elusive of Russian finds, an apartment. (They all eventually got out of Russia.) Unlike Philby, Maclean entertained obvious doubts about the USSR, and was in contact with some of the dissidents who tried to criticize the Communist party leadership. The only product of his years in Kuibyshev and Moscow was a book on international relations, *British Foreign Policy since Suez* (1972), which chiefly, but not entirely, followed the party line. It was a work with at least some pretensions to scholarship. He also taught classes at the Institute of World Economics in Moscow.

Kim Philby kept up a brave front to the end. His book, *My Silent War*, expressed his stubborn pride in refusing to go the route of so many deserters of "the god that failed," who had paraded their bitter disenchantment with Stalinism, and usually with Marxism, in a celebrated 1948 anthology bearing that title. A distinguished group, including Arthur Koestler, Ignazio Silone, and Burgess's one-time friend Stephen Spender, they cried *mea culpa* or pleaded their youth and naiveté, but they also acutely probed the deep flaws in the faith they had so innocently adopted. It had led them into a moral wilderness of intellectual prostitution where they told lies and sanctioned terrible crimes because the "good cause" required it—only to find that the cause was not good at all. They might, like Koestler, say they were not sorry they had had the experience, even though given the choice they would not do it again; it had a kind of soul-searing quality, like a passionate love affair gone sour. "How hard it is to break with somebody we have ceased to love!" the great seventeenth-century psychologist La Rochefoucauld had observed.

A considerable majority of the innumerable intellectuals and poets and novelists who had flirted with communism in the 1930s had to make the break in order to save their self-respect; they acknowledged their mistake and took some other road. But Philby disdained such self-abasement; he would never admit he was wrong. His masters treated him well, providing him with a sumptuous standard of living by Moscow standards. Friends sent him the cricket scores and crossword puzzles from England. Three months before his death in 1988 he appeared on Soviet television, recounting his triumphs as a spy and declaring that he regretted nothing. A British journalist wrote an admiring book about him, this man who had had the courage of his convictions and had thumbed his nose at the Anglo-American Establishment. British novelist Graham Greene considered Philby a good friend. Kim Philby certainly had led an adventurous life, though the final twenty-five years were spent in obscure retirement in a strange land. But toward the end he must have felt the pillars of his temple falling, as the Soviet economy crumbled and a massive rejection of the entire Bolshevik dictatorship began.

There is something epic about the Cambridge traitors, the Rosenbergs, and Alger Hiss, all of those who chose to withdraw their primary loyalty from their native country and give it to the land they thought represented the future of humanity. It was a tragic choice because it was so utterly misguided.

Their faith was based on total ignorance of Stalin's world of prison camps and murder. Stephen Spender, in his salad days an undergraduate Communist but wise enough to change, remarked revealingly that none of his pro-Soviet friends "had the slightest interest in any side of Russia which was not the Stalinist propaganda presentation." They had closed their minds, opting to disbelieve their own leaders and believe the Soviets. A mind once firmly closed is hard to reopen, and some of them could not do it until mountains of evidence finally convinced all but the most obdurate. As late as the 1950s, immense campaigns of abuse were launched against people who fled from Stalin's tyranny and tried to tell the truth about it: among others the cases of Victor Kravchenko and, in Australia, Vladimir Petrov, showed this.

A surprising number of writers in the 1930s never abandoned their Soviet faith, having made it a habit. One example: Sylvia Townsend Warner, a second-rank but quite well-known British fiction writer, a *New Yorker* favorite, was the author of subtle studies of private life. Like the Cambridge group a homosexual, she was anything but unsophisticated. Yet she became an enthusiastic Communist who wanted to get Stephen Spender purged from the party for his lack of sufficient orthodoxy. Her communism seemed to have nothing to do with her art. Her stories were utterly nongeneral, depicting the specifics of personal life—nothing to do with Marxist theory, which one is sure would have bored her profoundly had she understood it at all. Yet she never recanted, but defended Stalinism for the rest of her life, into the 1970s. Here was a lesser Blunt, a schizophrenic mixture of Communist and esthete—except that she never became a spy. In her case one feels that what kept her firm in her faith was simple inertia, the trouble it would be to find a new framework of thought, in effect forge a new identity. And was not anticommunism simply too vulgar?

In the early days of the Cold War, American diplomat George F. Kennan advised his country's policymakers that "Much depends on the health and vigor of our own society" in meeting the challenge of the Soviet Union. "World communism is like a malignant parasite which only feeds on diseased tissue," he stated. Cambridge commmunism fed on the diseased tissue of British society. The young men of the 1930s thought Britain vulgar, commercial, materialistic. One gets the feeling that in their eyes capitalism was repulsive not because it exploited and impoverished the masses—which they believed as a matter of dogma—but because it produced a low-brow culture.

We must turn back to Franz Kafka to understand how an esthetically sensitive temperament could be shocked to the depths of its being by the crass insensitivity of a "bourgeois" world. What we see in the case of the Cambridge traitors was a turning not to the ivory tower of art but to an attempted political revolution aimed at destroying the system they hated. The distinguished British writer Rebecca West, in her study of *The Meaning of Treason*, called them "mild-mannered desperadoes." Drunken, rowdy, sexually promiscuous, the Burgess-Maclean-Philby circle was not always so mild-mannered. Yet basically they were members of the civilized elite. It is true that the real poets, like the great W.H. Auden and, at Cambridge, Louis MacNeice, flirted with communism only briefly; the ones who stayed were likely to be less creative, though Blunt, as we know, was a scholar of very considerable ability. But all of them admired literature and art and music, despising the philistines of mainstream society for not doing so.

Among the most successful propaganda lines of the Soviet regime was its claim that science in the USSR, released from the bonds of private property, would be used for the good of all, not just a few. But, as it turned out, a narrow Marxian dogma perverted science in the USSR, as it also ruined literature. The only great poetry produced there came from Stalin's victims, like Osip Mandelstam.

POSTSCRIPT

The romance of the secret agent, which supplied the world with so much of its literature and cinema in recent decades (consider the novels of Ian Fleming and John Le Carré), now belongs to the past, it seems. Satellite photography and other high-tech devices supply information that once came from espionage. More important, the demise of Soviet Russia in the 1980s removed the indispensable partner in the great game. Alan Bennett, an English admirer of the moles, wrote in 1991: "The trouble with treachery nowadays is that if one does want to betray one's country there is no one satisfactory to betray it to." The jaded rebel of the post–Cold War years must envy Burgess and Philby for having had such a convenient spymaster and such an accessible alternative loyalty. Nevertheless, in early 1994 a senior CIA intelligence official was arrested in Washington and charged with spying for the Soviet Union and then for its successor, the Russian government. The great game seemed to go on. This was the first time a major CIA mole had been revealed.

On the other hand, internal subversion via "dirty tricks" is an art that continues to flourish. Or at least it is perceived that way. The authors of a book about British Prime Minister Harold Wilson allege numerous "covert actions" designed to discredit him in the 1970s.[11] Anyone nominated to a high government post must evidently be prepared to meet such tactics. The world has hardly gotten any cleaner since Burgess, Maclean, Philby, and Blunt betrayed their country's highest secrets to the Soviets. Do we dare hope that it ever will?

[11]Stephen Dorril and Robin Ramsay, *Smear! Wilson and the Secret State* (London: Fourth Estate, 1991).

13

Bertrand Russell: The Philosopher in Politics

THE MAKING OF A PHILOSOPHER

Bertrand Arthur William Russell, as he was christened, was born May 18, 1872, at Trelleck, Monmouthshire, Wales, of highly aristocratic lineage. His father, Lord Amberley, the son of a prime minister, came from a noble family that traced back to a hero and martyr of the Glorious Revolution. Almost equally aristocratic was Bertrand's mother, Kate Stanley, a pioneer feminist. One of Bertrand's godfathers was the great liberal economist and philosopher John Stuart Mill. So he came by his radical, nonconformist credentials honestly: an aristocratic radicalism, all the bolder for being asserted with the self-confidence, not to say arrogance, of those who knew they could get away with anything they felt like saying. His parents belonged to a mid-Victorian generation that knew Mill, Charles Darwin, religious controversy, new social ideas—a truly formative and turbulent period for the modern mind. Marx and Mazzini fitted into this picture.

Bertrand's strange, rather lonely childhood certainly goes far to explain his subsequent rebellious personality traits. Both of his parents died before he was four, his mother of diphtheria, which carried off his sister at the same time, his father eighteen months later of bronchitis. Though his parents had appointed two (irreligious) guardians, little Bertrand went with his older brother Frank to live with his grandparents, at Pembroke Lodge in south London; Lord John Russell soon died, and Bertrand's grandmother, Lady Frances

Russell, took charge of the boy. His education came chiefly from tutors and his grandparents' library, until he was sent to a "crammer" school in north London prior to entering Trinity College, Cambridge University, in 1890, on a mathematics scholarship. The Russell house swarmed with eminent relatives and other visitors from the high gentry of Great Britain, from whom Bertrand picked up knowledge. He was a precociously intelligent child, with little of what we would regard as normal social intercourse. Later he declared that he had an unhappy childhood and "in adolescence I hated life and was constantly on the verge of suicide."

It is no wonder that he was as unsuccessful in his private life as he was brilliantly successful in his intellectual career—something he acknowledged in 1905 as he contemplated the collapse of his marriage. "I have made a mess of my private life," he wrote in a letter. "I have failed to get or give happiness. . . . All my idealism has become concentrated on my work, which is the one thing in which I have not disappointed myself." In 1894, much against his grandmother's wishes, he had married Alys Pearsall Smith, from an American Quaker family living in England. Her brother was a writer of some distinction, and Alys had an earnest social conscience but nothing like the intellectual brilliance of Bertrand—who apparently expected it of her. Their marriage was one of those Victorian tragedies in which inexperienced people marry without really knowing each other. According to one of Bertrand Russell's great contemporaries, the French novelist Marcel Proust, lovers manufacture illusions about each other and then suffer cruel disappointment when experience reveals the truth. In 1901 Bertrand discovered that he no longer loved Alys and with brutal frankness told her this.

His career was advancing nobly. Russell studied under Alfred North Whitehead and was influenced at Cambridge by another prominent philosopher, G.E. Moore; he belonged to the Apostles society, where the brightest undergraduates met and debated with their teachers. It was the time of an exciting revolution in philosophy, which Bertrand joined. Like many gifted young people he found himself pulled in different directions; he wanted to be an economist, and in 1896 the first of his many books was a study of the German Social Democratic political party. But mathematics, he said, saved his sanity, and probably in flight from domestic unhappiness he threw himself into excruciatingly difficult work in logic and mathematics. A book about Leibniz's philosophy (1900) led to more than a decade of work with Whitehead on the epochal *Principia Mathematica* (1910–1913), an outgrowth of their *Principles of Mathematics* (1903).

This inquiry related to work being done on the Continent as well as by earlier British thinkers, including both great mathematicians and logicians. Its goal was to show that mathematical concepts derive from logical ones and that logic can be expressed in mathematical symbols, thus realizing Leibniz's idea of a universal language of logical symbols. DeMorgan and Boole had tried to apply mathematics to Aristotelian logic, developing equations that could be read as propositions. Whitehead and Russell reversed this, expressing logical propositions in mathematical form. A path had been blazed by the Viennese Gottlieb Frege, whose "single-minded pursuit of a demonstration that arithmetic had its foundations in pure logic alone, and that its fundamental concepts were derivable from purely logical ones" (P.M.S. Hacker), earned acknowledgment from Russell and Whitehead that "in all questions of logical analysis, our chief debt is to Frege." In the preface to *Principia Mathematica*, Russell also paid tribute to Georg Cantor, who prepared the way by his work on theory of aggregates or classes, and also to the Italian Giuseppe Peano's work on symbolic logic. Cantor's theory of infinite numbers has been called "one of the most powewrfully original conceptions in the whole of mathematics" (Roger Penrose). His theory of infinite sets "led to the Russell-Whitehead-Frege attempt to build the foundations of math on the principles of logic . . . , which effectively means on set theory."

All this, of which the work of Russell and Whitehead was the culmination, represented an attempt to establish secure foundations for mathematics, and merge logic with mathematics to create a precise method of scientific-philosophical inquiry—a perfect language, or language-structure, pure syntax without vocabulary as Russell called it. "On Denoting," a 1905 Russell paper, which sought to clarify one ambiguity in the way we use language, was part of this intense preoccupation with making language more exact and logical.

In seeking to establish arithmetic on secure logical foundations, Russell and Frege tried to demonstrate that the purely logical notions of identity, class, class-membership, and class-equivalence suffice for constructing the series of natural numbers. The "theory of types" was designed to overcome obstacles in the way of this goal, notably the paradox of "the class of classes that are not members of themselves."[1] *Principia Mathematica* is generally considered a landmark in the development of symbolic logic, and a truly innovative work, today requiring some amendment but still providing the basic framework. The Whitehead-Russell notation of logical symbols came to be widely adopted.

The very title summoned up comparisons with Isaac Newton. This abstract line of inquiry, beset with difficulties—"a monument of devotion to pure thinking," as Morris R. Cohen called it—left Russell exhausted, and was the most intensely arduous and difficult intellectual enterprise he ever undertook. The *Principia* brought Russell much renown, short of his fortieth birthday. Meanwhile, under G.E. Moore's influence Russell ventured into philosophy as a "realist" or logical empiricist, abandoning his earlier Plato-

---

[1]Russell illustrated this paradox by the story of how a group of secretaries, who by rule were excluded from membership in the clubs they worked for, decided themselves to form a club (of Excluded Secretaries) and hired a secretary whom they declared ineligible for membership in their club! Was he or she entitled or not to be a member of their club? There was also the barber who shaves everyone who does not shave himself. Does he shave himself?

nism and challenging the reigning idealist metaphysics. The young Austrian Ludwig Wittgenstein became Russell's student in 1911 and much influenced him. Among Russell's philosophical writings were *Problems of Philosophy* (1912); *Our Knowledge of the External World* (1914); *Mysticism and Logic* (1918). He visited the United States in 1914 lecturing on philosophy at Harvard and elsewhere.

It was hard to pin down a single Russell philosophical position. His colleague C.D. Broad once commented tartly, "As we all know, Mr. Russell produces a different system of philosophy every few years." But there were persistent characteristics: Philosophical methods should be modeled on those of science; they should pare away all useless abstractions and concentrate on logic rather than metaphysical speculation. Russell's "Logical Atomism" asserted (did it prove?) that the world contains facts, an objective realm not (for the most part) created by our minds, and not part of a great whole as the Hegelians claimed, but separate and discrete—the world is not like a bowl of jelly but a bag of shot, Russell declared. The problem is to match our language to this state of affairs. Russell described Logical Atomism as "the substitution of piecemeal, detailed, and verifiable results for large untested generalities recommended by a certain appeal to imagination."

This was a return to the Enlightenment, basically, in reaction against a century of Romanticism and Idealism. D'Alembert and the Encyclopedists had declared that the philosophical spirit is "a spirit of observation and exactness"; Voltaire had hailed "the light of common sense" bursting over Europe. It was the way of Locke and Newton, the revolt against metaphysics, the faith of Reason. Russell renewed this tradition. He was to be hailed as the Voltaire of the twentieth century. Yet there was another Russell, who knew that intuition or mysticism has a role in formulating beliefs, which reason then tests; imagination does after all come into play. "Even in the most purely logical realms, it is insight that first arrives at what is new."

RUSSELL IN POLITICS AND LOVE

Like his great predecessor Voltaire, Bertrand Russell was never to be content with pure thought. An interest in politics emerged early. As a Russell, he was almost expected to go into politics. What he went into was radical, minority-fringe politics. In 1907 he ran for Parliament on a votes-for-women platform, and in 1910 he campaigned for Philip Morrell, with whose wife, Lady Ottoline Morrell, he was soon to begin a passionate love affair. He had separated from poor Alys but did not seek a divorce.

In today's society people must live on several different levels, often not much related to each other. There is private life, the life of family and friends and personal relations, confronting young people with decisions about sex, marriage, choice of occupation. Second, there is the public, political arena.

This was an exceedingly lively one in Edwardian times, when urgent issues of social and political policy confronted the newly enfranchised masses. "The great issues of Free Trade and Protection, Home Rule for Ireland, the Disestablishment of the Church, and the Reform of the House of Lords," Herbert Read remembered, "were being debated with fervour and energy in every newspaper and at every street corner." He could have added other topics, notably the question of the welfare state and an income tax. The suffragettes, mainly from the educated upper class, launched their aggressive campaign for women's political rights. When fifty years later Bertrand took part in the Campaign for Nuclear Disarmament and introduced confrontational methods of aggressive "civil disobedience," he was only copying these genteel Edwardian ladies who threw themselves in front of horses and trains, went on hunger strikes, slashed pictures, and set fire to mail boxes.

And of course for people like Russell there was the additional realm of thought, literature, learning, the world of the mind—a growingly huge area, itself not very well organized or linked as among the domains of science, religion, philosophy, imaginative literature, music, the arts, the social sciences, and history. A rich, intoxicating presence saturated with echoes of all past historical epochs, it had been swelling in the book-saturated nineteenth century with its heroes and heroines of the printed page. And how was this mental world, this "noösphere," as a philosopher was to name it, linked to the other levels? How did social and political theory relate to the realities of politics, for example?

One connection: The year 1911 was rife with messages of sexual emancipation, free love, and feminism coming from the most advanced thinkers. The great Edwardian writers—George Bernard Shaw, H.G. Wells, Arnold Bennett—featured such themes. Margaret Sanger had begun her campaign for birth control. Russell once declared that Shaw was a rough British equivalent of Sigmund Freud, in that Shaw's plays brought to the forefront of respectable public notice a new recognition of hitherto mostly repressed questions about family and sexual relations. There were more explicit sexologists such as Havelock Ellis, not to speak of the unspeakable Aleister Crowley. In 1911, the year Russell embarked upon an affair with Lady Ottoline, his destined second wife, Dora Black, was reading H.G. Wells's novel about an "emancipated woman," *Ann Veronica*, and being converted to a life as the New Woman, who dared to have her romance and even her children outside the institution of marriage. Queen Victoria's successor on the throne, her grandson Edward VII, was setting a royal example of libertinism.

This "emancipation" movement sprang from many sources. For Britain, the death of Queen Victoria in 1901 had been a notable landmark; it removed a great weight of respectability and was the signal for an outburst of long repressed frankness about sex.

The British aristocracy had never practiced much at monogamy or Puritanism; it was said that this formed a bond between them and the proletariat against the middle classes. But Bertrand Russell had had to grow into his sexual boldness. Shy, repressed, and inexperienced as a youngster, pouring all his libido into intellectual creation, he spent the rest of his life making up for this early backwardness. Lady Ottoline was the first of two major mistresses who filled a large place in his life; there were many minor ones, and of his four wives the second and third ones at least were beautiful and passionate women. T.S. Eliot painted Russell as "Mr Apollinax," who combined passion with keen intellect. Nietzsche's Dionysus and Apollo, the twin horses of surging will and shaping reason, seemed united in this physically rather unimpressive British nobleman.

Lady Ottoline lavished hospitality on the celebrated "Bloomsbury Circle" that included Virginia Woolf and Lytton Strachey, and on other avantgarde literary figures. Bertrand and Lady Ottoline appear thinly disguised, and not very lovable, in D.H. Lawrence's *Women in Love* and in Aldous Huxley's *Crome Yellow*. Lady Constance Malleson, who went by the stage name of Colette, became the other important woman in Russell's life; he met her at a political meeting in 1916, and their friendship lasted on and off for many years—indeed, until the end of her life almost forty years later.

During World War I Russell was one of a relative few who opposed the war spirit; he helped found the neutralist Union for Democratic Control, later joined the No-Conscription Fellowship and wrote a series of essays about war and peace, printed in the books *Justice in Wartime* and *Principles of Social Reconstruction*. Dismissed from his lectureship at Trinity College, Cambridge, for antiwar utterances, he later suffered six months' imprisonment for writing that American troops would soon occupy England and break strikes. It was not an uncomfortable detention; one did not send the son of an earl to a plain jail, and Russell was able to get much writing done. Russell's position against the war was not based on pacifism, which he always was at pains to reject; there are some causes worth fighting for and it is necessary to do so, otherwise monstrous injustice ensues. He did not absolutely oppose even this war, but he was offended by the unfairness to Germany, the hysteria, the claims of moral righteousness, the censorship, the general illiberalism of wartime conditions. He thought Great Britain and the Allies partly to blame for the war, condemning British foreign policy with characrteristic extremism: "I cannot discover any infamy in the whole wide world which the Foreign Office has not done its best to support."

Needless to say such views were not popular during the conflict, but in the disillusioned post-1919 era they did not impair Russell's reputation as a political commentator; if anything they enhanced it. He went to Russia in 1920 to report on the new Red regime that emerged from the Bolshevik Revolution of late 1917 and the ensuing brutal civil war. Lenin's government, exciting to European radicals and abhorrent to conservatives, introduced bitter ideological conflict within the bewildered mind of postwar civilization. Russell was a nonconservative critic of the Communists. His book, *The Practice and Theory of Bolshevism* (1920) outraged the pro-Bolsheviks. Russell saw mainly a brutal dictatorship, led by a repulsively amoral terrorist. No doubt this was a more accurate picture than the rosy one Western radicals discerned. His earlier work on Marxism had left Russell with an aversion to what he regarded as a dogmatic religion, and his visit to Russia in 1920 left him with a persisting dislike of the USSR, rather paradoxical in one who had become a hero of the left wing.

His companion on the trip to Russia, and on one to China the year following, was not Colette, but Dora Black, the free-spirited recent graduate of Girton College, Cambridge, with whom Russell had started an affair in 1919, and who unlike Colette was willing to have children, something Bertrand now much wanted. In 1921 he was to divorce Alys and marry Dora, more than twenty years his junior. It was with some disappointment that admirers of Dora's love ethic greeted her decision to marry simply because a baby was coming, and she herself wrote, "I shall certainly never quite recover from the feeling of disgrace I had in marrying!" Practical considerations, and deference to "Bertie," who was recovering from an almost fatal bout with pneumonia in China, led her to agree to marriage, with reservations that were to prove troublesome in the future. For the time being she was very much in love with Russell ("Bertie") and delighted with the two children, born in late 1921 and in 1923.

In her book *The Right to Be Happy*, published in 1927 and quite successful in the United States, Mrs. Bertrand Russell (as she did not like to be known) argued that what made women happy was not only free and unrestricted sex, but also having children. The latter joy might, she wrote, "involve very nearly a life-long partnership, though not by any means strict marital fidelity," except maybe for "a few years," in order to "ensure the certainty of descent." She was as good as her word. She had other lovers (so did Bertrand), and at length bore two children by one of them. This proved too much for Bertrand, and when he sought a divorce she accused him of going back on their compact. His answer, which he gave with his customary candor, was that what his reason approved his emotions couldn't—a conclusion consistent with his philosophical position that ethics is not a matter for the scientific intellect. In fact, by that time Russell had cast his eyes elsewhere, and the Dora phase was drawing to a close. It lasted a decade; the separation came in 1932, followed by divorce in 1935 and his remarriage in 1936.

During their years together Dora and Bertrand lived with their two children in Cornwall, co-authored a book on *The Prospects of Industrial Civilization* (1923), and then between 1927 and 1932 ran an experimental school at Telegraph House on Beacon Hill in Sussex, a Russell family property. Russell wrote and lectured, going to the United States in 1924 and again in 1927 and 1929 on profitable speaking tours; the Americans paid him well to hear him stylishly insult them, as he observed. He ran for Parliament in 1923. Later Dora did too; the period 1924 to 1926 were exciting political years, featuring the first Labour government and the general strike of 1926. Russell's books included his popular explanation of Einstein's theories, another burning question of the hour (*The A B C of Relativity*); one of Russell's many talents was a flair for making difficult matters comprehensible. His interest in science was always strong; among his books of the 1920s and 1930s were *The Scientific Outlook* and *The Impact of Science on Society*. Dora was less sure about science, which she tended to identify with an abhorred "industrialism" and "mechanism," and which she understood only dimly. But in agreement with her he wrote provocatively about free love and trial marriage in *Marriage and Morals* and *The Conquest of Happiness*. They disagreed about Russia; Dora in general was a more passionate (and naive) political radical. *The Prospects of Industrial Civilization*, which they published in 1923, found them more or less agreeing on a socialist program. But their daughter Katherine says that Dora and Bertrand "quarreled about Russia for years."

As if a book a year, lecture tours, political campaigns, and love affairs were not enough to keep him busy, Russell, now approaching sixty, threw himself in partnership with his wife into running an experimental school for small children. He had persuaded himself that education was the most important of all subjects; how could tomorrow's better world come to pass, eliminating all the woeful errors of the past, unless the new generation was totally reeducated? If it could be, "one generation would suffice to solve all our social problems!" Out of this enthusiasm came two books on education, but within a few years Russell wearied of the school as well as of Dora; perhaps the two waning enthusiasms were connected.

This desire to indoctrinate mingled somewhat incongruously with a passion for total liberty in Russell's educational theory and practice. "Regimentation is the source of evil," Russell wrote in his essay on "Freedom and Authority" (in *Sceptical Essays*, 1928). Children must be free from authoritarian constraints. But they also must be given an intensive education in science and philosophy. Imaginative literature was not Russell's strong point; he read detective stories and sneered at poets. Dora was much more inclined to the imagination, but wrote embarrassingly bad poetry. Neither paid much attention to the exciting new frontiers of literature and the arts, although Russell befriended T.S. Eliot and may have had a brief affair with Eliot's unhappy first wife. Russell and D.H. Lawrence failed badly in an attempted wartime collaboration. On a few occasions Russell tried his hand without much success at fiction, mostly short stories (see especially *Satan in the Suburbs*, 1953).

The experimental school at Telegraph Hill was something of a scandal; callers claimed they had been greeted at the door by naked children, which is possible since the Bertrand Russell–Dora Black creed included sex education. Concealment and hypocrisy about "natural" bodily functions, "Puritan morality," joined Christianity and capitalism among the bad old ideas and habits that had to be extirpated. Telegraph House outdid both Montessori and A.S. Neill's Sommerhill in encouraging freedom and spontaneity. Later Russell admitted, "Many of the children were cruel and destructive. To let the children go free was to establish a reign of terror, in which the strong kept the weak trembling and miserable." Their daughter Katherine's account bears this out. When George Bernard Shaw visited the school, his immediate impulse was "Let's get out of here." The horrors were compounded by a rather Victorian (or Rousseau-like) regime of fresh air and cold showers, a remnant of Puritanism the Russells did not seem to have discarded. But Katherine remembered that the classes were intellectually strenuous, and rather conventional in subject matter. The children did not have much choice about what they learned.

The two Russell-Black youngsters not unpredictably turned out to have serious emotional problems. Katherine much later wrote a moving and critical book about an experience that seared her and almost destroyed her brother. Were her parents, those two eager world-savers, really profound egoists? Dora alleged it of Bertrand: "It may well be that it is not possible, if you spread your love over the human race, to have much left over to dispense within your home." For all Dora's altruistic protestations, one has to think the same of her: Dora's own "right to be happy" prevailed over other considerations. At a pinch the children would be left with servants while she dashed off to a conference of the World League for Sex Reform, a lecture in the Soviet Union or the United States, or a spate of electioneering.

RUSSELL AS A WORLD FIGURE

The death of his elder brother made Bertrand an Earl in 1932, with an obligation to sit in the House of Lords. The somewhat messy divorce from Dora, which left her embittered, was followed by Russell's third marriage, again to a younger woman, this time an Oxford student who had served as his secretary. Patricia, called "Peter" Spence (originally her name was Marjorie; in her autobiography Dora calls her Margery), was both beautiful and willing to have children; she was to bear Bertrand another son. Again, the marriage lasted a little more than a decade, beginning to dissolve by 1946. By the time of the divorce in 1952, Peter and Bertrand Russell had been estranged for some time. By then he had become a Nobel Prize winner, a television celebrity, and a name known all over the globe. He would soon be something like a World Power.

The flow of books continued, the subjects growing more political and less purely philosophical; *Education and the Social Order* was followed by *Freedom and Organization 1814–1914*, *Religion and Science*, and *Power, a New Social Analysis*, with an interlude titled *In Praise of Idleness*. In 1936 Russell had written a pamphlet called *Which Way to Peace?* in which with characteristic perverse clarity he declared that Britain must choose between war and capitulation to Hitler's Germany, and should prefer the latter—better Nazi than dead.

He held to this neutralist position until well into 1939; this was not unusual among intellectuals as well as others, so strong was the adverse reaction to World War I and the fear of another war.

Partly to evade the coming war, it seems, Russell took his family to the United States in 1938, first holding an interim university appointment in California. Then in 1940 he was appointed professor at City College of New York, but he came under attack as an atheist and a libertine; religious and public pressure caused the appointment to be revoked by the court. The brief filed against his appointment mildly characterized Bertrand as "lecherous, libidinous, lustful, venerous, erotomaniac, aphrodisiac, and irreverent." Not for the last time, Russell had become a storm center, a role he thoroughly enjoyed. An enormous controversy about academic freedom, which only the outbreak of major European war in 1940 muted, erupted over the Russell case.

Russell reneged on his neutralist stance, coming around to support the war against nazism. But he remained in the United States until 1944, teaching at Harvard and at the Albert Barnes Foundation in Philadelphia. At this time he published his *History of Western Philosophy*, said to have sold more copies than anything he ever wrote. That the British government failed to enlist him in public relations work in the United States is said to have been because he was too severe a critic of Stalin and the Soviets!

Russell returned to England in 1944, was restored to the Trinity fellowship he had lost in 1916, and given Newton's old chambers in Cambridge. Popular on British radio, later on television because of his quick wit and range of knowledge, he continued with his numerous lecture tours. Awarded the Order of Merit in 1949, he raked in the Nobel Prize for literature the following year. The famous Russell profile became familiar all over the world, and people wrote to him from every continent. New books included *Human Knowledge: Its Scope and Limits (1948); Authority and the Individual (1949);* and *New Hopes for a Changing World (1951)*. All this was but prelude to his emergence as a major public figure.

THE CAMPAIGN FOR NUCLEAR DISARMAMENT AND OTHER CAUSES

Bertrand Russell began his involvement in the nuclear disarmament movement in 1955, after getting the BBC to broadcast his warning that the world was on the brink of unprecedented disaster. Needless to say, he was not the only one dismayed by the emergence of super-atomic weapons and long-range missiles to deliver them, amid the conditions of Cold War hostility between Soviet and Western powers. Nor was the Campaign for Nuclear Disarmament (CND) his invention, as people seemed to think. It was something of a triumph of promotion and publicity that he was able to identify himself so strongly with these causes. Russell was given chief credit for initiating the

Pugwash Conferences. Held in Nova Scotia, financed by the Nova Scotia-born industrialist Cyrus Eaton of Cleveland, Ohio, these meetings brought together Soviet and Western nuclear scientists. They were still being held in 1987, the thirtieth anniversary of the first conference.

Russell's fourth marriage, to the American Edith Finch, accompanied increasing activity in CND meetings and rallies. In 1960/61 with Russell's support the Campaign for Nuclear Disarmament began aggressive "civil disobedience," marked by obstructions and sit-ins, which the Russells doubtless remembered the suffragettes having used in Edwardian times. Russell and his wife were themselves sentenced to a week's imprisonment for inciting civil disobedience. Always excitable, the aged gadfly became as a man possessed in his war with an imagined wicked and stupid ruling class leading the human race toward destruction. President John Kennedy and Prime Minister Harold Macmillan, he said, were "much more wicked than Hitler."

Leader of the crusade to save the world from nuclear war, Russell did not in fact have any clear idea exactly how this was to be done. The two sides of him, rational and emotional, were in conflict. The reasoning side of Russell's brain knew that there was no simple solution. You could not reverse science's relentless march; ban the H-bomb, he wrote, destroy all existing nuclear weapons, and it would do no good, for if war broke out the belligerents would hasten to manufacture them (*Common Sense and Nuclear Warfare*, 1959). Nor would a mere effusion of goodwill resolve international disputes: "I do not know what can be done" to remove mistrust between the great power blocs, he had written, confessing his "impotent perplexity" about the international standoff. His admired master was the stern realist Thomas Hobbes, who had seen no way to get two armed men in a room to throw away their guns simultaneously. "If one side is willing to risk nuclear war and the other is not," the one that does not will fall under the sway of the other.

At times, though not consistently, Russell declared that because "any world government is better than no world government," we would do well to give in to the Russians; better Red than dead! In fact, he continued to have no illusions about the Soviets; the option of those who simply saw the Communists as benign was not open to him. Right after 1945 he had joined Winston Churchill in trying to save Europe from Stalin (the Save Europe Now organization). In 1951 he wrote, "In the Soviet Union human dignity counts for nothing."

One of Russell's greatest embarrassments occurred when, having advocated preventive war against the Soviet Union in 1947 (if it did not accept internationalization of atomic energy), in 1959 he denied having said this; upon being confronted with the evidence, he could only apologize and say that he had completely forgotten that he had ever held such an opinion. The confusion is significant. The Russell intellect saw clearly the fallacies of schemes to abolish war. "Most of the suggestions I have seen struck me as silly," he stated. But the Russell spirit flamed forth in protest against the enormous evil, as he plunged into the movement to "ban the bomb," or at least re-move it from Great Britain's arsenal.

At the same time he began writing to international leaders to protest civil rights violations, a kind of one-man Amnesty International even before that organization's creation. These protests were surprisingly even-handed. A London columnist once annoyed Russell by snapping that Earl Russell should issue just one statement, that he is "in favor of any act calculated to render the West helpless in the face of international Communism," and then shut up! So it may have seemed. But in fact, as regards violations of civil liberties, Russell's complaints were addressed to Khrushchev, to Tito, to Castro, to the leaders of Poland and Romania as well as to those of Turkey, Algeria, Portugal, Greece. Anyone whether Communist or otherwise who suppressed freedom incurred the Russell wrath. It was a tribute to the depth and sincerity of his belief in absolute human freedom.

But in the great Cuban missile crisis of October 1962, during which he attempted to function as something like an international arbiter, Russell made no pretense of impartiality. He believed that there were no Russian missiles or nuclear weapons in Cuba; this was an American fable and President Kennedy a warmonger. "Your action is desperate. . . . End this madness," he wired Kennedy upon the American president's declaration of a naval block-ade against further Soviet shipments of nuclear arms to Cuba. (Both short-range missiles and nuclear warheads were already in Cuba, as subsequent re-search from all the involved countries has confirmed.) Nikita Khrushchev, with whom he had been pen pals since 1956, he asked to show restraint in the face of the "unjustifiable action" of the United States, until Russell and the United Nations could think of a plan.

Russell claimed credit for suggesting the trade-off of withdrawing American missiles from Turkey in exchange for Soviet renunciation of them in Cuba; but it appears that this idea came from other sources as well, and in any case was hardly the crucial factor in resolving the chilling crisis, though it played some part. Russell's rather megalomaniac account of the crisis in his book *Unarmed Victory* (1963) received cold reviews. The Soviet expert Robert Conquest called Russell's position "a defeat of intellect" (Russell threatened to sue). He was ridiculed in the satirical journal *Private Eye*.

On any showing, though, Russell's role as conscience of the world, which he shared with Jean-Paul Sartre, was extraordinary. Soon he and Sartre were to join forces in a "trial" of the Americans for alleged war crimes in Viet-nam—an enterprise that did not fare well. (See Russell's 1967 book *War Crimes in Vietnam*.) But he also condemned the Soviet intervention in Czechoslova-kia in 1968, One of his last (1970) manifestoes attacked Israel for "aggression" against Arabs; but in the same year he wrote a letter to the Polish Communist chief Gomulka accusing him of anti-Semitism.

During the last seven years of his life, from his home in Wales Russell ran the Bertrand Russell Peace Foundation; helping to finance it were funds from the sale of his letters and manuscripts to the highest bidder, which turned out to be Canadian again. (The collection housed at McMaster University in Hamilton, Ontario, has swollen since 1967 to become an impressive research library, touching the many areas Russell was involved in.) To say that Russell ran the foundation became a misstatement; it was, for a time at least, substantially taken over by a brash young American named Ralph Schoenman, Russell's secretary for several years and a director of the organization. A modish left-winger of boundless energy and almost no tact, Schoenman dashed around the world on foundation funds insulting world leaders. Russell had found him "indispensable" as an assistant during the Cuban missile crisis; he only learned later, Russell wrote two months before his own death, that Schoenman claimed credit for the telegrams to Khrushchev. Schoenman alienated Russell's friends and supporters and caused him to be ridiculed as senile, the old sage finally realized. The long memorandum Russell wrote in 1969 detailing his association with Schoenman is a pathetic document. Despite his final repudiation and dismissal of the American, Russell clearly had admired and depended on an immature campus radical of no political judgment, and in the end, it appears, dubious political morals. Jean-Paul Sartre's association with a similar young man suggests that these aging culture heroes hoped to preserve their youthful image in this way. These were, after all, the 1960s.[2]

The Autobiography of Bertrand Russell (3 vols., 1967–1969; compare the earlier BBC talks published as *Portraits from Memory* in 1956), Russell's final testament, quickly took rank as one of the century's leading personal accounts. Hardly a modest man, Russell like most public eminences was a narcissist; Virginia Woolf called him "a fervid egoist." But Russell's literary charm, never so evident as in his autobiography, depends in part on an ability also to deprecate himself, even laugh at himself, and of course laugh at the human race. He once published a history of the world, which is undoubtedly the shortest one ever written; it consists of one sentence, stating that, ever since its beginning, mankind has never refrained from any error of which it is capable.

Russell died peacefully on February 2, 1970, aged 97 years and 9 months, at his home Plas Penrhyn in northern Wales. He had almost succumbed to double pneumonia in China nearly fifty years earlier. The Japanese press actually reported his death. Had he died then, his philosophical reputation would not have been much different from what it is, for Russell did little with pure philosophy after 1914. The intervening years had seen the stream of books change in character from predominantly philosophical to social and political, from academic to popular or confrontational. One must ask whether

---

[2]Such behavior was not, however, confined to male culture heroes. The fashionable American painter Georgia O'Keeffe took up with a 27-year-old man at the age of 85, turning everything over to him as she abandoned her old friends.

the last half of Russell's long life was a wasted effort. But on any reckoning it was an amazing achievement in bridging the formidable gulf between the worlds of thought and action, life and work.

RUSSELL IN REVIEW

Russell's immense energy and range of interests, his long and active life, his ability as an intellectual of the highest caliber to become also a world-famous, headline-grabbing personality, were features of a life in some respects unparalleled in this century. His fellow Edwardian and socialist H.G. Wells probably wrote more books, but was far less a philosophical intellect. We have mentioned only a fraction of Russell's 75 or so works; additionally, he wrote about 2,500 articles and some 50,000 letters, while the lectures, talks, addresses numbered in the thousands also—Russell was a highly proficient and much sought-after speaker. He traveled in the United States, throughout Europe, China, Australia, and the Soviet Union, though he never wanted to return to the latter after the disillusioning experience in 1920. Having lived in the United States for several years, lectured throughout the country, and become involved in a famous controversy there in 1940, Russell was as well known in America as in Great Britain; but, as the collection of letters called *Dear Bertrand Russell* (1969) reveals, people wrote to him from all over the world. The main impact of Russell was therefore as a personality, and his chief significance lies in his life itself. This included his extraordinary romantic side, with the four wives, two long-time mistresses, and numerous other love affairs. He became prominently identified with a credo of sexual permissiveness or "free love," an outlook that, however, was hardly unusual in his generation of rebels fleeing Victorian morals and manners.

His thought in the end perhaps suffered from his amazing versatility and incredible facility. Russell wrote as readily as he talked, almost never revised; in this respect, at least, he seems to have resembled Shakespeare. His range extended from highly technical exercises in logic to books about love and marriage. Here was an outstanding philosopher who once wrote a column for the Hearst newspapers and appeared successfully on both radio and television. Additionally, he was an embattled political polemicist who enjoyed sailing against the wind. Despite Russell's high intelligence and literary genius such an enormous output was inevitably of uneven quality. In few specific areas has his thought made an enduring impact.

His early adventures in pure logic survive, of course, though the nonexpert may wonder to what purpose beyond the torture of university students. The hope that a reformed logical language would establish philosophy on a new basis of scientific certainty was destined to disappointment. In 1931 Kurt Gödel showed that some propositions in the *Principia* cannot be proved or disproved. The basic axioms of arithmetic thus might give rise to contradictions. (See *On Formally Undecidable Propositions of Principia Mathematica and Related Systems*, transl. R.B. Braithwaite.)

The new mode of philosophizing to which Russell and G.E. Moore contributed, along with Viennese "logical positivists," attacked traditional ontology and metaphysics as muddled thinking. Leaving the essentially irrational realm of morals and values to others, philosophers should concentrate on forging the right analytical tools for empirical science to use. Most of this program, which for the 1920s and 1930s was an exciting "revolution in philosophy," now is badly dated if not obsolete. But Russell remained a convinced rationalist, rejecting both the "common-language" philosophers and the existentialists. As he wrote more and more about morals and politics and less about logic and philosophy, Russell rather lost touch with the professional philosophers, who grew to regard him as obsolete while he scorned the analytical school deriving from his one-time student and friend Wittgenstein. He snapped that these philosophers concerned themselves only with the silly things silly people say. But the tendency today, which surely would have annoyed him, is to regard Wittgenstein as much the greater pure philosopher.

Russell also wrote a great deal about religion. It was an obsession from the start. He lost his belief in God to Mill and Darwin when a teenager, and he abhorred the suffocating Victorian piety in which he was brought up. Like Tolstoy his pet aversion was "the organized churches of the world." Russell's compulsive, often bitter nonconformism, perhaps stemming from his lonely childhood, included aggressive anti-Christian views. Some of his tracts were published by a low-brow Midwest American atheist press, headed by a renegade Catholic priest, putting Russell in company quite as demeaning for a great philosopher as the Hearst newspapers, if in a different way. In the manner of the Victorian "rationalists," he gleefully exposed what he felt to be Christian superstitions and vices, and was totally oblivious of all the efforts— associated with such august names as Karl Barth, Paul Tillich, Jacques Maritain, Martin Buber—to recapture a viable Christianity or Judaism. Strident and simplistic, Russell's diatribes against Christianity presented it simply as "irrational fanaticism" and accused it of causing virtually all of humanity's troubles. "The dragon of religion must be slain before mankind can enter the golden age," he declaimed. "The Christian religion, as organized in its churches, is the principal enemy of moral progress in the world." Again, "It seems to me that the people who have held to the Christian religion have been for the most part extremely wicked," he opined.

Analysis of Russell's frequent pronouncements on the subject of Christianity reveal that he usually equated it with antirational superstition fortified by hostility to the enjoyment of life and, most especially, by an intolerant persecutiuon of doctrinal deviations: a mixture of the Inquisition and Puritanism. In his group portrait of the Christian Church appeared the visages of Torquemada, Cotton Mather, the persecutors of Galileo, "Soapy Sam" Wilberforce and the anti-Darwinists, Mrs. Grundy, lean ascetics as well as fat bishops. The Church was not unlike Hitler's mythic Jew, in that Russell selected all its most unpleasant features to form one image of evil. Russell's own extreme intolerance, oddly, shone forth brightly in his attack on Christianity for its intolerance. His writings on this subject tend to be an embarrassment to his commentators: "Not one of Russell's more graceful efforts," Ronald Jager remarked. But he touched a responsive note in some quarters.

Russell's fairly consistent hostility to Soviet communism stemmed mostly from his feeling that it was basically another dogmatic and intolerant religion. "The most dangerous features of communism are reminiscent of the medieval church. They consist of fanatical acceptance of doctrines . . . and savage persecution of those who reject them" (*Why I Am Not a Christian*). He agreed with John Dewey that, having emancipated himself from one dogmatic creed, he was not about to bind himself to another!

Yet like Tolstoy, Russell felt the need for a faith, because he thought that "in order to value life it is necessary to value something other than mere life . . . some end outside human life." He had some mystical experiences when young, and in 1903 he wrote an impassioned essay titled "The Free Man's Worship" (later retitled "A Free Man's Worship"), which has often been reprinted. Faced with the fact that one is only a tiny, fleeting accident in the vast impersonal cosmos, that all one's achievements are destined to be "buried beneath the debris of a universe in ruins," a person can take comfort only in the freedom of his or her mind to formulate a faith, a "vision of the good." Russell hurls Promethean defiance back at a cruel fate.

Toward the end of his life Russell declared that "I have never found religious satisfaction in any philosophical doctrine that I could accept." But he never stopped trying. Meanwhile, he trusted his impulses. In his autobiography he claimed that from a mystical experience in his eighteenth year he emerged with three lifelong "passions," these being, in addition to the search for knowledge and for love, "unbearable pain for the suffering of mankind." This mystical experience grew out of an infatuation with the wife of his colleague, Alfred North Whitehead. Russell's lifelong experiments in erotic love, while in some ways not very unusual—he was an archetypal male philanderer trying to hold on to his youth—were certainly intensely interesting, and along with his writings on the subject they made a notable contribution to twentieth-century sexual history. Recent feminists are likely to downgrade his contribution to their cause, in his life if not his writings. But it can hardly be denied that Russell along with Shaw and Wells gave a decisive boost to the movement for women's rights; they may even be said to have created the movement.

One may say that Russell's chief religion was the fearless pursuit of truth. The enemies were credulity, misinformation, propaganda, as well as repression of the free mind. "The scientific temper is capable of regenerating mankind," he held. The paradox is that Russell himself often wrote hastily, angrily, and inaccurately about the events of the day that moved him deeply.

He was also willing on occasion to suggest censorship; he said he would ban the teaching of nationalism! Certainly he would have kept Christianity out of his utopia. Like many proclaimers of free speech he had his intolerant side.

And he did not think science capable of finding values. "The evils of the world are due to moral defects quite as much as to lack of intelligence," Russell once conceded, but added that "the human race has not hitherto discovered any method of eradicating moral defects; preaching and exhortation only add hypocrisy to the previous list of vices. Intelligence, on the other hand, is easily improved by methods known to every competent educator." Which, of course, hardly answers the question of what happens if intelligence is placed at the service of a moral defect.

Russell sometimes called himself a socialist but did not develop any distinctive conceptions of socialism—about which, indeed, he was usually ambivalent. State socialism might provide more justice in the distribution of wealth but at the cost of liberty. Russell was among those who never doubted that the "planned" economy would be far more efficient than what they saw as the chaos of capitalist market competition; he never recognized the value of the free market nor saw the flaws inherent in centralized planning. His dissent from the Stalinism fashionable among intellectuals in the 1930s was based on political considerations, not economic ones. The price of economic affluence might be too high in the form of loss of individual freedom.

His foremost concern was for liberty of the mind, and his passion and courage greatly advanced this cause, but his thoughts on the subject were basically those of John Stuart Mill. Russell may be credited with doing more than anyone to introduce the methods of aggressive "civil disobedience" that became the stock in trade of student revolutionaries in the turbulent 1960s. Mohandas Gandhi, however, had used such methods earlier, and he had learned it from Leo Tolstoy, who found it among other places in Henry David Thoreau, and so on back; Russell himself mentioned the early Christians. He can hardly have forgotten Emily Davidson and the militant suffragettes of his youth. Russell cannot claim a great deal of originality here. The "ban the bomb" movement fizzled out, in any case, after a couple of years. Russell certainly was in the vanguard of those who pointed out the urgency of the situation regarding nuclear weapons, but countless others did so too in the years just after the fusion (hydrogen) bomb and long-range missiles entered the arsenals of the superpowers in the late 1950s. As a propagandist for peace Bertrand might merit the response of A.E. Housman, who remarked, "If I were the Prince of Peace I would choose a less provocative ambassador"!

Russell's ethical, social, and political thought suffers from a strange ambivalence that was actually a source of its appeal: It is partisan and emotional, yet argued in an analytical, rational style, marked by great clarity laced with wit and paradox. "I like precision," Russell said. "I like sharp outlines. I hate misty vagueness." The world, unfortunately, especially the world of politics, is prone to vagueness and mistiness. Much of Russell's strength, like Karl

Marx's, stemmed from the brisk confidence with which he made unqualified judgments. Yet these might not be consistent with each other. We are reminded of what someone said of Voltaire, that he presented a "chaos of clear ideas." Indeed, Russell, like Jean-Paul Sartre, has frequently been compared to that great French Enlightenment skeptic and satirist.

For much of his life Russell thought reform of education the most important of all tasks. But here also he suffered from being a relative dilettante. What he wrote about education, while interesting, was not systematic enough to secure much of a place in the field of educational philosophy. As we know, after a few years he abandoned the experimental school he and Dora ran, seemingly regarding it as a failure. What remains are some curious fragments from a passionately committed life.

The most troubling contradiction in Russell is that he did not live up to his own creed of salvation through use of critical intelligence. He was often gullible, factually wrong in his appraisal of world affairs. He believed there were no Soviet missiles at all in Cuba; that was a fable made up in Washington, he claimed in 1962. He uncritically followed the Mark Lane theory on the assassination of President Kennedy and believed in the Rosenbergs' innocence. Then he denied that the Vietcong was Communist-dominated. As early as 1913 his friend George Santayana had noticed the "strange mixture" in Russell of "great ability and great disability." His later years of inspired prophecy, as his disciples saw it, seemed to others bizarre megalomania. Applicable to Russell is the frequent observation that the kind of thinking and writing appropriate to mathematics and science is absolutely wrong for politics and history; likewise, that, as Arthur Koestler noted, "Scientists, especially when they leave the particular field in which they have specialized, are just as ordinary, pig-headed and unreasonable as anybody else, and their unusually high intelligence only makes their prejudices all the more dangerous."

Russell's disciples, who organized Russell societies and published newsletters, tended toward the bizarre. The Russell Society Newsletter of February 1988, for example, carried news of a New Jersey attorney who had recently disrobed in public and who offered a certificate "unconditionally guaranteeing the following: When You Die, You Rot." Russellites were fervent atheists ("non-Godists," as Kathleen Nott called them), fanatical antinuclearists, or simply those who worshipped the departed sage as a kind of antiestablishment saint. The Bertrand Russell Society Annual Conferences in the United States brought together a strange blend of professional philosophers and amateur oddballs. Those attracted to the Russell cult were uncomfortably similar to Scientologists, Zen Buddhists, and shamanists. In a 1967 BBC broadcast discussion of Russell's legacy, Norman St. John-Stevas noted: "I think that the place he will be accorded in history, leaving aside the philosophic contribution, is in the gallery of great English eccentrics." What Bertrand would have made of this is hard to know. He prided himself on his nonconformity and individuality, but he surely aspired to more than a place alongside Lord Monboddo and Baron Corvo. He wanted to save the world.

The magazine *Private Eye* satirized him as a would-be nonagenarian superman, swimming the Atlantic before picketing the White House. Russell did indeed suffer from illusions of omnipotence; yet he *was* a unique figure in the world. This embattled personality with the razor-sharp brain, the quick wit, the ready phrase, the far-ranging knowledge, the incredible energy and passionate idealism became familiar all over the world. If not, as one philosopher declared, "the dominant figure of the century," Russell was one of its most interesting and influential ones.

Russell was most fascinating in his attempt to both live and think as a total person. "There is no longer a whole man confronting a whole world, but a human something floating about in a universal culture-medium," complained the hero of Robert Musil's *The Man without Qualities*. We have technicians of all sorts, whether in philosophy, science, or politics. To be a person who knows something of all of these and applies his knowledge to real life is a rarity. Russell made such an attempt, and if he partly failed, his courage and tenacity in trying should live on as an ideal.

14

Margaret Thatcher and the Economic Dilemma

THE SOCIALIST TURN

The age of statism in twentieth-century economic life with slight exaggeration might be said to have begun in England with one determined English woman and have ended with another. The first woman was Beatrice Potter Webb, who with the aid of her husband, Sidney, wrote a government paper in 1909 often considered the most significant expression of a new philosophy of economic welfare, one that challenged Victorian orthodoxy. Placing its faith in the individual entrepreneur, classical nineteenth-century liberalism had seen government, beyond strict limits, as an evil to be watched closely, and if necessary fought as a mortal foe of both liberty and material well-being. But in their minority report to a far-ranging official investigation of the British Poor Laws, the Fabian Socialists Sidney and Beatrice Webb argued that prevention of poverty is the responsibility primarily of government not of individuals. It is a social problem not a private one. Within a few years that principle was to be substantially accepted.

At the dawn of the twentieth century, a literature of reappraisal expressed considerable disappointment with the nineteenth century for not distributing widely enough the great wealth it had produced. L.T. Hobhouse remarked, "The nineteenth century might be called the age of Liberalism, yet its close saw the fortunes of that great movement brought to their lowest ebb." In the old Liberal Party itself, the party of John Bright and William Gladstone, people were talking now of the New Liberalism, almost directly opposite from the old liberalism in its attitude toward government's role in the economy. Two years after the Webb report a Liberal government in Britain secured passage of the National Insurance Act (1911), which a leading British newspaper called "the greatest scheme of social reconstruction ever attempted" in England. Modeled on the German system, it allowed the government to administer and contribute to a fund for insurance against unemployment. To pay for this and other rising expenses of government, Parliament in the same year passed an income tax amid scenes such as that body had not witnessed for two hundred years; its foes declared the tax to be contrary to basic individual rights, the first act of a veritable social revolution. Some members asserted a parallel with the illegal taxes of King Charles I. But the Fabian Socialists, the group to which the Webbs belonged, persuasively presented the case for a "collectivism" that, they said, was the inevitable result of modern industrial society with its vast enterprises, its complex interdependencies. Some private corporations, it was widely believed, had grown so big that only government could, and should, control them.

Social security systems and, needless to say, income taxes far in excess of the very modest ones enacted in 1911 are commonplace today in all countries pretending to any degree of modernization. The defenses of old-fashioned negative or *laissez-faire* liberalism suffered deep incursions during the Great Depression, and especially after World War II. Both world wars induced a kind of "war socialism" as the demand for speedy production of war materials in unprecedented quantities forced governments to plan their production while rationing consumer goods. In addition, the economic collapse of the 1930s dealt the old economic ideas devastating blows. At first most governments tried to follow the prescriptions of established economic theory by allowing the "natural" processes of recovery to operate, with the state's role confined largely to keeping out of the way. But the medicine of budget austerity and inflation avoidance failed to work.

Economic theories long considered valid had miscarried, evidently because actual conditions did not correspond to their highly idealized assumptions of perfect competition, international free trade, currency stability, and so forth. Desperate conditions forced abandonment of the apparently sterile program of doing nothing but wait for automatic adjustment to take place, amid hunger, unemployment, and bankruptcy. A host of ideas for curing or ameliorating economic woes burst forth.

At this moment the Soviet Union launched its ambitious program of planned economic growth, while the American New Deal encouraged experimental government intervention of various kinds, from attempting to fix industrial prices and wages to providing jobs for unemployed workers. To a considerable extent, the New Deal found theoretical justification in the brilliant Cambridge economist John Maynard Keynes. A Bloomsbury esthete, Keynes was also a sometime friend of the Communist moles, but he always thought Marxist economics misguided and simplistic. His vision preserved the private-property, capitalistic order while keeping it on track by using the fiscal and tax powers of the government as a balancing wheel. In times of economic depression governments should not hesitate to disperse more funds than they collect. (Keynes never intended that they should institutionalize overspending.) Keynes' *General Theory* (1936) provided the leading model of macroeconomic theory for the next three decades.

Even neoclassical economists wavered in their faith. The great names of free-market theory were literally driven into obscurity. A student of Ludwig von Mises has recalled how in the 1940s this distinguished Austrian economist, who had sought to demonstrate the unworkability of socialism, could not get a university post and was reduced to teaching part-time at a New York City business school.[1] The University of Chicago and other universities also rejected Mises's student and fellow Austrian Friedrich von Hayek, who would receive a Nobel Prize in economics in 1974. Unmitigated free-enterprise capitalism was relegated to the dark ages of human society; Karl Marx's predecessor and teacher Adam Smith, the founder of modern economics, became a byword for folly.

World War II, it was thought, demonstrated the ability of human intelligence to plan for full production. "Full Employment in a Free Society" was the title of an important wartime British study by William Beveridge, a belated convert to the welfare state. The expert use of government controls to help bring about recovery seemed even more necessary to war-shattered France and other parts of devastated Europe. That "planned production for use not profit" was superior to capitalism's chaos and greed, all right-thinking, that is, left-leaning intellectuals accepted in principle, if not always in the Russian practice. Such views came not just from Marxian dogmatists but from such anti-Communists as Albert Einstein and Bertrand Russell, the paladins of thought. The latter's hostility to Soviet communism, we recall, was entirely based on its lack of democracy and intellectual freedom, which he attributed not to socialism itself but mainly to Marxian dogmatism. "Private ownership of land and capital" Russell thought indefensible not merely on grounds of social justice but "on the ground that it is an uneconomical way of producing what the community needs." George Bernard Shaw's many lectures on this theme made the same point. The whole Western socialist tradition, rooted in Fabianism more than Marxism, took for granted the greater efficiency of socialism. The only concern was whether this efficiency might be bought at too high a price of liberty.

Sometimes the term was "collectivism," a bit less frightening than "socialism." Historian Paul Addison observed: "The intelligentsia worked with great success to establish collectivism as the conventional wisdom for all

---

[1]Richard Cornuelle, "New Work for Invisible Hands," *Times Literary Supplement* (*TLS*), April 5, 1991.

thinking people." "Collectivism" in British usage meant nationalization of some basic industries combined with centralized state administration of welfare and social security, along with trade unionism, the unions being given special powers and protection by government.

Great Britain's Labour party, rooted in the trade union movement, with a socialist tradition since 1918 and a platform pledged to nationalize basic industries, won the election of 1945, surprisingly defeating Winston Churchill's successful war government. It was the first clear victory for Labour in its forty-five-year history, and with a sense of jubilation at having conquered, the Labour government proceeded to begin to carry out its promises. This victory of socialism was supposed to herald the dawn of a new age, marked by a more compassionate as well as more efficient order, assuring abundance for all. In its six years in power Prime Minister Clement Attlee's Labour government installed a "cradle to grave" social security system, a national health program providing free medical care, and nationalization of a number of major industries, including steel and coal as well as the Bank of England.

THE TURN AGAINST SOCIALISM

The Labourites were scarcely the first to find the real world disillusioning. The band of socialist brethren who had worked over the years to win the right to install their program thought the victory had been won; the climax of all history had arrived and it only remained to celebrate the outcome. But in fact the struggle had only begun. Labour's six years in power between 1945 and 1951 did not produce much economic success. Social security was there to stay, and so was socialized medicine, despite many grumblings—probably Labour's biggest coup. But other nationalized industries proved inefficient. More important, transferring ownership did not in itself solve the real problem of expanding production and improving efficiency. The British economy relied heavily on exports, and here it was necessary to compete with other countries.

Labour never really recovered from the collapse of the socialist dream in its first term in office. Other European countries, including before long the despised and defeated Germans, seemed to do better by trusting basically to free enterprise. The Conservatives meanwhile had stolen Labour's clothes by going far toward accepting the managed economy and the welfare state; they rejected nationalization (though not until Mrs. Thatcher did they try to undo what Labour had done between 1945 and 1950) and successfully marketed their own economic program as more flexible than Labour's rigid straitjacket of state control. A strong tradition of paternalism existed in the Conservative party, reaching back to Benjamin Disraeli and Joseph Chamberlain, in social thought to Coleridge; the Tories in their way embraced the welfare state quite as warmly as did Labour.

There was a long Conservative term in office from 1951 to 1964—three consecutive general election victories in a row—while bitter arguments broke out within a frustrated opposition. These debates within Labour ranged an unrepentant hard left against a pragmatic, compromising group who believed the party must stop sounding the theme of class war, renounce nationalization, and gain middle-class support by moderate policies. Though in general the moderates prevailed, producing in Hugh Gaitskell the Labour party's leading figure of the post-1951 years until his untimely death in 1963, the split remained, even after Labour finally won an election in 1964.

A slim Labour victory that year led to a more substantial one in 1966, and the party held office until 1970, returning rather unexpectedly in 1974 for another five years. But it never really did well. At this time some harsh economic realities began to intrude themselves. Books begin to appear about "the end of the economic miracle" and "the passing of the Keynesian age." The word "stagflation" made its debut, a refutation in practice of something economic theory had held as axiomatic, that one could choose between inflation and unemployment. Now it seemed that one could have both—as it were, losing one's cake and not eating it too. Injection of government spending was a stimulant whose effect wore off, it seemed, requiring ever more of the drug.

Not Margaret Thatcher but the last Labour prime minister, James Callaghan, pointed out that it was no longer possible for a government to spend its way out of a recession. Rising social welfare costs raised taxes, which discouraged business investment. Government borrowing to finance perpetual budget deficits crowded out business loans and raised interest rates. Higher taxes reached the stage where an increase did not even bring in much additional revenue, and it actually cost jobs by raising the cost of goods. Increasingly generous minimum wage laws and unemployment grants diminished incentives, bringing declines in productivity; for higher salaries, workers produced less. Powerful trade unions kept wages ascending and hampered technological change by seeking to veto new and more efficient processes that made some workers redundant.

With Britain plagued by inflation (well into the 20 percent range), the Labour government was widely considered to be dominated by the unions, which had a vested interest in inflationary wage settlements, and also to some extent by the socialist left wing of the party, not numerous but influential, which pressed for increased public spending on welfare measures. When the government tried to restrain wage demands, the left became infuriated. The once fair-haired lad of Labour, Harold Wilson, resigned the prime ministership in 1976, completely disillusioned. (He later praised Mrs. Thatcher and criticized some of his own party.) Wilson's successor, James Callaghan, lacking the prestige of an elected leader, struggled in vain against the inflationary spiral, which caused a currency crisis; in order to get a desperately needed loan the British government had to submit to International Monetary Fund terms. At the end, in 1978/79, Labour collapsed spectacularly in a wave of strikes and confusion, as the trade unions rebelled against the Labour party leadership's attempt to hold back wage demands.

The failure of this last Labour government led to a shattering electoral rebuke to Labour in 1979, inaugurating a period of Conservative power that swept on to ever larger victories over the next decade. The 1980s belonged to the new Conservative leader, Margaret Thatcher. Labour was to split apart and then regroup as a very different kind of party.

This was part of a general crisis of socialism that extended all over the world and affected every country in some way. Its most notable manifestation was the decline and eventual collapse of the Soviet Union's administered economy. In France, a socialist president called off his program of government-fueled economic expansion in the 1980s and went over to a market-directed system; so also in Spain. Even Sweden wavered in its socialist faith.

In Britain, the failure of a great strike in protest against the newly elected Conservative government (May 14, 1980) revealed the decline in trade union power. In the next several years Margaret Thatcher was to push through Parliament a series of Employment and Trade Union acts that took away many of the immunities and privileges granted to organized labor. For example, workers had been compelled to pay dues to the union whether they wished to or not, and to go on strike if the union leadership ordered it. Employers had been compelled to punish workers who defied a union strike order. Unions at one time were not liable for damages resulting from strikes. It is fair to say that to most people many if not all of these privileges seemed excessive and unfair.

A general move to the right made its appearance midway in the 1970s. Deep disenchantment with public enterprises, including socialized medicine, marked this shift. At the same time new technology was bringing about a basic change in the economy. The service sector grew enormously at the expense of manufacturing. In other words, more people found employment in performing services, all the way from waiting on restaurant tables to giving financial advice, than in making things. In Great Britain, from 1955 to 1975 the percentage of jobs in the service industries rose from 46 percent to 57 percent of the total. Office jobs almost doubled in the same period. Computer technology tended to make the old-fashioned assembly-line factory obsolete and to provide new entrepreneurial growth. "The postindustrial society" became a favorite topic of discussion. This was a communications and not a heavy-industry economy; it demanded brains more than brawn. A decline in the number of manufacturing workers of the traditional sort was one reason for a decrease in trade union membership. The main sources of old-fashioned socialist militancy (e.g., the coal mines of Wales and the shipyards of Scotland) deteriorated with the decay of these industries in their nineteenth-century form. Trade union membership plummeted on average from 35 percent of the work force in 1980 to 28 percent in 1988 in the top ten industrial countries. For Britain, 41.5 percent of the work force was unionized as of 1988.

The British indulged in mordant self-analyses concerning their decline. There were dubious theories about the drying up of the entrepreneurial spirit. Thatcherites blamed the unions. Some argued that all societies lose their drive with success. The great Austrian-born economist Joseph Schumpeter thought that the work ethic and ambition found in early capitalism inevitably decayed; the scions of the great pioneer capitalists were either sybarites or socialists, while faceless corporate bureaucrats replaced them as business managers. The British were said to have lost their spirit of initiative; or they had too much of it but the wrong kind—nineteenth-century small-scale style. Evangelical religion was not strength but sentimental weakness. The British people were too civilized; or they had become barbarians. This considerable literature of self-examination testified to a national malaise, but failed to agree on a diagnosis.

Mrs. Thatcher for her part had no doubt that it was possible to revive individual pride, initiative, and work ethic after decades of being repressed by the dead hand of state regulation and union dominance. If only these weights were removed, and it was freed from heavy taxation, British enterprise, she thought, would respond by producing better goods more cheaply, and thus raise the standard of life. Between 1967 and 1975 Britain was the only major industrial country to show a decline in business spending on research and development. The result was that the country had become backward in technological innovation. Something dramatic must be done to turn this around.

This turn to the right, if such it was, came as a surprise. In 1975 the novelist Anthony Burgess, going George Orwell one better, wrote *1985*; predicting the past like most prophets, he foresaw a nightmare of inflation, trade union tyranny, Arab ownership of Great Britain—nothing about Thatcherism. That Mrs. Thatcher emerged so quickly out of the shadows in 1979 to take charge of a staggering country was a part of her success story.

THE COLLAPSE OF THE SOVIET SOCIALIST ECONOMY

Meanwhile, Margaret Thatcher was being upstaged in Russia. The spectacular decline and fall of the USSR did work to strengthen her own case against the socialist principle. The collapse of the Soviet economy came rather swiftly in the 1980s, with few among a distinguished corps of Sovietologists predicting it. A specialist symposium published in 1983 titled *The Soviet Economy: Toward the Year 2000* included such judgments as a prediction that the USSR's gross national product (GNP) would continue to grow at an annual rate of better than 3 percent to the year 2000, and that the odds were "overwhelmingly against" any fundamental economic reform. In reviewing this book Soviet expert Alec Nove, while suggesting a possible system crisis, added, "It would indeed be wrong to suggest that the Soviet Union is in any danger of collapse or disintegration."[2] The collapse and disintegration were in fact well underway.

The original fantasy of the Marxist-Leninist leaders of the Russian Revolution was an economic order without money or markets, somehow distributing the fruits of labor equally and justly with harmonious coordination of production. Marx had never explained how this could take place; it was just supposed to happen when the beast capitalism had been slain, ending the reign of selfishness and greed. It was always an illusion, yet with experience and experimentation the highly centralized and authoritarian Soviet Russian regime believed answers would be found. A lively debate took place in the 1920s, before Stalin arose to end debate by sheer force.

In 1922 Ludwig von Mises, the great Vienna economic theorist, alleged that only the market can provide a rational system of allocating resources. A planned economic system has no way to determine real costs of production. The attempt to decide on prices by administrative fiat can only lead to confusion and breakdown. "The motive force of the whole process which gives rise to the factors of production is the ceaseless search on the part of the capitalist and entrepreneur to maximize their profits by serving the customers wishes." Likewise there was a fatal flow in divorcing managerial performance and managerial reward. The most effective answer to von Mises's charge that a socialist economy was simply unworkable came from the Polish-born, University of Chicago economist Oskar Lange, who stipulated the necessity of "market socialism" with considerable decentralization of planning. Another line of theory saw the answer in stimulation of a market by elaborate use of mathematics. Such ideas, however, though sometimes suggested were never implemented in the USSR. Stalin's successor, Nikita Khrushchev, labored for economic reform but brought forth only a mouse; some changes in 1965 amounted to very little.

Stalin's command economy, with its obligatory output targets and physical allocation of producer goods, found its motivating force in the prison camp or firing squad. Doctored statistics persuaded the world for a time that it was a success. In the primitive stage of capitalist accumulation, and the building of an infrastructure, this state-administered and enforced program worked better than it did when a more complex consumer economy was needed. The appalling cruelty and loss of human lives entailed in Stalin's system was somewhat concealed from the outer world. Few saw, or wanted to see, the slave labor camps for a surprisingly long time. The threat of a firing squad rather than just bankruptcy did indeed function as a potent incentive for managers. Western observers, even experts, credited the Soviet economy with success. A representative evaluation by J.P. Nettl on the fiftieth anniversary of the Communist Revolution in 1967 paid tribute to "fifty years of concrete achievement" and spoke of "the enormous resurgence of Soviet indus-

---

[2]*Times Literary Supplement* (*TLS*), August 5, 1983.

try," impressive space technology, and growing interest from the Third World in Soviet methods. Nettl added, "The Soviet consumer will undoubtedly continue to be better off. . . . His rate of betterment will appear . . . extremely favorable in comparison with Western countries." Another standard textbook, Paul R. Gregory and Robert C. Stuart's *Soviet Economic Structure and Performance* (1974), declared, "The standard of living in the Soviet Union has risen rapidly and today stands at a level never before known in that country." And in 1984 (*The Soviet System in Theory and Practice*) Prof. Harry G. Shaffer saw the gap between the Soviet Union and the United States narrowing; with the Russian record before us, he wrote, "The West would be well advised not to underestimate the past performance nor the economic potential of the USSR."

Such judgments could be multiplied, though even the optimistic appraisals usually mentioned areas of concern. Shortages and low quality of goods, backward technology, and slowness to innovate plagued the Soviet economy. "Chronic shortage is the necessary consequence of a system that is dominated by bureaucratic coordination and that almost totally excludes market coordination," an East European economist pointed out. There was widespread corruption, and workers compensated for an absence of all but the most basic consumer goods by consuming lots of vodka. Some thought only the presence of a clandestine capitalist "second economy," estimated as high as 40 percent of GNP, enabled the supposedly socialist system to function at all. Against the predictions of the official ideology that its superior economic system would overtake and surpass the West, the Soviet Union fell further and further behind a dynamic international capitalism in the 1970s and 1980s. Disenchantment set in not only at home but among Third World countries that had hoped to find an easy road to economic development by emulating the Communists. They began to desert Moscow and line up for loans from the World Bank.

Most ironically, the Communist state displayed all the defects it accused capitalism of having: a privileged ruling class, a drugged proletariat, fetters on production, an "ideology" far out of touch with reality. In some ways the relaxing of terror under Stalin's successors made economic problems worse; with the prison camp no longer an incentive, the clumsy central planning apparatus fell into bureaucratic laxity. There were few penalties for inefficiency, no compelling budget constraints, minimal incentives to innovate, to improve quality, or to work harder. These all made for a slovenly, low-productivity system. Reformers' attempts to establish a market and some competition ran up against the powerful resistance of a huge entrenched Communist party and bureaucracy. This structure increasingly grew alienated from the people it was supposed to serve.

In the end the system ran out of excuses. There had always been some handy explanation, especially World War II and ensuing crises, for the expected utopia's failure to appear. Now at last none of them washed. A popular Soviet song declared "I don't believe in promises any more."

The remarkably rapid disintegration of the old order in the USSR and throughout Eastern Europe in 1989/90 could be explained by the simple fact that, having miserably failed, one whole economic system had to be replaced by another one. Between a system based on commands from central planning offices and one based on freely negotiated contracts, between bureaucratic allocation and a money-market determination of production and prices, there could be no middle ground. *Tertium non datur.* A "planned market economy" was a contradiction in terms. You can have a market economy within the framework of an order—indeed, you must have such an order, consisting of the basic rules. You can add, if you like, and this arguably was necessary, a variety of state counterweights and rescue operations. You can have, temporarily at least, a planned economy with a parallel market economy, though this is extremely awkward; or a different-sectored one—that is, two separate and unrelated economies, a schizophrenic situation that existed in Hungary for a number of years before 1989. But you cannot combine the planned and the market economy as an integral unit.

It was this siutuation that confronted the vast Soviet Union and led many to argue that the changeover, though bound to be agonizingly painful, was best done as quickly as possible. The new capitalists were now found in the lands of communism. To be sure, the persistence of the old cadres and the agony of change resulted in continual backsliding. An unhappy Boris Yeltsin followed an ultimately unsuccessful Mikhail Gorbachev as martyrs to the new revolution of capitalism. But there was no way to return to the old order of state socialism.

THATCHERISM IN ACTION

Someone noted that Mrs. Thatcher was the only prime minister in British history to give her name to an *-ism*. Dogmatic doctrines ran counter to the English heritage and temper. A determined and able woman took on just about the whole of that tradition and, for a time, won. Of course she made enemies. The intellectuals and university Establishment mostly hated her, the more so as she cut their subsidies. Though she was a distinguished (to say the least) alumna, Oxford University refused to grant her an honorary degree. Within the Conservative party, long dominated by landed aristocrats, this grocer's daughter was an anomaly. Trained as an industrial chemist, she was (happily) married to a businessman. Religious background: Methodist, not Church of England.

Initially her determination and obvious ability won Mrs. Thatcher respect, even awe. To challenge the "Oxbridge" intellectual elite—including its ally the BBC-ITV state monopoly of broadcasting and television—was as popular as to curb the powers of the trade union bosses. And economically there was early success in checking inflation. Great Britain did not have a grossly unbalanced national budget as did the United States. Other strokes of good fortune attended Mrs. Thatcher's early years in power. The discovery of oil in the North Sea, in British waters, was one. She even had a run at reviving the imperial spirit when Argentina attempted to wrest the Falkland Islands from British rule in 1982; the old lion's paw might be feeble but it was strong enough to beat off the inept Argentinians. The little Falklands War gave the public a welcome feeling of Britain *redevivus*.

At the same time, Mrs. Thatcher's government granted independence to Zimbabwe, the former Rhodesia, thus continuing the decolonization of Africa. The Anglo-Irish agreement of 1985 was a breakthrough in the long record of conflict in the Emerald Isle between Protestant North and Catholic South; it provided for contacts between the two sides that might lead to peace, though predictably extremists in both camps denounced it. (Since 1972 the British had ruled Northern Ireland directly from London. Irish Republican Army terrorism, including the assassination of Earl Mountbatten in 1979, paralleled Protestant "paramilitary" violence in the North.)

"Privatization," or the divestment in one way or another of direct government economic operations, was a popular feature of the Thatcher administration. The public might obtain shares in an erstwhile state-owned monopoly. British Telecom, which held a monopoly of telephones, became the property of two million shareholders in 1984, a transfer Mrs. Thatcher said "did more than anything else to lay the basis of a share-owning popular capitalism in Britain." Electricity, water, gas, British Airways, British Steel were similarly "divested"; in part or in whole, more than a score of privatizations took place between 1979 and 1993, with coal, railways, and the post office likely candidates for future privatization. People who lived in municipally owned public housing were encouraged to buy their homes, at generous prices and terms.

All over the world, from undeveloped Africa to Asia, South America, and then the former Communist economies of Eastern Europe and Russia, privatization in one way or another was the word. In Europe, Italy, France, and Spain welcomed it. New Zealand, which had pioneered in the welfare state, swung to the opposite pole in the 1980s, privatizing nationalized enterprises and slashing the state budget more determinedly than any other country. The great lesson of economic history in the last decades of the twentieth century seemed to be exactly the reverse of what had been preached in the first half: Private enterprise and free markets had to rescue the world from the failures of state ownership and central planning.

Mrs. Thatcher was no economic illiterate. Her intellectual mentor was Keith Joseph, and she drew also on Alfred Sherman and the Institute of Economic Affairs. But her choice of the free-market, antistatist position derived less from intellectual analysis than gut feeling. She inherited it from the English liberal past—liberal in the old-fashioned Adam Smith style, featuring robust dislike of the paternal state and a faith in the virtues of individual enterprise. After a long season of socialist fashions, the hour had come for this belief to make a comeback. You can give your money to the government, Mrs. Thatcher was fond of saying, and let it in its bumbling way do things for you; or you can keep it for yourself and invest it productively. Thatcherism was a matter of morality: restoring self-reliance, individual accountability, ending the dependency culture, freeing people from the paternal state. Hard work and frugality, the primeval capitalist virtues, were to be revived from near death. Like Cinderella, the homely bourgeois turned out to be worth more than her gaudy socialist sisters.

This austere creed never became wildly popular. In sweeping to three straight lopsided victories the Tories never actually won a majority of the voters. They profited from the collapse of a credible opposition. Seeking a haven somewhere between the shoals of competitive capitalism and state socialism, voters deserted Labour for a time for a third or rather a fourth party (in addition to the Liberals) made up of seceders from Labour who called themselves Social Democrats (SDs). With impressive leadership, the SDs for a time looked like the hope of a country caught between Labour socialism and Thatcher capitalism, neither of which it much liked. But the Social Democrats faltered. British election rules, as the Liberals long had had cause to complain (in vain), do not favor third parties; there is no proportional representation. The Social Democrats formed an awkward alliance with the Liberals; then the two merged outright to create a new party calling itself the Liberal Social Democrats. But the leading figure of the Social Democrats, Roy Jenkins, rejected the merger and led the Social Democratic rump into isolation. The new party tended to be just the old Liberals writ large, though not much larger than before. As this abortive center crumbled, most Labour moderates made their way back to the old party, now engaged in changing its image. (The Liberal Democrats, as they finally decided to call themselves, did hang around and were often a factor in local elections.)

A shattered British Labour party scarcely needed the impact of Thatcherism to jolt it into a drastic face-lifting. The 1979 debacle, followed by crushing electoral defeats, forced it to change on pain of extinction. Change it did in the 1980s. In 1980 the Labour conference voted overwhelmingly for unilateral nuclear disarmament, withdrawal from the European Community, massive extension of public ownership, a thirty-five-hour workweek. From that high point of leftism the party moved steadily away. By 1990 it had reversed all these positions completely. A typical case was that of Labour M.P. Margaret Beckett, once a Bennite,[3] now a Kinnockite (follower of the party leader Meil Kinnock) (she went on to become a leading aide of the next Labour leader, John Smith, in 1992); reminded that she had repudiated all her

---

[3]Anthony Wedgwood ("Tony") Benn was the classic, almost parodic figure of the ideological left in the Labour party. Like most enthusiastic socialists he was not a worker but an upper-class intellectual.

old views, she remarked simply, "The world has moved on; it's an entirely different place."[4]

In addition to hotly debated domestic issues of privatization, curbing the trade unions, reforming educational policy, introducing commercial television, restructuring local government, Britain's relation to the European Community (EC) constantly haunted politicians. The merger of economies that had begun with the 1957 Treaty of Rome among France, Germany, Italy and the three Low Countries (Belgium, Netherlands, Luxembourg) had broadened by the 1980s to include Denmark, Spain, Portugal, and Greece as well as Ireland and the United Kingdom. Austria and the other Scandinavian countries, including Finland, were next in line; with the breakup of the Soviet Union and the extinction of communism throughout Eastern Europe even more countries seemed likely to want in. In 1991 Poland, Hungary, and Czechoslovakia made approaches to membership.

The EC had extended its goal to nothing less than a completely united Europe. In 1984 the European Parliament adopted a blueprint for the establishment of a European Union, embodied subsequently in the Single Europe Act. Heads of government pledged that by 1992 all barriers to "the free movement of goods, persons, services and capital" within the EC would end.

The EC expected to move toward a common currency in the near future, despite Mrs. Thatcher's objections, and on the table was a proposal that the directly elected European Parliament elect the Commission's president, presently appointed by the Council of Ministers—a policy-making body in turn appointed by the various member nations, each of whom in effect thus exercised a veto power. That veto power was now being called into question.

Many thought that economic unity would inevitably entail political union; the powers eventually vested in a European central bank would have to be made accountable to a European Parliament. Not Mrs.Thatcher, to whom "true democratic accountability is through national parliaments." She had begun in 1980 by battling the EC over British contributions to the EC budget, which she thought unfair and which included agricultural subsidies she had little use for. The state interventionist philosophy, the *planification* outlook dominant in Brussels (where the powerful EC Commisssion sat) displeased her. It is interesting that the Labour party had opposed British membership in the Common Market because it thought it too capitalistic, whereas Mrs. Thatcher considered it socialistic. "We have not successfully rolled back the frontiers of the State in Britain, only to see them reimposed at a European level, with a European super-State exercising a new dominance in Brussels," the First Lady of Europe warned. While going along with limited economic integration, she continued to oppose Britain's entrance into a full European political union. She drew back before the proposal to replace the national currencies with a single European money.

---

[4]Reported in *The Economist*, October 8, 1990.

Nigel Lawson, Mrs. Thatcher's chancellor of the exchequer since 1983, resigned in 1989 in disagreement with her on this question; he wanted Great Britain to join the European Community's exchange rate mechanism (ERM), a prelude to currency integration, which Mrs. Thatcher finally did with some reluctance in 1990. Her successor, John Major, took Britain out of the ERM in 1992.

The fact is that her ambivalence on this issue had characterized the British position from the start. Britain had held aloof from the Common Market when it began in the 1950s, Winston Churchill explaining that England had historical ties to the British Empire and to North America in addition to Europe. The French president, Charles de Gaulle, then vetoed a British application for membership in the 1960s, because with some justification he doubted Britain's firm commitment to the European Community's goals. After the formidable de Gaulle's departure in 1970 Britain did join the EC, but there were always tensions in her relationship to it. At bottom, the British never felt like true Europeans; they were willing to enter into a business agreement but always hesitated when it came to marriage. On the question of surrendering British sovereignty to a European superstate, Margaret Thatcher was not out of step with British opinion. The isssue did split her party and distract her from domestic goals, however.

Other issues of foreign policy in a dramatically changing world called for her action. She was bold and courageous in extending a hand to Mikhail Gorbachev, as he struggled to liquidate the monstrous regime of Stalinist communism and democratize the Soviet Union. She backed George Bush in the war against Iraq in 1991, but she felt he had failed to see the process through by completely defeating and deposing the aggressor-dictator; Bush she thought less of than his predecessor. A part of the Reagan–Gorbachev era, she faded from the scene along with them.

THE END OF THATCHERISM?

A rapidly changing world finally overtook Mrs. Thatcher too. In November 1990 a veritable coup within the Conservative party ousted her as leader, replacing her, after a lively competition, with erstwhile cabinet member John Major. She had become overburdened with unpopular policies, especially a poll tax she had pushed for the financing of local government. The economy was sluggish and inflation was rising. Austerity did not seem to be paying off, an impatient electorate obviously thought. Public opinion polls registered a sharp decline in support for the Conservative government. Mrs. Thatcher had warned at the beginning that "things will have to get worse before they can get better." She was in the same boat as her friend Gorbachev. As in the USSR, to turn around an economy grown stagnant from long dependence on the state, and restore private initiative, would be a hard process. Decades of neglect of innovation and management could not be overcome in an hour. Mrs. Thatcher might have fortified herself with a quotation from Tolstoy: "The transition from state violence to a free, reasonable life cannot happen suddenly. Just as the state took thousands of years to take shape, so it will take thousands of years to disintegrate."

Initially voters welcomed her realism, and for a time her medicine seemed to work. Then doubts began to arise. The volatile electorate of a modern democracy makes extreme demands for instant miracles; patience is the least of its virtues.

Mrs. Thatcher did not go gently. It was a painful moment for both the party and for her; she undoubtedly felt betrayed. A minority stayed loyal to her, but, facing a general election no later than 1992, most Conservative members of Parliament opted for a new leader in time to repair the party's fortunes before then. Facing the inevitable, Mrs. Thatcher gave her approval to the choice of John Major as her successor, although she later had doubts about him, and bowed out as gracefully as possible. Politics, as she knew well, has small room for sentiment. Perhaps an understandable tendency to put election success ahead of principles caused her fall; unquestionably there were also personal resentments of her masterful style of leadership. Perhaps these were tinged with male rancor against a strong-willed woman. But after an uninterrupted decade in office, longer than any modern prime minster had ever enjoyed, the first woman to head a British parliamentary government had overstayed her time. Whether in rejecting her the Conservative party did not betray its principles was a question the answer to which depended on which Conservative party one meant, and what principles. The Tories also had a tradition of flexible realism and hostility to doctrinaires.

After being deposed as party leader, Mrs.Thatcher soon resumed her seat in Parliament, where she showed no loss of her abilities as a debater. Though professedly trying to avoid being a thorn in the side of John Major's government, she could not refrain from criticizing its policies, especially regarding the European Community.

The post-Thatcher Conservative government, trying to minimize its Thatcherite connections, made concessions to government programs and subsidies, moving closer to the Labour position as the time of another election approached in the spring of 1992. Would the results of this deficit spending lead again to economic crisis and the need for another round of austerity? A good part of the Thatcher reforms was not repealed, however. Even a Labour government was not likely to give the trade unions back the power they once had, much less (despite statements in the party's now antiquated constitution) renationalize hotels and steel mills.

The Tory victory in the election of April 1992 was rather unexpected; polls had suggested a tight race with possibly an edge to Labour. But the shadow of 1979 still hung over the Labourites; in the clutch, voters who might not like the Tories could not bring themselves to trust Labour. So John Major took office in his own right for another Conservative term, though with a much reduced parliamentary majority. Neil Kinnock resigned as Labour leader, replaced by a Scotsman named John Smith.

With conflicting views inside his cabinet, Prime Minister Major moved cautiously toward Europe. Britain could hardly stay out in the cold. At the Maastricht meeting in late 1991 Major succeeded in delaying the common currency unit, but Britain pledged to join it some time before the end of the century. Mrs. Thatcher asked for a referendum in Great Britain on this. Her criticism of Major breached primeval instincts of party loyalty, and she found herself once again in the wilderness.

But in June 1992 Denmark rejected the Maastricht treaty in a national referendum, and a subsequent French referendum resulted in a victory for it by such a narrow margin as to provide little boost for European Community morale. Major postponed ratification of the treaty by the British Parliament. Maastricht threatened to unravel amid wild currency disorders. At an Edinburgh meeting in late 1992 the British secured concessions to "subsidiarity," that is, greater local autonomy at the expense of the EC government in Brussels. Thatcherism seemed to be somewhat vindicated on this issue. Though the government of John Major managed to get the Maastricht treaty approved in Parliament after a furious debate and with some reservations, a sizable element in the Conservative party was now hostile to the European Community. On the Continent, expectations of early federation had diminished among its enthusiasts.

The end of the Thatcher story found no other woman on the political horizon in Britain. The all-male clubs had resumed their ascendancy in all the political parties. In an age of rampant feminism, masculine monopoly of political life was never stronger. The truth is that Mrs. Thatcher had never found much support among her sisters. Feminists who expected some female messiah to rescue the human race from the monstrous regiment of men did not think much of her; they were usually of the left, and revealed their primary loyalty to a (male-invented) ideology rather than to pure feminism. Here was a woman tougher than the men, asking discipline and austerity.

The basic restructuring that Mrs. Thatcher presided over in the 1980s outlasted her personal defeat. Nationalized industries stayed privatized, government was more decentralized, market disciplines were imposed on government services; higher education and the health services continued to undergo drastic changes, as indeed did elementary education, along "Thatcherite" lines.

On the other hand the impulse to soften the pains of competition continued to breed dependency on government programs. The free market is tolerated only because of a high degree of state-administered social security, making the risks of entrepreneurship more bearable. Western capitalism also includes, as a matter of course, government management of money and interest rates, as well as of military defense, along with a massive subsidy by the state of "infrastructure" in the form of roads, bridges, airports, and so forth. Government support for farm prices, a flagrant violation of the free market principle, is sacrosanct in all countries. In the United States "bailouts" of failed savings-and-loan institutions and banks by the federal government make any market test of efficiency virtually meaningless in this important area of economic life; Uncle Sam will always pick up the pieces at public expense, it seems. The enormous budget deficits of the United States, Italy, Sweden, and many other nations had not happened in Britain by 1993, but loomed on the horizon as a distinct possibility. When in October 1992, as a preparation for privatization, the British government sought to close down some deficit-making nationalized coal mines, a public outcry forced it to rescind the action.

"A market economy with counterweights," formula of the French socialists and in effect of British Labour, leaves open the question of whether the market or the counterweights will bulk the larger. The public, the French noted long ago, is free-enterprise for the profits and *dirigiste* for the losses; it wants the best of both worlds, and will cheerfully vote down any decrease in benefits or increase in taxes, while complaining about the deficit. Public opinion also generally approves of economic equality and wants to give special help to those with fewer material goods; but at the same time it complains not only about high taxes but about the scandals of "dependency" that arise from giving welfare payments to the poor. Long ago the political economists had argued that easy charity does economic harm in the long run by sapping the will to work and breeding an idle class. Such arguments now reappeared.

On the question of the free market versus state intervention, experts by no means agreed. Economic theorists were in fact in considerable disarray, as far as any consensus on major principles. Experts were in profusion, but they did not agree with each other; hence, they were of little value to leaders who must have definite prescriptions. (Give me one-handed advisers! Harry Truman once cried.) It was no wonder that, as one economist complained, "the pronouncements of amateur economists . . . and of noneconomists . . . command at least as much and probably more respect than those of professional economists." Offering models that do not pretend to describe any actually existing economy, the professionals drift further and further away from reality, and they find "no invariant laws . . . no certainties." Their sophisticated insights are not without application, but this is difficult, and in any case limited. They disagree on very basic things: "Whether in theory there are likely to be persistent market failures of a sort that would call for government interference if high levels of employment are to be achieved or, if intervention is called for, what the appropriate monetary and fiscal policy instruments are. . . . " "In both theory and practice the economic world is accepted as being a much more complex place than it was fifty or even twenty years ago."

Such reflections on the state of an art that, in technique, has become almost as intricate as nuclear physics suggest its limitations for practical purposes. Take your pick of economists.

Nor could philosophy, as Alistair MacIntyre pointed out, decide the issue between social and individual justice. One side points to the injustice of inequality, whereby some people, probably just luckier, have far more material goods than do others. The other asks whether it is fair for the state to take away from me that which I have earned and saved by arduous labor and self-denial to give it to others less motivated. Various evidence may be selected and doctored in support of both sides; rhetoric may be employed. But pure reason cannot decide the question. The answer is determined by a political struggle in which rhetoric and organization as well as special-interest groups play parts.

In the light of all this, the modern world seems condemned to struggle along with a muddled mixture of private and public economic practices and institutions, as it blunders from crisis to crisis. The dynamism of technological innovation and scientific research, bringing a flow of new products and techniques, could overcome this handicap of a stumbling public policy in lands such as Japan, the United States, or an integrated Western Europe; but the many critics of British society talked about the brain drain, lagging research, an antiquated educational system. A poll taken in 1993 indicated that nearly 50 percent of people in the United Kingdom would like to emigrate.

The England of Shakespeare and Newton, of Marx and Mazzini, had seemingly fallen far. Books analyzing the decline and fall of this modern empire began to appear almost annually.[5] No longer in possession of its far-flung colonial dependencies—"on dune and headland sinks the fire"—and now a poorer country than most of Western Europe, Britain's imposing cultural domination had shrunk too. British intellectual life was still vigorous, but the main global trends in ideas emanated from France, or the United States. The once mighty British lion seemed condemned to become a tame pussy cat, declining, as Athens had once done, into a musuem visited by tourists. (Though one of its poets, Philip Larkin, mused that this too was "going, going," the lanes and guildhalls of old England replaced by "concrete and tyres.") Or was such a fate possible for the country that had invented the Industrial Revolution?

Today, Stratford-on-Avon is a mecca for sightseers, equipped with deluxe hotels and a large modern theater, to which people from all over the world troop to take photographs of what is alleged to be Anne Hathaway's cottage. What the Bard would have made of this would be interesting to know. Would Newton be disappointed with the state of British science? It has

---

[5]One economic historian, W.D. Rubenstein, has argued that the indices of decline were misleading, because based on manufacturing production, the wealth of Britain has always lain in commerce and financial services more than industry. There may in fact have been no decline at all!

contributed much to the twentieth century, but Thomson, Rutherford, Chadwick, Turing the computer pioneer, the co-discoverers of penicillin Chain and Florey, belong to the first half of the century.

Our last personality featured in this book is the only one still alive as of this writing. As Lady Thatcher, she is still quite active, participating in speaking tours and literary projects. In 1993 she revisited Russia, now engaged in the monumental task of restructuring its economy around the free market, to shake hands again with her friends Mikhail and Raisa Gorbachev, whom she had befriended since 1984, and to be greeted by enthusiastic crowds.

Later that same year appeared the first volume of Mrs. Thatcher's memoirs, with more to come. Others who knew her will write theirs, and we will learn much more about her—perhaps more than we can absorb. The path from Shakespeare's day to the present has been one of progress in at least one way—the recording of information and the keeping of records. Future historians will base their estimations of Lady Thatcher not on a few garbled legends but on a huge mass of attested data. But we may be sure that this will not prevent violent controversy about her and her place in history. For she made herself a symbol of one of the chief issues of our own time and of other times, namely the role of the state in a free society.

From Queen Elizabeth I to Margaret Thatcher the question of the state versus the individual has remained a persistent issue in human affairs. We could reflect on other issues that have recurred in the lives of our handful of prominent men and women down the last four centuries: national loyalty challenged by the pull of conflicting beliefs, from Elizabeth I and the Catholics to Elizabeth II and the Communists; science battling mystery and ignorance—to create new forms of mystery and ignorance; racial hatreds, wars, and revolutions; the subjective consciousness of sensitive individuals at war with society's demands. The list is extensive. The questions remain.

Bibliographies
and Study Topics

The following brief bibliographies are not of course anything like complete, nor are the questions for further study and report meant to exhaust the endless possibilities. Teachers and students may well want to supply their own.

Shakespeare

Probably the best popular Shakespeare edition is *The Complete Works* (compact ed.), edited by Stanley Wells and Gary Taylor for Oxford University Press. David M. Bergeron and Geraldo U. De Sousa, *Shakespeare, A Study and Research Guide* (2nd ed., 1987), a selective annotated bibliography, includes aids to preparing a student research paper. The Shakespeare industry's trade journal is *The Shakespeare Quarterly*.

   Of the almost countless number of scholars, from Nicholas Rowe in 1704 to Peter Levi in 1989, who, undiscouraged by the near total lack of solid information, have tried to write a life of William Shakespeare, probably the most discriminating as well as interesting is S. Schoenbaum, *Shakespeare's Lives* (2nd ed., 1991). Schoenbaum adopted the strategy of showing us how all the biographers invented a Shakespeare of their own liking. His fascinating book is thus a history of Shakespeare's image, as well as a guide to all the lives and a study in the methods of historical detection. See also his *William Shakespeare: A Compact Documentary Life* (revised ed., 1987), and *Shakespeare and Others* (1985). E.A.J. Honigman, *Shakespeare: The "Lost Years"* (1985) may be compared with Russell Fraser, *The Young Shakespeare* (1989). Useful surveys include: John Russell Brown, *Discovering Shakespeare: A New Guide to the Plays*; Kenneth Muir, ed., *Interpretations of Shakespeare* (1987); A.M. Nagler, *Shakespeare's Stage* (1981); Geoffrey Bullough, *Narrative and Dramatic Sources of Shakespeare* (8 vols., 1957–1975). A study that questions some earlier ideas about the nature of the Elizabethan theater is John Orrell's *The Quest for Shakespeare's Globe* (1983). See also Bernard Beckerman,

Shakespeare at the Globe (1962). A work that highlights the theatrical context is Peter Thomson's *Shakespeare's Professional Career* (1992).

A selection from the vast corpus of Shakespeare criticism and interpretation might include A.C. Bradley, *Shakespearian Tragedy* (reprinted 1985); E.M.W. Tillyard, *The Elizabethan World Picture* (1943), a famous essay; G. Wilson Knight, *The Wheel of Fire* (1949). Those curious about the strange turns of recent critical analysis, where nothing is as it seems, should consult John Drakakis, ed., *Alternative Shakespeares* (1985) or Patricia Parker and Geoffrey Hartman, eds., *Shakespeare and the Question of Theory* (1985). *The Woman's Part: Feminist Criticism of Shakespeare*, edited by Carolyn Ruth Swift Lenz, Gayle Greene, and Carol Thomas Neely (1980), is a good introduction to a substantial body of feminist reactions to the Bard.

Some books about the Elizabethan age in general: Jo McMurtry, *Understanding Shakespeare's England: A Companion for the American Reader* (1989); G.R. Elton, *England under the Tudors* (1955); D.M. Dean and N.L. Jones, eds., *The Parliaments of Elizabethan England* (1990); John Guy, *Tudor England* (1988); A.L. Rowse, *The Elizabethan Renaissance* (1971, 1972). Colin Martin and Geoffrey Parker have produced the most up-to-date account of *The Spanish Armada* (1988). See also J.J. Scarisbrick, *The Reformation and the English People* (1985). On Shakespeare's London, see Ian W. Archer, *The Pursuit of Stability: Social Relations in Elizabethan London* (1991); Steve Rappaport, *Worlds within Worlds: Structures of Life in Sixteenth-Century London* (1989); J. Brewer and J. Styles, eds., *An Ungovernable People: The English and their Law in the Seventeenth and Eighteenth Century*.

The most notable films made from the plays are *Midsummer Night's Dream* (1935), stunningly directed by Max Reinhardt with a notable cast including James Cagney as Bottom and young Mickey Rooney as Puck; *As You Like It* (1936), with Laurence Olivier and Elizabeth Bergner; Olivier as director and star in *Richard III* (1956); Olivier's Oscar-winning *Hamlet* (1948), and outstanding *Henry V* (1946). *Henry V* was filmed again in 1989 by Kenneth Branagh. John Gielgud played *Julius Caesar* in 1970; Richard Burton and Elizabeth Taylor, *The Taming of the Shrew* in 1967 (cf. the Cole Porter musical version, *Kiss Me Kate*). Franco Ziffirelli directed an "accessible" *Romeo and Juliet* (1968) and Roman Polanski a gripping *Macbeth* (1971). Olivier and Orson Welles both made *Othello*. The BBC produced the entire Shakespeare cycle on television. For a full list, see *Shakespeare on Screen: An International Filmography and Videography*, eds. Kenneth S. Rothwell and Annabelle Henkin Melzer (1991); also Jack J. Jorgens, *Shakespeare on Film* (1977). But the movies keep coming; Kenneth Branagh's *Much Ado about Nothing* was a 1993 success. Among operas derived from Shakespeare plays are three of the best of Giuseppe Verdi's: *Otello, Macbeth,* and *Falstaff*.

Selected Topics

On the difficulties presented by the effort to get a "correct" Shakespeare text, see Fredson Bowers, *On Editing Shakespeare* (1966), also Alice Walker, *Textual Problems of the First Folio* (1953).

Was Shakespeare's marriage happy or unhappy? Evaluate the evidence. Controversies about Shakespeare's sonnets feature the arguments on behalf of the two main claimants for the "fair youth," and nominees for "dark lady." One treatment: Kenneth Muir, *Shakespeare's Sonnets* (1979); compare Joseph Pequigney, *Such Is My Love: A Study of Shakespeare's Sonnets* (1985).

Is Shakespeare's unflattering portrait of King Richard III, in his great play about that monarch, necessarily correct? See A.R. Myers, in *History*, June 1968 (Vol. LIII, No. 178); Rosemary Horrox, *Richard III: A Study of Service* (1989); Charles Ross, *Richard III* (1980).

H.N. Gibson, *The Shakespeare Claimants* (1962) examines and rejects the claims that have been made for someone other than Shakespeare being the author of some or all of the plays attributed to him. Evaluate and discuss the evidence. Compare Charlton Ogburn, *The Mysterious William Shakespeare* (1984). See Schoenbaum's *Lives*, pp. 385–451.

Newton

The best biography of Isaac Newton is Richard S. Westfall, *Never at Rest: A Biography of Isaac Newton* (1980); more accessible, perhaps, is A. Rupert Hall, *Isaac Newton: Adventurer in Thought* (1993). The genesis of Newton's epochal discovery may be followed in *The Preliminary Manuscripts for Isaac Newton's 1687 Principia*, with introduction by D.T. Whiteside (1989). A recent scholarly symposium is John Fauvel, Raymond Flood, Michael Shortland, and Robin Wilson, eds., *Let Newton Be!* (1988); another specialist collection is P.M. Harman and Alan E. Shapiro, eds., *The Investigation of Difficult Things: Essays on Newton and the History of the Exact Sciences* (1993). Among older books, John Herivel, *The Background of Newton's Principia* (1966); I. Bernard Cohen, *Introduction to Newton's Principia* (1971); Alexander Koyré, *Newton Studies* (1965). Mordechai Feingold, ed., *Before Newton: The Life and Times of Isaac Barrow* (1990) provides a gauge of how far Newton brought mathematics forward, via a picture of his predecessor at Cambridge. Alan Shapiro has edited *The Optical Papers of Isaac Newton* (1984); See also A. Rupert Hall, *All Was Light: An Introduction to Newton's Opticks* (1993). For the mathematically proficient, Niccolo Guicciardini, *The Development of Newtonian Calculus in Britain, 1700–1810* (1990), relates to the Newton-Leibniz controversy; see also A. Rupert Hall, *Philosophers at War: The Quarrel between Newton and Leibniz* (1980).

On Newton's apparently strange interest in alchemy, see Betty Jo Teeter Dobbs, *The Janus Face of Genius: The Role of Alchemy in Newton's Thought* (1991). A huge literature on alchemy may be approached via Claudia Kren, *Alchemy in Europe: A Guide to Research (1990)*. Garland Publishing Co. has issued editions of "Basil Valentine" and other alchemist tracts Newton was familiar with.

See also Frank Manuel, *The Religion of Newton* (1974); Richard Kroll, Richard Ashcraft, and Perez Zagorin, eds., *Philosophy, Science, and Religion in England 1640–1700* (1992); Richard S. Westfall, *Science and Religion in Seventeenth Century England* (1958); Tim Harris, Paul Seaward, and Mark Goldie, eds., *The Politics of Religion in Restoration England* (1990); John Brooke, "The God of Newton" in *Let Newton Be!*

More general accounts of the transition to a new "worldview" in the seventeenth century include such classics as Alfred North Whitehead, *Science and the Modern World* (1925); R.G. Collingwood, *The Idea of Nature* (1945); Alexander Koyré, *From the Closed World to the Infinite Universe* (1957); C.S. Lewis, *The Discarded Image* (1964); E.J. Dijksterhuis, *The Mechanization of the World Picture* (1986). More specific background is provided in Brian Vickers, ed., *English Science: Bacon to Newton* (1987).

The history of science bibliographies that are published annually in the journal *Isis*, and sometimes gathered together in a cumulative volume (Cumulative Bibliography for 1966–1975, 1980; for 1976–1985, 1989), can be a valuable research tool. *Bibliography of the History of Medicine* (National Library of Medicine, Washington, D.C.) can also help in locating sources in the sciences.

Robert Beddard, ed., *The Revolutions of 1688* (1991) is a recent assessment of the most significant event in English political history; cf. Stuart E. Prall, *The Bloodless Revolution* (1985). James T. Axtell's "Locke, Newton, and the Two Cultures," in John W. Yolton, ed., *John Locke: Problems and Perspectives*, may be supplemented by other studies of John Locke, both as philosopher and political theorist: John Dunn, *The Political Thought of John Locke*; Ruth W. Grant, *John Locke's Liberalism* (1987); Nathan Tarcov, *Locke's Education for Liberty* (1984); W.M. Spellman, *John Locke and the Problem of Depravity* (1988); Terence Hutchinson, *Before Adam Smith: The Emergence of Political Econ-*

omy, 1662–1776 (1988). The contribution John Locke's political theory made to the American Revolution is evaluated in John Phillip Reid, *The Concept of Liberty in the Age of the American Revolution* (1988) and in Steven M. Dworetz, *The Unvarnished Doctrine: Locke, Liberalism, and the American Revolution* (1990).

Some Topics

Thomas S. Kuhn's *The Structure of Scientific Revolutions* (1962) is a famous attempt to theorize about the basic shift in total outlook that went on in the seventeenth century. Compare the works cited above by Lewis, Whitehead, Koyré, and Collingwood.

A. Rupert Hall, "What Did the Industrial Revolution in England Owe to Science?," in Neil McKendrick, ed., *Historical Perspectives: Studies in English Thought and Society in Honour of J.H. Plumb* (1974) suggests a topic. See also E.A. Wrigley, *Continuity, Chance, and Change: The Character of the Industrial Revolution in England* (1988); C.A. Russell, *Science and Social Change 1700–1900* (1983). Thomas L. Hankins, *Science and the Enlightenment* (1985).

Rousseau

Maurice Cranston, *Jean-Jacques: The Early Life and Work of Jean-Jacques Rousseau* (1982), and *The Noble Savage: Jean-Jacques Rousseau 1754–1762* (1991), an ongoing definitive biography, may supersede admirable ones by Jean Guéhenno (2 vols. transl. 1966) and Lester G. Crocker (2 vols., 1968–1973). The immense literature of commentary, criticism, and interpretation includes Judith Shklar, *Men and Citizens: A Study of Rousseau's Social Theory* (1969); James Miller, *Rousseau: Dreamer of Democracy* (1984); Stephen Ellenburg, *Rousseau's Political Philosophy* (1977); Arthur M. Melzer, *The Natural Goodness of Man: On the System of Rousseau's Thought* (1990); Alfred Cobban, *Rousseau and the Modern State* (1965); Crocker, *Rousseau's Social Contract: An Interpretive Study* (1968).

Rousseau's *The Confessions* and *The Social Contract* are available from many publishers including Penguin Classics (translated and with introductions). Rousseau's *Collected Writings* are being edited by Roger Masters and Christopher Kelly for Dartmouth Press (4 vols., 1990–1994).

On Rousseau and the French Revolution: Norman Hampson, *Will and Circumstance: Montesquieu, Rousseau, and the French Revolution* (1983); Alan C. Kors, *D'Holbach's Coterie* (1976); Carol Blum, *Rousseau and the Republic of Virtue: The Language of Politics in the French Revolution* (1986); Joan McDonald, *Rousseau and the French Revolution 1762–1791* (1965); Lynn Avery Hunt, *Politics, Culture, and Class in the French Revolution* (1984); Gary Kates, *The Cercle Social, the Girondins, and the French Revolution* (1985); David P. Jordan, *The Revolutionary Career of Maximilien Robespierre* (1982); Alfred Cobban, "The Enlightenment and the French Revolution," in Earl J. Wasserman, ed., *Aspects of the Eighteenth Century* (1965); Roland N. Stromberg, "The *Philosophes* and the French Revolution," *The History Teacher*, May 1988; Emmet Kennedy, *A Cultural History of the French Revolution* (1989). The question of whether Rousseau is properly condemned for leading to "totalitarianism" is debated by J.L. Talmon, *The Origins of Totalitarian Democracy* (1960) and John W. Chapman, *Rousseau: Totalitarian or Liberal?* (1956).

Other cases of Rousseau's influence include: John P. Clark, *The Philosophical Anarchism of William Godwin* (1977); Mark Philip, *Godwin's Political Justice* (1987); Franco Venturi, *Utopia and Reform in the Enlightenment* (1970); Keith Ansell-Pearson, *Nietzsche contra Rousseau: A Study of Nietzsche's Moral and Political Thought* (1991); D.G.. Charlton, ed., *The French Romantics* (2 vols.,1984); Roger Scruton, *Kant* (1983); Meyer H. Abrams, *The Mirror and the Lamp* (1953); Northrop Frye, *A Study of English Romanticism* (1968); Geoffrey Hartman and David Thorburn, ed., *Romanticism: Vistas, Instances,*

Continuities (1973); Jerome J. McGann, *The Romantic Ideology: A Critical Investigation* (1983). The exact extent of Rousseau's influence on Romanticism is a good research topic. So is his impact on the novel; see such studies as Michael McKeon, *The Origins of the English Novel, 1600–1740* (1987); Ian Watt, *The Rise of the Novel* (1957). Also Hugh M. Davidson, "Dialectical Order in La Nouvelle Héloïse," in *Enlightenment Studies in Honor of Lester G. Crocker*, eds. Alfred J. Bingham and Virgil W. Topazio (1979).

The origins of self-identity and consciousness: John O. Lyons, *The Invention of the Self: The Hinge of Consciousness in the Eighteenth Century* (1978), and Charles Taylor, *Sources of the Self: The Making of the Modern Identity* (1992); Jean A. Perkins, "Contexts of Autobiography in the Eighteenth Century," in Bingham and Topazio, cited above; James Cox, "Autobiography and America," in J.H. Miller, ed., *Aspects of Narrative* (1971). The "reading revolution" is the theme of Robert Darnton, *The Literary Underground of the Old Regime* (1982), and "Readers Respond to Rousseau" in his *The Great Cat Massacre*; Roger Chartier, *The Cultural Uses of Print in Early Modern France* (transl. Lydia G. Cochrane, 1988); Robert Ellrich, *Rousseau and His Readers* (1969).

Those interested in Rousseau's music might consult Edward E. Lowinsky, "Taste, Style, and Ideology in Eighteenth Century Music," in Wasserman, *Aspects of the Eighteenth Century*. *On the Origin of Language: Jean-Jacques Rousseau and Gottfried Herder*, transl. John H Moran and Alexander Gode (1966) may be supplemented by Jacques Derrida's *On Grammatology*. Ronald Grimsley, *Rousseau and the Religious Quest* (1968) is by the editor of *Rousseau's Religious Writings* (1970); see also Ronald Ian Boss, "Rousseau's Civil Religion and the Meaning of Belief," *Studies on Voltaire*, Vol. 84.

On Rousseau and feminism, see: Victor G. Wexler, "Made for Man's Delight," *American Historical Review*, April 1975; Ruth Graham, "Rousseau's Sexism Revolutionized," in Paul Fritz and Richard Morris, eds., *Woman in the Eighteenth Century and Other Essays* (1976). Cf. Katherine Clinton, "Femme et Philosophe: Enlightened Origins of Feminism," *Eighteenth Century Studies*, Spring 1975; S.I. Spencer, ed., *French Women and the Age of Enlightenment* (1984).

Rousseau's quarrel with Hume is treated by Dena Goodman in an article in *Eighteenth Century Studies*, Winter 1991/92.

Further topic: The influence of Rousseau's *Emile* on education.

Catherine the Great of Russia

For background, John G. Garrard, ed., *The Eighteenth Century in Russia* (1973); Hans Rogger, *National Consciousness in Eighteenth Century Russia* (1961); Stephen K. Carter, *Russian Nationalism: Yesterday, Today, Tomorrow* (1990); Robert K. Massie, *Peter the Great: His Life and World* (1981); Paul Dukes, *Russia under Catherine the Great* (1967); Isabel de Madariaga, *Russia in the Age of Catherine the Great (1981)*; A.G. Cross, ed., *Russian Literature in the Age of Catherine the Great* (1976). James T. Billington, *The Icon and the Axe*, Thomas G. Masaryk, *The Spirit of Russia*, and N. Berdyaev, *The Russian Idea* are older classics searching for the key to Russia's enigmatic soul.

Isabel de Madariaga's *Catherine the Great, a Short History* (1990) is among the better biographies, along with John T. Alexander, *Catherine the Great: Life and Legend* (1988); also Marc Raeff, ed., *Catherine the Great: A Profile* (1972) and Joan Haslip, *Catherine the Great* (1977). More specialized studies include R.E. Jones, *The Emancipation of the Russian Nobility, 1762–85* (1973); David L. Ransel, *The Politics of Catherine the Great: The Panin Party* (1975); Allen McConnell, *A Russian Philosophe: Alexander Radishchev, 1749–1802* (1964); John P. LeDonne, *Absolutism and Ruling Class: The Formation of the Russian Political Order, 1700–1825* (1991) and his *Ruling Russia: Politics and Administration in the Age of Absolutism, 1762–96* (1984). A different side is presented in an art book, *Catherine the Great: Treasures of Imperial Russia from the Hermitage Museum* (1990).

American Bibliography of Russian and East European Studies, (annually from Bloomington, Indiana) is a valuable reference source.

Films

Catherine the Great with Douglas Fairbanks, Jr., and Elizabeth Bergner (1934). Jeanne Moreau played *The Great Catherine* in a 1967 film adaptation of a George Bernard Shaw play. Marlene Dietrich was *The Scarlet Empress* in a Josef von Sternberg movie of 1934. Mae West appeared in a 1944 Broadway production called *Catherine Was Great*.

Some Topics

Catherine and serfdom: See Paul Dukes, "Catherine and Serfdom," in William E. Butler, ed., *Russian Law* (1977).

A.G. Cross, "British Freemasons in Russia during the Reign of Catherine," *Oxford Slavonic Papers*, n.s. IV (1971), pp. 43–45.

The partition of Poland as a study in diplomacy and international politics.

Alexander I

The most helpful life of Alexander I in English is probably Allen McConnell, *Tsar Alexander I, Paternalistic Reformer* (1970). On the murder of his father by which Alexander came to power in 1801, see Roderick E. McGrew, *Paul I of Russia, 1754–1801* (1992). The notable Russian history specialist Marc Raeff has written on one of the tsars's close associates, *Michael Speransky, Statesman of Imperial Russia, 1772–1839* (1957), and Michael Jenkins on another, *Arakcheev, Grand Vizier of the Russian Empire* (1969).

M.K. Dziewanowski, *Alexander I: Russia's Mysterious Tsar* (1990), which suffers from the absence of bibliography and references, argues in favor of the often rejected legend of Alexander's survival after 1825 as a Siberian monk. See also Leo Tolstoy, "Posthumous Memoirs of Fyodor Kuzmich," in *Posthumous Works*, Vol. 1 (transl. A.J. Wolfe, 1919), and L.I. Strakhovsky, "Alexander I's Death and Destiny," *American Slavic and East European Review*, August 1961. Tolstoy relied on the Russian historian N.K. Schilder, who published biographies of Paul and Alexander 1901–1905.

Nigel Nicolson, *Napoleon 1812* (1985) is one of the most recent of many works on this epic historical drama. See also E.V. Tarle, *Napoleon's Invasion of Russia* (1942), for which this Soviet historian suffered imprisonment until Stalin changed the party line during World War II; Gunther E. Rothenberg, *The Art of Warfare in the Age of Napoleon*. Among novels, the most famous of course is Leo Tolstoy's *War and Peace*. The favorite game is to enumerate Napoleon's mistakes, or evaluate the tsar's strategy.

E.J. Knapton, *The Lady of the Holy Alliance* (1966) is one of the few scholarly studies in English of the remarkable Mme. Krüdener. In French, there is Francis Ley, *Mme. de Krüdener et son temps* (1961), also his *Alexandre I et sa Sainte Alliance* (1975). Probably the best treatment in English of Alexander's foreign policy and diplomacy (where a great many totally fail to understand him) is Patricia K. Grimsted's *The Foreign Ministers of Alexander I* (1969). W. H. Zawadzki, *A Man of Honour: Adam Czartoryski as a Statesman of Russia and Poland 1795–1831* (1993) is a new life of Alexander's friend and minister.

Patrick O'Meara's *K.F. Ryleev* (1984), a biography of one of the ringleaders of the Decembrists, who after Alexander's death attempted an ill-fated revolt against the tsardom, presents a good picture of the growing ferment among the intelligentsia during the tsar's later years. See Philip Pomper, *The Russian Revolutionary Intelligentsia* (1970); Tibor Szamuely, *The Russian Tradition* (1974); Franco Venturi, *Roots of Revolution: A History of the Populist and Socialist Movements in Nineteenth Century Russia* (1960).

Marx

Biographically, David McClellan, *Karl Marx, His Life and Thought* (1973); Terrell Carver, *Marx and Engels: The Intellectual Relationship* (1983); William J. Brazill, *The Young Hegelians* (1970). Broader surveys of the context of Marx's life and thought include James T. Billington, *Fire in the Minds of Men: Origins of the Revolutionary Faith* (1980); O.H. Taylor, *The Classical Liberalism, Marxism, and the Twentieth Century* (1960); Ronald Meek, *Smith, Marx, and After* (1977). The earlier socialist tradition may be glimpsed in Keith Taylor, *The Political Ideas of the Utopian Socialists* (1982); Frank E. Manuel, *The New World of Henri Saint-Simon* (1956); Christopher H. Johnson, *Utopian Communism in France: Cabet and the Icarians, 1839–1851* (1974); Robert L. Hoffman, *Revolutionary Justice: The Social and Political Theory of P.-J. Proudhon* (1972).

    Among the almost numberless studies of Marx's thought: Leszek Kolakowski, *Main Currents of Marxism* (2 vols., 1978–1980); R.N. Hunt, *The Political Ideas of Marx and Engels* (2 vols., 1974–1984); Jon Elster, *Making Sense of Marx* (1985); N. Scott Arnold, *Marx's Radical Critique of Capitalist Society* (1990); Thomas Sowell, *Marxism, Philosophy, and Economics* (1985); M.C. Howard and J.C. King, *The Economics of Marx* (1976); Leonard Wessell, *Prometheus Bound: The Mythic Structure of Karl Marx's Scientific Thinking* (1984).

Later Marxists

G.H.R. Parkinson, ed., *Marx and Marxisms* (1982); Peter Gay, *The Dilemma of Democratic Socialism: Bernstein's Challenge to Marx* (1952); J.P. Nettl, *Rosa Luxemburg* (1966); George Lichtheim, *Marxism in Modern France* (1966); Walter L. Adamson, *Marx and the Disillusionment of Marxism* (1985); Neil McInnes, *The Western Marxists* (1972); J.G. Merquior, *Western Marxism* (1986); Paul Piccone, *Italian Marxism* (1983); Robert Gorman, *Neo-Marxism: The Meanings of Modern Radicalism* (1982); Eugene Lunn, *Marxism and Modernism* (1984); John Roemer, ed., *Analytical Marxism: An Anthology* (1986); Alex Callinicos, *Althusser's Marxism* (1976) Jack Lindsay, *The Crisis in Marxism* (1981); Michael Kelly, *Modern French Marxism*.

    Marx and Nationalism: See Horace B. Davis, *Nationalism and Socialism: Marxist and Labor Theories of Nationalism to 1917* (1967). *Marx's reception in other parts of the world*: Arif Dirlik and Maurice Meisner, eds., *Marxism and the Chinese Experience* (1989); also Dirlik's *Origins of Chinese Communism* (1989). *Class*: Peter Calvert, *The Concept of Class* (1982); P.N. Furbank, *Unholy Pleasure; or the Idea of Social Class* (1985); Frank Parkin, *Marxism and Class Theory: A Bourgeois Critique* (1979). *Lenin and Marx*: Alain Besançon, *The Rise of the Gulag: Intellectual Origins of Leninism* (1981); David W. Lovell, *From Marx to Lenin: An Evaluation of Marx's Responsibility for Soviet Authoritarianism* (1984).

    See also Paul Thomas, *Marx and the Anarchists* (1980); François Furet, *Marx and the French Revolution* (1988); S.W. Prawer, *Karl Marx and World Literature* (1976); Margaret A. Rose, *Marx's Lost Aesthetic: Karl Marx and the Visual Arts* (1984).

Mazzini

Among biographies, supplementing the older standard by Bolton King (1902–1905) is Gwilym O. Griffith, *Mazzini: Prophet of Modern Europe* (1970) and especially Denis Mark Smith, *Mazzini* (1994). See also Luigi Salvatorelli, *Thought and Action in the Risorgimento* (1970); Denis Mack Smith, *Victor Emanuel, Cavour, and the Risorgimento* (1971), also his *Cavour* (1985) and *Garibaldi* (1969); Fred Kaplan, *Thomas Carlyle: A Biography* (1984). The popular early twentieth-century historian George Macaulay Trevelyan wrote a classic life of Garibaldi in three volumes (1907–1911, reprinted 1948, 1971).

    Giuseppe Mazzini: Selected Writings, edited by N. Gangulee, was published in London in 1945.

Studies of nationalism include Eugene Kamenka, *Nationalism: The Nature and Evolution of an Idea* (1976); Elie Kedourie, *Nationalism* (1960); Anthony D. Smith, *Theories of Nationalism* (1983); Arnold J. Toynbee, *Nationality and the War* (1915). Interesting and important are George L. Mosse, *The Nationalization of the Masses: Political Symbolism and Mass Movements in Germany from the Napoleonic Wars through the Third Reich* (1975) and Eugen F. Weber, *Peasants into Frenchmen: The Modernization of Rural France, 1870–1914* (1976). See also the books on Russian national consciousness cited under Catherine the Great. Also Horace Davis, cited under Marx.

On the somewhat related question of race, see Michael D. Biddiss, ed., *Images of Race* (1979); George L. Mosse, *Toward the Final Solution: A History of European Racism* (1977); Michael P.Banton, *The Idea of Race* (1977).

Answers to the question, to what extent, and how legitimately, did fascist doctrines make use of Mazzini, may be found in such works as Denis Mack Smith, *Mussolini* (1981); A.J. Gregor, *Young Mussolini and the Intellectual Origins of Fascism* (1979); Alexander De Grand, *Italian Fascism: Its Origins and Development* (1982).

Max Weber

Max Weber's widow, Marianne Weber, wrote one of the best lives, translated as *Max Weber: A Biography* (1975). See also Reinhard Bendix, *Max Weber: An Intellectual Portrait* (1960); Dirk Käsler, *Max Weber: An Introduction to his Life and Work* (1988); Arthur Mitzman, *The Iron Cage: An Historical Interpretation of Max Weber* (1970). Stanislav Andreski, ed., *Max Weber on Capitalism, Bureaucracy and Religion* (1983) is a judicious selection of texts; also H.H. Gerth and C. Wright Mills, eds., *From Max Weber* (1967). A brief introduction is Frank Parkin's *Max Weber* (1982); also Donald G. Macrae, *Max Weber* for the Viking Modern Masters series (1974); Dennis Wrong, *Makers of Modern Social Science: Max Weber* (1970). For Weber in a wider context, see Raymond Aron, *Main Currents of Sociological Thought* (2 vols., 1967); Robert A. Nisbet, *The Sociological Tradition* (1966); Arthur Mitzman, *Sociology and Estrangement* (1973); Wolf Lepenies, *Between Literature and Science: The Rise of Sociology* (transl. 1988).

The famous Weber thesis on the nature of modern capitalism might be approached via Gordon Marshall, *In Search of the Spirit of Capitalism: An Essay on Max Weber's Protestant Ethic Thesis* (1982); Wolfgang Schluchter, *The Rise of Western Rationalism: Max Weber's Developmental History*, transl. Guenther Roth (1986); Roth and Schluchter, *Max Weber's Vision of History* (1979). Roth has an essay on "Weber's Relationship to Marxism" in Bendix and Roth, eds., *Scholarship and Partisanship: Essays on Max Weber* (1971); cf. Robert J. Antonio and Ronald M. Glassman, eds., *A Weber-Marx Dialogue* (1985) and Anthony Giddens, *Capitalism and Modern Social Theory* (1971).

Equally celebrated are the Weberian modes of authority, treated in Bendix, *Kings or People: Power and the Mandate to Rule* (1978), and Vatro Murvar, ed., *Theory of Liberty, Legitimacy and Power: New Directions in the Intellectual and Scientific Legacy of Max Weber* (1985). Weber's own view of politics is the subject of Wolfgang Mommsen, *Max Weber and German Politics, 1890–1920* (1984); Ilse Dronberger, *The Political Thought of Max Weber* (1971); Raymond Aron, "Max Weber and Power Politics," in Otto Stammer, ed., *Max Weber and Sociology Today* (1971).

Curie

There is a useful sketch of Mme. Curie's scientific methods and achievements by Jean Wyart in *Dictionary of Scientific Biography* (1973); likewise in the same reference work are articles on Frederic Joliot and Irene Joliot-Curie. Probably the best biography to date is Rosalynd Pflaum, *Grand Obsession: Madame Curie and Her World* (1989), although it leaves something to be desired. Others, more popular than epochal, can be found in Robert Reid, *Marie Curie* (1974); daughter Eve Curie (transl. Vincent Sheean), *Madame Curie* (1937), valuable for printing letters from a correspondence later lost during World War II; Françoise Giroud, *Une femme honorable* (1981). Marie herself wrote a tribute to her husband, *Pierre Curie* (transl. Charlotte and Vernon Kellogg), which first appeared in 1923 (reissued 1963) and which contains some autobiographical notes. See also an article on Marie Curie by Helena Pycior in Pnina G. Abir-am and Dorinda Outram, eds., *Uneasy Careers and Intimate Lives: Women in Science, 1789–1979* (1987). Professor Pycior is working on a Curie biography.

Theodore Zeldin, *France, 1848–1945*, especially Vol. 2 (1977), is a fine portrait of Mme. Curie's France. The movie about her life, *Madame Curie* (1943), was directed by Mervyn LeRoy.

Other scientists: David Wilson, *Rutherford: Simple Genius* (1983) is a fairly adequate study of one of Curie's friendly rivals in the exciting world of twentieth-century physical science. Others of the towering figures whose lives and work occasionally impinged on that of the Curies are almost too numerous to mention; Albert Einstein, James Chadwick, Lise Meitner, Otto Frisch, and Niels Bohr must certainly be included. They have all received quality biographical and scientific study, and have sometimes written their own memoirs: cf. Frisch's *What Little I Remember* (1991). Useful general accounts of the stupefying scientific revolution of the Planck-Einstein-Curie era are Christa Jungnickel and Russell McCormmach, *Intellectual Mastery of Nature: Theoretical Physics from Ohm to Einstein* (2 vols., 1986); P.M. Herman, *Energy, Force and Matter: The Development of Nineteenth-Century Physics* (1982); Stephen Brush, *The History of Modern Science: A Guide to the Second Scientific Revolution, 1800–1950* (1988). The story of the scientific origins of nuclear energy can be followed in Richard Rhodes, *The Making of the Atomic Bomb* (1986) and Margaret Gowing, *Britain and Atomic Energy, 1939–1945* (1965).

L. Badash's *Radioactivity in America: Growth and Decay of a Science* (1979) treats a special topic.

Women in science: See in addition to Pnina G. Abir-am and Dorinda Outram as cited above, Jonathan R. Cole, *Fair Science: Women in the Scientific Community* (1979) and Jonathan R. Cole and Harriet Zuckerman, eds., *The Outer Circle: Women and the Scientific Community* (1991).

Kafka

Biographies include Ernest Pawel, *The Nightmare of Reason: A Life of Franz Kafka* (1984); Peter Mailloux, *A Hesitation before Birth: The Life of Franz Kafka* (1989). See also Marthe Robert, *Franz Kafka's Loneliness* (1982); Ritchie Robertson, *Kafka: Judaism, Politics, and Literature* (1985). Max Brod's *Kafka, a Biography* (1947) is uniquely important. On Kafka's romances, see Margarete Buber-Neumann, *Milena* (transl. Ralph Manheim,1989); Jane Černa, *Kafka's Milena* (transl. A.G. Brain, 1989); Kafka, *Letters to Felice*. Some doubt has been cast on the accuracy of Gustav Janouch's *Conversations with Kafka* (transl. 1971). Anthony Northey's *Kafka's Relatives* (1990) is of some interest.

Writings: In English, Schocken Books published ten volumes of "The Kafka Library" in the 1970s, including the three novels, the stories, diaries, and letters. A briefer selection is *The Basic Kafka*, introduction by Erich Heller (1979). The Critical Edition of Kafka's works being published by Fischer at Frankfurt, Germany, not yet translated into English, outmodes previous versions.

Topics of interest in Kafka biography include his relationship with Felice, with Milena, and other women; with his father; his relation to Zionism, and to Judaism in general; his illness. For studies dealing with Kafka's city, see Pavel Eisner, *Franz Kafka and Prague* (1950); Heinz Politzer, "Prague and the Origins of Rilke, Kafka, and Werfel," *Modern Language Quarterly*, Vol. 16, pp. 49–63 (1955); Hans Tramer, "Prague, City of Three Peoples," *Leo Baeck Institute Year Book*, 1964, pp. 305–339. See also Gary B. Cohen, "Jews in German Society, Prague 1860–1914," *Central European History*, March 1977. Among books that address the larger question of Jewish identity in the German world are Marsha Rozenblitt, *The Jews of Vienna, 1867–1914* (1985); Steven Beller, *Vienna and the Jews 1867–1938* (1989); H.I. Bach, *The German Jew . . . 1730–1930* (1985); Sander L. Gilman, *Jewish Self-Hatred* (1986); also George Mosse, *Germans and Jews* (1970), and Peter Gay, *Freud, Jews, and Other Germans* (1978).

Literary studies: In 1978 (*TLS*, April 7), Robert M. Adams reflected on the vastness of the Kafka industry, and the process of "infinite exegesis" by which academic industries of this sort are self-augmenting. He found some 10,000 studies, which fifteen years later, of course, had exploded to many times that. A small sampling: Charles Bernheimer, *Flaubert and Kafka* (1982); Patrick Bridgwater, *Nietzsche and Kafka* (1974); Erich Heller, *Kafka* (1974); A. Peter Foulkes, *The Reluctant Pessimist* (1967); Anthony Thorlby, *Kafka, a Study* (1972); Angel Flores and Homer Swander, eds., *Franz Kafka Today* (1973). The varying interpretations of *The Trial* and *The Castle* constitute perhaps the most interesting Kafka topic. In 1978 (*TLS*, April 7), Robert M. Adams reflected on the vastness of the Kafka industry, and the process of "infinite exegesis" by which academic industries of this sort are self-augmenting. He found some 10,000 studies, which fifteen years later, of course, had exploded to many times that.

Films have been made of *The Trial* (Orson Welles, director, 1963) and *The Castle* (Rudolf Noelte, 1968). A film called *Kafka* (1991) is only loosely related to the novelist. *Metamorphosis* was adapted into a ballet-musical.

Hitler

Probably the best biographies are Joachim Fest, *Hitler* (1975) and Werner Maser, *Hitler: Legend, Myth, and Reality* ((1974); for other perspectives see also Rudolf Binion, *Hitler among the Germans* (1976) and R.G.L. Waite, *The Psychopathic God* (1977). Special aspects of Hitler's career are the subject of such monographs as Harold J. Gordon, *Hitler and the Beer Hall Putsch* (1972); Eberhard Jäckel, *Hitler's Weltanschauung* (1972); Peter Pulzer, *The Rise of Political anti-Semitism in Germany and Austria* (revised ed., 1988). *Hitler: Memoirs of a Confidant*, ed. Henry Ashby Turner, Jr. (1985), and Albert Speer, *Inside the Third Reich* (1970) are among the more revealing accounts by those who knew Hitler well.

A selection from the vast literature on the Nazi regime includes: John Gillingham, *Industry and Politics in the Third Reich* (1985); Michael Burleigh and Wolfgang Wipperman, *The Racial State: Germany 1933–45* (1992); D.J.K. Peukert, *Inside Nazi Germany* (1987); Ian Kershaw, *The Hitler Myth: Image and Reality in the Third Reich* (1987); Edward N. Peterson, *The Limits of Hitler's Power* (1969).

The war: Harold C. Deutsch, *Hitler and His Generals* (1974); Anthony Read and David Fisher, *The Deadly Embrace: Hitler, Stalin, and the Nazi-Soviet Pact, 1939–41* (1988); Norman Rich, *Hitler's War Aims* (1974); David Irving, *Hitler's War* (1977), a leading revisonist attempt to de-criminalize the Nazi leader. See Graham and Bidwell, *Tug of War* (1986) on Hitler's determination to defend Italy at all costs, 1943–1945. John Erickson's *Stalin's War with Germany* (1975) is one of the best accounts of the war's greatest chapter. On Germany and the atomic bomb, see Mark Walker, *German National Socialism and the Quest for Nuclear Power, 1939–49* (1990). Hugh Trevor-Roper's classic account of *The Last Days of Hitler* is still in print (latest edition 1987).

Klemens von Klemperer, *German Resistance against Hitler* (1992); Peter Hoffman,

History of the German Resistance, 1933–1945 (1977); Patricia Meehan, *The Unnecessary War: Whitehall and the German Resistance to Hitler* (1992); and Victoria Barnett, *For the Soul of the People: Protestant Protest against Hitler* (1992) are scholarly studies of Hitler's futile but often heroic adversaries within Germany.

Leading accounts of the genocide against the Jews are Christopher R. Browning, *The Path to Genocide: Essays on Launching the Final Solution* (1992); Gerald Fleming, *Hitler and the Final Solution* (1984); Raul Hilberg, *The Destruction of the European Jews* (1985); Lawrence L. Langer, *Versions of Survival: The Holocaust and the Human Spirit* (1982). Walter Laqueur's *The Terrible Secret* (1981) deals with the strange failure of the world to believe the Holocaust was happening.

Kafka's friend Ernst Weiss, a physician turned novelist who committed suicide in 1940, wrote a novel about Hitler in World War I titled *The Eyewitness* (transl. 1977). *Hitler films: Night and Fog*, directed by Alain Resnais. *Triumph of the Will*, directed by Leni Riefenstahl, the 1934 propaganda documentary; *Hitler, a Career*, a German-made movie by Hitler biographer J.C. Fest. Others include *The Secret Life of Adolf Hitler*; *Inside the Third Reich*, based on Albert Speer's famous memoirs; *The Wannsee Conference*; *The Desert Fox* (1951), devoted to General Rommel. Films about World War II, of lesser or greater fidelity to fact, are too numerous to mention. An electronic guide covering 5,000 films turns up 241 under WWII.

Topics

What was Hitler's exact role in ordering and carrying out out the "Final Solution"? Why did people refuse for so long to accept the existence of the murder camps? What best explains the German failure to match the Allied achievement in building atomic weapons?

Blunt

Generally on the Red generation: David Caute, *The Fellow Travellers* revised ed. 1988); Neal Wood, *Communism and British Intellectuals* (1964); R.H.S. Crossman, ed., *The God That Failed* (1950); Raymond Aron, *The Opium of the Intellectuals* (1952); Samuel Hynes, *The Auden Generation* (1977); Paul Hollander, *Political Pilgrims* (1981). Some of the best books about the Cambridge spies are John Costello, *Mask of Treachery* (1988); Nigel West, *Molehunt* (1988); Boris Penrose and Simon Freeman, *Conspiracy of Silence: The Secret Life of Anthony Blunt* (1986); Harry Chapman Pincher, *Too Secret Too Long* (1984) and *Their Trade Is Treachery* (1981); Andrew Boyle, *The Climate of Treason* (revised ed., 1979); Douglas Sutherland, *The Fourth Man* (1980); Nicholas Bethell, *The Great Betrayal* (1984); Andrew Sinclair, *The Red and the Blue: Cambridge, Treason, and Intelligence* (1986); Robert J. Lamphere, *The FBI–KGB War* (1988). An outstanding biography of a key figure is Anthony Cave Brown, *"C": The Secret Life of Sir Stewart Menzies, Spymaster to Winston Churchill* (1987); the same historian earlier wrote *Bodyguard of Lies* (1975).

In a class by itself is Peter Wright's *Spycatcher* (1987), the best-selling memoirs of the former MI5 assistant director that the British government banned in Britain and tried to suppress elsewhere. Some criticisms of Wright's book may be found in Anthony Glees, *The Secrets of the Service: A Story of Soviet Subversion of Western Intelligence* (1987). Other interesting autobiographies include Michael Straight, *After Long Silence* (1982), and Kim Philby, *My Silent War* (1968), written by the unrepentant Soviet agent after he fled to Moscow. Alan Bennett's *An Englishman Abroad* (1982, on TV 1983), also *The Old Country* (1978), were based on Guy Burgess in Moscow. See also Eleanor Philby, *The Spy I Loved*; Robert Cecil, *A Divided Life: a Biography of Donald Maclean* (1988).

Books such as David Kahn, *The Codebreakers*, and Wladyslaw Kozaczuk, *Enigma: How the German Machine Cipher Was Broken*; Peter Calvocoressi, *Top Secret Ultra* (1981);

Charles Cruickshank, *Deception in World War II* (1980); John Masterman, *The Double Cross System in the War of 1939–45* (1972) present the story of how intelligence work contributed to winning World War II. William Stevenson's *A Man Called Intrepid* (1976) is about a man named William Stephenson, who was the British liaison in the United States during World War II for highly confidential matters like Ultra.

Wesley K. Wark, ed., *Spy Fiction, Spy Films, and Real Intelligence* (1991) asks the question: How true to life are these widely read and viewed novels and movies of the James Bond vintage?

John Lewis Gaddis, "Intelligence, Espionage, and Cold War Origins," *Diplomatic History*, Spring 1989 (Vol. 13, No. 2) assesses the damage the moles did to Allied policy, and how much help they gave the USSR. Lawrence Badash, *Kapitza, Rutherford and the Kremlin* (1985) is among studies of Soviet espionage and nuclear weapons. See also Robert Chadwell Williams, *Klaus Fuchs, Atom Spy* (1987). Published in 1994, the memoirs of Pavel Sudoplatov, a Soviet intelligence officer under Stalin, claimed that Robert Oppenheimer himself, the head of the American atomic bomb project at Los Alamos during World War II, passed secret information to Soviet agents (*Special Tasks: The Memoirs of an Unwanted Witness*).

Bertrand Russell

Alan Ryan, *Bertrand Russell: A Political Life* (1988); Ronald W. Clark, *The Life of Bertrand Russell* (1976); Andrew Brink, *Bertrand Russell: The Psychobiography of a Moralist* (1990); and Caroline Moorehead, *Bertrand Russell* (1992) are the leading biographies. See also the article on Russell by T.A.A. Broadbent in *Dictionary of Scientific Biography*. Russell's own classic *Autobiography* was published in three volumes, 1967–1969, but is available in a single-volume paperback. He also published *My Philosophical Development* (1959) and *Portraits from Memory* (1956). Indispensable vitae come from his second wife, Dora Russell, *The Tamarisk Tree* (1975), and from Katherine Tait, *My Father Bertrand Russell* (1976). Robert Gathorne-Hardy edited *Ottoline at Garsington* (1975).

Alistair Cooke has a critical sketch of Russell in his *Six Men* (1977)—the others including Charlie Chaplin and Humphrey Bogart. Biographies of people close to Russell include Sandra Jobson Darroch, *Ottoline: The Life of Lady Ottoline Morrell* (1976) and Miranda Seymour, *Ottoline Morrell* (1992); Brian McGuinness, *Wittgenstein, A Life*, Vol. 1 (1988); Victor Lowe, *Alfred North Whitehead, The Man and His Work*, Vol. 1 (1985); Michael Dummett, *Frege, Philosopher of Language* (1973); Paul Levy, *G.E. Moore and the Cambridge Apostles* (1979).

Fictional treatment: Russell not only is "Mr. Apollinax" in T.S. Eliot's poem by that title, but he is also generally considered to be Joshua Malleson in D.H. Lawrence's novel *Women in Love* and Mr. Scogan in Aldous Huxley's *Crome Yellow*. Colette (Lady Constance Malleson) wrote about her long-time lover in her novel *The Coming Back* (1933).

Perhaps the most useful selection from Russell's voluminous publications is Robert E. Egner and Lester E. Denonn, eds., *The Basic Writings of Bertrand Russell* (1961). Selections of special appeal and interest are *Dear Bertrand Russell . . . : A Selection of His Correspondence with the General Public (1969), 1950–1968*, Barry Feinberg and Ronald Kasrils, eds., and, from the same editors, *Bertrand Russell's America: A Documented Account, 1896–1945* (1974). *Philosophical Essays* (1966) contains some of his most popular philosophical writing. In 1983 the Bertrand Russell Archives at McMaster University in Hamilton, Ontario, began publishing the *Collected Papers of Bertrand Russell*, a projected 28 volumes. They also put out a semiannual journal, *Russell*. Nicholas Griffin, ed., *The Selected Letters of Bertrand Russell*, Vol. 1, 1884–1914 (1992) is one of the results of the McMaster project.

Critical assessments of Russell's thought appear in George W. Roberts, ed., *Bertrand Russell Memorial Volume* (1979); Kenneth Blackwell and John E. Thomas, eds., *Russell in Review* (1976); Paul A. Schilpp, ed., *The Philosophy of Bertrand Russell* (1944); A.J. Ayer, *Bertrand Russell* (1972); David Pears, *Bertrand Russell and the British Tradition in Philosophy* (1967); Ronald Jager, *The Development of Bertrand Russell's Philosophy* (1972); Peter Hylton, *Russell, Idealism, and the Emergence of Analytic Philosophy* (1990). Helpful on the mathematics side is Jan van Heijenoort, *From Frege to Gödel* (1967). See also Joseph Warren Dauben, *Georg Cantor* (1990).

Special Topics

Russell and World War I: Jo Vellacott, *Bertrand Russell and the Pacifists in the First World War* (1981), and G.H. Hardy, *Bertrand Russell and Trinity* (1970). Harry T. Moore, ed., *D.H. Lawrence's Letters to Bertrand Russell* (1948) documents one side of a celebrated mis-collaboration between Lawrence and Russell; see also article by George J. Zytaruk in *Russell*, Vol. 3, No. 1 (1983).

Russell as educator: See Joe Park, *Bertrand Russell on Education* (1964); Arthur Zilversmit, *Changing Schools: Progressive Education Theory and Practice, 1930–1960* (1993). Russell's own writing on education includes *Education and the Social Order* and *On Education*. Russell's notoriously liberal views on sex and marriage may be found in his *Marriage and Morals* and *The Conquest of Happiness*; see also his wife Dora's *The Right to be Happy*.

CCNY affair: See John Dewey and Horace Kallen, eds., *The Bertrand Russell Case* (1941).

Russell and socialism: See "Why I Am a Socialist," in his *In Praise of Idleness and Other Essays*. Compare Friedrich A. Hayek, *The Fatal Conceit: The Errors of Socialism* (1988).

For Russell's connection with the Campaign for Nuclear Disarmament movement, and "civil disobedience," see Richard Taylor, *Against the Bomb: The British Peace Movement, 1958–1965* (1988). Film: "Bertie and the Bomb," BBC, 1984.

For Russell's role in the 1962 Cuba missile crisis, see Raymond L. Garthoff, *Reflections on the Cuban Missile Crisis* (1989); James G. Bright and David A. Welch, *On the Brink: Americans and Soviets Reexamine the Cuban Missile Crisis* (1990); Robert Smith Thompson, *The Missiles of October* (1992). Russell's account was in *Unarmed Victory* (1963).

Anyone interested in a purely philosophical or logical Russell topic might choose his "theory of types" as an answer to the problem of sets or classes and how this was of critical importance in establishing an unshakable logical foundation for mathematics. See also A.R. Garciadiego Dantan, *Bertrand Russell and the Origins of the Set-Theoretic Paradoxes* (1992).

Thatcher

A Thatcher biography is Hugo Young, *One of Us* (1991). Varying appraisals of her political achievements include Peter Jenkins, *Mrs. Thatcher's Revolution: The Ending of the Socialist Era* (1989); Robert Skidelsky, ed., *Thatcherism* (1989); Shirley Robin Letwin, *The Anatomy of Thatcherism* (1992); Ian Gilmour, *Dancing with Dogma: Britain under Thatcherism* (1992). Leo Abse's *Margaret, Daughter of Beatrice* (1993) is an attempt at psychoanalyzing Mrs. Thatcher. *Special episodes*: David Butler and Dennis Kavanaugh, *The British General Election of 1987* (1988); also by the same scholars, *The British General Election of 1992*. Also see Charles C. Hanson, *Taming the Trade Unions* (1991); as background, Martin Holmes, *The Labour Government, 1974–1979* (1985). Geoffrey Smith's *Reagan and Thatcher* focuses on this special relationship. Alan Watkins, *A Conservative*

Coup (1991), provides an account of the deposing of Mrs. Thatcher in late 1990. Memoirs by those closely associated with her include Nigel Lawson, *The View from No. 11: Memoirs of a Tory Radical* (1992), and, less weightily, Bernard Ingham, *Kill the Messenger* (1991), by Mrs. Thatcher's chief press secretary. In late 1993 the first volume of Mrs. Thatcher's own autobiography, *The Downing Street Years, 1979–1990*, was published. See also Timothy Raison, *Tories and the Welfare State: A History of Conservative Social Policy since the Second World War* (1990).

   On economic theory: Walter Eltis and Peter Sinclair, eds., *Keynes and Economic Policy: The Relevance of the "General Theory" after Fifty Years* (1989); F. von Hayek, *The Fatal Conceit: The Errors of Socialism* (1988). J.R. Shackleton and Gareth Locksley, eds., *Twelve Contemporary Economists* (1981); Peter Giles and Guy Routh, ed., *Economics in Disarray* (1984); Thomas Blinder, *Hard Heads, Soft Hearts* (1989). More generally, David Willetts, *Modern Conservatism* (1992); Barry Cooper, Allan Karnberg, and William Mishler, *The Resurgence of Conservatism in Anglo-American Democracies* (1988). The various theories presented to account for Great Britain's alleged decline in power and wealth may be inspected in Bernard Elbaum and William Lazonick, eds., *The Decline of the British Economy* (1986); see also Corelli Barnett, *The Collapse of British Power* (1972) and *The Audit of War: The Illusion and Reality of Britain as a Great Nation* (1986). Cf. W.D. Rubenstein, *Capitalism, Culture, and Decline in Britain, 1750–1990* (1993).

   Among numerous books on the collapse of the socialist economies of eastern Europe are Janos Kornai, *Contradictions and Dilemmas: Studies on the Socialist Economy and Society* (1986); Victor Nee and David Stark, eds., *Remaking the Economic Institutions of Socialism, China and Eastern Europe* (1989); Alec Nove, *The Economics of Feasible Socialism* (1989); Marshall I. Goldman, *USSR in Crisis: The Failure of an Economic System* (1983); Michael Barratt Browne, ed., *The Challenge: Economics of Perestroika* (1988). On the issue of socialism's viability, see Joseph Schumpeter, *Capitalism, Socialism, and Democracy* (1942); and Arnold Heertje, *Schumpeter's Vision* (1982). Finally, compare the evaluations of Thatcher by Letwin and Gilmour in works cited above.

Index